PICTORIAL PRICE GUIDE
TO AMERICAN ANTIQUES

PICTORIAL PRICE GUIDE
TO AMERICAN ANTIQUES

and Objects Made for the American Market

OVER 5000 OBJECTS IN 300 CATEGORIES
ILLUSTRATED AND PRICED

BY

Dorothy Hammond

A Dutton Paperback

E. P. DUTTON
New York

Library of Congress Catalog Card Number: 77-72038

ISBN: 0-525-47445

Published simultaneously in Canada by Clarke, Irwin & Company Limited, Toronto and Vancouver

10 9 8 7 6 5 4 3 2 1

First Edition

CONTENTS

KEY to ABBREVIATIONS

Every item listed within this volume is keyed to either a dealer price, or an auction value. The letter "D" denotes "Dealer", whereas the letter "A" denotes an "Auction" price. The two letters that follow indicate the state, and the numbers indicate the year.

Abbreviations for the states included are:

Alabama . . . . .AL	Maine . . . . .ME	Ohio . . . . .OH
Arizona . . . . .AZ	Maryland . . . . .MD	Oklahoma . . . . .OK
Arkansas . . . . .AR	Massachusetts . . . . .MA	Oregon . . . . .OR
California . . . . .CA	Michigan . . . . .MI	Pennsylvania . . . . .PA
Colorado . . . . .CO	Minnesota . . . . .MN	Rhode Island . . . . .RI
Connecticut . . . . .CT	Mississippi . . . . .MS	South Carolina . . . . .SC
Delaware . . . . .DE	Missouri . . . . .MO	South Dakota . . . . .SD
Florida . . . . .FL	Montana . . . . .MT	Tennessee . . . . .TN
Georgia . . . . .GA	Nebraska . . . . .NE	Texas . . . . .TX
Idaho . . . . .ID	Nevada . . . . .NV	Utah . . . . .UT
Illinois IL	New Hampshire . . . . .NH	Vermont . . . . .VT
Indiana . . . . .IN	New Jersey . . . . .NJ	Virginia . . . . .VA
Iowa . . . . .IA	New Mexico . . . . .NM	Washington . . . . .WA
Kansas . . . . .KS	New York . . . . .NY	West Virginia . . . . .WV
Kentucky . . . . .KY	North Carolina . . . . .NC	Wisconsin . . . . .WI
Louisiana . . . . .LA	North Dakota . . . . .ND	Wyoming . . . . .WY

ACKNOWLEDGMENTS

This book would not have been possible without the gracious assistance of auction companies who have so generously provided photograph illustrations to make this undertaking a reality. The author expresses deepest appreciation to: Richard A. Bourne Company, Inc., Hyannis Port, Ma.; Robert C. Eldred Company, Inc., East Dennis, Ma.; Garth Auctions Inc., Delaware, Oh.; Laws Auctions & Antiques, Manassas, Va.; Pennypacker Auction Centre, Kenhorst, Reading, Pa.; Robert W. Skinner Inc., Bolton, Ma.; and Woody Auction Company, Douglas, Ks.

The following individuals were also most cooperative in providing photographs and assistance. Thanks are especially due to: Joel and Kate Kopp, America Hurrah, New York, N.Y., for the cover photograph; Ginny Barber, Garth Auctions Inc.; Joan Cawley, White Buffalo Gallery, Wichita, Ks.; H. G. Doran, Wichita, Ks.; Sarradah Hapburn, Maryville, Mo.; Tom King, Garth Auctions Inc.; Carolyn Lerke Antiques, Wichita, Ks.; George & Beverly Mann, Gay Nineties, Wichita, Ks.; Helen McClure; Mae Moore; Tom Porter, Garth Auctions Inc.; Evelyn Phillips, Portchester, N.Y.; Grant Rine; Fred & Harriet Schuster, Platte Purchase Antiques, Gower, Mo.; Ron & Onalea Slade, White Eagle Antiques, Wichita, Ks.; Mona Smith, Cranberry Shop, Wichita, Ks.; and United Art & Antiques, Beverly Hills, Ca.

Special Acknowledgment is also due to: Barbara Hart for proof reading; and to Gail S. Hendry, the person who so cheerfully organized the hundreds of illustrations — sometimes over and over again, and to Bill Whitaker for assisting. Additionally, I am very grateful to A. W. Styer III, Reading, Pennsylvania for helping to provide many fine photographs.

Finally, to my editor, Cyril I. Nelson at E. P. Dutton Company, I would like to give special thanks for permitting the production of this book to be done here in Wichita, in order that I could follow its progress more closely. And I would especially like to thank my production director, Leonard Mainzer of McCormick-Armstrong for being so very amiable from the very beginning to the end of this horrendous project. And to James L. Adkins for assisting.

INTRODUCTION

Pictorial Price Guide to American Antiques and Objects Made for the American Market is the first fully illustrated price guide ever published, consisting of over 5,000 items. The format has been structured to provide a special visual delight to readers — especially for the beginning collectors — which will increase their knowledge and appreciation for antiques and collectibles immeasurably.

The many illustrations have been conveniently arranged into 26 sections: Advertising, Art Nouveau, Banks, Baskets, Bottles & Flasks, Ceramics, Clocks, Decoys, Dolls, Furniture, Glass, Kitchenwares, Lighting, Metals, Miniatures, Orientals, Paintings, Pictures and Prints, Photography, Shaker Items, Textiles, Toleware, Tools, Toys, Weathervanes, Woodcarvings and Miscellaneous. The latter includes photographs of multiple items, in addition to many singular objects, when there were not enough photographs available in a particular field for a complete section.

From the beginning, the goal was to include over 5,000 different items. Additionally, all illustrations in each section were to be arranged in alphabetical sequence, but as the preparation of the book progressed it appeared advisable to separate some illustrations due to the length of captions. Hence, a comprehensive index has been included for quick reference.

The majority of the items illustrated date from the nineteenth century or early twentieth century. Every effort has been made to include the circa of earlier items when possible, in addition to as much historical background information as space permitted. Extensive coverage has been given to the Ceramic, Glass and Furniture sections of this book.

Every entry is keyed to either a dealer's price or an auction price, the year the item was either noted in an antiques shop or show, or at an auction. A state abbreviation is also included for the readers' convenience since prices vary in different locations.

All entries included were either noted or purchased from antiques shops or antiques shows across the country, or sold at auctions from late 1975 through January 1977. Every effort has been made to note the condition of every item when available to the writer. Interestingly enough, damaged glass and ceramics, or furniture with some restoration, has become more acceptable with each passing year, because of the scarcity of good antiques. In such instances, rarity and age determine values.

As antiques and collectibles continue to be among the best investments in America, record prices were set during 1976 for many single items as well as for entire auctions. Furniture from all periods is still at the top of the market in popularity. As collectors have become more selective, it has become a challenge to find furniture of quality and design that prove enjoyable, and a good investment. Prices paid for dolls and toys also reached record heights. Art Nouveau and Art Deco items are now a focus of interest, with the best of these styles commanding the highest prices.

Interest has intensified rapidly in recent months for objects that are decorative rather than functional. Prices of art glass and cut glass are again on the upswing. Moreover, the value of all types of opalescent glass has soared in recent months. Also, there have been noticeable price increases in American glasswares from the second quarter of the present century — Fenton, Imperial, McKee, Heisey and others.

The scarcity of early kitchenwares has created a new market for items manufactured from the 1900s through the 1930s. Budget-bound collectors have found this to be a fertile field.

Every effort has been made to record prices as accurately as possible in this book. However, the writer cannot be responsible for any clerical or typographical errors that may have occurred.

Dorothy Hammond

8 ADVERTISING

During the 1800s, manufacturers began using a variety of objects as giveaways to advertise their products. As a result, collecting early examples is a fascinating field. Regardless of shape or size, most are actually works of art, made especially to capture the attention of the public.

(D-IA. '76)
Advertising Tin, German Chocolates . .$48.50

(D-CO. '76)
ADVERTISING CONTAINERS *(Row I, Left to Right)*
Huntley & Palmers Biscuit Tin, Books, Multi. Colors, 1903 . . . .$95.00
Huntley & Palmers Biscuit Tin, Books, Red, 1901 . . . .$95.00
Mayo's Tobacco Co. Brownie, Store Keeper $290.00
Dixie Queen Plug Cut Tobacco, Lunch Pail Ty;e $45.00
(Row II)
Huntley & Palmers Biscuit Tin, Marble Column, Hinged Lid $65.00
Huntley & Palmers Biscuit Tin, Satchel $75.00
Hang Bag Cut Plug Tobacco Tin, ...$65.00
George Washington Cut Plug $35.00

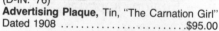

(D-IN. '76)
Advertising Plaque, Tin, "The Carnation Girl"
Dated 1908 . . . .$95.00

(D-IA. '76)
ADVERTISING CARD
Jewel Stoves & Ranges, 5" x 7" $7.50

(D-IA. '76)
ADVERTISING CARD
McLaughlin Coffee, 5" x 7" $6.00

(D-OH. '76)
Diamond Dyes, Cabinet Complete W/Dividers,
Refinished $300.00

(D-CO. '76)
ADVERTISING CARD
Buckeye Mowers & Binders, 4" x 7½"$10.00

(D-CO. '76)
ADVERTISING CARD
Broadmead Dress Goods, 5" x 7" $5.00

ADVERTISING CARD (D-IA. '76)
Monitor Rake, 5" x 7" $15.00

(D-IA. '76)
ADVERTISING CARDS
(Left)
Stickney Mustard, 3" x 4" $3.00

(Right)
The Detroit Evening Journal, 3¼" x 5" $18.00

(D-IA. '76)
(Left)
Hires' Rootbeer, 3" x 5" $8.50
(Right)
Hard A Port Cut Plug Tobacco, 2½" x 4" ...
....$4.00

(D-IA. '76)
(Left)
Ayer's Cathartic Pills, The Country Doctor,
Dated 1883, 2½" x 4½" $10.00
(Right)
Eagle Brand Milk, 3½" x 5" **$8.00**

(D-OH. '76)
(Left)
Wonder Flour,Dated 1895, 3½" x 5½" .$6.00
(Right)
Stickney Mustard, 3" x 4" $3.00

(Left)   (D-MO. '76)
Walter A. Wood Binders, Mowers, Horse-rakes, Reapers, Dated 1890, 4" x 6" ...$8.00
(Right)
Buckeye Lawn Mower, 3½" x 6" $10.00

(Left)   (D-MO. '76)
Clark's O.N.T. Spool Cotton, 3" x 4½" .$3.00

(Right)
Hampden Watches, 3¼" x 4½" $8.00

(D-CO. '76)
(Left)
Heinz Baked Beans, 3½" x 5" $10.00
(D-IL. '76)
(Right)
Safety Oil Can, 3" x 5½" $3.50

(D-KS. '76)
Ayer's Hair Vigor For The Toilet, 2¾" x 4½".
....$8.00

(Left)   (D-CO. '76)
J & P Coats, Best Six Cord, 3" x 4¼" .$5.00
(Right)
Stickney & Poor's Pure Sage, 3" x 4" .$3.50

(D-CO. '76)
ADVERTISING POSTER
Winner Plug Tobacco, Lithograph by Hoen &
Co., Richmond, Va., 10½" x 10¼" $20.00

(D-CA. '76)
**Smoke Old Judge Cigarettes - Best In The
World.** Dated 1888 ....$15.00

(Left)   (D-W.V. '76)   (D-CO. '76)
Stickney & Poor's Spices, 3" x 4" $3.00
(Right)
Clark's O.N.T. Spool Cotton, Hard To Beat,
3" x 4¼" **$4.00**

D-MI. '76)
AMC Perfect Cereal, 4" x 6½" $5.00

10   ART NOUVEAU & DECO

The term is French, meaning "new art", which became popular after 1890 and continued well into the 20th century. The style is characterized by free-flowing organic designs, insects, and the feminine form, encompassing all of the decorative and functional arts from architecture to furniture, metals and art glass. The Art Deco period started at the Paris Exposition of 1925 and flourished through the 1930s. Its varied characteristics include zigzag lines resembling a lightning bolt, simplicity, and the usage of two sharply contrasting colors such as black and white, or others.

(D-CA. '76)   *United Art & Antiques*
Pair of Bronze Gypsies by Emice Guillemin, 14" H. French $2,300.00

(DA-CA. '76)   *United Art & Antiques*
Bronze & Ivory Figure By Chiparus, 9½" H. French $1,500.00

(D-CA. '76)   *United Art & Antiques*
Bronze (Gold) Nude Woman By Barrias, 34" H. French $3,500.00

← (D-KS. '76)   *Gay Nineties*
Bronze Book Ends $45.00

(D-CA. '76)   *United Art & Antiques*
Bronze & Ivory By Chiparus, 12" H. French ..
.... $3,000.00

(D-CA. '76)   *United Art & Antiques*
Black Bronze & Ivory Woman On Rust Colored Marble Base, Unsigned, 10" H. French ..
.... $900.00

(D-CA. '76)   *United Art & Antiques*
Bronze & Ivory Figure By Maurice Bouvar, 16½" H. French $3,000.00

The production of mechanical and still banks began during the mid-1800s and continued well into the present century. A mechanical bank displays some type of action when a coin is inserted, whereas a still bank does not have any moveable parts. Although reproductions continue to have their effect on values, old banks in good original condition with no repairs increase in price with each passing year.

(D-CA. '76)
STILL BANKS
(Left to Right)
Elephant, Iron, Orig. Paint Fair $45.00
Horse, Black Beauty, Iron, Paint Good .$45.00
Rooster, Iron, Paint Good $38.50
Bank, Tin, Orig. Paint Good $35.00

(D-WI. '76)
Bank, Still, Postal, 3¾" H. $45.00

(D-WA. '76)
Bank, Mechanical, Eagle & Eaglets . .$325.00

(A-PA. '75)   *Pennypacker Auction Centre*
MECHANICAL BANKS
(Top Row)
Trick Pony $260.00
Eagle & Eaglets $110.00
(Bottom Row)
Uncle Remus $130.00
Organ Bank, Medium Monkey $90.00

(D-OH. '76)
Bank, Mechanical, Pelican, Rabbit In Mouth
. . . .$550.00

(A-PA. '76)   *Pennypacker Auction Centre*
BANKS
(Left to Right)
William Tell, Mechanical $190.00
Tammany, Mechanical $65.00
Sitting Bulldog, Still $20.00
Creedmore, William Tell, Mechanical $115.00

(D-KY. '76)
Bank, Still, Cash Register, 5" H. $55.00

12 BASKETS

Basketry is considered one of our oldest crafts. During the decades following the first colonization, the need for containers was immense and, since materials were abundant, the art flourished until the present century when basket factories were established and mass-produced containers became available.

Over the years, a variety of materials were used to produce baskets of various shapes and sizes. The earliest types made by the colonists were sturdy splint baskets usually of oak, ash or hickory. The hand-cut splints were thick and irregular, and handles were carved by hand.

Presently, baskets are enjoying much popularity among collectors. If one's taste preference doesn't include a Shaker, Nantucket or American Indian basket — an interesting collection can be assembled inexpensively.

At one time, the arts and crafts of the latter were valued only by natural history enthusiasts, but today there is recognition of the artistic merit of the American Indians who, after all, are the only native Americans. Although the majority of their baskets available to the collector were made during the present century — these have a certain historic value in addition to their monetary value, as they reflect a continuing development of the tribal arts.

(D-KS. '76)   *White Buffalo Gallery*

Pima (Az.) Coiled Tray, Willow & Devil's Clay, Ca. 1920, 16'' Diam. $300.00

(D-AZ. '76)

Apache Indian Basket, W/Wild Turkey Decoration, 7'' H., 14'' Diam. $250.00

(A-PA. '76)   *Pennypacker Auction Centre*

Sewing Basket, Stenciled W/Crescent Moon & Stars, Yellow, Red & Green, 10'' L. . . .$450.00
Basket, Stenciled, 7'' Diam. $200.00
Basket, Salmon Decor., Long Handle, 14'' L. $100.00
Basket, W/Lid, Tobacco Juice Coloring, 21'' L., 16'' W., 13'' H. $300.00
Basket, Tobacco Stenciling, Red & Yellow Bands, 2 Handles, 11'' Diam. $225.00
Basket, Blue, Green & Red Decor., 11'' Diam. $160.00
Basket, Bright Yellow Bands Stenciled W/Red & Blue Leaf Design, Round At Top, Rect. At Base $160.00

(D-KS. '76)   *White Buffalo Gallery*

Yokut Indian Gambling Tray (Central Ca.), Ca. 1900, Rattlesnake Design Known As "Tulare." Made From Black Rootlets & Strips Of Bark $795.00

(D-KS. '76)   *White Buffalo Gallery*

Pima Indian (Arizona), Ca. 1920, Olla Shape Coiled Storage Basket. Made From Willow & Devil's Claws W/Red Polychrome Decor., 10'' H. $400.00

(D-IL. '76)

Basket, Covered Picnic Hamper, Splint Having Synthetic Dyes Of Red, Green & Brown Stain, 11½'' H., 20'' L., 15'' W. $75.00

(D-KS. '76)   *White Buffalo Gallery*

(Left to Right)
Mission Indian Basket (S. Ca.), Made From Sumac & Juncus, Ca. 1920 . . . .$250.00
Pauite Beaded Basket (Nv.), Beads Attached To Surface After Basket Was Made . . .$225.00
Hupa Cap (Lower Klamath River, Ca.), Made From Graperoot, Willow, Hazel, Fern & Other Minerals, Designs Applied By False Embroidery On Exterior Only $240.00

(A-PA. '76)   *Pennypacker Auction Centre*

Fowl Basket, Pa. $260.00
Nut Gathering Basket $260.00

(D-ME. '76)

Covered Sweet Grass Basket, W/Red & Green Dyed Designs, 4½'' H., 6½'' Diam. $28.00

(D-VT. '76)
Wooden Fruit Basket Mkd. On Base "Massachusetts, Pat. Pending 1882; 16" H. ..$45.00

(D-KS. '76)
Amish Splint Basket, 8" W., 12" L., 8" H. . . .
. . . .$35.00

(D-PA. '76)
Splint Egg Basket, 5½" H., 9" L. $28.00

(A-PA. '76) *Pennypacker Auction Centre*
Rice Straw Basket, Chinese, Peafowl Decor.
. . . .$290.00
Rice Straw Basket $110.00

(A-PA. '75) *Pennypacker Auction Centre*
Straw Basket $90.00

(D-MI. '76)
Splint Egg Basket, 12" H. $55.00

(D-W.V. '76)
Sewing Basket, Double-Decker $55.00

(D-KS. '76) *White Buffalo Gallery*
Chemehuevi Indian Basket, Ca. 1920, 5¼" H.,
6½" Diam. $800.00

(D-KS. '76) *White Buffalo Gallery*
Panamint Indian Basket, Ca. 1930; Origin,
Death Valley; Decor. W/Orange & Brown Butterflies, Yellow & Black Bird Perched On Branch,
3¾" H., 7" Diam. At Top $1,750.00

(D-KS. '76) *White Buffalo Gallery*
Pomo Indian Basket, Boat Shaped, Ca. 1900;
Possibly Used For Storage Of Religious Paraphernailia, Decor. W/Flat Bone Buttons &
Feathers — Black, Yellow & Red (Woodpecker),
4¼" D., 17" L. $2,500.00

(D-KS. '76) *White Buffalo Gallery*
Nevada Shoshone Indian Basket, Ca. 1900,
3½" H., 6" Diam. $585.00

(D-KS. '76) *White Buffalo Gallery*
Pomo Indian Basket, Ca. 1920, Decor. W/
Black Feathers Around Top, 2½" H., 5½" Diam.
. . . .$450.00

(A-PA. '76) *Pennypacker Auction Centre*
(Center)
Unusual Splint Woven Basket W/Two Whittled Handles & Bent Rim; Two Extra Colored Bands For
Body Decor., Square At Base, Round Top 10" Diam. $75.00
(Left to Right)
Two Rye Straw Baskets, Smaller Ex. 8" Diam.; Larger Basket 11½" Diam., Pr. $42.50

14   BOTTLES & FLASKS

Glass containers have been an integral part of American history for more than 300 years. In 1608 at Jamestown, the colonists established the first colonial furnace to produce glass — probably window glass and bottles. However, glassmaking didn't develop rapidly until the late 1700s, and the majority of the bottles produced were used to contain spirits of various kinds — wines, rum, gin and later whiskey.

One of the truly American aspects of early glass bottle making was the production of historical and pictorial flasks. During their heyday — 1815-1875 — over 700 different subjects were made.

The nineteenth century proved to be a fertile ground for patent medicines and bitters. There were few Doctors and epidemics were numerous. Almost everyone relied upon patent and proprietary medicines for alleviating aches and pains. Between 1840-1906 at least 450 different styles were produced.

From the mid-19th century, improved methods of food preservation resulted in the growth of a tremendous need for glass containers. The most famous of the early food containers was the Mason jar which was patented November 30, 1858. Automatic production of both food and beverage containers didn't begin until after the turn of the century.

Today, bottle collecting is considered to be a major American hobby. When the earlier examples became scarce, collectors turned to contemporary bottles — Avon, Beam, cologne, etc, creating a brisk market for all types.

(A-OH. '76)   *Garth's Auctions, Inc.*

ROCKINGHAM POTTERY
(Row I, Left to Right)
Bottle, Man Smoking Pipe, 7⅝" H. $120.00
Bottle, Lady W/Generous Proportions, Skinny Neck & Bunn, Tiny Glaze Flaws, 8" H. $55.00
Bottle, Man Seated W/Cane, 8¾" H. $115.00
(Row II, Left to Right)
Bottle, Man W/Tall 3-Cornered Hat, 7¾" H. $115.00
Bottle, Quatrefoil Shaped House W/Thatched Roof, Old Flake On Base, 7½" H. $85.00
Bottle, Shoe, Molded Laces, Drk. Glaze, 6½" H. $35.00
Bottle, Double Gemel W/Molded Rose Design, 7¼" H. $85.00

(A-OH. '76)   *Garth's Auctions, Inc.*

(Row I, Left to Right)
Blown Flask, Green, Applied Lip, 5½" H. ....
.... $70.00
Sapphire Blue Bottle, 12 Sided, McK. 243-3, Ex McKearin Coll., 9" H. $100.00
Blown Bottle, Lt. Olive-Green, 9½" H. ....
.... $17.50
Pepper Sauce Bottle, Aqua, "E.R.D. & Co. Pat'd Feb. 17, 1874" On Base; "E.R. Durkee, N.Y." On Bottom, 7¾" H. $20.00
Blown Bottle, Aqua, High Kick-Up, 6½" H. ...
.... $17.50
Blown Flask, Pale Yellow-Green, Applied Lip, 5" H. $35.00
(Row II, Left to Right)
Bottle, Amber, "Valentine's Meat Juice", 3¼" H. $6.00
Oyster Shaped Bottle, Threaded Metal Cap, Worn Paint $25.00
Flask, Amber, Threaded Metal Cap, 4¾" H. ..
.... $10.00
Medicine "Sample" Bottles, (2), Aqua, Both "Dr. Kilmer's Swamp Root Kidney Remedy, Binghamton, N.Y.", 3⅛" & 4¼" H. ....
.... $7.50
Medicine Bottle, Pale Green, "The Crescent Polish Co., Van Wert, Ohio", Partial Paper Label, 4½" H. $7.00
(Row III, Left to Right)
Blown Medicine Bottles, Aqua, (2), 4½" & 4¾" H. $8.00
Essence Bottles, (2), Aqua, "Hires Improved Root Beer, Philadelphia, Pa.", 4½" H. & "Genuine Essence", 4½" H. $4.00
Medicine Bottles, (2), Aqua, "Dr. King's New Discovery, H.F. Bucklen & Co., Chicago, Ill.", 4½" H., & "Chamberlain's Colic Cholera Diarrhoea Remedy, Des Moines, Iowa", 4½" H. ...
.... $6.00
Medicine Bottles, (3), Aqua, "Otto's Cure, B.H. Bacon, Rochester, N.Y.", 2¾" H.; "Kemp's Cough Balsam, O.F. Woodward, Leroy, N.Y.", 2¾" H.; "Mrs. Winslow's Soothing Syrup, Curtis & Perkens, Proprietors", 5" H. $6.00

(A-PA. '76)   *Pennypacker Auction Centre*

HISTORICAL FLASKS
(Row I, Left to Right)
Westford Eagle, ½ Pt., Deep Olive Green, GII-65 .... $100.00
Willington Eagle, Pt., Olive Amber, GII-64 ...
.... $90.00
Washington-Taylor, Qt., Brilliant Green, GI-54
.... $100.00
(Row II, Left to Right)
Cornucopia, ½ Pt., Yellow Amber, GIII-10 ...
.... $75.00
Cornucopia, ½ Pt., Deep Blue-Green $190.00
Cornucopia, Pt., Deep Peacock Green, GIII-17 .... $250.00

(Left to Right) (A-PA. '76) *Pennypacker Auction Centre*
Masonic Flask, Eagle, Aqua, GIV-37, Pt. ....
.... $240.00
Traveler's Companion Flask, 8-Pointed Star; Reverse W/Ravenna Glass Co. Around 8-Pointed Star, Bluish Aqua $130.00
Grapes-Sheaf Flask, GX-3, Aqua, ½ Pt. .....
.... $110.00
Double Gemel Bottle, White Loopings & Sm. Applied Blown Circular Foot, Aquamarine .....
.... $195.00
Zanesville Bottle, Globular, 24 Ribs Swirled To Left, Lt. Green, 8¼" H. $340.00
Pitkin Flask, Chestnut Shape, 32 Ribs In Broken Swirl To Right, Mantua, Lt. Green, 7" H. ...
.... $220.00

(A-OH. '76)   *Garth's Auctions, Inc.*
(Row I, Left to Right)
Zanesville Globular Bottle, Red-Amber,
Swirled, 7½" H. $250.00
Zanesville Globular Bottle, Green, Swirled,
7½' H. $825.00
Zanesville Globular Bottle, Golden-Amber,
Swirled, 7½" H. $405.00
(Row II, Left to Right)
Flattened Globular Bottle, Aqua, Swirled, 18
Ribs, Excellent Impression, 7¼" H. $55.00
Zanesville Globular Bottle, Brilliant Amber,
Melon Ribbed, 24 Ribs, Shallow Broken Blister
On 1 Rib, 7½" H. $525.00
Flattened Globular Bottle, Aqua, Swirled,
24 Ribs, 6⅝" H. $65.00

(A-OH. '76)   *Garth's Auctions, Inc.*
(Row I, Left to Right)
Blown Ludlow Bottle, Green, 5½" H. .$55.00
Blown Bottle, Green, ½ Post, Flattened, Circu-
lar, Pewter Collar & Threaded Cap, 5" H. .....
....$40.00
Cornucopia Flask, Yellow-Amber, Rev: Bas-
ket Of Produce, Chip On Lip, 5" H. $55.00
Blown Flask, Pale Green, 21 Vertical Ribs,
4¾" H. $65.00
(Row II, Left to Right)
Flask, Green, Blown In 2-Part Mold, Applied
Ring On Neck, Pontiled, 6¾" H. $40.00
Blown Bottle, Olive-Green, 8½" H. $30.00
Flask, Chestnut, Aqua, 5" H. $25.00
Cornucopia Flask, Olive, Rev: Urn W/Pro-
duce, 6¾" H. $45.00
(Row III, Left to Right)
Flask, Red-Amber, Eagle W/"Ohio" & Shep-
ard & Co.", Rev: Masonic, 6½" H. $210.00
Violin Flask, Olive-Amber, Check In Neck, 7" H.
....$180.00
Cornucopia Flask, Bluish Green, Rev: Urn
W/Produce, 6⅝" H. $175.00

(A-OH. '76)   *Garth's Auctions, Inc.*
(Row I, Left to Right)
Calabash Bottle, Aqua, Union & Clasped
Hands, Rev: Eagle & "A.R.S.", Chip On Lip,
8¾" H. $35.00
Calabash Bottle, Green, Eagle & Shield, Rev:
Plain, 8¾" H. $65.00
Calabash Bottle, Aqua, Washington, Rev:
Tree, 9" H. $90.00
Calabash Bottle, Aqua, Union & Clasped
Hands, Rev: Eagle & D"A.R.S.", 9" H. .$35.00
(Row II, Left to Right)
Flask, Aqua, "Summer", Rev: "Winter", 7¼" H.
....$15.00
Flask, Aqua, Eagle & "Continental", Rev:
Indian & "Cunningham & Co., Pittsburgh, Pa.",
9¼" H. $50.00
Flask, Aqua, Eagle & Banner W/"A. & Co.",
Rev: Union & Clasped Hands, 8½" H. .$30.00
Flask, Aqua, "Gen. Taylor Never Surrenders",
Rev: "The Father Of His Country", 7¼" H. .....
....$15.00
(Row III, Left to Right)
Flask, Aqua, Eagle & Shield, Rev: "For Our
Country", 7" H. $45.00
Flask, Aqua, "For Pike's Peak", Rev: Eagle,
7½" H. $20.00
Flask, Green, Double Eagle, 9" H. ...$110.00
Flask, Aqua, "Dyottville Glass Works, Philada,
Gen. Taylor Never Surrenders", Rev: "The
Father Of His Country", 7" H. $25.00

(A-OH. '76)   *Garth's Auctions, Inc.*
(Row I, Left to Right)
Globular Bottle, Amethyst, Flake On Lip, 12" H.
....$65.00
Cathedral Bottle, Brilliant Aqua, Iron Pontil,
14¼" H. $310.00
Blown Bottle, Sapphire Blue, Base Stamped
"3000" In A Square, 10½" H. $25.00
(Row II, Left to Right)
Blown Jar, Peacock Green, Pontiled, Minor
Flake On Bottom Edge, 9" H. $95.00
Blown Jar, Apple Green, Pontiled, Rim Has
Turned Over Lip, 7" H. $50.00
Ink Bottle, Cobalt, "Carters", 9¾" H. ..$25.00
Blown Jar, Lt. Cornflower Blue, Pontiled, 9¼" H.
....$75.00

(A-OH. '76)   *Garth's Auctions, Inc.*
(Row I, Left to Right)
Bottle, Amber, "Rex Kidney & Liver Bitters, The
Best Laxative And Blood Purifier", 9½" H. ....
....$2.00
Bottle, Amber, "Hoster, Col. O.", 11½" H. ....
....$4.00
Bottle, Drk. Teal Blue, 14" H. $10.00
Bottle, Amber, "Zincari Bitters", Bulbous Neck,
Iridescent Exterior, 12" H. $17.50
(Row II, Left to Right)
Flask, Eagle & "Liberty", Green, Rev: "Willing-
ton Glass Co., West Willington, Conn.", 9" H. .
....$55.00
Bottle, Puce, Ludlow, Applied Handle & Iron
Pontil, Attrib. To South Jersey As Little Brown
Marshallville Jug, 6¼" H. $140.00
Flask, Chestnut, Olive-Green, 5¼" H. .$62.50
Flask, Drk. Amber, Sheaf W/Crossed Rake &
Pitch Fork, Rev: "Traveler's Companion",
9¼" H. $85.00

(A-PA. '76)   *Pennypacker Auction Centre*
HISTORICAL FLASKS
(Left to Right)
Eagle, Half-Pint, Brilliant Greenish-Aqua $90.00
Eagle, Half-Pint, Brilliant Aqua $110.00
Washington-Eagle, Quart, Bluish-Aqua ......
....$85.00
Double Eagle, Half-Pint, Aqua $70.00

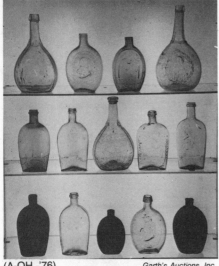

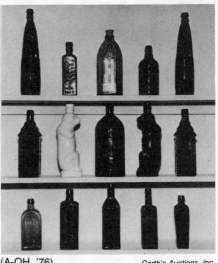

(A-OH. '76)   Garth's Auctions, Inc.

(A-OH. '76)   Garth's Auctions, Inc.

(A-OH. '76)   Garth's Auctions, Inc.

(Row I, Left to Right)
Calabash Flask, Aqua, Man Shooting Gun, Dog, Tree, Fence; Reverse: Man W/Whip, Horse, Tree, 9¼" H. $85.00
Flask, Aqua, Bust Of Washington, "The Father Of His Country"; Reverse: Bust Of Taylor, "Gen. Taylor Never Surrenders", 7" H. $65.00
Zanesville Shepard Flask, Aqua, GIV-32, 6⅝" H. $275.00
Calabash Flask, Aqua, Jenny Lind, GI-99. Sick. 10" H. $70.00

(Row II, Left to Right)
Flask, Green, Pint, "For Pike's Peak", Reverse: Eagle & "Credo", 7¾" H. $75.00
Flask, Aqua, Pint, Double Sheaf Of Wheat Ties W/A Loop In Center, 7⅞" H. $80.00
Calabash Flask, Aqua, Union & Clasped Hands; Reverse: Eagle & Banner, 9¼" H. $50.00
Flask, Blue, Pint, Union & Clasped Hands, "W. Frank & Sons, Pitts"; Reverse: Cannon & Flag, 7⅜" H. $75.00
Flask, Aqua, Pint, "Champion"; Reverse: "Balt. Md." Mck. Pl. 251, No.'s 11 & 12, 8¼" H. $85.00

(Row III, Left to Right)
Flask, Olive, Pint, Star W/Eye & "A.D."; Reverse: Star W/Arm & Fist & "G R J R", Flake On Base, McK. Pl. 251, No.'s 16 & 17, 7½" H. $105.00
Flask, Green-Aqua, Pint, Girl On Bicycle, Banner "Not For Joe"; Reverse: Plain. Sick. 7⅝" H. $65.00
Cornucopia Flask, Olive-Amber, Pint, GIII-7, 5¼" H. $85.00
Flask, Aqua, Pint, "Washington"; Reverse: "G. Z. Taylor", Sick., 7⅛" H. $50.00
Cornucopia Flask, Green-Yellow, Pint, GIII-4, 6⅞" H. $105.00

(Row I, Left to Right)
Stoneware Bottle, "Wm. Edwards & Co., Cleveland, Ohio", Orig. Threaded Stopper, 11¼" H. $50.00
Blown Demi-John, Olive Green, 11¼" H. $70.00
Paneled Bottle, Cobalt Blue, 11¼" H. $82.50
Rockingham Bottle, Coachman, 9½" H. $75.00

(Row II, Left to Right)
Opalescent Bottle, Crumpled Look, Threaded Metal Cap, 5-3/5" H. $25.00
Medicine Bottle, "Dr. Sullivan's Sure Solvent, A Reliable Tonic", Orig. Contents Label & Box, 7⅝" H. $3.00
Bitters Bottle, Amber, "Lash Bitters", Orig. Contents, 9½" H. $3.00
Bitters Bottle, Aqua, "Atwood's Jaundice Bitters—Moses Atwood, Georgetown, Ma.", 6⅜" H. $2.00
Medicine Bottle, Amber, "Warner's Safe Remedies Co., Rochester, N.Y. U.S.A.", Orig. Contents, Label & Box, 9¼" H. $20.00
Sapphire Blue Bottle, "Strong Gobb & Co., Wholesale Druggist's, Cleveland, Ohio, 6½" H. $25.00

(Row III, Left to Right)
Bottle, Amber, "Jno. Wyeth & Bro., Philadelphia, Liq. Ext. Malt", 9" H. $7.00
Bottle, Red Amber, "Highrock Congress Spring C & W., Saratoga, N.Y.", 9½" H. $35.00
Gin Bottle, Olive, Bottom Marked By Star & 8 Dates, 10½" H. $17.50
Gin Bottle, Olive, Bottom Marked By 3 Concentric Rings, 9" H. $12.50
Bottle, Drk. Green, "Congress & Empire Spring Co., Saratoga, N.Y., 7¾" H. $32.50

(Row I, Left to Right)
Bottle, Ear Of Corn Shape, Amber, "National Bitters", Base Marked "Patent 1867", 12½" H. $190.00
Bottle, Green, "Pine Tree Tar Cordial, Phila., L.Q. Wishart's Patent 1859, 8" H. $40.00
Carter Ink Bottle, Cobalt, Gothic Arches, 9¾" H. $45.00
Bottle, Drk. Green, "Congress Water - Etc.", Flake On Lip, 7½" H. $12.00
Bottle, Ear Of Corn Shape, Amber, "National Bitters", Base Marked "Patent 1867", 12" H. $200.00

(Row II, Left to Right)
Bottle, Amber, "Drake's 1860 Plantation X Bitters, Patented 1862, 10" H. $45.00
Bear Bottle, Milk Glass, 11" H. $105.00
Bottle, Amber, "Warner's Safe Cure", 11" H. $155.00
Bear Bottle, Black Glass, 11" H. $125.00
Bottle, Lt. Amber, "Drake's 1860 Plantation X Bitters, Patented 1862", 10" H. $85.00

(Row III, Left to Right)
Bottle, Aquamarine, "Gargling Oil, Lockport, N.Y.", 7¼" H. $12.50
Bottle, Drk. Amber, "Dr. J. Hostetter's Stomach Bitters", 8½" H. $5.00
Bottle, Amber, "Boyles Hop Bitters 1872", 9½" H. $20.00
Bottle, Amber, "H.E. Bucklen & Co., Chicago, Ill., Electric Bitters", 8⅝" H. $12.50
Gin Bottle, Olive, Roughness On Lip, 7½" H. $10.00

← (A-MA. '75)   Richard A. Bourne Co. Inc.
BOTTLES AND FLASKS
(Row I, Left to Right)
"Warner's Safe Kidney & Liver Cured" Bottle, Deep Reddish-Amber, 1½ Pt. $15.00
"P. Horan, #5 W. 27th St., N.Y." ½ Pt. $10.00
"Chance & Duncan N.Y." Bottle Slightly Sick $30.00
(Row II, Left to Right)
Whiskey Flask, Scarce Dark Yellow-Green Pt. $80.00
"Flora Temple" Whiskey, Rare Deep Amber, Pt., Rare, Crack Across Face Of Front .$10.00
Eagle-Cornucopia Pt. Flask, Amber ...$60.00

(A-MA. '75)   Richard A. Bourne Co. Inc.

(Left to Right)
"Greeley's Bourbon Bitters", Qt. Dark Amber $90.00
"Globe Tobacco Co." Amber Barrel-Shaped Bottle, Arrangement For Screw Top, Pat. Date Oct. 10, 1882 .... $20.00
Amber Blown Chestnut Bottle, Heavy Lipped, 10½" H. $50.00

(A-OH. '76)

(Row I, Left to Right)

Bottle, Amber, "Tippecanoe", Base Marked "Rochester, N.Y." $70.00

Bottles, (2), Aqua, "Thompson's Wild Cherry Hygenia Phosphate, Chicago", 8" H. (Pictured) & "Ayres Sarsaparilla, Lowell, Mass., U.S.A.", 8½" H. $6.00

Bottle, Amber, "Dr. C.W. Robacks Stomach Bitters, Cincinnati, Ohio", 9½" H. $120.00

Soda Bottles, (2), Aqua, "One Tall" W/Tall Man & Cane, 9" H. (Pictured), Also "The Giering Bottling Co., Youngstown, Ohio", W/Anchor, 7¾" H. $3.00

Log Cabin Bottle, Amber, "Holtzerman's Patent Stomach Bitters", 9⅞" H. $140.00

(Row II, Left to Right)

Octagonal Bottle, Aquamarine, "Rumford Chemical Works", Bottom Marked "Patented March 10, 1868", Chipped Lip, 7¾" H. $3.00

Elephant Bottle, Amber, "Old Sol", 8½" H. $9.00

Milk Glass Bottle, White, "Hartwig Kantorowicz Pozen Hamburg, Germany", 9" H. $50.00

Bottles, (2), Drk. Amber, Moses, "Facsimile Of First Poland Water Bottle, Hiram Ricker & Sons, Inc.", 8¾" H. (Pictured); & Clear Figural Bottle, Man W/Umbrella, 8¾" H. $2.00

Bottle, Aqua, "Wm. Betz Mineral Water, Salem, Ohio", Iron Pontil, 7⅝" H. $182.50

(Row III, Left to Right)

Bottles, (2), Aqua, "Dr. Kilmer's Swamp Root Cure, Binghamton, N.Y.", 8¼" H. (Pictured); & Amber "Dr. J. Hostetter's Stomach Bitters", Base Marked "W.McC. & Co." 9" H. $7.00

Bottle, Amber, "Warner's Kidney & Liver Cure, Rochester, N.Y.", 9½" H. $10.00

Fish Bitters Bottle, Amber, 9¾" H. $7.00

Bottle, Golden Amber, "Dr. M.M. Fenner's Peoples Remedies, Fredonia, N.Y. U.S.A., Kidney & Backache Cure, 1872-1898", 10¼" H. $17.50

Medicine Bottles, (2), Aqua, "Indian Sagwa, Healy & Bigelow", 8⅝" H. (Pictured), & Cobalt Blue "Sanford's Radical Cure", Small Chip On Lip, 7⅝" H. $17.50

(A-OH. '76)

(Row I)

White Milk Glass Bitters Bottle, "Harwin Kantorowicz, Posen Hamburg, Germany", 9¼" H. $40.00

Aqua Medicine Bottle, "C. F. Haskell Coloris Capilli Restitutor". Flake on Lip, 7⅜" H. $12.50

Brilliant Red Amber Bottle, Whittled Mould. "Hartwig Kantorowicz Posen, Wrokerstr No. 6 Germany". Marked With "H.K." And Star Of David, 10" H. $25.00

Blue Octagonal Bottle, "C. Meimstreet & Co. Troy, N.Y." 7" H. $10.00

(Row II)

Golden Amber Bitters Bottle, "Doyles Hop Bitters", 9½" H. $15.00

Amber Bitters Bottle, "The Great Tonic, Dr. Caldwell's Herb Bitters", Small Broken Blister Almost To The Shoulder, 12½" H. $62.50

(A-MA. '76)

(Row I, Left to Right)

Flask, Washington-Taylor Portraits, McKearin GI-55, Pale Green $80.00

Scrolled Flask, Pt., McKearin IX-11a, Aquamarine $50.00

Medicine Bottle, ½ Pt., Two Mold W/Pontil, Bearing Name "F. Brown, Druggist, Cor. Chest & So. St. Philada", Pale Aqua $17.00

(Row II, Left to Right)

Eagle-Cornucopia Flask, Pt., McKearin GII-72, Drk. Olive $130.00

Coventry Flask, Pt., McKearin GIII-4, Basket Of Fruit & Cornucopia, Olive Amber $70.00

Coventry Flask, Pt., McKearin GIII-4, Basket Of Fruit & Cornucopia, Deep Olive Green $75.00

(Row III, Left to Right)

Carter's Ink Bottle, Pt., Gothic Panels, Cobalt Blue; Together W/**Whiskey Bottle,** ½ Pt., Med. Green $50.00

Plantation Bitters Bottle, Qt., Amber . $40.00

Doyle's Hop Bitters Bottle, 1872, Amber $15.00

(A-PA. '76)

(Row I, Left to Right)

Masonic Flask, Olive Green, GIV-24, ½ Pt. $270.00

Masonic Flask, Olive Amber, GIV-21, Pt. $160.00

Zanesville Bottle, Globular, 24 Ribs Swirled To Right, Deep Amber, 1¾ Qt. $500.00

Flask, Star & Arm Above "C.R.J.A.", Reverse W/Seeing Eye On Six Pointed Star Above "A.D." McKearin #251-16-17, Amber, Pt. ... $190.00

Pitkin Flask, Connecticut-Keene, 36 Rib, Flake On Side Of Neck, Olive Green, 5" H., ½ Pt. $140.00

(Row II, Left to Right)

Flask, Railroad W/Eagle On Reverse, Deep Amber, GV-8, Pt. $185.00

Free Blown Bottle, McKearin, Deep Olive Green, 5½" H. $55.00

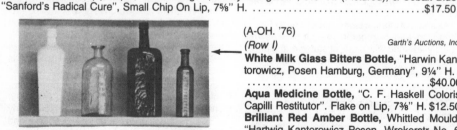

ABC PLATES - Alphabet plates were made especially for children as teaching aids. They date from the late 1700s, and were made of various material including porcelain, pottery, glass, pewter, tin and ironstone.

ADAMS ROSE dinnerware was made by Adams & Son in the Staffordshire District of England from 1820-1850. The ware is decorated with brilliant red roses and green leaves on a white ground.

AMPHORA ART POTTERY was made at the Amphora Porcelain Works in the Teplitz-Turn area of Bohemia during the late 19th and early 20th centuries. Numerous potteries were located here.

BATTERSEA ENAMELS - The name "Battersea" is a general term for those metal objects decorated with enamels, such as pill, patch, and snuff boxes, door knobs, etc. The process of fusing enamel onto metal — usually copper — began about 1750 in the Battersea District of London. Today, the name has become a generic term for similar objects — mistakenly called "Battersea."

BELLEEK porcelain was first made a Fermanaugh, Ireland in 1857. Today, this ware is still being made in buildings within walking distance of the original clay pits according to the skills and traditions of the original artisans. Irish Belleek is famous for its thinness and delicacy. Similar type wares were also produced in other European countries as well as the United States.

BENNINGTON POTTERY - The first pottery works in Bennington, Vermont was established by Captain John Norton in 1793; and, for 101 years, it was owned and operated by succeeding generations of Nortons. Today, the term "Bennington" is synonymous with the finest in American ceramics because the town was the home of several pottery operations during the last century — each producing under different labels. Today, items produced at Bennington are now conveniently, if inaccurately, dubbed "Bennington". One of the popular types of pottery produced here is known as "Rockingham". The term denotes the rich, solid brown glazed pottery from which many household items were made. The ware was first produced by the Marquis Of Rockingham in Swinton, England — hence the name.

BISQUE -The term applies to pieces of porcelain or pottery which have been fired, but left in an unglazed state.

BLOOR DERBY — "Derby" porcelain dates from about 1755 when William Duesbury began the production of porcelain at Derby. In 1769, he purchased the famous Chelsea Works and operated both factories. During this Chelsea-Derby period, some of the finest examples of English porcelains were made. Because of their fine quality, in 1773, King George III gave Duesbury the patent to mark his porcelain wares "Crown Derby". Duesbury died in 1796. In 1810, the factory was purchased by Robert Bloor, a senior clerk. Bloor revived the Imari styles which had been so popular. After his death in 1845, former workmen continued to produce fine porcelains using the traditional Derby patterns. The firm was reorganized in 1876 and in 1878, a new factory was built. In 1890, Queen Victoria appointed the company "Manufacturers to Her Majesty," with the right to be known as Royal Crown Derby.

BUFFALO POTTERY - The Buffalo Pottery of Buffalo, New York, was organized in 1901. The firm was an adjunct of the Larkin Soap Company which was established to produce china and pottery premiums for that company. Of the many different types produced, the Buffalo Pottery is most famous for their "Deldare" line which was developed in 1905.

CANARY LUSTRE earthenware dates to the early 1800s, and was produced by potters in the Staffordshire District of England. The body of this ware is a golden yellow and decorated with transfer printing, usually in black.

CANTON porcelain is a blue-and-white decorated ware produced near Canton, China from the late 1700s through the last century. Its hand-decorated Chinese scenes have historical as well as mythological significance.

CAPO-di-MONTE, originally a soft paste porcelain, is Italian in origin. The first ware was made during the 1700s near Naples. Although numerous marks were used, the most familiar to us is the crown over the letter "N". Mythological subjects, executed in either high or low relief and tinted in bright colors on a light ground, were a favorite decoration. The earlier ware has a peculiar greyish color as compared to later examples which have a whiter body.

CARLSBAD porcelain was made by several factories in the area from the late 1800s and exported to the United States. When Carlsbad became a part of Czechoslovakia after World War I, wares were frequently marked "Karlsbad." Items marked "Victoria" were made for Lazarus & Rosenfeldt, Importers.

CASTLEFORD earthenware was produced in England from the late 1700s until around 1820. Its molded decoration is similar to Pratt Wares.

CHELSEA KERAMIC ART WORKS - The firm was founded in 1872 at Chelsea, Massachusetts by James Robertson & Sons, and closed in 1889. In 1891, the pottery was reopened under the name of The Chelsea Pottery, U.S. The first and most popular blue underglaze decoration for the desirable "Cracque Ware" as the rabbit motif — designed by Joseph L. Smith. In 1893, construction was started on the new pottery in Dedham, Massachusetts and production began in 1895. The name of the pottery was then changed to "Dedham Pottery", to eliminate confusion with the English Chelsea Ware. The famed crackleware finish became synonymous with the name. Because of its popularity, over fifty patterns of tableware were made.

CHINESE EXPORT PORCELAIN was made in quantity in China during the 1700s and early 1800s. The term identifies a variety of porcelain wares made for export to Europe and the United States. Since many thought the product to be of joint Chinese and English manufacture, it has also been known as "Oriental or Chinese Lowestoft."

As much of this ware was made to order for the American and Europeran market, it was frequently adorned with seals of states or the coats of arms of individuals, in addition to eagles, sailing scenes, flowers, religious and mythological scenes.

COALPORT porcelain has been made by the Coalport Porcelain Works in England since 1795. The ware is still being produced at Stroke-on-Trent.

COPELAND-SPODE - The firm was founded by Josiah Spode in 1770 in Staffordshire, England. From 1847 W.T. Copeland & Sons, Ltd., succeeded Spode, using the designation "Late Spode" to their wares. The firm is still in operation.

COPPER LUSTRE - See Lustre Wares

CORONATION items of pottery, glass, etc., with the images of a monarch and the date, have been produced as souvenirs for many years.

CUP PLATES were used when cups were handless and saucers were deep. During the early 1800s, it was very fashionable to drink from a saucer. Thus, a variety of fancy small plates were produced for the cup to rest in. The lacy Sandwich examples are very collectible.

DAVENPORT pottery and porcelain were made at the Davenport Factory in Longport, Staffordshire, England by John Davenport — from 1793 until 1887 when the pottery closed. Most of the wares produced here — porcelains, creamwares, ironstone, earthenwares and other products — were marked.

DEDHAM - See Chelsea Art Works

DELFT - Holland is famous for its fine examples of tin-glazed pottery dating from the 16th century. Although blue and white is the most popular color, other colors were also made. The majority of the ware found today is from the late Victorian period and, when the name Holland appears with the Delft factory mark, this indicates that the item was made after 1891.

DORCHESTER POTTERY was established by George Henderson in Dorchester, a part of Boston, in 1895. Production included stonewares, industrial wares, and later some decorated tablewares. The pottery is still in production.

DOULTON - The Pottery was established in Lambeth in 1815 by John Doulton and John Watts. When Watts retired in 1854, the firm became known as Doulton & Company. In 1901, King Edward VII conferred a double honor on the company by the presentation of the Royal Warrant, authorizing their chairman to use the word "Royal" in describing products. A variety of wares have been made over the years for the American market. The firm is still in production.

DRESDEN, see Meissen

FAMILLE ROSE is a Chinese export porcelain dating from the late 1700s to 1800. It has a pink opaque body.

FLOWING BLUE ironstone is a highly glazed dinnerware made at Staffordshire by a variety of potters. It became popular about 1825. Items were printed with the patterns (oriental), and the color flowed from the design over the white body so that the finished product appeared smeared. Although purple and brown colors were also made, the deep cobalt blue shades were the most popular. Later wares were less blurred, having more white ground.

GAUDY DUTCH is the most spectacular of the Gaudy wares. It was made for the Pennsylvania Dutch market from about 1785 until the 1820s. This soft paste tableware is lightweight and frail in appearance. Its rich cobalt blue decoration was applied to the biscuit, glazed and fired — then other colors were applied over the first glaze — and the object was fired again. No lustre is included in its decoration.

GAUDY IRONSTONE was made in Staffordshire from the early 1850s until around 1865. This ware is heavier than Gaudy Welsh or Gaudy Dutch, as its texture is a mixture of pottery and porcelain clay.

GAUDY WELCH, produced in England from about 1830, resembles Gaudy Dutch in decoration, but the workmanship is not as fine and its texture is more comparable to that of spatterware. Lustre is usually included with the decoration.

GIBSON GIRL PLATES were created by Charles Dana Gibson at the turn of the century, and were made by Royal Doulton. They were of semi-porcelain, with scenes printed in underglaze black, and blue petalled borders. The first series included 24 different scenes. The second set was composed of 12 plates in 9-inch size, each centered with a different Gibson Girl head, printed in black, with a bowknot blue border.

HISTORICAL STAFFORDSHIRE — The term refers to a particular blue-on-white, transfer-printed earthenware produced in quantity during the early 1800s by many potters in the Staffordshire District. The central decoration was usually an American city scene or landscape, frequently showing some mode of transportation in the foreground. Other designs included portraits and patriotic emblems. Each potter had a characteristic border which is helpful to identify a particular ware, as many pieces are unmarked. Later transfer-printed wares were made in sepia, pink, green and black, but the early cobalt blue examples are the most desirable.

HULL POTTERY was made in 1803 by the Acme Pottery Company in Croaksville, Ohio. Their art pottery line was produced in 1917 and was discontinued in 1950.

HUMMEL figurines, based on the drawings of Berta Hummel — German born artist and nun, were first made in 1934. All Hummel items today are extremely collectible, including collectors' plates.

IMARI ware is named for the Japanese port of Imari, from which porcelain made in neighboring villages was exported. The body of this ware was pure white, hard, fine, and very durable. Early pieces were modeled on Chinese blue and white wares or colored with enamels with red predominating. Because potteries in the area worked independently, many different shapes and patterns were produced. Since the colorful ware was extremely popular, European factories of the 18th and 19th centuries imitated the designs. Thus, the name has come to mean any pattern of this type.

IRONSTONE is a heavy, durable, utilitarian ware made from the slag of iron furnaces, ground and mixed with clay. Charles Mason of Lane Delft, Staffordshire, patented the formula in 1813. Much of the early ware was decorated in imitation of Imari, in addition to transfer-printed blue ware, flowing blues and browns. During the mid-nineteenth century, the plain white enlivened only by embossed designs became fashionable. Literally hundreds of patterns were made for export.

JASPERWARE is a very fine grained, smooth, unglazed ware first introduced by Josiah Wedgwood in 1774. Its mat surface is always decorated with white relief ornaments — usually cameo designs. Blue is the most common color (many variations); however, lavender, sage-green, olive-green, yellow and lilac were made. Jasper Ware made by Wedgwood is almost always clearly marked.

KATE GREENAWAY Kate Greenaway was born in Hoxton, England in 1846 and lived until 1902. Her interesting illustrations first appeared at the height of the Victorian period, and the child-like figures that she created in old English costumes had great appeal. Her designs appear on glass, china and metals.

K.P.M. — is part of one of the marks used by the Meissen Factory Konigliche Porzellan Manufaktur during the 18th century. Other German firms also included the letters with their marks on wares produced during the 19th century and 20th century.

LEEDS POTTERY was established by Charles Green in 1758 at Leed, Yorkshire, England. Early wares are unmarked. From 1775, the impressed mark, "Leeds Pottery" was used. After 1800, the name "Hartly, Green & Co." was added, and the

impressed or incised letters "L P" were also used to identify the ware

LIMOGES — The name identifies fine porcelain wares produced by many factories at Limoges, France since the mid-1900s. A variety of different marks identify wares made here including Haviland china.

LIVERPOOL POTTERY — The term applies to wares produced by many potters located in Liverpool, England from the early 1700s, for American trade. Their print-decorated pitchers — referred to as "jugs" in England — have been especially popular. These featured patriotic emblems, prominent men, ships, etc., and can be easily identified as nearly all are melon-shaped with a very pointed lip, strap handle and graceful curved body.

LUSTRE WARES — John Hancock of Hanley, England invented this type of decoration on earthenwares during the early 1800s. The copper, bronze, ruby, gold, purple, yellow, pink and mottled pink lustre finishes were made from gold — painted on the glazed objects, then fired. The latter type is often referred to as "Sunderland Lustre". Its pinkish tones vary in color and pattern. The silver lustres were made from platinum.

MAJOLICA — The name identifies fancifully designed and brilliantly colored lead-glazed earthenwares. During the mid-1800s, it was made in quantity in England and later in the United States. Its popularity continued until the turn of the century. The best known Majolica produced here was made by Griffen, Smith & Hill Co., Phoenixville, Pa. during the late 1800s.

MEISSEN PORCELAIN, the first true porcelain in Europe, was produced by a process discovered by Johann Freidrich Bottger, under the patronage of August II Elector. This ware was first made in Dresden, Saxony, about 1708. Later, the factory was moved to nearby Meissen, giving the ware an interchangeable nomenclature.

METTLACH, Germany, located in the Zoar Basin, was the location of the famous Villeroy & Boch factories from 1836 until 1921 when the factory was destroyed by fire. Steins (dating from about 1842) and other stonewares with bas relief decoration were their specialty.

MINTON — The Minton pottery was established by Thomas Minton at Stroke-On-Trent in 1793. Early wares were generally unmarked, but after 1862, all items produced here were clearly marked.

MOCHA WARE — This banded creamware was first produced in England during the late 1700s. The early ware was light weight and thin, having colorful bands of bright colors decorating its cream-colored to very light brown body. After 1840, the ware became heavier in body and the color was oftentimes quite light — almost white. Mocha Ware can easily be identified by its colorful banded decorations — on and between the bands, including feathery ferns, lacy trees, seaweeds, squiggly designs and lowly earthworms.

MOORCROFT POTTERY — W. Moorcroft Limited, Potters, was established at Cobridge, England in 1913 by William Moorcroft. Today, the firm is still in operation and is now managed by Walter Moorcroft, son of the founder. Practically all of the fine art pottery produced by the firm was handcrafted on the potter's wheel and then decorated. Because of the exceptionally high temperature at which the colors are fired, its surface has an unusual brilliance. Moorcroft Pottery is well marked. After its founder's death, the mark (signature) was changed to the letters WM in script, or showed only the impressed mark MOORCROFT, in addition to the words "Made in England", in green.

MORIAGA is a term used to identify colorful Japanese pottery to which a raised overglaze decoration has been added, resembling elaborate cake decoration.

MUSTACHE CUPS were first made at Longton, Stroke-on-Trent, England in 1930 by Harvey Adams. The cups became popular in the United States following the war with Mexico, when men cultivated the hair of the upper lip. The purpose of this cup was to permit a gentleman to drink without letting his mustache touch the liquid. This was accomplished by a raised lip guard attached to the rim of the cup, or a fixed internal ledge attached to one side, each having a small opening through which the liquid could drain into the mouth.

NEWHALL porcelain was made at the Newhall Porcelain Manufactory at Shelton, Staffordshire, England, beginning in 1872. During the first quarter of the nineteenth century, the factory also made bone porcelain.

NILOAK POTTERY with its prominent swirled, marbleized designs, is a 20th century pottery first produced at Benton, Arkansas in 1911 by the Niloak Pottery Company. Production ceased in 1946.

NIPPON porcelain has been produced in quantity for the American market since the late 19th century. After 1891, when it became obligatory to include the country of origin on all imports, the Japanese trademark "Nippon" was used. Numerous other marks appear on this ware identifying the manufacturer, artist or importer. The hand painted Nippon examples are extremely popular today and prices are on the rise.

NORITAKE porcelain was made in Japan after 1904. It was manufactured by Nippon Toki Kaisha at Nagoya, Japan, and the company is still in operation. One of the most popular dinnerware patterns produced is "Azalia." The Larkin Soap Company included dinner sets in this pattern on their premium lists. The ware was also sold in stores.

OCCUPIED JAPAN — The term includes items exported to the United States from Japan during the years 1945 through 1952. This also applies to an array of small items marked "Made in Occupied Japan."

QUIMPER POTTERY has been made in France for almost 300 years. This ware is usually decorated with bright hand decorated provencial scenes. The joined letters HB written in script is found on the early pieces dating from 1782. Quimper is still being made in France, and since it is decorated by hand, standardization is impossible. Its variations in color and irregularities of pattern are one of its charms. Marks include "Henriot" or "H-B," with the name "Quimper," — and after 1891, "France" was added to the mark.

REDWARE is one of our most popular forms of country pottery. It has a soft, porous body and its color varies from reddish-brown tones to deep wine or light orange. It was produced in mostly utilitarian forms by potters in small factories or by potters working on their farms, to fill their everyday needs. Glazes were used to intensify the color. The most desirable examples are the slip-decorated pieces.

ROCKINGHAM, See Bennington Pottery.

ROOKWOOD POTTERY — The Rookwood Pottery began production at Cincinnati, Ohio in 1880 under the direction of Maria Longworth Nichols Storer, and operated until 1960. The name was derived from the family estate, "Rookwood", because of the "rooks" or "crows" which inhabited the wooded areas. All pieces of this art pottery are marked, usually bearing the famous flame mark, and the reversed letter "R" placed back to back with the letter "P". The flames surrounded the letters. However, several marks were used prior to the impressed "Rookwood" name first used in 1882. The RP monogram was adopted in 1886 and, in 1887, a flame was placed over the RP along with another flame.

ROSE MEDALLION ware dates from the eighteenth century. It was decorated and exported from Canton, China in quantity. The name generally applied to those pieces having medallions with figures of people alternating with panels of flowers, birds and butterflies. When all the medallions were filled with flowers, the ware was differentiated as Rose Canton.

ROSENTHAL PORCELAIN was first produced in Selb, Bavaria in 1880, and the factory is still in operation, specializing in quality tablewares and figurines.

ROSEVILLE POTTERY — The Roseville Pottery was organized in 1890 in Roseville, Ohio. The firm produced utilitarian stoneware in the plant formerly owned by the Owens Pottery. In 1898, the firm acquired the Midland Pottery of Roseville, also producers of stoneware, and the Linden Avenue Plant at Zanesville, Ohio, originally built by the Clark Stoneware Company. In 1900, an art line of pottery was created to compete with Owens and Weller lines. The new ware was named "Rozane", and it was produced at the Zanesville location. Following its success, other prestige lines were created. The Azurine line was introduced about 1902.

ROYAL BAYREUTH manufactory began in Tettau in 1794 at the first porcelain factory in Bavaria. Wares made here were on the same par with Meissen. Fire destroyed the original factory during the late 1800s. Much of the wares available today were made at the new factory which began production in 1897. These include Rose Tapestry, Sunbonnet Baby novelties and the Devil and Card items. The Royal Bayreuth blue mark has the 1794 founding date incorporated with the mark.

From 1946 to 1949, the firm reproduced some Tapestry and Devil and Card items, using the Royal Bayreuth crest, but the color of the mark was changed to light green.

ROYAL BONN — The trade name identifies a variety of porcelain items made during the 19th century by the Bonn China Manufactory, established in 1755 by Clemers August. Most of the ware found today is from the Victorian period.

ROYAL DOULTON wares have been made from 1901, when King Edward VII converted a double honor on the Doulton Pottery by the presentation of the Royal Warrant, authorizing their chairman to use the word "Royal" in describing products. A variety of wares have been produced for the American market. The firm is still in production.

ROYAL DUX was produced in Bohemia during the late 1800s. Large quantities of this decorative porcelain ware were exported to the United States. Royal Dux figurines are especially popular.

ROYAL WORCESTER — The Worcester factory was established in 1751 in England. This is a tastefully decorated porcelain noted for its creamy white lustreless surface. Serious collectors prefer items from the Dr. Wall (the activator of the concern) period of production which extended from the time the factory was established to 1785.

R. S. PRUSSIA porcelain was produced during the mid-1800s by Erdman Schlegelmilch in Suhl. His brother Reinhold founded a factory in 1869 in Tillowitz in lower Silesia. Both made fine quality porcelain, using both satin and high gloss finishes with comparable decoration. Additionally, both brothers used the same R.S. mark in the same colors, the initials being in memory of their father, Rudolph Schlegelmilch. It has not been determined when production at the two factories ceased.

SALOPIAN table wares were first produced by the Caughley Factory of England during the mid 1770s. The ware is delicate and fragile. Early pieces were generally marked with the letter C or S, a crescent, or with various Chinese style numerals in underglaze blue. The impressed mark "Salopian" appears on many later wares which appealed to the Pennsylvania Dutch.

SARREGUEMINES POTTERY was made in Germany during the 18th century and later in France by Utzschneider & Co., where much soft paste porcelain, biscuit figures, artistic stonewares and even majolica have been produced. The latter is lighter in weight than English majolica. Items bear the impressed mark "Sarreguemines," and the firm is still in operation.

SATSUMA is a Japanese pottery having a distinctive creamy crackled glaze decorated with bright enamels and oftentimes Japanese faces. The majority of the ware available today includes the mass produced wares dating from the 1850s. Their quality does not compare to the fine early examples.

SGRAFFITO is a type of scratched or incised line decoration on brown earthenware which was covered with light slip, then incisions were cut through the slip. This type of ornamentation was almost exclusively the work of Pennsylvania artisans. Flowers and birds were the most typical decoration. Examples were rarely used for ordinary utilitarian purposes, but were given as gifts. Signed pieces are especially prized.

SHENANDOAH POTTERY — The term identifies pottery and stoneware produced in the Shenandoah Valley by various potters during the last century.

SILVER RESIST ware is similar to Silver Lustre with the exception that a pattern appears on the surface.

SPATTERWARE is a soft paste tableware, laboriously decorated with hand-drawn flowers, birds, buildings, trees, etc., with "spatter" decoration chiefly as a background. It was produced by almost every export potter in Staffordshire, Scotland and Wales, for the American market. A variety of patterns were produced in considerable quantity from the early 1800s to around 1850.

To achieve this type decoration, small bits of sponge was cut into different shapes — leaves, hearts, rosetts, vines, geometrical patterns, etc. — and mounted on the end of a short stick for convenience in dipping into the pigment.

SPONGEWARE, as it is known, is a decorated white earthenware. Color — usually blue, blue/green, brown/tan/blue, or blue/brown — was applied to the white clay base. Because the color was often applied with a color-soaked sponge, the term "spongeware" became common for this ware. A variety of utilitarian items were produced — pitchers, cookie jars, bean pots, water coolers, etc. Marked examples are rare.

STAFFORDSHIRE is a district in England where a variety of pottery and porcelain wares have been produced by many factories in the area.

STICKSPATTER — The term identifies a type of decoration that combines hand painting and

transfer-painted decoration. "Spattering" was done with either a sponge or a brush containing a moderate supply of pigment. Stick-spatter was developed from the traditional Staffordshire spatterware, as the earlier ware was time-consuming and expensive to produce. Although the majority of this ware was made in England from the 1850s to the late 1800s, it was also produced in Holland, France and elsewhere. Examples of this later were occasionally marked.

STONEWARE is a weighty dense glazed pottery made from clay mixed with flint or sand, or made from very siliceous clay that vitrifies when heated to form a durable, nonporous base. Most stoneware is salt-glazed. When not salt-glazed, it was coated with slip glaze, having a smooth finish.

SUNBONNET BABIES were created by Bertha Corbett and appeared in the Sunbonnet Babies Primer in 1902. The Royal Bayreuth China Company produced a full line of children's dishes decorated with these charming little figures. See Royal Bayreuth.

SUNDERLAND LUSTRE - See Lustre Wares

TEA LEAF is a lightweight stone china decorated with copper or gold "tea leaf" sprigs. It was first made by Anthony Shaw of Longport, England during the 1850s. By the late 1800s, other potters in Staffordshire were producing the popular ware for export to the United States. As the result, there is a noticeable version in decoration.

VAN BRIGGLE POTTERY was established at Colorado Springs, Colorado in 1900 by Artus Van Briggle and his wife Anna. Most of the ware was marked. The first mark included two joined "A's", representing their first two initials. The firm is still in operation.

VILLEROY & BOCH - See Mettlack

WEDGWOOD POTTERY was established by Josiah Wedgwood in 1759 in England. A tremendous variety of fine wares have been produced through the years including basalt, lustre wares, creamware, jasperware, bisque, agate, Queen's Ware and others. The system of marks used by the firm clearly indicates when each piece was made.

Since 1940, the new Wedgwood factory has been located at Barleston.

WELLER POTTERY — Samuel A. Weller established the Weller Pottery in 1872 in Fultonham, Ohio. In 1888, the pottery was moved to Piece Street in Putnam, Ohio — now a part of Zanesville, Ohio. The production of art pottery began in 1893 and, by late 1897, several prestige lines were being produced including Samantha, Touranda and Dickens' Ware. Other later types included Weller's Louwelsa, Eosian, Aurora, Turada and the rare Sicardo which is the most sought after and most expensive today. The firm closed in 1948.

WHIELDON ware was made by Thomas Whieldon during the 1700s in Little Fenton in Staffordshire, England. Whieldon ware is commonly associated only with the creamware decorated with mottled green, brown, blue, yellow and grey glaze, resembling tortoise shell. Whieldon also made a variety of wares molded in the shape of vegetables — melons, cauliflower, cabbage, etc., in addition to teapots and milk jugs.

YELLOWWARE is an unadorned form of earthenware produced in the United States from the 1840s. Its body texture is finer, less dense and vitreous than stoneware. Colors vary from deep yellow to pale buff, having a clear glaze. Forms were almost always utilitarian.

ZSOLNAY porcelain is a soft paste porcelain made in Funkirchen, Hungary after 1855. Items are usually decorated and enamelled in brilliant colors and glazed.

(D-CA. '76)
Children's Dishes, Buster Brown Tea Set, 21 Pcs. $290.00

(A-MO. '76)   *Woody Auction Company*
R. S. Prussia Parrot Vase, 8¾" H. . . $950.00

(D-LA. '76)
Sarreguemines Covered Dish, Melon Shaped W/Leaf-Shaped Underplate, Mkd. "Sarreguemines, France." $85.00

(D-CA. '76)
Porcelain Tea Strainer, Unmarked $45.00

(D-IL. '76)
R. S. Prussia Bowl, Deep Red Iris W/Floral Center, 11" Diam. $125.00

(A-MO. '76)   *Woody Auction Company*
R. S. Prussia Chocolate Set, Melon Boy $2,800.00

(A-MO. '76)
(Left to Right)   *Woody Auction Company*
R. S. Prussia Pitcher, 7" H., Floral Decor. $350.00
R. S. Prussia Pitcher, 7½" H., Floral Decor $275.00
R. S. Prussia Pitcher, 9" H., "Swan" $450.00
R. S. Prussia Pitcher, 8½" H., "4 Seasons" $2,800.00
R. S. Prussia Pitcher, 6½" H., "Ostrich" $3,000.00
R. S. Prussia Pitcher, 7" H., "Turkeys" $650.00
R. S. Prussia Pitcher, 7" H., "Shepherd" $2,000.00

(D-FL. '76)
Sarreguemines Plate, Mkd., Military Scene, 8½" Diam. $18.00

(A-PA. '76)
Historical Blue Staffordshire Platter, 16½",
Almshouse, New York, Beauties Of America,
Ridgway $460.00

(A-PA. '76)
Historical Blue Staffordshire Platter, 16½",
Mendenhall Ferry, Spread Eagle Border, Joseph
Stubbs, Chipped $170.00

(A-OH. '76)
HISTORICAL BLUE STAFFORDSHIRE
(Row I, Left to Right)
Plate, "LaGrange, The Residence Of The Marquis LaFayette", Impressed "E. Wood & Sons, Burslem",
10⅛" Diam. $130.00
Soup Plate, "Pine Orchard House, Catskill Mountains", Impressed "E. Wood & Sons, Burslem",
10¼" Diam. $200.00
Plate, "Table Rock Niagara", Impressed "Wood", 10" Diam. $200.00
(Row II, Left to Right)
Plate, "Beauties Of America, City Hall, New York, J. W. Ridgway", 9¾" Diam. $105.00
Platter, "Hoboken In New Jersay", STubbs, 12⅝" L....................................$295.00
Plate, "Bank Of The United States, Philadelphia", Stubbs, 1 Section Of Edge Professionally Repaired,
10¼" Diam. $85.00
(Row III, Left to Right)
Plate, "Dartmouth", Impressed "E. Wood & Sons, Burslem", 8½" Diam. $210.00
Soup Plate, "Beauties Of America, Octagon Church, Boston, J. & W. Ridgway", Some Wear,
9¾" Diam. $105.00
Plate, Nahant Hotel Near Boston", 8¼" Diam. $135.00

(A-OH. '76)
HISTORICAL BLUE STAFFORDSHIRE

Left to Right)
Platter, English Scene Of People On Country Road, 17" L. $75.00
Platter, "Beauties Of America, Alms House, New York, J. & W. Ridgway", Knife Scratches, 16½" L.
....$240.00
Platter, "Fair Mount Near Philadelphia", 21" L. $385.00

(A-PA. '75)   *Pennypacker Auction Centre*

HISTORICAL BLUE STAFFORDSHIRE
(Left to Right)

Plate. 10", Bank Of United States, Phila., Spread Eagle Border, Joseph Stubbs $200.00
Soup Plate, 10", Table Rock, Niagara, Shell Border, Circular Center, Enoch Wood & Sons .
. . . . $190.00

(A-PA. '75)   *Pennypacker Auction Centre*

HISTORICAL BLUE STAFFORDSHIRE
(Left to Right)

Deep Plate, 9", Quebec, Marked "Robert Laurence Cincinnati", Proof $130.00
Pitcher, 5¾" H., 6½" L., Boston State House, Reverse Side: New York City Hall, Rose Border, Joseph Stubbs $410.00

(A-PA. '75)   *Pennypacker Auction Centre*

HISTORICAL BLUE STAFFORDSHIRE
(Left to Right)

Platter, 9½" x 6¾", St. Paul's Church, Boston, Beauties Of America, John & William Ridgway
. . . . $380.00
Creamer, 5" H., 6" W., Commodore MacDonnough's Victory, Shell Border, Irregular Center, Enoch Wood & Sons, Proof $575.00
Teapot, 7¾" H., 10½" W., Commodore Mac-Donnough's Victory, Shell Border, Irregular Center, Enoch Wood & Sons $525.00

Garth's Auctions, Inc.

(A-PA. '75)   *Pennypacker Auction Centre*

HISTORICAL BLUE STAFFORDSHIRE
(Left to Right)

Plate, 10", Boston State House, John Rogers & Son $100.00
Plate, 10", Fair Mount near Philadelphia, Spread Eagle Border, Joseph Stubbs $120.00
Plate, 10½", Blenheim, Oxfordshire, W. Adams
. . . . $85.00

(A-OH. '76)
HISTORICAL BLUE STAFFORDSHIRE
(Row I, Left to Right)
Platter, "Alms House Boston", Impressed Stevenson, Sm. Flake On Back Edge, 16½" L. .$310.00
Plate, "Commodore MacDonnough's Victory", Impressed "Wood", 10⅛" Diam. $220.00
(Row II, Left to Right)
Soup Plate, "Beauties Of America, Octagon Church, Boston, J & W Ridgway", 9⅞' Diam. $130.00
Teapot, George Washington At Tomb, Impressed "Wood", Damaged, 7½" H. $200.00
Plate, Steamboat, "Union Line", Impressed "Wood & Sons", 10¼" Diam. $230.00
(Row III, Left to Right)
Plate, "Fair Mount Near Philadelphia", Impressed "Wood", 10¼" Diam. $110.00
Plate, "Landing Of Gen. Lafayette At Castle Garden, New York", Impressed "Clews Warranted Staffordshire", Pinpoint Rim Flake, 7¾" Diam. $120.00
Plate, "Harvard College", Stevenson, 10" Diam. $175.00

(A-PA. '76)   *Pennypacker Auction Centre*

Historical Blue Staffordshire Vegetable Dish, Covered, 11¾" L., 9" W., Woodlands Near Phila., Spread Eagle Border, Joseph Stubbs $800.00

(A-OH. '76)   *Garth's Auctions, Inc.*

HISTORICAL BLUE STAFFORDSHIRE
(Row I, Left to Right)
Platter, "Upper Ferry Bridge Over The River Schuylkill", Minor Edge Wear & Knife Scratches, 18¾" L.
....$225.00
Plate, "Beauties Of America, City Hall, New York, J. W. Ridgway", Med. Blue, 9⅞" Diam. $105.00
(Row II, Left to Right)
Plate, "Water Works, Philadelphia", Stevenson, 10" Diam. $250.00
Saucer, "Franklin Tomb", Impressed "Wood", Repaired $35.00
Plate, Table Rock Niagara", Impressed "E. Wood & Sons, Burslem", Sm. Hairline, 10" Diam. ....
....$120.00
(Row III, Left to Right)
Soup Plate, "Fair Mount Near Philadelphia", 9¾" Diam. $170.00
Soup Plate, "Landing Of Lafayette At Castle Garden, N.Y.", Impressed "Clews Warranted Staffordshire", 10" Diam. $240.00
Plate, "Fair Mount Near Philadelphia", Med. Blue, 10¼" Diam........................$100.00

(A-OH. '76)   *Garth's Auctions, Inc.*
HISTORICAL BLUE STAFFORDSHIRE
(Left to Right)
Plate, Impressed "Wood", 7⅝" Diam. $165.00
Plate, "John Geddes, Verreville Pottery, Glasgow", Mismarked Because View Is Park Theater, N.Y., Hairline, 10" Diam. $60.00
Plate, "View Of Trenton Falls", Impressed "Wood & Sons, Burslem", Eagle Mark, 7½" Diam. ....
....$190.00

(A-OH. '76)   *Garth's Auctions, Inc.*
HISTORICAL BLUE STAFFORDSHIRE
(Row I, Left to Right)
Plate, "Park Theater, New York", Stevenson, 10" Diam. $90.00
Plate, "Upper Ferry Bridge Over The River Schuylkill," Minor Flake On Base, 8¾" Diam. $70.00
(Row II)
Soup Plate, "Harvard College," Stevenson, 10" Diam. $165.00
(Row III)
Plate, "Mitchell & Freeman's China & Glass Warehouse, Chatham Str. Boston," Impressed "Adams Warranted Staffordshire," 10¼" Diam. $300.00
(Row IV, Left to Right)
Creamer, George Washington At Tomb, Repaired Flake, 4¾" H. $100.00
Plate, DeWitt Clinton W/Scene Of The Erie Canal, Two Sm. Old Flakes On Rim, 10¼" Diam. $130.00

HISTORICAL BLUE STAFFORDSHIRE
(Left to Right)

Plate, 10", New York From Brooklyn Heights, Floral Border, Andrew Stevenson $400.00
Plate, 7", Masonic Hall, Phila., Beauties of America, John & William Ridgway $375.00
Toddy Plate, 5¼", State House, Boston, Beauties Of America, John & William Ridgway .....
.... $200.00

Historical Blue Staffordshire Platter, 18¾" L. x 15½", Upper Ferry Bridge Over River Schuylkill, Spread Eagle Border, Joseph Stubbs .....
.... $420.00

HISTORICAL BLUE STAFFORDSHIRE
(Left to Right)

Plate, 8½", Boston State House, With Chaise, Enoch Wood & Sons $100.00
Cup, 2½" H., 4" W., American Eagle On Urn, Ralph & James Clews, Chip On Rim .. $30.00
Pitcher, 6½" H., 7½" W., The Landing Of The Fathers At Plymouth, Enoch Wood & Sons, Rare
.... $800.00

Flowing Blue Staffordshire Teapot, Sugar & Creamer, "Chusan" Patt. by J. Clementson, W/6 Matching C/S's, Set $850.00

HISTORICAL BLUE STAFFORDSHIRE
(Left to Right)

Plate, 10½", A Winter View Of Pittsfield, Mass., Pittsfield Elm, James & Ralph Clews $170.00
Soup Plate, 9¾", Octagon Church, Boston, Beauties Of America, John & William Ridgeway, Age Mark, ... $140.00

HISTORICAL BLUE STAFFORDSHIRE
(Left to Right)

Plate, 10", Harvard College, Ralph Stevenson & Williams $150.00
Plate, 10½", Pease & Plenty, James & Ralph Clews, Age Mark On Reverse $120.00

HISTORICAL BLUE STAFFORDSHIRE
(Row I, Left to Right)
Plate, "Beauties Of America, Library, Philadelphia, J. W. Ridgway", Med. Blue, 8¼" Diam. $125.00
Platter, English Scene Of Cows & Ruins, 16¾" L. $95.00
Plate, States Plate, Impressed "Clews Warranted Staffordshire", 8½" Diam. $160.00
(Row II, Left to Right)
Plate, "The Boston State House", Impressed "Rogers", Lt. Blue, 9¾" Diam. $60.00
Soup Plate, "A View Near Philadelphia", 9¾" Diam. $70.00
Plate, "The Boston State House" (W/Chaise), Unmarked, Lt. Blue, 9¾" Diam. $55.00
(Row III, Left to Right)
Plate, English Scene Of Cows & Ruins, Med. Blue, 10" Diam. $35.00
Toddy, Med. Blue, 5⅜" Diam. $160.00
Plate, English Scene Of Shepherd & Sheep, Lt. Blue, 10" Diam. $25.00

(A-OH. '76) *Garth's Auctions, Inc.*

White Clay Dog, Hand Molded Seated Dog W/ Basket,Tooled Details, Drk. Brown Glaze, Handle Of Basket Repaired & Sm. Repair On Base, 5¼" H. $45.00
Redware Bear, Hand Molded W/Coleslaw Coat, Head Comes Off Revealing Sander, Bear's Paws Hold Ink Well, Sander Insert Is Repaired, Minor Damage To Coat, 9" H. $110.00
Redware Chicken, Drk. Brown Glaze, Minor Flake On Comb, 5" H. $145.00

(A-MA. '76) *Richard A. Bourne Co. Inc.*
(Row I, Left to Right)
Ironstone China, Mulberry, Handleless Cup & Saucer, "Washington Vase" Pattern; Covered Vegetable Dish, "Jeddo" Pattern, W. Adams & Son, Invisible Crack & Minor Chip On Foot; Pair Of Shell Form Relish Dishes, "Leipsic" Pattern, J. Clements & Son $55.00
(Row II)
Platters, Matching Pair, "Corea" Pattern, J. Clements & Son, Both Discolored & Darkened W/Age, Both Fitted W/Handmade Hangers, 13½" L. & 16" L. $25.00
(Row III, Left to Right)
Ironstone Platter, Mulberry, "Corean" Pattern, 13½" L. $35.00
Staffordshire Platter, Mark Of Henderson & Kane's Importers, New Orleans, Blue & White W/ "Exchange Hotel, New Orleans" In Center, Davenport Anchor Mark, 1 Sm. Flake On Back Edge, Slight Wear, 19" L. $40.00

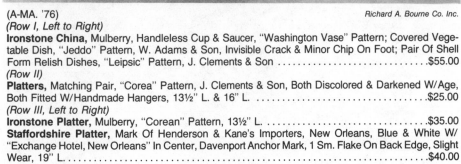

(A-OH. '76) *Garth's Auctions, Inc.*
(Left to Right)
Earthenware Dog, Hand Molded, Begging Dog /Basket, Tooled Work Details, Amber Glaze, 6¾" H. $90.00
Redware Pepper Pot, Clear Glaze W/Drk. Brown Band, Glaze Wear On Top Around Holes, 5" H. $315.00
Redware Jar, Ovoid, Applied Handles & Wide Flared Lip, Clear Glaze W/Splotches Of Drk. Brown, Minor Old Chips & Sm. Repairs On Rim, 8" H. $125.00
Redware Seated Dog, Hand Molded, Clear Glaze W/Splotches Of Brown, 3¾" H. $95.00
Redware Pitcher, Clear Glaze W/Splotches Of Drk. Brown, Minor Chips, 6" H. $160.00

(A-MA. '76) *Richard A. Bourne Co. Inc.*

Staffordshire Figural Vases, Pr., Glaze Wear To High Points, Serpents Heads' Repaired, 11½" H. $175.00

DEDHAM POTTERY PLATES

(Row I, Left to Right)

Plate, Tapestry Lion Pattern, (Pre-1929), 8½" Diam. $100.00

Plate, Polar Bear Pattern, (Pre-1929), Circular Signature Of Maud Davenport In Border, Sm. Chip On Underside Of Rim, 8¼" Diam. $70.00

Plate, Elephant Pattern, (1929-1943), 8⅜" Diam. $110.00

(Row II, Left to Right)

Plate, Turtle Pattern, (1929-1943), 8½" Diam. $220.00

Plate, Quail Pattern, (Pre-1929), Scalloped Border, 3 Small Scallops Over Sheaf Of Wheat & Lge. Scallop Over Quail Alternating; "L" Signature On Reverse, 8¾" Diam. $300.00

Plate, Moth Pattern, (Pre-1929), Minor Imperfections In Edge, 3 Slight Nicks, 8⅝" Diam. $60.00

(Row III, Left to Right)

Plate, Duck (Tufted) Pattern, (Pre-1929), 8½" Diam. $80.00

Plate, Horse Chestnut Pattern, (1929-1943), Signed By Maud Davenport, 8½" Diam. $250.00

Plate, Birds In Potted Orange Tree Pattern, (Pre-1929), 8¾" Diam. $60.00

(Row IV, Left to Right)

Plate, Raised Pineapple Border, By Chelsea Pottery Co. W/Clover Mark, Few Tiny Nicks In Foot Ring Only, 10" Diam. $130.00

Plate, Wild Rose Pattern, (Pre-1929), Crack Across Back Of Plate Runs From Edge To Dish Ring On Opposite Side, Barely Visible In Front, 8½" Diam. $50.00

Plate, Poppy Pattern, (Pre-1929), 1 Tiny Nick & Several Bubbles In The Rim Glaze, 8¾" Diam. $90.00

DEDHAM POTTERY   (A-MA. '75)

(Row I, Left to Right)   Richard A. Bourne Co., Inc.

Plate, Grouse Pattern, (Pre-1929), Minute Rim Flake, 8¾" Diam. $250.00

Plate, Turtles Pattern, (Pre-1929), 8⅜" Diam. $175.00

(Row II, Left to Right)

Plate, Dolphin Pattern, (Pre-1929), Serpentine Edge & Dolphin Going Clockwise, 8¾" Diam. $275.00

Plate, Grape Pattern, (Pre-1929), Incised Signature Only, 8⅝" Diam. $50.00

(Row III, Left to Right)

Plate, Turkey Pattern, (Pre-1929), 10" Diam. $75.00

Plate, Snowtree Pattern, (Pre-1929), 9⅞" Diam. $70.00

(Row IV, Left to Right)

Plate, Magnolia Pattern, (Pre-1929), Unusual Cloudy Glaze In Center, 10" Diam. $50.00

Plate, Azalea Pattern, (1929-1943), Design Of Leaves, 10" Diam. $80.00

(Row V, Left to Right)

Plate, Grape Pattern, (Pre-1929), 10⅛" Diam. $70.00

Plate, Duck Pattern, (Pre-1929), 10" Diam. $60.00

(Row VI, Left to Right)

Plate, Iris Pattern, (Pre-1929), 9⅝" Diam. .....
....$60.00

Plate, Horsechestnut Pattern (Pre-1929), 9¼" Diam. $35.00

ART POTTERY

Weller Jardiniere, Marked "Lowelsa", Nasturtiums Against Multi-Colored Ground Of Drk. Browns & Greens, 16½" Diam., 12½" H. $100.00

(Row I, Left to Right)

Saucer-Based Candlesticks, (1 Of 2), Dorchester Pottery Co., Blueberry Pattern, Marked, Diam. of Largest 5½" $50.00

Rabbit Paperweight, Van Briggle Pottery, Plum Color, Signed, 2¾" L. $120.00

Covered Sugar & Creamer, Pr., Dorchester Pottery, Blueberry Pattern, Signature & "C.A.H." On Bottom $30.00

(Row II, Left to Right)

Lidded Pitcher, Dorchester Pottery, Marked, Pussy Willow Pattern, 4¾" H. $45.00

Covered Pitcher, Dorchester Pottery, Marked, Pine Cone Pattern, 4¾" H. $35.00

Lidded Pitcher, Dorchester Pottery, Marked, Blue Floral Pattern, 5" H. $50.00

(Row III, Left to Right)

Covered Casserole, Dorchester Pottery, marked, Blue Scrolled Band Around Lid & Base, 6½" Diam. $60.00

Pitcher, By The Chelsea Keramic Art Works, Aqua W/Brown Streaking & Greek Fret Borders, Impressed Mark "CKAW" In Bottom, Tiny Nick On Corner Of Pouring Spout, 8" H. ...$325.00

Creamer, By The Chelsea Keramic Art Works, Blue-Gray, Incised Decor. Of Flowers, Leaves & Stems. Signature "CKAW" In Bottom, 4⅜" H. $400.00

(Row I, Directly Above, Left to Right)

Whieldon Plate, Octagonal, Rope-Molded Border, 8¾" Diam. $200.00

Whieldon Plate, Octagonal, Deep Color, 2 Minor Flakes Off Rim, 8⅜" Diam. $175.00

Whieldon Plate, Detailed Raised Border Design, 9½" Diam. $150.00

(Row II, Left to Right)

Whieldon Plate, Scalloped Gadroon-Style Rim, 1 Tiny Glaze Flake, 9½" Diam. ..$100.00

Whieldon Plate, Scalloped Rim, Raised Design, 1 Minute Rim Flake, 9¼" Diam. $100.00

(Row III, Left to Right)

Whieldon Plate, Unusual Decor. Of Brown & Green Cross On Cream-Colored Ground, Border Professionally Retouched, 9⅝" Diam. .....
....$125.00

Whieldon Plate, Feather Edge Molding & Scalloped Rim, Davenport-Type Rosette Mark Impressed in Base, 9¼" Diam. $100.00

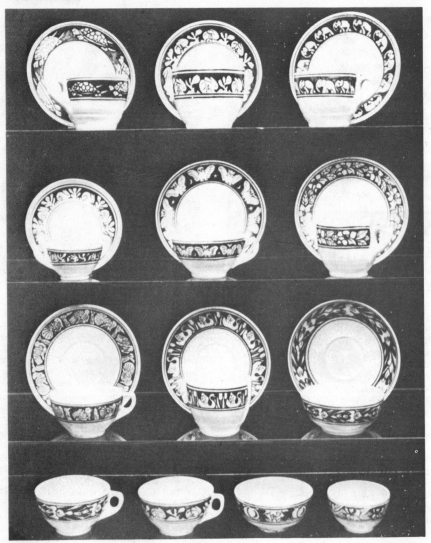

Richard A. Bourne Co. Inc.

(A-MA. '75)   *Richard A. Bourne Co. Inc.*

DEDHAM POTTERY

(Row I, Left to Right)

Tankard-Shaped Creamer, Turtle Pattern, Small $150.00

Sugar Bowl, Turtle Pattern, Small $85.00

Bowl Or Handleless Cup, Lobster Pattern, Tiny Rim Nick $110.00

Bowl Or Handleless Cup, Crab Pattern, Small $125.00

Footed Sherbet W/Two Handles, Rabbit pattern $85.00

(Row II, Left to Right)

Mug, Elephant Pattern, 3½" H. $150.00

Mug, Turtle Pattern, Incised JD Signature (Josephine Day), 3½" H. $150.00

Mug, Rabbit Pattern, Blue X Mark Under Blue Rabbit Mark On Bottom, Slightly Misshapen, 3½" H. $80.00

Mug, Rabbit Pattern, Quite Misshapen To An Oval Shape, 3½" H. $50.00

(Row III, Left to Right)

Pint Mug, Rabbit Pattern, W/Fruit & Leaf Band Around Top, Incised Signature "Dedham Pottery" $125.00

Quart Mug, Rabbit Pattern, W/Fruit & Leaf Band Around Top, Incised Signature "Dedham Pottery" $150.00

Creamer, Rabbit Pattern, Dated 1931, W/7 Rabbits Instead Of Usual Eight, Age Cracks In Bottom $50.00

Covered Sugar Bowl, Rabbit Pattern ..$80.00

(Row IV, Left to Right)

Goblets, (1 Of 3), Rabbit Pattern, Incised Mark In Bottom, "D" & "9/1", 4⅞" H. $400.00

Covered Marmalade Jar, Azalea Pattern, 2 Age Cracks Approx. 2" L. $70.00

Covered Marmalade Jar, Swan Pattern, Incised Mark "D9", Possibly By Josephine Day $225.00

Squat Covered Jar, Rabbit Pattern $75.00

(Row V, Left to Right)

Creamer, Turkey Pattern $110.00

Tankard-Shaped Creamer, Rabbit Pattern, 5¼" H. $90.00

Covered Sugar Bowl, Rabbit Pattern, W/ Incised Mark "DP", Cover Fits Loosely .$40.00

Squat Covered Sugar Bowl, Rabbit Pattern $40.00

(A-MA. '76)

DEDHAM POTTERY

(Row I, Left to Right)

Cup & Saucer, Turtles Patt., Cup Repaired $75.00

Cup-Shaped Bowl W/Saucer, Rabbit Patt. $50.00

Cup & Saucer, Elephant Patt., Flaking Of Glaze On Underside Of Saucer $70.00

(Row II, Left to Right)

Cup & Saucer, Small, Rabbit Patt., Age Crack On Rim Of Saucer $60.00

Cup & Saucer, Owl Patt. $250.00

Cup & Saucer, Azalea Patt. $40.00

(Row III, Left to Right)

Cup & Saucer, Turkey Patt. (Rare) $50.00

Cup & Saucer, Swan Patt., Handle Broken Off Cup $25.00

Bowl & Saucer, Iris Patt. $50.00

(Row IV, Left to Right)

Cup, Iris Patt. $15.00

Cup, Rabbit Patt. $17.00

Small Bowl, Horsechestnut Patt. $40.00

Very Small Bowl, Azalea Patt. $40.00

(A-MA. '76)   *Richard A. Bourne Co. Inc.* →

Pratt Ware Toby Jug, English, 10"H.

.... $200.00

(A-MA. '75) *Richard A. Bourne Co. Inc.*

DEDHAM POTTERY
(Row I, Left to Right)
Cup & Saucer, Elephant Pattern $125.00
Cup & Saucer, Turtle Pattern, Scratched Saucer $125.00
Cup, Polar Bear Pattern $30.00
(Row II, Left to Right)
Cup & Saucer, Azalea Pattern, Sm. Chip In Rim Of Saucer, Slight Crack Caused By Chip $50.00
Cup & Saucer, Azalea Pattern $60.00
Cup & Saucer, Rabbit Pattern, Oversized $90.00
(Row III, Left to Right)
Creamer, Rabbit Pattern $70.00
Creamer, Rabbit Pattern, Incised Mark "Dedham Pottery" W/Blue Rabbit Mark, Pale Blue $60.00
Covered Marmalade Jar, Rabbit Pattern, Sm. Chip Inside Of Cover $100.00
Covered Sugar Bowl, Rabbit pattern, Dedham Tercentenary Piece $80.00
(Row IV, Left to Right)
Low Covered Sugar Bowl, Rabbit Pattern $40.00
Squat Sugar Bowl, Small, Rabbit Pattern, 1" Age Crack One Side $40.00
Sugar Bowl, Rabbit Pattern, Faint Incised Mark Inside Cover, Illegible $60.00
Sugar Bowl, Rabbit Pattern, Faint Illegible Incised Mark Inside Cover, ½" Age Crack In Rim, Minute Nick On Inside Cover Inset Ring $25.00

(A-MA. '76) *Richard A. Bourne Co., Inc.*
(Row I, Left to Right)
Staffordshire Pug Dog Figure, Miniature, W/Hairline, 3¾" H. $15.00
Staffordshire Figure Of Man, Represents Winter, One Of Set Of Four Seasons Series, 7½" H. $40.00
Staffordshire Bust Of William Shakespeare, Mid-19th C., Incised Underglaze Signature "E" In Back Of Bust, 8½" H. $160.00
(Row II, Left to Right)
Toby-Style Pitcher, Depicting "The Watchman", 9" H. $80.00
Whieldon Salt Glaze Toby Jug, Ca. 1770, Pro. Repair To Hat, 8¾" H. $325.00
Whieldon-Type Toby Jug, Ca. 1770, Faint Age Crack & Sm. Flake Off Back Of Hat, Sm. Flake Off Foot $325.00
Toby Jug, Representing The Squire, Ca. 1840, 11½" H. $200.00
(Row IV)
Staffordshire Dog Figures, Pair, Reddish-Brown Decor. On White, Each Holding Basket In His Mouth, 8½" H. $150.00

(A-MA. '76) *Richard A. Bourne Co. Inc.*
(Row I, Left to Right)
Staffordshire Plate, 18th C., Overglaze Decor., Signed "Turner", Faint Rim Nicks, 8½" Diam. $50.00
Staffordshire Pearlware Plate, Polychromed, Decor. Of Landscape W/Castle, Raised Figures Of Birds & Insects Around Rim, 1½" Crack In Rim, 8½" Diam. $15.00
Leeds-Type Pearlware Plate, Underglaze Decor. Of Flower In Center & Floral Garland Border, 7⅞" Diam. $60.00
(Row II, Left to Right)
Davenport Plate, Impressed Mark & Spatter Decorated Border W/Floral Decor. In Center, Sm. Edge Flakes, 8⅜" Diam. $20.00
Gaudy Staffordshire Plate, Scalloped Rim, Underglaze Decor. Of Queen's Roses, Impressed Propeller Marks, 9" Diam. $30.00
Wedgwood Plate, Ca. 1810-20, Second Period, Decor. Of Pink Roses, Blossoms, Leaves & Stems, Impressed Wedgwood Mark, Black Rim Stripe, 9" Diam. $20.00
(Row III, Left to Right)
Gaudy Staffordshire Plate, Underglaze Decor. Of Queen's Roses, 9" Diam. $10.00
Strasbourg Faience Plate, Ca. 1775-1800, Tin Glaze & Colorful Polychrome Decor., Sm. Flakes On Rim, 9" Diam. $30.00
Gaudy Staffordshire Dinner Plate, Green Decor. W/Red Flowers & Pink Lustre Striping, 10½" Diam. $15.00

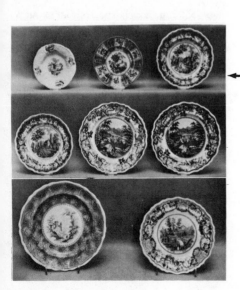

(A-MA. '76) *Richard A. Bourne Co. Inc.*

STAFFORDSHIRE
(Row I, Left to Right)
Plate, White W/Lavender Transfers W/Landscape In Center, Exotic Birds & Flowers In Border Alternating W/Raised Border Design, 6" Diam. $10.00
Lavender Plate, Eastern Plants, 6¾" Diam. $5.00
Blue Plate, "The Residence Of The Late Richard Jordan, New Jersey" By J. H. & Co., Faint Age Crack In Center, 7¾" Diam. $30.00
(Row II, Left to Right)
Lavender Plate, "The Residence Of the Late Richard Jordan, New Jersey" By J. H. & Co., 2 Tiny Rim Nicks, 7⅝" Diam. $35.00
Black & White Plate, "Nr Hudson, Hudson River" By Clews, 9" Diam. $40.00
Black & White Plate, Nr. Hudson, Hudson River" By Clews, 9" Diam. $40.00
(Row III, Left to Right)
Two-Color Plate, By Davenport, Center W/Pink Landscape Of Fisherman Surrounded By Broad Green Outer Border Of Pine Cones, 9½" Diam. $25.00
Pink & White Plate, "View Near Conway, N. Hampshire, U.S." By Adams, 9" Diam. $55.00

(A-MA. '76)   Richard A. Bourne Co. Inc.

(Row I, Left to Right)
Davenport Cup Plate, Eagle Decor. & Blue Rayed Border Design, 3⅞" Diam. $200.00
Ironstone China Cup Plate, Drk. Blue Decor. Of Amer. Eagle W/Flag, Shield, Arrows & Olive Branch Perched On Globe, 1/3 Broken Off & Reglued, 4" Diam. $5.00
Ten-Sided Cup Plate, Eagle, Flag, Shield & Arrows In Blue Design In Center, 3¾" Diam. $80.00
Cup Plate, Blue Spatter Border & Brown Eagle W/Flag, Shield & Arrows In Center, Age Cracks, 3¾" Diam. $35.00
(Row II, Left to Right)
Blue Staffordshire Child's Plate, Raised Rosettes Around Border & Pink Eagle W/Spread Wings Perched On Branch & Labeled "The Eagle", 5" Diam. $70.00
Leeds Octagonal Plate, Underglaze Eagle Decor. In Blue, Yellow & Green W/Green Rayed Border Design, 6" Diam. $80.00
Staffordshire Child's Plate, Titled "American Eagle", Polychromed Eagle W/Crossed Flags Beneath Over Globe W/Areas Of No. America Identified, Alphabet In Relief Around Border, 6" Diam. $20.00
(Row III, Left to Right)
Leeds Plate, Polychromed Eagle Decor. In Red, White, Blue, Yellow, Green & Drk. Brown, Blue Raised Border Design, 7½" Diam. $40.00
Staffordshire Child's Plate, "The Eagle And Nest", W/Eagle's Nest & Eagle In Pink On White Ground, Raised Floral Border Design, Mkd. Cardiff & Swansea, 6" Diam. $10.00
Liverpool Plate, Polychrome Floral Border & Black Transfer Of "Jefferson" W/Arms Of America On Top Surrounded By Lge. Bouquet Of Flowers, 7¼" Diam. $40.00
(Row IV, Left to Right)
Presidential Plate, By Tressemannes & Vogt, Limoges, France; On Back "France Decore Pour M.W. Beveridge, Washington, D.C., Harrison 1892", 7¼" Diam. $30.00
French Porcelain Plate, Polychrome Decor. Of Eagle W/Shield Clutching Arrors & Olive Branch & Holding Banner "E Pluribus Unum" W/Star Formed By Stars Over Its Head; Black, Gold & Sepia Border Design, 7" Diam. $60.00
Staffordshire Plate, Blue-Green Border Design & Amer. Eagle W/Flag, Banner, Arrows Olive Branch Flying Over What May Be Hudson River In Center & Done In Pink, 5¾" Diam. . . $15.00

(A-MA. '76)   Richard A. Bourne Co. Inc.

(Row I, Left to Right)
Decorated Spode China, (Partial Service - 3 Pcs. Illus.), Made For the American Market, Ca. 1810-1820; 7 Cups, 7 Saucers & Matching Waste Bowl, Polychrome Decor. Of American Arms Together W/Band Of Gold Stars On Blue Band Around Rims, Age Crack In Waste Bowl, Faint Age Crack In Center Of One Saucer $700.00
Liverpool Teapot, Black Transfer Scenes Of Amer. Steamboat One Side & Amer. Sailing Vessel W/Eagle & Anchor On Other; Sm. Landscape Ornaments On Cover, Pink Lustre Striping & Designs, 2 Faint Age Cracks In Bottom, Pro. Repair To Cover $80.00
(Row II, Left to Right)
Castleford-Style Pearlware Sugar Bowl, Raised Designs In Panels $70.00
Castleford-Type White Stoneware Teapot, Raised Decor. In Panels, Great Seal Of The U.S. On One Side, Liberty's Head Within Wreath On Opposite, Foliate Designs, Panels Outlined In Blue Enamel, Pressed Numeral "36" In Base, Sm. Chip Along Top Edge Of Pot $175.00
Staffordshire Teapot, Lavender, Eagle - Riding On Shell By H. Rall & Son, Faint Age Cracks One Side $50.00
(Row III, Left to Right)
Liverpool Jug, Portrait Of John Adams Surrounded By Justice & 2 Other Figures On One Side & The Great Seal Of The U.S. Surrounded By Chain Of 15 States On Other, Age Cracks In Bottom, 8½" H. $1,300.00
Liverpool Jug, Transfer Portrait Of "Captain Jones Of The Macedonian" Framed Within Trophy Of Flags, Arms & Ship On One Side; Captain Hull Of The Constitution Framed Within Trophy Of Flags, Arms & His Ship On Other; Great Seal Of The U.S. Below Spout W/Word "America" Beneath, Pink Lustre Striping, 6½" H. $200.00
Ironstone Pitcher, Transfer Portrait Of Washington W/Polychromed Flag & Liberty Cap Plus Eagle & Banner On Both Sides, Flower-Like Border Designs, Illegible Impressed Mark In Bottom, 9½" H. $75.00
(Row IV, Left to Right)
Ironstone Chamber Set, Underglaze Blue Decor. Of Eagle, Flag, Shield & Arrows In Center & Repeated 3 Times Around Border Of Wash-Bowl, Design On Either Side Of Pitcher, Washbowl Has Age Crack On Side $60.00
Flowing Blue Ironstone China, (1 Of Partial Set), "America" By Thomas Ford & Co., Pattern Registered Nov. 21, 1846, Consists Of 17¾" Platter, Handleless Cup & Saucer & 9⅜" Plate, Cup & Plate Chipped $125.00

(A-MA. '76)   Richard A. Bourne Co. Inc.

(Row I, Left to Right)
Silver Resist Jug, Eagle On One Side & Marine Scene W/Ships On Other & Anchor Under Pouring Spout, Pouring Spout Pro. Repaired, 8¾" H. $950.00
Lustre Jug Or Pitcher, Transfer Scene On One Side Depicting Liberty & Various Patriotic Symbols W/Eagle In Center, Eagle Under Spout & Same Panel Repeated On Opposite Side, Pro. Res. To Upper Rim Of Pitcher, 7½" H. $900.00
Staffordshire Jug Or Pitcher, "Washington" — "Lafayette" By Ric'd Hall & Son, Beneath Spout, Produced "In Commemoration Of The Visit Of Gen'l Lafayette To The U.S. Of America In The Year 1824" Around Rim, Slight Age Crack In Bottom, 7¼" H. $300.00
(Row II, Left to Right)
Sunderland Lustre Jug, Overall Pink Spatter Lustre Surrounding Portraits Of Admiral Perry, Trophy Of Arms & Ships One Side & Pike Enclosed W/Trophy Of Arms On Other, Pro. Repair To Base, 8" H. $900.00
Liverpool Jug, Polychrome Decor., Transfers Of "Abbas And Abra" W/Verse On One Side & Amer. Ship W/Banner "Success To The Trade" On Other, & The Great Seal Of The U.S. Under Pouring Spout W/Script Citing Jefferson Dated 1804, Several Age Cracks, Sm. Spout Chip, 9½" H. $250.00
Liverpool Jug, Polychrome Transfer Of Amer. Ship One Side, Washington's Portrait Within Banner Of 15 States On Other, & The Great Seal Of The U.S. W/Initials "WRK" Under Spout, Pouring Spout Pro. Repaired Years Ago, 9½" H. $400.00
(Row III, Left to Right)
Liverpool Jug, Polychromed Transfer Scene On One Side Depicting Musical Group, On Other Side Are Transfer Initials "PPF", Transfer Frame Of Flowers; The Great Seal Of The U.S. In Orange, Yellow, Black & Green Under Pouring Spout, 9¾" H. $300.00
Liverpool Jug, Lavender Transfers Of Washington's Tomb In Landscape Beneath Which Are 2 Oval Portraits, Presumably Of Jefferson W/Verse Around Frame & Beneath; Opposite Side Is Portrait Representing An Amer. Militiaman W/Flag & Landscape Containing Figures, Ships, Cannon, Etc. Under The Spout An Amer. Ship, 4 Roses Painted In Blue Around Upper Shoulder, Pro. Repairs To Handle, Spout & Rim, 12¼" H. $500.00

(A-MA. '76)   Richard A. Bourne Co. Inc.

(Row I, Left to Right)
Child's Creamware Mug, Bearing Arms Of America In Iridescent Brown W/Banner Wishing Success To Our Agriculture, Trade, Manufacturers & Sailor's Rights, Sm. Inner Rim Chip, 2" H. $125.00
Child's Creamware Mug, Transfer In Brown Of Eagle Perched Over "Munroe" Which In Turn Surrounded By Flowers, 2½" H. $450.00
Child's Staffordshire Mug, Eagle On Each Side In Green & "The Golden Rule/And Its Universal/Adoption" Framed On Cross W/ Eagle Perched Above, Green Inner Border Design, 2⅜" H. $40.00
English Porcelain Mug, Lowestoft Style W/ Eagle Decor. In Black Flanked By Tea Leaves & Serpentine Border Around Upper Rim, 2¼" H. $50.00

(Row II, Left to Right)
Pink Lustre Child's Mug, Transfer In Brown Of Arms Of America & Banner W/"May Success Attend Our Agriculture Trade And Manufacturers", Together W/"A Present For My Dear Girl", 2⅜" H. $125.00
Leeds-Type Mug, Reddish-Brown Transfer Of Eagle Bearing Portraits Of "Lafayette" & "Washington", 2½" H. $275.00
Staffordshire Mug, Eagle On Shell In Black,
(Cont. top next column)

Attrib. To R. Hall & Sons, Scroll Label In Center States "Prosper/Commerce", 3" H. $60.00
Child's Staffordshire Mug, Lge. Transfer Scene Of Child, Landscape & Eagle Above Which Is Written "E. Was An Eagle & Chained To A Perch; F. Stands For Fanny Returning From Church"; On Inside Is "G. Is a Goldfinch a Very Nice Bird; H. Is A Hammer The Noise You Have .....", 2⅝" H. $85.00

(Row III, Left to Right)
Staffordshire Mug, Transfer Scene Of "Lafayette The Nation's Guest" On One Side, "Washington His Country's Father" On Other, On The Front The Amer. Arms W/Words "Republicans Are Not Always Ungrateful" & Registered Mark Of Hall & Sons Underneath, 2⅜" H. ..$200.00
Child's Staffordshire Mug, Attrib. To R. Hall & Sons, Eagle Riding Shell On Either Side In Pink & Label Which Reads "Prosperous/Freedom" On Front, 1 Minute Rim Nick, 2⅜" H. ..$50.00
Staffordshire Mug, W/Amer. Arms Either Side In Pink & Framed Label In Front Which States "The Land Of Liberty", 2⅜" H. $100.00
Child's Staffordshire Mug, Eagle Riding Shell On Each Side In Pink W/Label In Scrolled Frame On Front Which Says "America The Land Of Liberty", Slight Age Crack One Side, 2½" H. $40.00

(Row IV, Left to Right)
Child's Staffordshire Mug, Attrib. To R. Hall & Sons, Eagle Riding Shell On Either Side & Scrolled Frame Label "Forgetmenot" In Blue, 2½" H. $40.00
Centennial Porcelain Mug, Portrait Of George Washington Flanked By Flags & Guarded By Eagle In Black Transfer Scene On One Side & "A Memorial/Of/The Centennial/1876" On The Other; On Base "Manufactured For J. M. Shaw & Company", "Trademark Registered 1876", Minute Flake On Bottom Of Foot Ring, 3" H. $40.00
Child's Staffordshire Mug, Attrib. To R. Hall & Sons, Eagle Riding Shell On 2 Sides & Scrolled Frame Motto In Center "The United States Of America", Transfers In Brown Highlighted By Polychromed Greens & Blues, 3" H. ..$200.00
Chinese Export Porcelain Cup, Handleless, American Arms In Sepia & Gold $80.00
(Row V)
English Porcelain, Partial Set Consisting Of Handleless Cup Together W/Handled Cup & Deep Saucer, All W/Matching Decor. In Black Of American Arms & Serpentine Lines & Inner Border Designs, Saucer Has Star-Shaped Age Crack $40.00

(A-MA. '76)   Richard A. Bourne Co. Inc.
(Row I, Left to Right)
Leeds Toddy Plate, W/Amer. Eagle Decor. & Green Rayed & Scalloped Border Design, 5½" Diam. $300.00
Chinese Export Porcelain Saucer, Or Dish W/ Eagle Decor., Flag, Shield, Stars & "E Pluribus Unum" Banner, Inner Border Decor. Is Garland Of Grapes, 3 Rim Chips W/8 Faint Hairline Cracks, Ea. Approx. 1" L., 5½" Diam. .$275.00
(Row II, Left to Right)
Bennington Graniteware Presentation Pitcher, Eagle Decor. In Scrolled Panel Against Drk. Blue Ground W/Red & Gold Foliate Decor., Marked On Base "A Lincoln 1863" Within Scroll, 9½" H. $400.00
Early Liverpool Jug, W/Transfer Decor. Of Amer. Ship On One Side & Compass Rose W/ Verse On Other, Minor Rim Nick, Several Age Cracks In Rim, 6⅝" H. $225.00
(Row III)
Liverpool Jugs, Pr., Identical W/Transfers: Amer. Full-Rigged Ship On One Side, The Names "Daniel & Elizabeth Cashman" Framed Within Garland Of Flowers W/Barrels & Kegs On One Of Which Sets A Glass Of Wine At The Bottom, & A Newspaper Named "The Sun" On Top Of Wreath; On the Other Side Is Scene Of Washington's Tomb W/Liberty, Indians & Other Mourning Figures Within Chain Made Up Of Orig. Thirteen States, 1 Jug Has Age Cracks In Bottom & Pro. Repair To Handle, Heights 9¾" & 9⅞" $700.00

(A-MA. '77)   Richard A. Bourne Co., Inc.
STAFFORDSHIRE

(Row I, Left to Right)
Cup Plate, Pink Lustre Floral & Leaf Decor., 3⅝" Diam. $5.00
Pink Cup Plate, "Canova", By Mayer, Age Crack In Rim, 3⅞" Diam. $5.00
Pale Lavender Cup Plate, "Canova", By Mayer, 4" Diam. $15.00

(Row II, Left to Right)
Dark Blue Cup Plate, Unidentified Scene W/ Hunter, Dogs & Building, 3⅞" Diam. ...$35.00
Blue Cup Plate, Oriental Landscape W/Temples, Junks, Mountains, Etc., 3¾" Diam. $20.00
Cup Plate, "Fishers", By C. F. & M., Boy & Girl In Landscape Done In Several Colors W/Blue Heart Border, 3⅞" Diam. $20.00

(Row III, Left to Right)
Medium Blue Toddy-Sized Plate, Landscape W/Ladies & Man Watching Waterfall, 4¾" Diam. $20.00
Child's Plate, W/Motto "Not To Oversee Workmen Is To Leave Your Purse Open", 4⅝" Diam. $60.00
Brown & White Toddy Plate, "Neptune" Pattern, By Alcock, 4⅝" Diam. $10.00

(Row IV, Left to Right)
Commemorative Plate, "Victoria Regina Crowned 28 Of June 1838", & Below Legend Raised Floral Rosettes In Border, 6" Diam. $45.00
Child's Plate, W/Transfer Of "England's Hope, Prince Of Wales", Raised Fruit & Flowers In Border, 6½" Diam. $35.00

(A-OH. '76)   *Garth's Auctions, Inc.*

(A-OH. '76)   *Garth's Auctions, Inc.*

(Row I, Left to Right)
English Soft Paste Bowl, Blue & White Oriental Decor, Marked W/Crescent, 7½" D. $75.00
Historical Blue Staffordshire Plate, "Park Theater, New York," By Stevenson, Flake On Rim, 10" D. $95.00
Canary Luster Bowl, Purple Luster Foliage & Polychrome Enameled Flowers, Red Over Glaze Enamel Has Flaked, 7" D. $167.50
(Row II, Left to Right)
Pratt Ware Teapot, Embossed & Decor. W/4 Colors, Widow Warburton Finial, Finial Glued & Lid Chipped, Sm. Hairline At Top Of Handle, 6¾" H. $45.00
Historical Blue Staffordshire Pitcher, Tower W/Flags & Shields & "Washington, Independence — J.P. Jones," Hairline At Spout & Base Of Handle, 6¼" H. $175.00
Porcelain Creamer, New Hall, 3¼" H. $27.50
Pratt Ware Creamer, Embossed & Decor. W/4 Colors, 4½" H. $145.00
(Row III, Left to Right)
Historical Blue Staffordshire Plate, "Landing Of General Lafayette At Castle Garden, New York, 16 August 1824," Impressed "Clews," Sm. Flake On Rim, 9" D. $125.00
Historical Blue Staffordshire Plate, Mythological Battle Scene W/2 Horse & Riders In Sky, Impressed "E. Wood & Sons," Glaze Wear, 9¼" D. $35.00
Historical Blue Staffordshire Plate, "Commodore MacDonnough's Victory," 9¼" D. . . . $240.00

(Row I, Left to Right)
Staffordshire Lamb, 2" H. $65.00
Pratt Fox Creamer, Swan Handle, Old Chips & Enamel Has Some Wear, 5" H. $170.00
Miniature Creamer, Blue Transfer Design, Marked "Spodes Tower", 2¼" H. $22.50
(Row II, Left to Right)
Earthenware Cup, Bearded Man's Head W/ Serpent Tail Handle, 3¾" H. $85.00
Pratt Creamer, Winged Animal Forms Spout, Handle Is Serpent, Polychromed, 3¼" H. $120.00
Earthenware Cup, Baccus, Clear Glaze W/ Dripping Drk. Brown, Whieldon Like Colors, 4" H. $105.00
(Row III, Left to Right)
Mocha Pepper Pot, Grey-Blue W/Cats Eyes In Ochre, Brown & White, Flakes On Top, 5" H. $225.00
Earthenware Desk Set, Base W/Shell & Dog & Inserts For Ink & Sander, White Clay W/Amber, Blue & Brown Glaze, Impressed Mark On Base Not Distinguishable, Chips, Research Indicates 18th C. Portuguese, 5½" L. (A-OH. '76) $55.00
Mocha Pepper Pot, Blue & Tan Bands W/Drk. Brown, Blue & White Spots, 4" H. . . . $150.00

(A-OH. '76)   *Garth's Auctions, Inc.*
(Row I)
Spatterware Soup Plates, Pr., Stick Spatter, "Made In Belgium", 11" Diam. $60.00
. . . .$60.00
Soft Paste Creamer, W/Satyr's Face, Polychrome Enameling, 4¾" H. $120.00
(Row II)
Gaudy Staffordshire Plates, Pr., Mkd. "Staffordshire England", 9¾' Diam. $65.00
Soft Paste Toddy Plate, Polychrome Transfer Design Of Pheasant & Blossoms, 5¼" Diam. $50.00
(Row III, Left to Right)
Staffordshire Plate, Octagonal, Black Transfer "The Gleaner" W/Additional Enamel & Blue Stripes, Registry Mark, 5½" Diam. $20.00
Gaudy Staffordshire Plate, Red, Yellow, Ochre, Green & Black, 9" Diam. $30.00
Staffordshire Plate, Black Transfer "The Doves" W/Additional Enamel & Blue Stripes, Minor Edge Roughness, 5½" Diam. $17.00

(A-MA. '76)   *Robert C. Eldred Co., Inc.*
Chinese Export Porcelain Bull's Head Tureen & Matching Platter. Tureen Is Modeled In Two Sections W/Upstanding Gray Horns & Ears & Flared Nostrils For Escaping Steam. Decor. W/ Flowers In Famille Rose Enamels. Tureen 13" L. Platter 16½" L., Ca. 1765 . . . .$4,800.00

Spatterware Chamber Set, W/Blue Transfer Of Eagle & Shield Decor. . . . .(D-PA. '76) $325.00

(A-MA. '76)   Richard A. Bourne Co. Inc.

Spatterware
(Row I, Left to Right)
Plate, Peafowl W/Red Spatter Border, 7⅜" D. $150.00
Cup, Handleless W/Peafowl & Pink Spatter $25.00
Plate, Peafowl W/Red Spatter Border . $170.00
(Row II)
Sugar Bowl, W/Red Spatter & Queen's Rose Decor., Rim Chip . . . . (A-OH. '76) $75.00
Saucer, Peafowl W/Green Spatter Decor. $70.00
Saucer, Blue House W/Green Spatter Trees, Red Border $80.00
Saucer, Brown Spatter Border, Red Floral Center W/Gr. Leaves $20.00
(Row III)
Cup & Saucer, Brilliant Blue Spatter $40.00
Saucer, Rainbow Lavender & Green Spatter, Cracked $10.00
Saucer, Tan Spatter On Border W/Red & Blue Floral Center $40.00
Saucer, Red & Green Spatter Panels . $30.00
(Row IV)
Creamer & Bowl, Child's Set, Blue Spatter $60.00
Plate, Blue Spatter, 8¾" D. $15.00

Spatterware, All Pieces Have A Blue Spatter Border W/Blue Transfer Of Eagle Clutching Arrows In Front Of A Shield. . . . . '76)
(Row I, Left to Right)
Plate, 9" D., Platter, 11" D., Waste Bowl, 3 pc. $175.00
(Row II)
Pitcher, Hexagon Shape, 6" H. $110.00
Platter, Lg. 15¼" $170.00
Pitcher, Hexagon Shape, Age Crack On Side, 7¾" H. $40.00

(D-TX. '76)
Staffordshire Hen On Nest $90.00

(A-MA. '76)   Richard A. Bourne Co. Inc.
Rockingham Glazed Pottery
(Row I, Left to Right)
Soap Dish $20.00
Soap Dish W/Vertical Panels $30.00
Bowl, Paneled Sides, 6" D. $40.00
Bowl, Paneled Sides, 8" D. $30.00
(Row II)
Vegetable Bowl, 9⅛" L. $65.00
Toby Creamer, 6" H. $30.00
Toby Jug, 8" H. $100.00
Open Sugar Bowl, Oval, 7¾" L. $90.00
(Row III)
Bowl W/Gothic-like Decor. In Relief, 11" D. . . $70.00
Vegetable Bowl, 9¼" L., Flared Rim . $90.00
Bowl, Minor Damage to Rim, 11" D. . . $70.00
(Row IV)
Pitcher, Hunter W/Game & Dogs In Relief, 9" H. $45.00
Pitcher, Strawberries In Relief, Minor Crack In Base, 9½" H. $55.00
Pitcher, Tulips In Relief, 9" H. $30.00

(A-MA. '76)   Richard A. Bourne Co. Inc.
Pottery
(Row I, Left to Right)
Bowl, Rockingham Glaze, Flaring Rim, 9½" D. $25.00
Bowl, Rockingham Glaze, 9½" D. $50.00
Bowl, Rockingham Glaze, Flaring Rim, 7⅜" D. $25.00
(Row II)
Pie Plate, Rockingham Glaze, 9¾"D. $55.00
Milk Pan, Rockingham Glaze, 12⅛" D. $60.00
Pie Plate, Rockingham Glaze, 9¾" D. $60.00
(Row III)
Bowl, Blue/White Sponged Decor. On Gray, 9¼" D. $60.00
Bowl, Blue/Brown Sponged Decor. On Gravy, 9¼" D. $70.00
Pitcher, W/Tan & Brown Splotches, 8" H. . . . . Garth's Auctions, Inc. (A-OH. '76) $60.00

(A-PA. '76)   Pennypacker Auction Centre
Historical Blue Staffordshire Plate, 9¾", Dam & Water Works, Phila., Henshall, Williamson & Co. $220.00
Gravy Boat, 7" L., 3½" H., State House Boston, Ridgway, Handle Repair $45.00

(A-PA. '76)   Pennypacker Auction Centre
Historical Blue Staffordshire Platter, 15¼" x 11¾", Landing Of Lafayette, Clews . . .$500.00

(A-VA. '77)
Commemorative Pitcher, From Liverpool, Portraits Of Franklin & Washington, Ca. 1790-1820, 6" H. $150.00
Commemorative Pitcher, From Liverpool, Portrait Of Washington, 1 Panel Showing Washington's Tomb, Ca. 1800 .... $275.00
Commemorative Pitcher, From Liverpool, Portraits of Washington & Lafayette, 6" H. $175.00

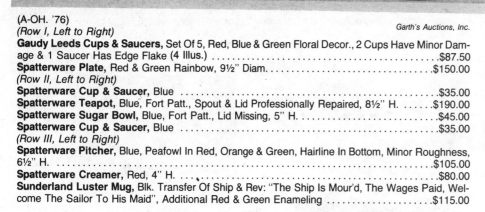

(A-OH. '76)
(Row I, Left to Right)

Gaudy Leeds Cups & Saucers, Set Of 5, Red, Blue & Green Floral Decor., 2 Cups Have Minor Damage & 1 Saucer Has Edge Flake (4 Illus.) $87.50
Spatterware Plate, Red & Green Rainbow, 9½" Diam. $150.00
(Row II, Left to Right)
Spatterware Cup & Saucer, Blue $35.00
Spatterware Teapot, Blue, Fort Patt., Spout & Lid Professionally Repaired, 8½" H. $190.00
Spatterware Sugar Bowl, Blue, Fort Patt., Lid Missing, 5" H. $45.00
Spatterware Cup & Saucer, Blue $35.00
(Row III, Left to Right)
Spatterware Pitcher, Blue, Peafowl In Red, Orange & Green, Hairline In Bottom, Minor Roughness, 6½" H. $105.00
Spatterware Creamer, Red, 4" H. $80.00
Sunderland Luster Mug, Blk. Transfer Of Ship & Rev: "The Ship Is Mour'd, The Wages Paid, Welcome The Sailor To His Maid", Additional Red & Green Enameling $115.00

(A-MA. '77)

Gaudy Dutch Type Tea Service, English, Early 19th C., Typical Gaudy-Dutch Decor. W/Blue Area Under Glaze, Other Colors Of Polychrome Decor. Over Glaze, Highlighted By Pink Lustre Striping Around Rims, Handles & Foot Rings, Pattern Bears Strong Resemblance To Number Of Known Gaudy Dutch Patterns But Is Not Exactly Like Any, Consists Of Teapot, Creamer & Lidded Sugar Bowl, Waste Bowl (1½" Rim Crack), 2 Tea Plates, 11 Cups & 11 Saucers (A Few Cups & Saucers Have Minor Flaking Of Green Decor.) 3 Cups W/Age Cracks & 1 W/ Slight Rim Nick $375.00

(D-TX. '76)
Doulton, Jug or Pitcher, W/English Reg. No. $300.00

(D-KS.)
Handkerchief Plate, 8½" Diam. $25.00

(D-AR. '76)
Majolica Cheese Dish, English $85.00

(A-PA. '75)
SPATTERWARE
(Left to Right)
Sugar Bowl, Blue W/Wild Horses Pattern In Red, Sm. Chip On Lid $100.00
Soup Plate, Yellow Border, Green Leaves, Blue Thistle Flower Center, 9¼" $400.00
Miniature Cup & Saucer, Blue W/Red Star Flower Style Center $150.00
Coffeepot, Rainbow, Red, Green, Yellow & Blue Decor., Sm. Repair On Spout $300.00

(A-PA. '75)
(Left to Right)
Spatterware Plate, 8¼" $130.00
Spatterware Soup Plate, 10", Red, Green & Blue Closed Star Center $160.00
Woods Rose Soft Paste Plates (4), 6¾" $100.00

(A-PA. '75)
SPATTERWARE
(Left to Right)
Cup & Saucer, Rainbow, Red & Yellow $300.00
Creamer, Rainbow, Blue & Purple, 3½" $250.00
Plate, Green, 9" $150.00
Cup & Saucer, Yellow & Pink, Blue Flowers $220.00

(D-PA. '76)
(Left to Right)
Spatterware Plate, Mkd. ''R. Hammersley, Gem'',Cobalt Blue Eagle Center, Stick Border, 9" Diam. $85.00
Spatterware Plate, Blue/White "Snowflake" Pattern, 9" Diam. $75.00

(A-PA. '75)
SPATTERWARE CUPS & SAUCERS
(Row I)
Blue Tulip Star Pattern, Pair $150.00
(Row II, Left to Right)
Blue W/Thistle Center $110.00
Red & Blue Rainbow Pattern $125.00
(Row III)
Red W/Peacock Center $65.00

(D-CT. '76)
Spongeware Cup & Saucer, Blue & White, Large $65.00

(D-N.J. '76)
Stickspatter Plate W/Running Rabbit Border, 9½" Diam. $85.00

(D-N.J. '76)
Spatterware Plate W/Plumb Center, 9" Diam. $90.00

(A-PA. '75)   *Pennypacker Auction Centre*
Adams Rose Plate, 9½" $30.00

(D-N.Y. '76)
Coalport Porcelain Bowl, Footed & W/Cover $90.00

(D-CT. '76)
Coronation Souvenir Pitcher Of King Edward VIII $65.00

(A-CA. '76)   *Woody Auction Company*
Weller Sicard Vase, Sgn., Chrysanthemum Decor., 12" H. $625.00

(D-VA. '76)
Royal Crown Derby Teapot, Six Cups/Saucers, Sugar, Creamer & Tray $650.00

(D-LA. '76)
Meissen Plate, (1 Of 6, Each W/Different Center Decor.), W/Augustus Rex Monogram In Blue Underglaze, 9" Diam., Set $600.00

(D-WI. '76)
Spongeware Pitcher, Blue & White, 9¼" H. $75.00

(D-MO. '76)
Decorative KPM (German) Plate, Decal Fruit Center, Gold Trim, 8¾" Diam.........$65.00

(A-PA. '76)   *Pennypacker Auction Centre*
Leeds Pottery Platter, Green Border W/Yellow & Blue Floral Decor. In Center, 12" x 15½", ...$390.00

(A-OH. '76)   *Garth's Auctions, Inc.*
(Row I, Left to Right)
Leeds Plate, Green Feather Edge, Eagle Decor. & 15 Stars, 8" Diam. $410.00
Leeds Waste Bowl, 4 Colors, 4½' Diam. $110.00
Leeds Plate, Green Feather Edge, Eagle Decor. & 15 Stars, Minor Wear Around Edge, 8" Diam. $360.00

(Row II, Left to Right)
Soft Paste Bowl, Blue Oriental Transfer, 4⅜" Diam. $35.00
Leeds Octagonal Plate, Blue Feather Edge, Eagle Decor. & 13 Stars, 7½" Diam. $925.00
Leeds Creamer, Cup Shape, 4 Colors, 2⅝" H. $70.00

(A-PA. '75)   *Pennypacker Auction Centre*
Blue Delft Plaque, 526-135-T Perfect, Holland Street Scene W/Church, 20" L. $170.00

(A-PA. '75)   *Pennypacker Auction Centre*
(Left to Right)
Handleless Cup W/Saucer, Red Rose & Blue Leaf Decor $70.00
Leeds China Plate, Green, Orange, Brown & Yellow, 8¾" $190.00
Leeds China Miniature Pitcher, 3" $150.00
Leeds China Plate, Orange, Blue & Green, 7¾" $190.00

(D-MO. '76)
Rosenthal Cake Plate Decor. W/Lilacs, Gold Trim, 12" Diam., Mkd. $55.00

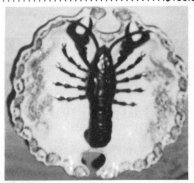

(D-MO. '76)
Child's Cup, Beatrix Potter's Character Attached To Side $22.50

(D-MD. '76)
Lobster Bowl, 2 Sections, Mkd. "Carlsbad, Austria" $45.00

(D-ME. '76)
Oyster Plate, Unmarked, 9¼" Diam. . .$22.50

(A-MA. '77) Richard A. Bourne, Co., Inc.
(Row I, Left to Right)
Newhall-Type Creamer, Decor. Of Flowers
....$15.00
Newhall Creamer, Decor. Of Flowers ..$15.00
Newhall-Type Creamer, Decor. Of Medallions
Of Flowers, Slight Area Of Roughage On Rim
....$10.00
(Row II, Left to Right)
Newhall-Type Teapot, Decor. Of Medallions Of
Flowers, Signed "Herculaneum", Minor Nick
In Tip Of Spout $40.00
Gaudy Welsh Milk Pitcher, Decor. Of Flowers
In Blue & Orange, Copper Lustre Highlights,
Handle Check, Age Crack Beside Spout ......
....$35.00
(Row III, Left to Right)
Staffordshire Tea Plate, Pair, (1 Illus.), Raised
Border Designs W/Queen's Rose Decor., One
Has Nearly Invisible Star-Shaped Age Crack,
6½" Diam. $15.00
Staffordshire Plates, (4), (1 Illus.), Each One
W/Decor. Of Queen's Rose, Raised Cross-
Hatching In Border & Double Pink Lustre Band
Around Border, One Has Age Crack, One-6¾"
Diam.; Three-7¾" Diam...............$25.00
(Row IV, Left to Right)
Staffordshire Tea Plates, Pair, (1 Illus.), Decor.
Of Roses & Ribbons, 7⅝" Diam. $30.00
Staffordshire Tea Plates, (2), (1 Illus.), Similar
Floral Decor., Differences In Scalloped Borders,
7¾" Diam. $25.00

(A-MA. '76) Richard A. Bourne Co., Inc.
(Row I, Left & Right)
Bloor Derby Serving Dishes, Pr., English,
Early 19th C., Royal Blue Border Design W/Gold
Decor. Encircling Painted Still Life Of Fruit On
Table Top, Circular Underglaze Red Bloor
Derby Mark, Perfect Cond., 9¼" x 9½" ....
....$500.00
(Center)
Davenport Dessert Service, 23-Pc. (1 Illus.),
Mid-19th C., Compote, W/Different Flower, Blue
& Gold Borders, Damage To 1 Plate & 3 Serving
Dishes, Plates: 9¼" Diam., Oblong Serving
Dish: 11½" L., Circular Dishes: 9½" Diam.,
Compote: 11½" Diam., 8" H. $700.00
(Row II)
**Royal Crown Derby Footed Tureen W/Pr.
Matching Sauce Tureens & Stands,** Early
19th C., Drk. Blue & Burnished Gold W/Panels
Of Flowers In Natural Colors, Lge. Tureen Pro-
fessionally Repaired At One End, Other Handle
Broken Off & Refastened, Foot Of One Sauce
Tureen Broken Off & Refastened As Has One
Handle, Several Age Cracks $450.00
(Row III)
Davenport Dessert Service, 23-Pc. (3 Illus.)
....$700.00

(A-OH. '76)
Garth's Auctions, Inc.

ENAMELED BATTERSEA TYPE BOXES
 1. Lady Warming Hands, Pink Base Damaged $70.00
 2. Cock Fight,"Business", Inside Lid Lgn.,
Blue Base $175.00
 3. Early Ship, "A Trifle From Bristol'.. Repaired $55.00
 4. Boxers, "Set To", Blue Base $160.00
 5. Racing, Blue Base $175.00

(A-MA. '76) Richard A. Bourne Co., Inc.
(Row I, Left to Right)
**Mason's Patent Ironstone China Dessert
Plates,** (1 Of 12), Polychrome Chinoiserie
Decor., Slightly Worn In Centers Of Plates,
1 W/Lge. Chip Professionally Repaired W/
Rivets, 8" Diam. $350.00
Copeland Porcelain Dessert Plates, (1 Of 18),
By W. T. Copeland & Sons, Plates Have Blue &
Gold Panels On White Alternating W/3 Panels
Of Hand Painted Exotic Birds W/Single Bird In
Center, Decor. Different On Each Plate, Decor.
2 W/Age Cracks Across Center, 9½" Diam.
....$325.00
Samson Plates, (1 Of 17), Each W/Pink Ribbon
Decorated W/Berries & Leaves Around Rim &
Bouquet Of Flowers In Center, 9½" Diam. .....
....$250.00
(Row II, Left to Right)
Meissen Service Plates, (1 Of 8), Reticulated
Borders W/Lattice-Like Panels Alternating
W/Foliage Panels, All Panels W/Raised Flowers,
Center Is Royal Blue W/Different Romantic
Scene In Center Highlighted In Gold, Underglaze
Blue Crossed Swords Mark, 10" Diam. ....
....$900.00
Copeland Spode Service Plates, (1 Of 12),
Broad Green & Gold Borders W/Ivory-Colored
Medallions, Heavy Gold Garlands & White Cen-
ters, 10" Diam. $300.00
Meissen Plates, (1 Of 15), Each W/Royal Blue
Border & 3 Floral Panels, Different Romantic
Transfer Scenes In Center, Oval Meissen Mark,
Some Variation Of Color In Blue Borders, 9¾"
Diam. $300.00
(Row III)
Paragon China Service Plates, (1 Of 12),
Commemorating The Coronation Of King
Edward VIII, May 12, 1937, Decor. W/The
British Arms In Center & Around Border
"Edward VIII, King And Emperor", 19½" Diam.
....$225.00
Minton China Service Plates, (1 Of 12), Bou-
quet Of Flowers In Center, Lt. Pale Green Trac-
eries Of Leaves In Border W/Red & Black Keyed
Border Design, 10½" Diam..........$150.00

 6. Amorous Couple, "I Love Too Well To Kiss
& Tell." Pink Base, Damaged $55.00
 7. Black & White Box W/Blue Base, Inscribed
"Accept This Trifle From A Friend, Whose Love
For Thee Will Never End." $125.00
 8. Black & White Box W/Pink Base, Inscribed
"Remember Him Who Gives This Trifle." Damaged $125.00
 9. Blue Box, W/White Birds, "A Friend's Gift"
....$105.00
 10. Floral Top W/Yellow Base $85.00

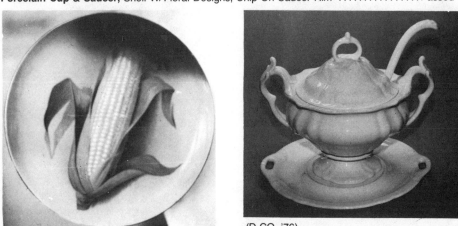

Garth's Auctions, Inc.

(A-OH. '76)
(Row I, Left to Right)
Porcelain Creamer, English, 18th C., Transfer & Polychrome Free Hand Oriental Decor., 4'' H. $40.00
Salopian Cup & Saucer, Floral Acorn Pattern, Saucer Damaged & Not Pictured $10.00
Soft Paste Cup & Saucer, Blue Transfer W/Angel Carrying Banner W/German Inscription "Den Menschen Een Walbehagen" $45.00
Soft Paste Creamer, Oriental Decor. In Blue Transfer W/Polychrome Enamel, Marked W"R" Incircled By Rays, 3¾'' H. $35.00
(Row II, Left to Right)
Leeds Cup & Saucer, Floral Decor. In 4 Colors, Chip On Foot Of Handleless Cup $55.00
Salopian Cup & Saucer, Oriental Scenery, Tiny Flake On Cup Rim $195.00
Leeds Cup & Saucer, Blue Vintage, Minor Roughness $45.00
(Row III, Left to Right)
Porcelain Cup & Saucer, English, 18th C., Transfer & Polychrome Free Hand Oriental Decor., Saucer Has Crows Foot . . . . .Passed
Strawberry Cup & Saucer $345.00
Porcelain Cup & Saucer, Shell W/Floral Designs, Chip On Saucer Rim . . . . .Passed

(D-MO. '76)
Coffeepot, Porcelain Body, Pewter Trim, 1½'' H.
. . . .$90.00

(D-N.Y. '76)
Pratt Jug, Adm. Duncan (1831-1904), 9½'' H.
. . . .$145.00

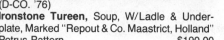

(D-MO. '76)
Hanging Plate Sgn. "Beck", Realistic Ear Of Corn On Shaded Pink Ground $45.00

(D-CO. '76)
Ironstone Tureen, Soup, W/Ladle & Underplate, Marked "Repout & Co. Maastrict, Holland" Petrus Pattern $190.00

(D-IL. '76)
Kewpie Plate, Rose O'Neill, 7 Action Kewpies, Rudolstadt, 7'' Diam. $90.00

Gaudy Welsh Washbowl & Pitcher, Pink W/Rose & Blue & Copper Lustre Decor., 19" H. Pitcher, 12½" W. Washbowl $350.00

(Left to Right)
Copper Lustre Goblet, 5", Pink Lustre Band Decor. $10.00
Copper Lustre Goblet, 4½", Chinese Poly-chrome Decor. $10.00
Silver Resist Lustre Pitcher, 5½", Polychrome Bird Center, Slightly Worn, #225 ......$37.50

(Left to Right)
Whieldon Ware Plate, 9½" $120.00
Spatterware Plate, Red, 9½" $140.00
Spatterware Plate, Red, 9" $170.00

COPPER LUSTRE
(Left to Right)
Pitcher, 5¼" $37.50
Pitcher, 5½" $25.00
Pepper Pot, Sandy Sunderland Lustre Base, 4½" $42.50
Bowl, Blue Band Decor. $15.00

LEEDS
(Left to Right)
Plate, Green Edge, 9" Diam. $275.00
Creamer, 3¾" $475.00
Cup & Saucer, Brown & Yellow Stripe, Orange Swirl Border, Green Leaf Center $110.00

Prattware Group Figure, Soft Paste, "The Baptism", Handle On Baby Basket Missing, ...
....$190.00

(A-OH. '76) *Garth's Auctions, Inc.*

(Row I, Left to Right)
Copper Luster Pitcher,Blue Band W/Floral Design, Edge Chip, 6½" H. $40.00
Copper Luster Pitcher, Putty Colored Band W/Floral Design, 5¾" H. $35.00
Copper Luster Creamer, Pale Green Band W/Purple Luster Floral Design, Sm. Spout Chip, 4¼" H. $10.00
Copper Luster Creamer, White & PuttyColored Band W/Copper & Purple Luster & Reddish-Orange Enamel In Floral Design, Spout Chips, 3¾" H. $10.00
Copper Luster Pitcher, Blue Band W/Floral Design, Sm. Chip On Spout, 3¼" H. $5.00
(Row II, Left to Right)
Copper Luster Sugar Bowl, Blue Edge, Chips, 5½" H. $5.00
Copper Luster Creamer, Blue Stripes, 2½" H. $12.50
Silver Luster Teapot, 8" H. $50.00
Copper Luster Creamer, Sanded Finish, 3" H. $7.50
Copper Luster Pitcher, Blue Band, 5¼" H. $37.50

(Row III, Left to Right)
Copper Luster Creamers, (2), One Plain, One W/Putty Colored Band, 2½" H. $10.00
Copper Luster Creamer, Blue Band W/Floral Design, Chips On Spout, 3¼" H. $5.00
Copper Luster Creamer, Blue Band W/Embossed Polychrome Scene, 3½" H. $27.50
Copper Luster Creamer, Putty Colored Band W/Floral Design In Purple Luster, 4⅜" H. $22.50
Copper Luster Pitcher, White Band W/Floral Design In Purple Luster & Red & Green, 5¼" H. $15.00

(D-MO. '76)
Sunbonnet Babies By Royal Bayreuth China Co.
(Left to Right)
Pitcher, Washing, 4" H. $145.00
Pitcher, Mending, 3½" H. $165.00
Pitcher, Washing, 3" H. $135.00

(A-MA. '76) *Richard A. Bourne Co. Inc.*
(Row I)
Mettlach Tumblers, (6), Each W/Different Human Figure On One Side, Green Villeroy & Boch Mettlach Signature, Brown "Geschutzt", All W/Numeral "2327", 2 Sm. Chips In Rim, (2 Illus.) $140.00
(Row II)
Mettlach One-Liter Lidded Stein, Russian Phoenix Bird Or Eagle In Black, Silver & Gold On Front; W/"VB", Green Villeroy & Boch Stamped Mark, Impressed "2204", "1", "01", "29", "C", & "Gesgesch", ...$600.00

(D-IL. '76)
Carlsbad China Vase, Austria, 11" H. .$90.00

(D-GA. '76)
Limoges Pitcher W/T & V Mark, 12" H. .....
.................................$95.00

(D-N.C. '76)
Mustache Cup & Saucer, Mkd. Germany. Note Partially Covered Top For Lip Guard ....
.....................................$60.00

(D-MS. '76)
Sunderland Lustre Mustache Cup & Saucer W/Inscription Written On Opposite Side In Black $85.00

(D-N.Y. '76)
IRISH BELLEEK
(Left to Right)
Mustache Cup & Saucer, 1st Mark ..$150.00
Basket, Woven W/Delicate Applied Flowers In Pastel Colors, 2nd Black Mark, 5¾" Diam.
.................................$125.00

(D-IA. '76)
French Limoges Lemonade Set, Pitcher, Tray & 8 Glasses, Sgn. $200.00

(D-MO. '76)
Pap Boat (Infant Feeder) Porcelain, 5½" L. . . .
. . . .$20.00

(D-WA. '76)
Amphora Vase, 20" H. (Bohemian) Ca. 1900 .
. . . .$250.00

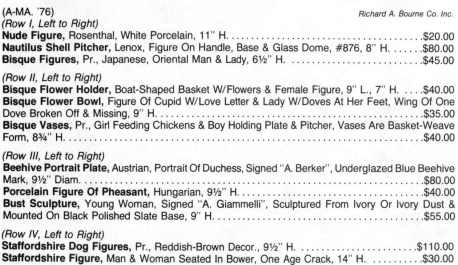

Richard A. Bourne Co. Inc.

(A-MA. '76)
(Row I, Left to Right)
Nude Figure, Rosenthal, White Porcelain, 11" H. $20.00
Nautilus Shell Pitcher, Lenox, Figure On Handle, Base & Glass Dome, #876, 8" H. $80.00
Bisque Figures, Pr., Japanese, Oriental Man & Lady, 6½" H. $45.00

(Row II, Left to Right)
Bisque Flower Holder, Boat-Shaped Basket W/Flowers & Female Figure, 9" L., 7" H. $40.00
Bisque Flower Bowl, Figure Of Cupid W/Love Letter & Lady W/Doves At Her Feet, Wing Of One
Dove Broken Off & Missing, 9" H. $35.00
Bisque Vases, Pr., Girl Feeding Chickens & Boy Holding Plate & Pitcher, Vases Are Basket-Weave
Form, 8¾" H. $40.00

(Row III, Left to Right)
Beehive Portrait Plate, Austrian, Portrait Of Duchess, Signed "A. Berker", Underglazed Blue Beehive
Mark, 9½" Diam. $80.00
Porcelain Figure Of Pheasant, Hungarian, 9½" H. $40.00
Bust Sculpture, Young Woman, Signed "A. Giammelli", Sculptured From Ivory Or Ivory Dust &
Mounted On Black Polished Slate Base, 9" H. $55.00

(Row IV, Left to Right)
Staffordshire Dog Figures, Pr., Reddish-Brown Decor., 9½" H. $110.00
Staffordshire Figure, Man & Woman Seated In Bower, One Age Crack, 14" H. $30.00

(D-CA. '76)
Royal Doulton Umbrella Stand, 22" H. . . . . . .
. . . .$125.00

CHALKWARE
(Left to Right)
Fruit Basket, 13" H. $250.00
Basket Of Pears, 6½" H. $210.00

CHALKWARE
(Left to Right)
Doves, Pr., On Tree Stump, Cherry Decor $325.00
"Moses In The Bullrushes" $210.00

(D-MA. '76)
Pitcher, Blue/White Porcelain, Cherub & Grapes Pattern By U.S. Pottery Co., Bennington, Vt. (1852-1858) 6½" H. $1,200.00

(D-CA. '76)
ABC Plate, Porcelain, 7¼" Diam. $45.00

(Row I, Left to Right)
Chalkware Reclining Dog, Red, Orange, Yellow & Black, 3½" L. $25.00
Chalkware Watch Case, Bright Colors, 11¾" H. $95.00
Chalkware Garniture, Red & Yellow, Repaired & Sm. Hole, 10½" H. $35.00
(Row II, Left to Right)
Chalkware Standing Dogs, Pr., Free Standing Front Legs, Brown, Blue, Orange & Yellow, 8¼" H.
....$150.00
Chalkware Roosters, Yellow, Red & Black, Base Repair, 6" H. $425.00

Garth's Auctions, Inc.

(A-OH. '76)

(Row I, Left to Right)
Salopian Mug, Brittania & Other Figures Transfer, 4¾" H. $100.00
Salopian Bowl, Deer & Cottages Transfer, 6¼" D. $205.00
Canary Luster Pitcher, Silver Floral Band, Old Chip On Rim & Crow's Foot, 4¾" H. $265.00
(Row II, Left to Right)
Canary Luster Covered Bowl, Enameled Brick Red Roses & Green Leaves, 3¼" H. $400.00
Canary Luster Urn Shaped Jar, Applied Satyr Marks & Black Transfer Of Boy & Cow, Hairlines In Base, 5" H. $90.00
Canary Luster Cup & Saucer, Brick Red Transfer Of Tea Party, Saucer Has Impressed Signature, "Sewell" $200.00

(D-CT. '76)
Parian Porcelain Vase, Decorated W/Grapes & Vines, 8½" H. $45.00

(D-TX. '76)
'71 Annual Goebel Hummel Collector Plate
...................................$450.00

(D-OH. '76)
"Little Red Riding Hood" Cookie Jar, "Hull" Pottery, 13½" H. $28.50

(D-MO. '76)
Limoges Platter, W/8 Matching Plates (not illus.), Mkd. & Sgn. By The Artist "Duval" .....
...................................$550.00

(D-KS. '76)
HUMMEL FIGURINES, Ca. 1952
(Left to Right)
Little Gabriel, 5' H. $28.50
New Baby, 5½" H. $35.00
Goose Girl, 4" H. $30.00

(D-CA. '76)
Buffalo Pottery Bowl, Geranium Pattern, Blue/White, 6½" H. $85.00

(D-LA. '76)
Moorcroft Bowl, Cobalt W/Fruit In Center & Around Exterior, Sgn. In Green Script & Impressed Word "Moorcroft", 10" Diam. ......
...................................$75.00

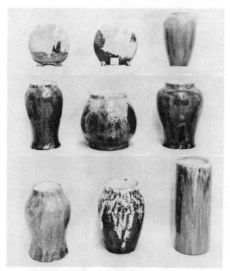

(A-MA. '75)   Richard A. Bourne Co. Inc.

CHELSEA & DEDHAM POTTERY
(Row I, Left to Right)

Flat Globular Footed Vase, By Chelsea Keramic Art Works, Robertson & Sons, Prior To 1889, Decor. W/Marine Seascape, Mkd. In Base, 2⅜" D., 6¼" W., 6¼" H. $650.00

Flat Globular Vase, By Chelsea, Robertson & sons, Decor. W/Landscape In Green & Blue, Mkd. "HCR", 1 Leg Has Professional Repair, 2½" D., 6½" W., 6¼" H. $350.00

Dragon's Blood Pottery Vase, By Chelsea Keramic Art Works, 7¾" H. $175.00

(Row II, Left to Right)

Olive Brown Pottery Vase, By Chelsea, Mkd. W/Incised Signature "Dedham Pottery RW CRV", Chips On Bottom Of Feet, 9" H. ....
....$200.00

Bowl-Shaped Vase, By Chelsea, Mottled Brown & Silvery-Grey, Possibly Silveria, Mkd. "Dedham Pottery AW & HCR", 8" Diam., 7½" H. ....
....$400.00

Pottery Vase, By Chelsea, Deep Green W/Deeper Green Runs, Mkd. "Dedham Pottery HCR" W/Various Penciled & Painted Numbers, 9" H. $300.00

(Row III, Left to Right)

Pottery Vase, By Chelsea, So-Called Silveria Type W/Mottled Runs Of Grey, Green, Brown & Various Other Colors, Repaired Crack In Bottom, Mkd. "Dedham Pottery", "HCR", 8¾" H.
....$400.00

Pottery Vase, By Chelsea, Drk. Mottled Brown W/Runs Of White, Green & Pale Blue-Green Down Sides, Number Of Open Bubbles In Runs Create Rough Areas (Occurred During The Making), Signed On Bottom "Dedham Pottery", W/Painted & Penciled-On Numerals, 8¾" H. ...
....$400.00

Cylindrical Pottery Vase, Brown Flint-Like Enamel, Mkd. "Dedham Pottery HCR 1-8-48", Penciled & Painted-On Numerals & Label Stating "Made 1848 No Duplicates", 4¾" Diam., 11½" H. $300.00

(A-MA. '75)   Richard A. Bourne Co. Inc.

(Row I, Left to Right)

Rookwood Vase, Decor. Of Lge. Yellow Flower W/Green & Brown Leaves, Dated 1906, 6⅝" H.
....$125.00

Art Nouveau-Style Rookwood Vase, Multi-colored Floral Design & Pastel Shading, Dated 1920, 9⅛" H. $150.00

Rookwood Vase, Globular, Plain W/Slightly Embossed Design, 1927, 3½" H. ...$20.00

Rookwood Paperweight Or Bookend, Ivory-

(A-MA. '75)   Richard A. Bourne Co., Inc.

ART POTTERY
(Row I, Left to Right)

Globular Jug, Handle & Pouring Spout, Low-elsa Ware By Weller, Handle Broken & Reglued, 5½" H. $20.00

Rookwood Or Weller Bottle, Mounted As A lamp, Height Of Vase & Stand-9" $25.00

Rookwood Vase, Yellow Tulips W/Green Leaves Against Deep Red-Brown Ground, Marked W/12 Flame Points Indicating 1899, Decorator Charles Schmidt, 6" H. $100.00

(Row II, Left to Right)

Rookwood Vase, Gray Blueberries Against Purple-Blue Ground Which Shades To Peach-bloom Color At Top, Dated 1927, Decorator Harriet E. Wilcox, 9½" H. $70.00

Rookwood Vase, Mottled Green, Aqua & Blue-Gray, Dated 1930, Decorator Janet Harris, Chips In Foot, 11½" H. $25.00

Weller Vase, Marked "Eocean", Jonquils & Leaves Against Green Background Fading To Ivory At Bottom, Age Crack In Bottom, 9¼" H.
....$30.00

White, Dated 1930, In The Form Of Pair Of Geese, 4" H. $50.00

(Row II, Left to Right)

Roseville Vases, Pair, Embossed Flowers, Each Fitted W/Handle, 7¼" H. $20.00

Weller Vase, Blue Jasperware-Style, Hunting Scene On The Side In White On Deep Blue, Signed On Bottom "Weller Pottery", 8" H. ....
....$50.00

Weller Boat-Form Planter, Signed On Bottom "Weller", Slight Edge Roughage, 9⅝" L. $30.00

(A-MA. '76)   Richard A. Bourne Co., Inc.

LIVERPOOL POTTERY
(Row I, Left to Right)

Jug, Amer. Eagle Holding Banner, Inner Rim Chip, Sm. Chip In Pouring Spout, Age Crack & Sm. Repair To Hole In Bottom, 5¾" H.$250.00

Jug, Qt., Lowestoft Form W/Interlaced Strap Handle, Amer. Eagle W/Banner, Arrows & Olive Branch & "James Leech" Beneath On One Side, Cracks On Handle $250.00

Jug, Qt., Pink Lustre Striping, Transfer Of Portrait Of George Washington & "Captain Jones Of The Macedonian" $250.00

(Row II, Left to Right)

Jug, W/Transfer Portrait Of James Madison One Side, Eagle Under Spout & Trophy Of Arms W/ . Eagle, W/Phrase, "Pease, Plenty & Independence". Age Cracks, 7¾" H. $400.00

Jug, Qt., Pink Lustre Decor., Portrait Of Captain Jones Of The Macedonian Within Trophy Of Arms & Ship On One Side, & Captain Hull Of The Constitution On Other; 2 Age Cracks In Rim, 5¼" H. $350.00

Jug, Transfer Portrait Of Commodore Rogers On One Side & Amer. Eagle W/Banner Shield, Arrows & Olive Branch Within Frame Of A Chain, Pro. Repair About Spout, 7" H. $250.00

(Row III, Left to Right)

Jug, W/Eagle Clutching Banner, Shield, Arrows & Olive Branch W/Decor. Has Arms Of The U.S., W/Verse On One Side & Scene W/Classical Ruins, Angel & Female Figure Bearing Proclamation Saying "July 4, 1776 America Declared Independent", Cracks & Chips, 8" H. .$200.00

Jug, Transfer Scene W/Amer. Full-Rigged Ship On One Side, Eagle Under Spout & Lge. Oval Scene Of Washington Being Borne To Heaven By Angels. Sm. Age Crack, 8" H. $300.00

(Row IV, Left to Right)

Jug, W/Transfer Scene Of British Ship W/Label "A Merchantman Becalmed" On One Side, Eagle W/Banner, Shield & Olive Branch Under Spout & Masonic Arms On Other; Pro. Repair To Spout, 2 Cracks Near Lower Handle, 8¼" H. $375.00

Jug, W/Portrait Of Commodore Decatur W/Verson On One Side, & Transfer Portrait Of Commodore Perry W/Verse, Repaired, Part Of Transfer Repainted, 7¾" H. $150.00

(D-N.J. '76)
Rookwood Vase, Indian On Dark Brown Ground, 9" H. $195.00

(D-AR. '76)
Niloak Pottery Vase, Blue W/Pink & White, 12½" H. $45.00

(D-CO. '76)
Van Briggle Bowl, Blue, 5" H. $35.00

(D-CA. '76)
Mettlach Pitcher & Tumbler, (1 of 6), Sgn. Mettlach, V & B. Ca. 1900 . . . .$500.00

(D-TN. '76)
Newcomb Pottery Vase, Cattails, 11" H. . . . .
. . . .$75.00

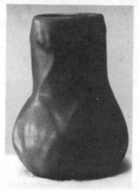

(D-KS. '76)
Van Briggle Pottery Vase, Mulberry Color, 6" H. $18.00

(D-NE. '76)
Weller Vases, Dickensware, 11½" H., Figures On Brown Ground $375.00

(D-AR. '76)
Weller Pitcher, Blue Jay, 8" H. $55.00

(D-FL. '76)
Zsolnay Vase, Ivorıne, 12" H. $225.00

(D-WA. '76)
Weller Pitcher, Dickensware, 11½" H. . . . .
. . . .$95.00

(A-MA. '76)   Richard A. Bourne Co. Inc.

STONEWARE
(Row I, Left to Right)
Jar, Cobalt Blue Decor. Of 4 Flowers Around Entire Body, 8¼" H. $40.00
Crock, 2-Gal., By Pottman Bros., Fort Edward, N.Y., Ca. 1870, Cobalt Blue Decor. Of Birds, Chips In Bottom $70.00
Crock, 2-Gal., Cobalt Blue Decor. Of Scrolled Leaf & Numeral "2" $45.00
Jug, 1-Gal., By E. & L. Norton, Bennington, Vermont, Cobalt Blue Decor. Of Leaf Or Flower, Chips At Rim, Sgn. $60.00
(Row II, Left to Right)
Jug, 2-Gal, By Cowden & Wilcox, Harrisburg, Pa., Ca. 1870-90, Cobalt Blue Decor. Of Flower. Sgn. $60.00
Bowl, Salt Glaze, Flat Rim, Cock & Flower Framed In Incised & Blue Fired-On Design, 13" Diam. $140.00
Jug, 1-Gal, By Sipe & Sons, Williamsport, Pa., Cobalt Blue Decor. Of Lge. Leaf $45.00
(Row III, Left to Right)
Crock, 4-Gal., By Haxstun, Ottman &Co., Fort Edward, N.Y., Cobalt Blue Decor. Of Bird, Molded-On Handle $50.00
Jug W/Pouring Lip, 19th C., Approx. 4-Gal., Cobalt Blue Decor. Of Tulips & Scrolled Leaves, Sm. Chip In Pouring Lip, 15½" H. $75.00
Foot Warmer, Salt Glaze, Sgraffito Decor., Carrying Handle, Cracks Around Neck & Sides, ...$200.00

(D-VT. '76)
Pottery Pitcher, Blue & White W/Embossed Leaves & Branches, 7½" H. $95.00

(A-MA. '76)   Richard A. Bourne Co. Inc.
(Row I, Left to Right)
Pottery Jar Or Vase, Incised Design Under Glaze Of Flowers, Circles & Egg-Like Shapes, Drk. Brown Mottled Glaze W/Touches Of Green, 6¼" H. $290.00
Redware Cup, Pa., W/Dabbed-On Decor. Of Reddish-Brown Glaze $110.00
Slipware Dish, Pa., Yellow Double Line Decor. On Reddish-Brown Glaze, 7⅜" Diam. ....
..................................$50.00
Redware Pottery Dish, Pa., Reddish-Brown Glaze W/Brown Mottling, 6⅜" Diam. ...$45.00
(Row II, Left to Right)
Turk's Head Pottery Mold, Mottled Tan & Brown Glaze, 7" Diam. $50.00
Swirled Turk's Head Mold, Mottled Brown & Lt. Green Glaze, 1 Chip On Rim, 8¾" Diam. ...
..................................$25.00
Swirled Turk's Head Mold, Pa., Red Glaze, Crack In Side & Minor Nicks, 9½" Diam. .....
..................................$20.00
(Row III, Left to Right)
Redware Turk's Head Mold, Pa., Drk. Mottling Around Rim, 8" Diam. $40.00
Turk's Head Mold, Reddish-Brown Glaze & Black Sponge Mottling, Sm. Edge Chips, 9¼" Diam. $25.00
Pie Plate, Pa., Lt. Brown Glaze Inside Only, Faintly Visible 2" Crack, 1 Slight Nick, 8¼" Diam. $10.00
(Row IV, Left to Right)
Redware Jar, Pa., Late 18th-Early 19th C., Reddish-Brown Glaze & Dribbled-On Yellow Decor., Nick In Rim, 6¾" H. $125.00
Redware Pottery Jar, Pa., Dashed-On Drk. Brown Decor. Over Reddish-Brown Glaze, Crack On Base, 7¼" H. $45.00
Wide-Mouthed Crock, Early Ct., Fisheye Glaze In Reddish Brown & Deep Gray, 8¾" Diam., 8⅝" H. $60.00
Jar, Early Pa., 19th C., Molded-On Handles, Zig-Zagged Incised Lines Around Neck, 8" H. $70.00

(A-MA. '75)   Richard A. Bourne Co. Inc.
(Row I, Left to Right)
Chelsea Vase, Mottled Red On Green Ground W/Iridescent Blue-White Mottling, Mkd. "Dedham Pottery HCR", Conjoined Initials, Minor Damage On Foot, 7½" H. $650.00
Chelsea Vase, Elongated Tear-Drop Shape, Red & Silvery-Blue On Moss-Green Ground,

(Cont. next column)

"Dedham Pottery" & Initialed Twice W/Conjoined Initials "HCR", Foot Damage Minor, 8⅞" H. $750.00
Chelsea Vase, Yellow, Brown & Green Mottling, Bulbous W/Elongated Wide Cylindrical Neck, Minor Imperfections On Base, Heavy Glaze, 6⅞" H. $150.00
Chelsea Vase, Silveria Type W/Many Shades Of Mottled Green W/Flecks Of Blood-Red & Touches Of Yellow-Green At Top, Mkd. "Dedham Pottery", Painted & Penciled Numbers, Slight Damage On Foot, 8" H. $250.00
(Row II, Left to Right)
Chelsea Vase, Silveria-Type, Olive & Yellow-Green W/Mottled Runs Of Blue-Black & Blue W/Touch Of Red, Mkd. "Dedham Pottery" W/Conjoined Initials Of "HCR", Penciled & Painted Numbers, 7¼" H. $500.00
Chelsea Vase, Apple-Green Glaze, "Dedham Pottery", Penciled Numbers, Minor Imperfections, 7¼" H. $125.00
Chelsea Vase, Mottled Olive-Green Glaze, Mkd. "Dedham Pottery", Painted On Number, Chip In Neck Reglued, Smaller Chip In Same Area, 8¼" H. $50.00
(Row III, Left to Right)
Decorated Redware Vase, Signed "HCR" On Bottom, Together W/Note "This Redware Vase Was Made In Chelsea", Signed "Charles F. Davenport", Decor. Worn, 7⅞" H. $100.00
Blood Red Vase, By Chelsea, Impressed Signature "CKAW" In Bottom, 7⅜" H. ...$400.00
Vase, By Chelsea, Yellow-Green Mottled Glaze W/Lge. Imperfection One Side At Shoulder, Glaze Brown At Top, Mkd. "CKAW" On Bottom, 6¾" H. $200.00
(Row IV, Left to Right)
Gourd-Form Vase, Chelsea, Drk. Deep Grey Glaze, Mkd. On Bottom "CKAW", 7½" H. ...
..................................$425.00
Vase, Chelsea, Deep Grey-Black Glaze W/Touches Of Red At Bottom, Unsigned, 3 Imperfections, 6¼" H. $100.00
Chelsea Redware Acanthus Leaf Vases, (1 Of Pr.), Green W/Deeper Green Raised Acanthus Leaves Together W/Slip Which Reads: "These Acanthus Leaf Vases Were Made In Chelsea, Charles F. Davenport", Few Flakes In Decor., 7½" H. $300.00

(A-MA. '76)   Richard A. Bourne Co. Inc.
(Row I, Left to Right)
Oblong Vegetable Dish, Rockingham Glaze, Lt. Color W/Drk. Green & Brown Splotches In Center, 10¼" L. $160.00
Bennington-Type Oblong Vegetable Dish, Rockingham Glaze, Sm. Chip One End, 8½" L. $140.00

(Row II, Left to Right)
Bennington Book Flask, "Departed Spirits", Drk. Mottled Brown Rockingham Glaze, 5½" H. $170.00
Bennington Flint Enamel Book Flask, 1 Sm. Chip In Bottom, 5¼" W., 6¾" H. $225.00
Bennington Book Flask, Rockingham Glaze, 5¼" W., 6½" H. $150.00
Bennington Book Flask, Rockingham Glaze, Incised Title "Dante" On Long End, Chips On Bottom, 3⅞" W., 5¾" H. $120.00
(Row III, Left to Right)
Bennington Candlesticks, Pair, One Flint Enamel, One W/Rockingham Glaze, 9½" H. $450.00
Bennington Glaze Candlesticks, Pair, One W/Chip In Upper Rim Of Socket, 9¾" H. $325.00

(D-WA. '75)
Wedgwood Bowl, Agate Ware, Mkd. .$300.00

(A-PA. '75)   *Pennypacker Auction Centre*
Capo Di Monte Covered Vases, 12" T., Pair. $400.00
Center, **Meissen Compote,** Crossed Sword Mark, 17" T., Minor Repair $925.00

(D-PA. '76)
Spatterware Plate, 9½" Diam., French $90.00

(D-ME. '76)
Spongeware Plate, Blue & White, 10" Diam. $125.00

(A-MA. '76)   Richard A. Bourne Co., Inc.
(Row I, Left to Right)
Rockingham Glaze Ink Bottle, English, 19th C., Form Of Man's Hear Wearing Night Cap, Chips On Foot Ring $60.00
Rockingham Glaze Bank, Form Of Miniature Sheraton Chest, 2 Lge. Chips In Coin Slot, 2⅝" W., 1¾" D., 2¼" H. $20.00
Rockingham Glaze Salt, Possibly English, Round, Footed $25.00
Rockingham Brilliant Glaze Bottle, Or Vase, 6" H. $10.00
Dark Brown Glazed Mug, Reeded Applied Handle, Triple Bank Of Dots Around Upper Rim $20.00

(Row II, Left to Right)
Rockingham Glaze Mug, Applied Handle $40.00
Rockingham Glaze Mug, Ohio, Applied Handle, Age Crack In Base $20.00
Rockingham Glaze Mug, Applied Handle $35.00
Rockingham Glaze Mug, Ohio, Paneled Sides & Applied Handle $40.00
(Row III, Left to Right)
Rockingham Glaze Mug, By Bennett Brothers, Baltimore, Maryland, Frog Inside & 2 Toby's On Outside $170.00
Rockingham Glaze Mug, Applied Reeded Handle, Large $65.00
Rockingham Glaze Mug, Applied Handle, Large $45.00
(Row IV, Left to Right)
Rockingham Glaze Dish, Scalloped Rim, 9" Diam. $140.00
Rockingham Glaze Cake Dish, Rounded & Fluted Corners, Flaring Sides, Approx. 9" Sq. $100.00

(D-MS. '76)
Wedgwood Jasper Ware Bowl, Blue & White, Mkd., 6½" H. $65.00

(D-MO. '76)
PEORIA POTTERY
(Left to Right)
Canning Jar W/Drk. Brown Glaze & Incised Mkd. "Peoria Pottery" $18.50
Canning Jar W/Drk. Brown Glaze, Barrel Shaped, Also Bears Incised Mark $22.50

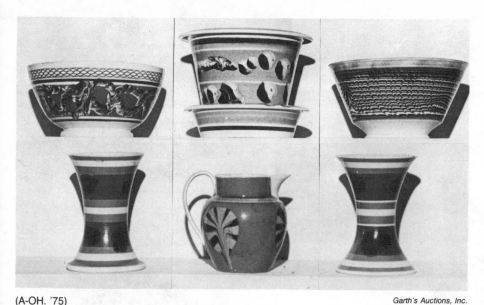

Garth's Auctions, Inc.

(A-OH. '75)

(Row I, Left to Right)

Mocha Bowl, Orange Tan Band W/Brown Stripes & Earth Worm Decor., 6⅜" Diam. $250.00
Mocha Flower Pot, 2-Pc., Blue Bands W/Cats Eyes; Yellow, White & Brown Stripes, Chips, Rare Form, 4¾" H. $475.00
Mocha Bowl, Sqwiggly Decor. In Green, Brown, Blue & White, 6¼" Diam. $350.00

(Row II, Left to Right)

Mocha Spill Holders, Pair, Terra Cotta Bands W/Black Seaweed Decor., Wide Blue & White Stripes, Inside Flake On One, Other Has Small Repair, 5⅛" H. $400.00
Mocha Creamer, Orange Tan W/Blue & Black Balloons & Embossed Green Stripe, Chip On Spout, 4½" H. $425.00

(D-IN. '76)
Mocha Bowl, Earthworm On Blue, 4¼" H., 9½" Diam. At Top $450.00

Pennypacker Auction Centre

(A-PA. '76)
Mocha Ware Cream Pitcher, Earthworm Design, Blue, Green & Brown, Rim Flake & Spider In Base, 5" H. $425.00
Leeds Pitcher, Minor Chips, 6" H. . . . $160.00
Mocha Ware Mug, Chain & Stripe Patt., Minor Chips, 5" H. $110.00

Pennypacker Auction Centre

(A-PA. '76)
MOCHA WEAR
(Left to Right)

Mustard, Earthworm Design, Lt. & Drk. Brown, 3" H. $375.00
Cup, Stripes Of Blue, Yellow & Mocha, Minor Flake On Base, 3" H. $180.00
Bowl, Marbleized Design, Minor Rim Flakes, 5¼" Diam. $100.00
Salt Shaker, Seaweed Design, Blue & Brown, Minor Flakes, 4¼" H. $150.00
Cup, Marbleized Design, Hairlines & Rim Chip, 5" H. $110.00

Pennypacker Auction Centre

(A-PA. '76)
MOCHA WEAR
(Left to Right)

Pitcher, Stripes & Waves Design, Brown, Blue, Green & Mocha, 7½" H. $120.00
Pitcher, Seaweed Design, Brown & Mocha, Hairline & Sm. Base Chip, 6½" H. $180.00
Pitcher, Cats Eye & Earthwork Design, Blue, Green & Brown, Hairline & Rim Chips, 8" H. $190.00

(D-MO. '76)
Pottery Whiskey Bottle, "Quinn's Quality Quantity" $75.00

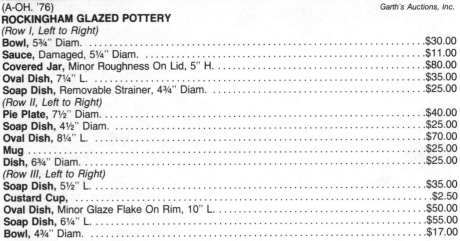

Garth's Auctions, Inc.

(D-MN. '76)
Delft Platter, Mkd. "Jan Van Putten Co., Delft, Holland" Ca. 1850 . . . .$135.00

(A-OH. '76)
ROCKINGHAM GLAZED POTTERY
(Row I, Left to Right)
Bowl, 5¾" Diam. $30.00
Sauce, Damaged, 5¼" Diam. $11.00
Covered Jar, Minor Roughness On Lid, 5" H. $80.00
Oval Dish, 7¼" L. $35.00
Soap Dish, Removable Strainer, 4¾" Diam. $25.00
(Row II, Left to Right)
Pie Plate, 7½" Diam. $40.00
Soap Dish, 4½" Diam. $25.00
Oval Dish, 8¼" L. $70.00
Mug $25.00
Dish, 6¾" Diam. $25.00
(Row III, Left to Right)
Soap Dish, 5½" L. $35.00
Custard Cup, ...$2.50
Oval Dish, Minor Glaze Flake On Rim, 10" L. $50.00
Soap Dish, 6¼" L. $55.00
Bowl, 4¾" Diam. $17.00

(D-MT. '76)
Gibson Girl Plate, The Day After Arriving At Her Journeys End, 10" Diam. $55.00

(D-KY. '76)
Quimper Platter, Peasant Woman, Sgn., 11 x 16½" L. $45.00

(A-PA. '76)
SHENANDOAH POTTERY *(Left to Right)*
Wash Bowl & Pitcher $975.00
Hanging Wall Vase, Applied Bird $675.00
Double Sander $275.00

Pennypacker Auction Centre

Pennypacker Auction Centre

(A-PA. '76)
Shenandoah Type Pitchers, Pr., Yellow, Green & Chocolate Decor., 9" H. $42.50
Shenandoah Redware Spitoon, Green & Brown Slip Decor $150.00

(A-PA. '76) *Pennypacker Auction Centre*
Redware Mold, 8" $330.00

(A-OH. '76) *Garth's Auctions, Inc.*
(Row I, Left to Right)
Rockingham Covered Jar, Sm. Rim & Lid Chips, 5" H. $100.00
Rockingham Pitcher, 8" H. $95.00
White Clay Jar, Shiny Drk. Brown Glaze, 6" H. $15.00
(Row II, Left to Right)
Redware Jar, Covered, Surface W/Applied Molded Heades & Arched Panels W/Figure Of Cardinal & Churchman & "Ambrosius"; Interior Has White Slip Decor. W/Green Dasher & Covered W/Clear Glaze; Exterior Has Shiny Drk. Brown Glaze, Minor Wear, 7¾" H. $65.00
Graduated Bowls, Set Of 3, Green & Brown Glaze, 7", 6" & 5" Diam. $95.00
(Row III, Left to Right)
Rockingham Creamer, Rim Chip, 4¼" H. $25.00
Stoneware Bird Watering Fountain, 5½" H. $30.00
Mixing Bowl, Brown & Green Glaze, 9" Diam. $40.00
White Clay Hanging Planter, Exterior Has Multicolored Dripping Glaze, Brown, Green, Blue & Yellow, Chips, 7" L. $22.50
Rockingham Mug, 3¾" H. $40.00

(A-PA. '75) *Pennypacker Auction Centre*
Redware Fat Lamp $1,250.00

(A-PA. '75) *Pennypacker Auction Centre*
Slip Decorated Redware Plate, 9¾" Diam. $250.00

(A-PA. '75) *Pennypacker Auction Centre*
(Left to Right)
Earthen Bottle, Brown W/Streaked Ochre Glaze $65.00
Redware Crock, Orange Shaded To Green, 3" H. $120.00
Redware Cream Pitcher, Greenish Orange Speckled Glaze, 4½" H. $75.00
Redware Jar, Reddish Brown Glaze W/Yellow Slip, 1 Handle Broken $45.00
Redware Jar, W/Pierced Holes $20.00

(A-PA. '76) *Pennypacker Auction Centre*
Redware Slip Cup (White Clay "Slip" Was Poured From This Type Cup To Decorate Pie Plates, Etc., Quills Were Inserted To Produce A Fine Line) $220.00

(A-VA. '77)
Laws

Stoneware Crock, Molded Lip, Applied Handles, Cobalt Blue Decor. W/Amer. Eagle & Inscription, 12-Gal., 22" H...........$325.00

(A-PA. '76)   *Pennypacker Auction Centre*
REDWARE (*Left to Right*)
Fish Mold, Circular, Berks County $180.00
Food Molds, Pr., Fish Shape, Berks Co. .....
.....................................$320.00

(A-PA. '76)   *Pennypacker Auction Centre*
Redware Roof Tile, 3 Applied Purple Martins, Attrib. To Ohio Valley Area, Early 20th C., ...
.....................................$675.00

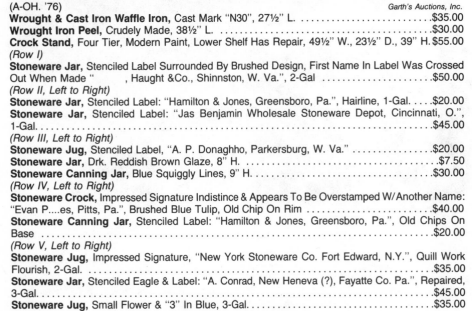

(A-OH. '76)   *Garth's Auctions, Inc.*
Wrought & Cast Iron Waffle Iron, Cast Mark "N30", 27½" L. $35.00
Wrought Iron Peel, Crudely Made, 38½" L. $30.00
Crock Stand, Four Tier, Modern Paint, Lower Shelf Has Repair, 49½" W., 23½" D., 39" H. $55.00
(*Row I*)
Stoneware Jar, Stenciled Label Surrounded By Brushed Design, First Name In Label Was Crossed Out When Made "   , Haught &Co., Shinnston, W. Va.", 2-Gal $50.00
(*Row II, Left to Right*)
Stoneware Jar, Stenciled Label: "Hamilton & Jones, Greensboro, Pa.", Hairline, 1-Gal. $20.00
Stoneware Jar, Stenciled Label: "Jas Benjamin Wholesale Stoneware Depot, Cincinnati, O.", 1-Gal. $45.00
(*Row III, Left to Right*)
Stoneware Jug, Stenciled Label, "A. P. Donaghho, Parkersburg, W. Va." $20.00
Stoneware Jar, Drk. Reddish Brown Glaze, 8" H. $7.50
Stoneware Canning Jar, Blue Squiggly Lines, 9" H. $30.00
(*Row IV, Left to Right*)
Stoneware Crock, Impressed Signature Indistince & Appears To Be Overstamped W/Another Name: "Evan P....es, Pitts, Pa.", Brushed Blue Tulip, Old Chip On Rim $40.00
Stoneware Canning Jar, Stenciled Label: "Hamilton & Jones, Greensboro, Pa.", Old Chips On Base $20.00
(*Row V, Left to Right*)
Stoneware Jug, Impressed Signature, "New York Stoneware Co. Fort Edward, N.Y.", Quill Work Flourish, 2-Gal. $35.00
Stoneware Jar, Stenciled Eagle & Label: "A. Conrad, New Heneva (?), Fayatte Co. Pa.", Repaired, 3-Gal. $45.00
Stoneware Jug, Small Flower & "3" In Blue, 3-Gal. $35.00

(A-PA. '75)   *Pennypacker Auction Centre*
Redware Bowl, Yellow & Green Slip Decor. On Red Ground, Bethlehem Moravian, 12" Diam.
.....................................$130.00

(A-PA. '75)
Pennypacker Auction Centre

STONEWARE
(Left to Right)
Crock, 13" H., Blue Decor., Stamped "Sam'l Irvine, Newville, Pa." $175.00
Crock, 13¼" H., Blue Decor. $45.00

(D-OH. '76)
Stoneware Bean Pot, Boston Baked Beans Embossed On One Side, Opp. Side, Dutch Girl & Boy, Cobalt Blue On Grey Ground ..$125.00

(A-PA. '75)
Pennypacker Auction Centre
Beer Pitcher, Incised Decor. W/Cobalt Blue, Attrib. To Carl Wingender, Haddonfield, N.J., ...$80.00
Stoneware Butter Crock, Blue, Orig. Lid, 1½ Gal. $75.00

(A-PA. '76)
STONEWARE
(Left to Right)
Pennypacker Auction Centre
Jug, Blue Decor., Signed "G. W. Fulper Bros., Flemington, N.J., 1-Gal. $55.00
Crock, Bird Decor., "Whites, Utica", 2-Gal. $150.00
Crock, Blue Tulip Decor., Ear Handles, 3-Gal. $57.50
Crock, Blue Flower Decor., "M. Woodruff, Cortland", 3-Gal. $90.00

(A-PA. '75)
Pennypacker Auction Centre
Stoneware Crock, Blue Decor., Marked "Eagle Pottery, James Hamilton & Co., Greensboro, Pa.", 21" H., 12-Gal. $350.00

(A-PA. '76)
STONEWARE *(Left to Right)*
Pennypacker Auction Centre
Crock, Bird On Stump Decor., Evan B. Jones, 5 Gal. $250.00
Cooler, Brushed Decor., 5-Gal. $250.00
Crock, Blue Parrot Decor., Signed "E. L. Norton Co., Worcester, Mass.", 4-Gal. $175.00

STONEWARE
(Left to Right)
Crock, Bird Decor., 1½-Gal. $90.00
Crock, Bird Decor., 2-Gal. $80.00
Crock, Blue Decor., Form Of Leaf, "Whites, Utica", 2-Gal. $40.00
Jug, Cobalt Decor., "Whites, Utica", 2-Gal. $45.00
Jug, Blue Decor., Signed "Courtland", 2-Gal. $75.00

STONEWARE
(Left to Right)
Jug, Blue Tulip Decor., Marked Camden & Wilcox, Harrisburg, 1½ Gal. $55.00
Jug, Blue Leaf & Floral Decor., By T. F. Connoley, New Brunswick, N.J., 2-Gal $60.00
Jug, Blue Floral Decor., Marked F. B. Norton & Co., Worcester, Mass., 1½ Gal. $60.00

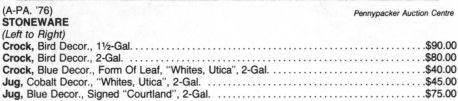

STONEWARE
(Row I, Left to Right)
Butter Crock, Embossed Deer Hunting Scene Highlighted W/Blue, Repaired Lid, 9½" Diam. $35.00
Butter Crock, Embossed Deer Hunting Scene Highlighted W/Blue, Minor Flake On Lip, 7¼" Diam.
....$40.00
Butter Crock, Embossed Deer Hunting Scene Highlighted W/Blue, 6" Diam. $45.00
(Row II, Left to Right)
Bowl, Embossed Peacocks, 8¼" Diam. $10.00
Pitcher, Embossed Swan, 8" H. $22.50
Bowl, Embossed Flowers, 10" Diam. $12.50

Stoneware Butter Tub W/Embossed Surface Decor. & Cobalt Leaves $85.00

Crock, Blue Decor., J. Norton & Co., Bennington, Vt. $310.00

(Row I, Left to Right)
Redware Pottery Jar, J. E., Late 18th C., Mottled Glaze Of Browns & Greens, Age Cracks & Minor Nicks In Rim, 5¼" H. $80.00
Redware Bean Pot, N.E., Late 18th-Early 19th C., Greenish-Brown Glaze W/Drk. Flecks, Illegible Impressed Signature Inside Near Upper Rim, 5¼" Diam., 4¾" H. $60.00
Redware Pottery Jar, Ma., Greenish-Gray & Reddish-Brown Mottling & Fish-Eye Glaze, 3⅞" Diam., 4" H. $110.00
(Row II, Left to Right)
Scant Pint Jug, Unusual Pinkish-Brown Glaze W/Black Mottling Overall & Applied Strap Handle $350.00
Redware Jar, N.E., Heavy Green Skin-Like Glaze, 6¾" H. $200.00
Turk's Head Redware Mold, Possibly Ma., Early 19th C., Mottled Green & Brown Glaze, 7½" Diam. $60.00

(Left to Right)
Pottery Jug, Grotesque Face, Green Glaze, 1 Handle, Signed On Base, 9¼" H. $60.00
Pottery Jug, Grotesque Face, Drk. Brown Glaze, 2 Handles & 2 Faces, Signed On Base, 9" H. $80.00

(A-PA. '75)
STONEWARE

Pennypacker Auction Centre

(Left to Right)
Crock, Blue Decor., "#6 A. P. Donaghho, Fredericktown, Washington County, Pa." 17" . .$220.00
Jug, Blue Decor., "Harrisburg" $35.00
Crock, Blue Decor., "Philip Eller, East Berlingham, Pallery, Pa." $200.00

(A-PA. '75) *Pennypacker Auction Centre*

(Left to Right)
Stoneware Pitcher, Blue Decor., 10½" ......
....$125.00
Butter Crock, Blue Decor., 5½" H., 8½" W. . .
....$100.00
Jug, Blue Decor., Marked "Witt, Farrar & Co., Geddes, N.Y.", 11" $125.00

(D-IA. '76)
Stoneware 5 Gal. Churn, Cobalt Decor., 16½" H. W/Orig. Cover $85.00

(A-MA. '76) *Richard A. Bourne Co. Inc.*
(Row I, Left to Right)
Mettlach Half-Liter Stein No. 1453 . .$225.00
Mettlach One-Liter Stein No. 812 . . .$350.00
(Row II, Left to Right)
Mettlach Stein No. 1169, Large Size, Bottom Portion Of Handle Missing $150.00
Mettlach Stein No. 3177, Large Size .$400.00

(D-IA. '76)
Stein, Military, German, Lithophane, 10½" H.
...................................$125.00

(A-PA. '75) *Pennypacker Auction Centre* ➔

GERMAN STEINS
(Left to Right)
Stein W/Lithophane Base, 9¼" H.....$55.00
Stein W/Lithophane Base, 8" H. $55.00
Stein W/Lithophane Base, 10½" Portrait .....
...................................$35.00

(A-PA. '75) *Pennypacker Auction Centre*

GERMAN STEINS EACH WITH LITHOPHANE BASE
(Left to Right)
9½" $37.50
10½" $47.50
7½" $35.00

The earliest clocks were brought to America by the first settlers. Although craftsmen were working here as early as the seventeenth century, clocks did not become common in homes until after 1800. Their manufacture in quantity began in 1840, when Chauncey Jerome, a Waterbury clockmaker began replacing wooden movements with rugged interchangeable brass-geared works which eventually led to mass production. Today, all types of clocks — tall, wall and shelf — are avidly collected. And the demand is so great that great numbers of old clocks have been imported from Europe in recent years.

Recommended reading: THE AMERICAN CLOCK by William H. Distin and Robert Bishop (E.P. Dutton & Company, Inc.). This new release includes a comprehensive pictorial survey of American clocks from 1723-1900, and includes a listing of 6153 clockmakers.

(A-PA. '75)   *Pennypacker Auction Centre*

Banjo Clock, Mahogany Case, E. Howard & Co. Boston $400.00

(A-PA. '75)   *Pennypacker Auction Centre*

Willard Patent Banjo Clock, Reversed Painting Of Ships At Sea & Shield $1100.00

(D-MO. '76)

Mantel Clock "The Boston", 8 Day, Half Hour Strike $125.00

(A-PA. '75)   *Pennypacker Auction Centre*

Chippendale Case Grandfather's Clock, Brass Moon Dial $1400.00

(A-PA. '75)   *Pennypacker Auction Centre*

Carved Wooden Clock, 8-Day Works, 20" Spread Eagle Top, 16" Eagle on Side, 29" H. $775.00

(A-MA. '75)   *Richard A. Bourne Co. Inc.*

Tall Clock, Amer., Late 18th Or Early 19th C., Brass Works W/Iron Face, Wrought Iron Hands, Calendar Dial & Second Hand, Fret Needs Repair, Sm. Quarter Turning Missing From Top Of Left Hand Column, 90½" H. $2,100.00

(A-PA. '75)   *Pennypacker Auction Centre*

Victorian Ansonia Hanging Wall Clock, Cherry Case, Jenny Lind Medallion At Top, 51" T. $350.00

(A-PA. '75)   *Pennypacker Auction Centre*

Ansonia Hanging Wall Clock, Oak, 38" T. $220.00

(A-MA. '75)   *Richard A. Bourne Co. Inc.*

Pillar & Scroll Clock, Chauncey Ives, Bristol, Conn., Early 19th C., Complete & Running, Replaced Brass Finials, 31" H. $1000.00

(D-CO. '76)

Shelf Clock, Seth Thomas $325.00

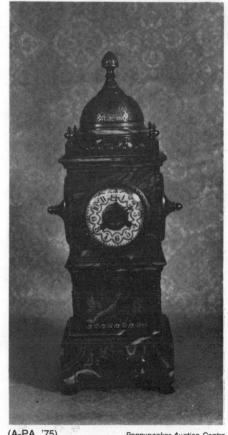

(A-PA. '75)   *Pennypacker Auction Centre*

Calendar Shelf Clock, Wagon Spring $750.00

(A-MA. '76)   *Richard A. Bourne Co. Inc.*

Banjo Clock, W/Eglomise Throat Glass, Lower Panel Depicts American & British Ships Engaged In Battle. Dial Reads "Warranted By P. Whiting, Concord," Gilt & Natural Wood Case, 42" H. $1400.00

(A-PA. '75)   *Pennypacker Auction Centre*

Mantle Clock, Brown Marble W/Brass, Porcelain Dial, J.E. Caldwell, Phila., Pa., 22" H. $525.00

(A-MA. '76)   Richard A. Bourne Co. Inc.
(Row I, Left to Right)
Rotary Pendulum Clock, Briggs, Circular
Wooden Base W/Glass Dome, 8" H. .$250.00
Wag-On-The-Wall Clock, Continental 19th C.,
Brass Works & Painted Wooden Dial, Iron
Weights & Pendulum, Sm. Chips On Wooden
Dial, Height Of Dial - 7½" $200.00
China Cased Shelf Clock, French Brass Works,
9⅞" H. $125.00
Shelf Clock, German, 19th C., Marked "Vinzenz
Radermacher In Wein" On Dial, Fruitwood &
Other Woods, Applied Marble Columns & Urn
At Top, Bronze Ormolu Mounts, 18½" H. .....
.................................$150.00
Shelf Clock, Marked "Regulator Going One
Year/Without Winding" On Porcelain Dial,
Polished Slate Face W/Glass Door In Back,
Glass Plate In Top, Few Sm. Chips On Case,
Back Door Glass Cracked In Two Places,
14¼" H. $250.00
(Row II, Left to Right)
Empire Ogee Shelf Clock, Waterbury Clock
Co., 8 Day & 30 Hr. Brass Movement, Rosewood
& Mahogany Veneered Case, Some Veneer Off
& Missing, 18¾" H. $100.00
Victorian Mantle Clock, Seth Thomas, Wooden
Gallery Around Top, 2 Finials Missing, 19" H.
.................................$80.00
Victorian Steeple Clock, Ansonia Brass &
Copper Works, 8 Day & 30 Hr. Brass Movement,
Mahogany & Rosewood Veneered Case,
19¾" H. $130.00
Regulator Wall Clock, Wm. L. Gilbert Clock
Co., Glass Face Reverse Painted, Walnut Case
W/Minor Carving On Bottom, Orig. Label On
Brass, 37¾" H. $275.00

(A-PA. '75)   Pennypacker Auction Centre
Victorian Hanging Wall Clock, Walnut Case,
Jenny Lind Head Top $300.00

(Left)
(D-OK. '76)
Seth Thomas, W/Reverse Painting Of Indian
Chief, 25" H. $300.00
(Right)
(D-MO. '76)
Seth Thomas Pillar Clock, W/Reverse Paint-
ing $150.00

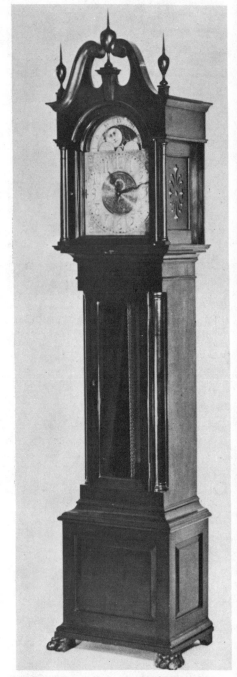

(A-MA. '76)   Richard A. Bourne Co. Inc.
Mahogany Cased Tall Clock, Engraved Brass
Dial, Moon Phase Calendar Dial, Second Hand
& May Be Adjusted For Silent Or Strike Opera-
tion, Label Of "E. P. Sundberg & Co., Fargo,
North Dakota", 101" H. $875.00

(Left)
(D-CT. '76)
Ingraham Shelf Clock, ...$350.00
(Right)
(D-S.C. '76)
New Haven Banjo Clock, W/Reverse Painting
And Eagle Finial $290.00

(D-CO. '76)
Shelf Clock, Maker Unknown, Oak Case .....
..............................$275.00

(D-CT. '76)
Mantel Clock, E. Ingraham, Briston, Conn. ....
..............................$350.00

(Left)

(A-VA. '77)   *Laws*

English Japanned Tall Case Clock, 18th C., Hood W/Double Finialed Roof Top, Molded Lip, Arched Door & Pillared Sides, Lge. Arched Door & Ogee Molded Base, Case W/Hand Painted Garden Scenes & Geometric Devices Overall, Brass Works & Face Marked Wm.Gill, Maidstone W/Overall Ormolu Decor. & Date Slide At Bottom, Ca. 1800, 9" D., 18" W., 86" H.
................................$3,250.00

(Right)

(A-VA. '77)   *Laws*

Cherry Tall Case Clock, Molded Scrolled Pediment Top & Arched Framed Door Flanked By 2 Bulbous Turned Columns, Slender Body W/Long Cabinet Door Is Connected To Molded Base W/Double Inset Columned Corners Shaped Skirt, Turned Feet $800.00

(Left)

(A-VA. '77)   *Laws*

"Rittenhouse" Tall Cased Clock, Queen Anne Case W/Plateau Pediment Top W/3 Plinths, Lower Molded Arch Above The Conforming Door Which Is Flanked By Twin Turned Columns, 8-Day Movement Has Silvered Chapter Ring & Lunette Stating "David Rittenhouse, 1763, Norriton", All Framed By Cast Spandrels & Calendar Slide At Lower Section, Running Cond. $7,500.00

(Right)

(A-VA. '76)   *Laws*

Chippendale Flat Top Tall Case Clock, English, Mahogany, Engraved Brass Dial W/ Calendar, Signed "Allan Fontos", Ca. 1800, 10" D., 19" W., 82" H.............$1,500.00

(Left)

(A-VA. '76)   *Laws*

English Tall Case Clock, Molded Top, Inlaid Banding & Arched Door Hood, Finely Shaped Skirt, Bracket Feet, Hand Painted Dial W/Floral Decor., Signed John T. Finmore, London / .....
...............................$1,000.00

(Right)

(A-VA. '77)   *Laws*

Waltham Tall Case Clock, Ogee Molded Arch Pediment, Moon Dial W/Elab. Ormolu Work, Whittington, St. Michaels & Westminster Chimes, Marked A. Stowell & Co., 16" D., 24" W., 92" H. $2,000.00

(D-MI. '76)
Sessions Mantle Clock, Half Hour Strike ....
................................$150.00

(A-VA. '77)   *Laws*
(Row I, Left to Right)
Empire Shelf Clock, Stenciled Center Crest, Twin Stenciled Column Sides & Resting On Carved Leaf & Claw Feet, Reverse Painting On Glass Of Town Scene, Signed Riley Whiting, Winchester, Conn., Retains Orig. Paper Label, Wooden Works, Ca, 1835, 17½" W., 27" H.
................................$250.00
Triple Decker Shelf Clock, Walnut Case W/ Crown Above Arched Inset Hand Decorated Panel, Flanked By Two Three-Quarter Turned Corinthian Columns, Claw Feet, Orig. Paper Label Stating "8 Day Repeating Brass Clock Manufactured & Sold By C. Jerome & Co., Richmond, Va.", Running Cond., Ca. 1835-37, 6" D., 18" W., 40" H. $700.00

(Row II)
Chauncey Jerome Shelf Clock, Ogee Cased W/Double Paneled Door, Glass Top & Reverse Painted Bottom Panel, Retains Partial Paper Label, "Patented Brass Clocks, Chauncey Jerome, New Haven, Conn.", Ca. 1850, 15" W., 26" H............................$130.00

60 DECOYS

Of all the different types of folk art, few have as undisputed an American heritage as the decoy. It was one of man's earliest and most essential tools developed as a result of his attempt to survive. Although most serious collectors of decoys prefer the earlier hand-carved varieties, there is a tremendous interest in the machine made examples as well as the handsomely carved and decorated contemporary decoys being produced today.

(A-MA. '76)   Richard A. Bourne Co. Inc.

(Row I, Left to Right)

Buffleheads, Drake & Hen, Identified & Signed By L.T. Ward W/Date 1959 on Bottom; 1 Marked "Hollow White Pine", Carved & Raised Primary Feathers, Content Head Position ... $1500.00

Bufflehead Drake, Dated 1966, Fitted W/Metal L.T. Ward Label, Carved Primary Feathers, Graining On Head & Body, Content Head Turned Left, Fancy Grade $1200.00

(Row II)

Hooded Mergansers, By L.T. Ward, Identified on Bottom W/"Lophodytes Cucullatus", Signed, Dated 1964, Semi-Content Heads, Raised & Carved Primary Feathers $1100.00

(Row III, Left to Right)

Surf Scoter, By Ward Bros., Marked On Bottom "My Compliments/Steve Ward"; Head Turned Right $750.00

Black Duck, By L.T. Ward Brothers, Identified, Signed & Dated 1958, Marked "Best Grade" on Bottom; Balsa, Head Turned Left, Raised & Crossed Wing Tips W/Carved Covert Feathers ····················· $850.00

(Row IV)

Mallards, Hen & Drake, Hen Signed, Premier Grade, Dated 1949 On Bottom; Drake Is Signed, Dated 1962, Delux Grade; Both W/Turned Heads, Raised Wings & Carved Primary Feathers Hen W/Carved Covert Feathers As Well ......
.... $1700.00

(A-PA. '76)   Pennypacker Auction Centre

Red Head Duck Decoys, Pr., Susquehanna, Red, Yellow & Green Paint, Signed "Glieberknech, Hellam, Pa.", ...$300.00

(D-MO. '76)

Miniature Mallard Decoys, Papier Mache, Mkd. "Carry-Lite, Milwaukee, Wis." Pair $35.00

(A-MA. '76)   Richard A. Bourne Co. Inc.

(Row I, Left to Right)

Green-Winged Teal, Drake & Hen, Carved Primary Feathers, Signed On Bottom By L.T. Ward, Dated 1962 .... $1200.00

(Row II)

Pintails, Drake & Hen, Both W/Carved Covert & Primary Feathers, Signed L.T. Ward, Dated 1960 .... $1700.00

(Row III.)

Old Squaw Drake, Preening, Carved Covert & Primary Feathers. Identified on Bottom W/ "Clangula Hyemalis", Signed L.T. Ward, Dated 1964 ....(A-MA. '76) $3000.00

Mallard Drake, Preening, Carved Covert Feathers, Signed L.T. Ward, Dated 1959 .....
.... $1000.00

(Row IV)

Canada Goose, Carved Primary Feathers, By L.T. Ward/1967, Grained Head $1500.00

(A-MA. '76)   Richard A. Bourne Co. Inc.

Pair Of Buffleheads. Drake And Hen, Wooden Bodies, Both In Content Position With Slightly Turned Heads, Both With The Brand "Cigar".
...................................$190.00

(A-MA. '76)   Richard A. Bourne Co. Inc.

DECOYS

(Row I, Left to Right)

Black-Bellied Plover, Walnut Base, Repainted.
....$45.00

Canada Goose, Hollow Carved, Stripped & Finished In Natural Wood. $90.00

Black-Bellied Plover, Brand Of E. C. Cole, Hit W/Shot. $80.00

(Row II, Left to Right)

Canvasback Drake, Mason, Premier Grade, Hit W/Shot. $50.00

Canvasback Drake, Mason, Standard Grade.
....$40.00

Canvasback Hen, Mason, Challenge Grade.
....$45.00

(Row III, Left to Right)

Mallard Drake, Dodge Decoy Factory, Repainted $35.00

Mallard Drake, Dodge Decoy Factory, Worn Paint, Retouched $15.00

Scaup Drake, Mason, Minor Age Split In Body Block, Worn $20.00

(Row IV)

Mallard Drake & Hen, Pr. Pratt Decoy Factory, Paint Worn, Age Splits In Body Blocks. .$35.00

(A-MA. '76)   Richard A. Bourne Co. Inc.

Pair of Scaup. Drake And Hen, By Will Heverin, Each With Carved Initials Under Tail, "LP". Slightly Weathered $200.00

(A-MA. '76)   Richard A. Bourne Co. Inc.

(Row I)

Canvasbacks, Drake & Hen, Turned Heads & Keels, Signed & Dated, Drake 1938, Hen 1940; Neck Of Hen Broken & Reglued, Repainted, By L.T. Ward Bros. $600.00

(Row II)

Pintails, Drake & Hen, Turned Heads, Ca. 1926, Signed & Identified On Bottom, Marked "Restored & Repainted 1961, Steve Ward, L.T. Ward Bro." $700.00

(Row III)

Canada Goose, Cedar, Ca. 1938, Signed On Bottom & Under Tail, Ward Bros., Repainted, Neck W/Repaired Break & Crack Visible .....
.... $500.00

(Row IV)

Balsa Canada Goose, By Steve Ward, Crisfield, Maryland, 1947, Painted By Lem Ward, Signed On Bottom, Cracking Around Neck Joint $600.00

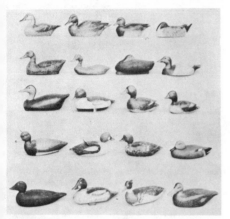

(A-MA. '75)   Richard A. Bourne Co., Inc.

DECOYS
(Row I, Left to Right)
Pintail Hen, By Ray Baliel, Rio Vista, Calif., Ca. 1935, Balsa Body, Repainted, Minor Wear To Paint $75.00
Mallard Hen, By Walter Poelzer, Milwaukee, Wis., Deep Body, Carved Wing Details, Turned Head $300.00
Widgeon Hen, By Walter Poelzer, Deep Body, Carved Wing Details, Turned Head, Paint Weathered & Worn, Chip Or Mar On Tail $300.00
Sleeping Pintail, California, Cork Body, Tip Of Tail Broken Off, Possibly Retouched Paint $25.00

(Row II, Left to Right)
Black Duck, Deeply Carved Wing & Tail Feathers Detail, Rough Finish, Repainted ..$50.00
Pintail Hen, From Petosky, Mich., Primitive Style, Carved Head, Worn Orig. Paint, Orig. Glass Eyes, Repaired Break At Neck .$150.00
Sleeping Black Duck, From Sag Harbor, Long Island, Cork Body, "W. F. Halsey" Brand Either Side Of Keel, Possibly Repainted $40.00
Canvasback Hen, By Ken Harris, Harris Brand On Bottom & Name Of Weldon Daly, W/Dates 1925-1969, Orig. Paint, Worn On Top Of Head & End Of Tail $35.00

(Row III, Left to Right)
Black Duck, By Ken Harris, Ca. 1936, Harris Brand On Bottom, Unused Cond. $35.00
Goldeneye Hen, By Ken Harris, Balsa Body, Harris Brand On Bottom, Marred On Right Side, Hit By Shot, Orig. Paint Weathered ...$25.00
Canadian Scaup Hen, Ca. 1925, Deep Carved Wing & Tail Feather Detail, Head Turned Slightly To Right, Bill Broken & Repaired, Orig. Paint.. ....$50.00
Canadian Goldeneye Hen, Ca. 1925, Deep Carved Wing & Feather Detail, Chip In Tail & Tip Of Right Wing, Orig. Paint $40.00

(Row IV, Left to Right)
Canadian Redhead Drake, By Robert Paquette, Wing & Feather Carving, Head Turned Slightly To Left, Hit By Shot On Left Side $110.00
Canadian Goldeneye Drake & Hen, Pr., By Robert Paquette, Wing & Feather Carving, Hen W/Head Turned Head Slightly To Right, Used Cond., Orig. Paint Worn On Hen $275.00
Gadwall Hen, Cork Body, Head Tucked Down In Sleepy Attitude, Traces Of Brand Visible Near Anchor Ring, Orig. Cond. $400.00

(Row V, Left to Right)
New England Decoy, Possibly A Goldeneye, Repainted Black, Carved Wing & Tail Feathers, Paint Weathered, Chip In Back, Age Split In Body $40.00

(A-MA. '76)   Richard A. Bourne Co., Inc.

DECOYS
(Row I)
Early Canvasback Hen, Strong Similarity To Work Of Dick Howlett, Well Preserved, Old Paint Weathered $80.00
Canvasback Drake, By Severn E. Hall (North East Maryland), Signed & Dated 1946, Cork Body, Shows Little Use $70.00
(Row II)
Pair Of Canvasbacks, Drake & Hen, By Capt. John Glenn, Hen Bears Brand "AWW" & Pencil Identification W/Date 1949, Old Paint Weathered, Paint On Hen More Worn Than That On Drake, Hen Has Age Split In Body $90.00
(Row III)
Canvasback Drake, By Capt. Ben Dye, Note On Bottom Indicates Decoy Is From Perry K. Barnes' Rig Of Charlestown, Maryland, Old Weathered Paint W/Some Marring In Light Colored Areas $325.00
Scaup Drake, By George Washington ("Wash") Barnes, Old Paint W/Comb Graining On Back, Neck Has Clean Break $125.00

Goldeneye Drake, New England, Hollow-Carved, Head Turned To Left, Orig. Paint, Worn, Hit By Shot $60.00
Red-Breasted Merganser Drake, Head Turned Left, Hollow-Carved, Note On Bottom Indicates It Was Used On Hope Bay, Rhode Island, Horsehair Comb, Old Paint $225.00
Black Duck, By Bob Kerr, Signed & Dated 1958 On Bottom, Carved Wing, Feather & Tail Details $100.00

(A-MA. '76)   Richard A. Bourne Co., Inc.

IMPORTANT WORKING DECOYS

(Row II)
Pair Of Canvasbacks, By Mason's Decoy Factory, Premier Grade, Hen Is Branded "Bartholomay", Orig. Paint Remains Bold, Small Shot Groove In Head Of Drake, Paint On Hen Is Less Well Preserved And Flaking, Drake's Neck Has Been Repaired $600.00
(Row III)
Scaup Drake, By H. Keyes Chadwick (Oak Bluffs, Martha's Vineyard, Mass. 1868-1959), Branded W/The Name "Foote", Good Orig. Paint, Slightly Weathered, Age Split In Bottom, Rare $325.00
Black Duck, By A. Elmer Crowell (East Harwich, Mass., 1862-1951), Bears Oval Decoy Brand, Orig. Paint Worn To A Fine Patina $375.00
(Row IV)
Rare Brant, Cobb Island, Virginia, Slightly Down-Turned Head, Chip On Upper Base Of Bill, Orig. Paint Weathered $900.00
Hollow-Carved Brant, By Nathan Roland ("Rowley") Horner (Manahawkin, New Jersey), Good Condition, Probably Repainted ..$240.00

(A-MA. '76)   Richard A. Bourne Co., Inc.

DECOYS
(Row I)
Pair Of Canvasbacks, Drake & Hen, By Carroll "Wally" Algard (Charlestown, Maryland), Orig. Paint Showing Wear On Sides, Heads & Breasts $150.00
(Row II)
Redhead Drake, From Charlestown, Maryland Area, Orig. Paint Weathered $275.00
Canvasback Hen, By Capt. Ben Dye, Ca. 1880, Possible Orig. Paint Worn To A Fine Patina, Bears Mackdy Stamp $375.00
(Row III)
Pair Of Redheads, Drake & Hen, By Henry Lockard, Orig. Paint, Both Have Been Hit On Right Side By Shot, Well Preserved ..$550.00
(Row IV)
Canvasback Drake, By Leonard Pryor, Old Paint, Possibly Orig. W/Some Retouching, Flaking On Both Sides To Bare Wood $80.00
Canvasback Hen, Very Old, Noted On Base It Came From The Rig Of Ralph Murphy's Grandfather Out Of Charlestown, Maryland, Orig. Paint Weathered $125.00

(A-MA. '75)
SHORE BIRD DECOYS
(Row I, Left to Right)
East Coast Yellowlegs, Early, Bill Possibly Old Replacement, Orig. Paint Worn To Natural Wood, Sm. Chip In End Of Tail $60.00
Virginia Robin Snipe, Possibly From Cobb Island, Lightly Hit By Shot In Right Breast & Left Side, Old Paint Weathered $130.00
Cape Cod Yellowlegs, Early, Metal Rod For Bill, Bill Possibly Replacement, Orig. Paint Slightly Worn $75.00
Massachusetts Curlew, 19th C., Part Of Tail Chipped Away, Lightly Hit By Shot On Left Side, Orig. Paint & Bill $200.00
(Row II, Left to Right)
Shore Bird, Possibly Plover, Almost Shadow Decoy, Metal Bill Possibly Replacement . . . . . .
. . . .$50.00
Shore Bird, Possibly Plover, Almost Shadow Decoy, Metal Bill Possibly Replacement . . . . . .
. . . .$90.00
East Coast Plover, Early, Branded On Bottom "AHGM", Sm. Groove Right Side Of Head, Orig. Nail Bill, Orig. Paint Weathered & Worn . . . . . .
. . . .$45.00
Cape Cod Yellowlegs, Early 19th C., Sm. Shot Holes On Right Side, Copper Wire Bill Possibly Replacement $110.00
(Row III, Left to Right)
Cape Cod Yellowlegs, Early, Orig. Paint, Copper Wire Bill A Replacement $60.00
Feeding Ruddy Turnstone, Early, Possibly From New Jersey, Old Paint $70.00
Black-Bellied Plover, Early, Nail For Bill, Beady Tack Eyes, Orig. Cond. $80.00
(Row IV, Left to Right)
Cape Cod Yellowlegs, Early, 19th C., Orig. Paint, WoodenBill $100.00
Cape Cod Yellowlegs, Early, 19th C., Copper Wire Bill Possibly A Replacement, Hit Both Sides By Shot, Left Side W/Indentations, Orig. Paint $100.00
Massachusetts Feeding Yellowlegs, Bill Reglued, Split In Head, Orig. Paint . . .$125.00
East Coast Black-Bellied Plover, Possibly Orig. Paint $130.00
(Row V, Left to Right)
East Coast Yellowlegs, Copper Wire Bill, 2 Sm. Holes On Right Side, Bill Possibly Replacement & Loose, Orig. Paint $80.00
Shore Bird, Possibly Dowitcher, Carved Wing Details, Lt. Color W/Touches Of Gray Overall & Black-Tipped Tail $80.00
Plover, Early, Traces Black Breast Paint Visible $100.00
Black-Bellied Plover, Cape Cod, Carved Initials Under Tail, "JPN" $90.00

(A-MA. '75)
METAL FOLDING SHORE BIRDS
(Row I, Left to Right)
Tin Black-Bellied Plover, 1874 Pat. Date, Orig. Paint $40.00
Tin Golden Plover, 1874 Pat. Date, Worn & Slightly Dented On Sides, Orig. Paint . .$40.00
Tin Plover, 1874 Pat. Date, Minor Scratches, Orig. Paint $65.00
(Row II, Left to Right)
Tin Golden Plover, Almost Unused, Orig. Paint $50.00
Tin Ruddy Turnstone, 1874 Pat. Date, Orig. Paint Flaking $70.00
Tin Yellowlegs, Orig. Paint, Some Flaking, Rust $25.00
(Row III, Left to Right)
Tin Yellowlegs Or Dowitcher, Almost Unused. $40.00
Tin Common Snipe, Orig. Paint, Worn On Sides Of Wings $50.00
Tin Golden Plover, Hit By 2 Shot, Orig. Paint.
. . . .$15.00
(Row IV, Left to Right)
Tin Plover, Oct. 1874 Pat. Date, Orig. Paint. Some Rusting & Flaking $30.00
Tin Yellowlegs, Unused Cond. $60.00
Tin Yellowlegs, Unused Cond. $50.00
(Row V, Left to Right)
Tin Yellowlegs Shadow Decoy, Flat W/Fold-Up Wings, Orig. Paint, Minor Flaking Of Paint & Some Rust $35.00
Tin Yellowlegs, Set Of 12, Oct. 27, 1874 Pat. Date On Inside, Orig. Box W/8 Orig. Stick-Ups, Orig. Cond. $350.00

(A-MA. '76)
OLD CHESAPEAKE GUNNING DECOYS
(Row I)
Early Canvasback Drake, By Capt. Ben ("Daddy") Holly, Paint Not Orig., Weathered . .
. . . .$175.00
Canvasback Drake, By Robert F. McGraw, High Neck, Paint Weathered, Probably Orig. . . . .
. . . .$120.00
(Row II)
Canvasback Drake, By Will Heverin, Old Paint Probably Not Orig., Weathered $60.00
Redhead Drake, By Will Heverin, Repainted, Two Slight Mars In Head $90.00
(Row III)
Oversized Canvasback Drake, By Madison R. Mitchell, Clean Break In Neck Reglued, Paint Orig. & Weathered, A Little Retouching . . . .
. . . .$75.00
Early Canvasback Hen, By Robert F. McGaw, High Neck, Paint Orig. & Weathered, Age Split In Body $80.00
(Row IV)
Rare Early Canvasback Drake, By Robert F. McGaw, Branded "Wilkins" On Bottom, Age Split In Bottom Runs Length Of Bird, Old Paint & Weathered $65.00
Early Canvasback Drake, By Samuel T. Barnes, High Neck, Neck Has Been Crudely Repaired At Base, Paint Weathered & Flaking . . .$70.00

(A-MA. '76)
DECORATIVE DECOYS BY NORRIS E. PRATT
(Row I)
Pair Of Large Scaup, Carved Wing Tips, Made In 1969 & Painted By Lem Ward In 1969, Both W/Keels, Unused $125.00
(Row II)
Pair Of Balsa Canvasbacks, Made In 1970 & Painted By Lem Ward In 1970, Raised Carved Wings, Style Of Ward Decoys Of 1920's & 1930's Unused $275.00
(Row III)
Pair Of Canvasbacks, Drake & Hen, Made In 1961 & Painted By Lem Ward, Both W/Turned Heads, unused$240.00
(Row IV)
Pair Of Wood Ducks, Drake & Hen, Made In 1954, Painted By Lem Ward In 1959, Both W/ Slightly Turned Heads & Raised Wing Tips, Unused $500.00

Richard A. Bourne, Co., Inc.

ILLINOIS RIVER & OTHER MIDWESTERN DECOYS

(A-MA. '75)   Richard A. Bourne Co., Inc.

(Row I, Left to Right)

Mallard Drake, By G. Bert Graves, Peoria, Ill. (18??-1944), W/Signature "B. Graves Decoy Co. Peoria, Ill.", Split On Neck Repaired $400.00

Canvasback Drake, By G. Bert Graves, Branded W/Name "Athan", Weight Removed, Partially Repainted $175.00

Hollow-Carved Mallard Drake, By Hector Whittington, Oglesby, Ill., Head Turned To Right, Unused Cond. $260.00

Hollow-Carved Mallard Hen, By Hector Whittington, Unused Cond. $125.00

(Row II, Left to Right)

Scaup Hen, Removable Head Which Is Stored In Base Of Body Block When Not In Use, Original Paint $150.00

Pintail Drake, Hollow-Carved, Repainted By Edna Perdew, Sm. Chips In Paint . . . $225.00

Mallard, Hollow-Carved, By Perry Wilcoxsen, Brand "HLR" On Bottom, Bears Date Reference "8-12-18", Orig. Paint Worn $160.00

Swimming Black Duck, Hollow, Painted Initials "GH" On Bottom, Orig. paint $125.00

(Row III, Left to Right)

Scaup Drake, By Robert A. Elliston, Bureau, Ill. (1849-1915), Orig. Signed Elliston, Weight On Bottom, Chip On Right Underside Of Tail, Orig. Paint $500.00

Squaw Drake, By Hector Whittington, Dated Jan. 4, 1973, Signed, Unused $90.00

Squaw Hen, By Hector Whittington, Dated Jan. 4, 1973, Signed, Unused $85.00

Mallard Drake, "JRW Maker", Ca. 1895-1905, Orig. Paint, Tip Of Bill Replaced, Sm. Shot Grooves In Back $200.00

(Row IV, Left to Right)

Greater Scaup Drake, By Frank Strey, Oshkosh, Wis., Pencilled Initial Signature On Bottom Twice, Unused Cond. $60.00

Greater Scaup Hen, By Frank Strey, Unused Cond. $40.00

Redhead Drake, By Frank Strey, Head Slightly To Left, Unused Cond. $65.00

Scaup Drake, By Frank Strey, Carved Wing Details, Traces Of Signature & Address On Bottom In Pencil, Orig. Paint Weathered . . . $60.00

(Row V, Left to Right)

Scaup Drake, By Ben Schmidt, Center Line, Michigan, Carved Wings, Unused Cond. $100.00

Canvasback Hen, By Ben Schmidt, Carved Wing Feathers, Little Use $150.00

Mallard Hen, By Ben Schmidt, Wing Carving & Feather Carving Over Entire Body, Signed On Bottom In Pen, Orig. Cond. $275.00

Canvasback Drake, By Ben Schmidt, Carved Wings & Some Feather Carving, 1 Sm. Shot Groove In Back, ... $175.00

FACTORY DECOYS

(A-MA. '75)

(Row I, Left to Right)

Mallard Drake, Mason's Decoy Factory, Premier Grade, Bird Hit On Right Side By Shot, Restored Cond., Repainted By Kenneth E. DeLong Of Hyannis, Ma. $100.00

Redhead Drake, Mason's Decoy Factory, Detroit Grade, Age Split In Left Side Of Body, Orig. Paint Weathered & Worn, Scratches $30.00

Scaup Drakes, Pr., Mason's Decoy Factory, Detroit Grade, Weathered & Worn $30.00

(Row II, Left to Right)

Mallard Drakes, Pr., Dodge Decoy Factory, Both Hit By Shot, Retouched, Paint Weathered, Head Loose On One $60.00

Mallard Hen, Dodge Decoy Factory, Lge. Shallow Chip In Tail, Orig. Paint Weathered & Worn, Head Loose $30.00

Scaup Drake, Mason's Decoy Factory, Challenge Grade, Snake Head, Traces Of White Paint On Bill, Orig. Paint Weathered & Worn, Age Split On Left Side Of Body, Hit By Shot On Right Side $55.00

(Row III, Left to Right)

Mallard Hen, Mason's Decoy Factory, Premier Grade, Hollow-Carved, Orig. Paint Weathered & Worn, Lge. Split In Body Block W/Lge. Piece Missing $50.00

Scaup Drake & Hen, Pr., Possibly Early Decoys By Dodge, Drake W/Comb Carving On Back, Hen W/Head Turned To Left, Worn Orig. Paint. $60.00

Scaup Drake, Mason's Decoy Factory, Detroit Grade, Age Split In Bottom Of Body Block, Orig. Paint Retouched, Hit By Shot On Left Side $15.00

(Row IV, Left to Right)

Scaup Drake & Hen, Pr., Mason's Decoy Factory, Standard Grade, Both Heads Loose, Hen W/Mar In Top Of Bill, Orig. Paint Weathered & Worn $45.00

Mallard Drake, Mason's Decoy Factory, Standard Grade, Orig. Paint, Hit By Shot, Glass Eyes Missing, Chip On Upper Part Of Head, Head Loose $30.00

(Row V, Left to Right)

Scaup Drake, Used Cond., Weathered $20.00

Mallard Drake, Unknown Maker, Orig. Paint Weathered & Worn $10.00

Redhead Drake, Unknown Maker, Hollow-Carved, Orig. Paint Weathered & Worn $20.00

(A-MA. '76)   Richard A. Bourne Co. Inc.

OLD CHESAPEAKE GUNNING DECOYS

Pair of Canvasbacks. Drake And Hen, By Norris E. Pratt, Circa 1922, Identified On Bottom. Slight Age Split To Hen's Body $125.00

(A-MA. '76)   Richard A. Bourne, Co., Inc.

IMPORTANT CHESAPEAKE BAY WORKING DECOYS

(Row I)

Pair Of Canvasbacks, Drake & Hen, By Scott Jackson (Charlestown, Maryland), Both Birds Bear Brand Of L. Pennock, Paint Appears To Be Orig., Slight Age Split In Drake's Head & Slight Age Split In Body Block Of Hen $500.00

(Row II)

Pair Redheads, Drake & Hen, By Samuel T. Barnes, Orig. Paint Showing Little Wear $200.00

(Row III)

Pair Of Canvasbacks, Hen & Drake, By John F. McKenney (Chestertown, Maryland), Carved Signature On Bottom. Hen Completely Orig., Paint Flaking On Sides, Drake W/Some Orig. Paint And Retouching $200.00

(Row IV)

Pair Of Scaup, Drake & Hen, By Samuel T. Barnes, Early Pair, Small Split In Drake's Body Filled, Both W/Orig. Paint $300.00

(A-MA. '76)   Richard A. Bourne Co. Inc.

DECOYS

(Row I)

Pair Of Mallards. Drake And Hen, With Cork Bodies, Each Branded On The Bottom "Cigar". $110.00

(Row II)

Black Duck. With Cork Body, Brand "Cigar". CONDITION: Unused $70.00

Black Duck, With Cork Body, Brand "Cigar". $80.00

(Row III)

Pair Of Scaup. Hen And Drake, With Cork Bodies, Signed In Pencil On Bottom "Delbert 'Cigar' Daisey/October 1970" $80.00

Garth's Auctions, Inc.

Richard A. Bourne Co., Inc.

(A-OH. '76)
MINIATURE WOODEN DECOYS
(Row I, Left to Right)
Merganser Drake, "Bennie Daisey, Chincoteague, Va.", 7½" L. $30.00
Ex Samaha, Crudely Carved, 5½" L. $40.00
Merganser Hen, 7½" L. $20.00
(Row II, Left to Right)
Teal Drake, "Old Pekin Carver", 5½" L. $40.00
Teal Hen, "Old Pekin Carver", 5⅝" L. $25.00
Decoy, 5⅜" 1" L. $50.00
Decoy, Signed & Dated 1953 ....$50.00
(Row III, Left to Right)
Decoy, Signed & Dated "1953", 6½" L. $20.00
Mallard Drake, "A. Bennett, Joliet Area", 6⅛" L. ...$35.00
Decoy, Chip On Tail, 6½" L. $22.50
(Row IV, Left to Right)
Decoy, Possibly By Crowell, 3¾" L. $85.00
Decoy, Crudly Carved & Painted, Mdk. "A. Dole", 6½" L. ..$20.00
Sleeper, Mallard Hen, 5½" L. $35.00
Decoy, Possibly by Crowell, 4⅛" L. $95.00

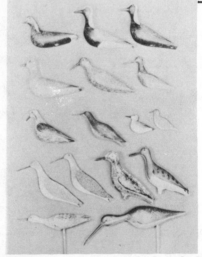

(A-MA. '75)
Richard A. Bourne Co., Inc.
SHORE BIRD DECOYS
(Row I, Left to Right)
Golden Plover, Ca. 1855, By Father Of H. B. Chandler, Turned Head, Orig. Cond. . .$800.00
Black-Bellied Plover, Ca. 1900, By Sherman Or Simmons, Nephew Of H. B. Chandler, Orig. Cond. $175.00
Golden Plover, Ca. 1880, By Sherman Or Simmons, Nephew Of H. B. Chandler, Orig. Cond. $325.00
(Row II, Left to Right)
Young Golden Plover, Ca. 1880, Bird In First

Plumage, Orig. Cond. $325.00
Eskimo Curlew, By Ed Tolson's Father, Ocracoke Inlet, North Carolina, Ca. 1870, Lightly Hit By Shot On Left Side $250.00
Dowitcher, Ca. 1875-1880, By Father Of H. B. Chandler, Orig. Cond $275.00
(Row III, Left to Right)
Beetlehead Plover, Ca. 1890, By P. Hall, Cod Pond, Accord, Ma., Turned Head, Orig. Cond. $475.00
Yellowlegs, Ca. 1890, By Fred Gardiner, Accord, Ma., Orig. Paint Worn & Pigmented ..
...................................$400.00
Sandpiper, By Herb Kendall, Sag Harbor, Long Island, Orig. Cond. $225.00
Sandpiper, By H. Young, Hingham, Ma., Ca. 1910, Flat, Almost Unused $250.00
(Row IV, Left to Right)
Yellowlegs Shadow Decoy, Ca. 1910, By H. Cushing, Duxbury, Ma., Nail For Bill, Orig. Cond.
...................................$70.00
Yellowlegs Shadow Decoy, Ca. 1910, By H. Cushing, Nail For Bill, Orig. Cond. $70.00
Folding Tin Yellowlegs, (1 Of 4), W/Sticks, Orig. W/Minimal Amount Of Rust, Sticks Old But Not Orig. $100.00
Folding Tin Yellowlegs, (1 Of 2), W/Sticks, 1 W/Minor Flaking Of Paint, Orig. Sticks .$80.00
(Row V, Left to Right)
Running Yellowlegs, By Elisha Burr, Hingham, Ma., Carved Wing Details & Head, Hit Both Sides By Shot, Old Paint $600.00
Feeding Curlew, Both Carved Wing Tips Chipped & Worn Slightly $425.00

(A-MA. '75)
CANADIAN DECOYS
(Row I, Left to Right)
Hollow-Carved Black Duck, By Ken Anger, Dunnville, Ontario (1905-1961), Carved Feather Details, Orig. Paint, Some Flaking $220.00
Hollow-Carved Redhead Drake, By Ken Anger, Ca. 1951, Carved Wing Details $325.00
.....................................$325.00
Hollow-Carved Redhead Hen, By Ken Anger, Ca. 1951, Carved Wing Details $250.00
Black Duck, By Ken Anger, Carved Wing Details, Unused Cond. $250.00
(Row II, Left to Right)
Scaup Drake, By Ken Anger, Carved Wing Details, Orig. Paint $225.00
Scaup Hen, By Ken Anger, Slightly Turned Head, Carved Wing Details, Orig. Paint. ......
.....................................$250.00
Black Duck, By Ken Anger, Carved Wing Details, Unused Cond. $250.00
Hollow-Carved Black Duck Feeder, By Ken Anger, Bird Made Without Head, Carved Wing Details, Struck By One Shot, Orig. Paint ......
.....................................$50.00
(Row III, Left to Right)
Hollow-Carved Canvasback Drake, By Ken Anger, Carved Wing Details, Orig. Paint, Weathered & Worn, Struck By Three Shot .$300.00
Hollow-Carved Canvasback Hen, By Ken Anger, Carved Wing Details, Paint Weathered & Worn, Lightly Struck By Shot $175.00
Scaup Hen, By Bob Paquette, Detailed Wing & Feather Carving, Retains Orig. Paint, Weathered & Worn, Lightly Struck By Shot $120.00
Goldeneye Drake, By David W. Nichol, Hollow-Carved, Hunting Decoy, Carved Feather Details.
.....................................$150.00
(Row IV, Left to Right)
Scaup Drake, By Orel LaBoeuf, Carved Wing & Feather Details, Sleepy Attitude, Orig. Paint, Shot Furrow On Bill & Head $175.00
Scaup Hen, By Gilbert Joval, Carved Feather Details, Unused Cond. $50.00
Black Duck, By Ernest Fox, Carved Wing Details, Unused Cond. $60.00
Scaup Drake, By Ernest Fox, Carved Wing Details, Dated 1957, Unused Cond. $40.00
(Row V, Left to Right)
Goldeneye Hen, By Orel LaBoeuf, Carved Wing & Tail Feathers, Orig. Paint Weathered, Age Split In Body $100.00
Scaup Drake, By E. Chantel, Ca. 1920, Carved Wing & Tail Feathers, Orig. Paint Weathered $80.00
Black Duck, By Jean Boucher, Lake St. Peter, Quebec, Carved Wing & Tail Feathers, Unused cond. $40.00
Goldeneye Drake, By E. Chantel, Ca. 1920, Carved Wing & Tail Feathers, Painted Eyes, Orig. Paint Weathered $70.00

Over the years, dolls have been made primarily as playthings for children in all parts of the world. Their very progress reflects the development of our human whimsey, ingenuity and sophistication. There are porcelain, bisque, papier-mache, wax, rubber, metal, celluloid, plastic and composition dolls. Additionally, there is an array of homemade dolls made from rawhide, nuts, apples, corn shucks and rags.

Dolls dating from the nineteenth and early twentieth century are the ones for which most collectors search. However, because of their scarcity, the end result is that more and more collectors are moving into the contemporary field — especially the younger collectors. Prices of antique as well as later dolls have increased to the point of the ridiculous in most areas because of demand. Today, collecting dolls has become almost a mania with adult collectors.

(Left)
(D-N.Y. '76)
Parian Doll, W/Glass Eyes, Kid Body, Original Clothes, Late 19th C., 20" T.........$550.00

(Right)
(D-N.Y. '76)
Dolly Madison Doll, Glass Eyes Parian, Blue Molded Ribbon In Hair, 22" T........$700.00

(Left)
(D-N.Y. '76)
Parian Doll, Painted Eyes, Deeply Combed Hair, Orig. Clothes, 24" T...........$450.00

(Right)
(D-N.Y. '76)
Parian Doll, Known as "Dagmar", Molded Blouse Front, Orig. Clothes, 13" T. ...$375.00

(Left)
(D-N.Y. '76)
China Doll, "Low Brow", Kid Body, Old Clothes, 16" T..............................$110.00

(Right)
(D-N.Y. '76)
Parian Doll, Painted Eyes, Sausage Curls, Orig. Clothes, Ca. 1860, 10" T......$325.00

(Left)
(D-N.Y. '76)
Milliner's Model, Flat Wood Feet, Wooden Hands, Kid Body, Ca. 1850, 14' T.....$250.00

(Right)
(D-N.Y. '76)
China Doll, Kid Body, Orig. Clothing, 16" T.
.... $275.00

(Left)
(D-N.Y. '76)
Bisque, German Doll, Turned Head On Stationary Shoulder Plate, 18" T...........$475.00

(Right)
(D-N.Y. '76)
Bisque Shoulderhead, German, Bisque Arms To Elbow, P.W. Eyes, Kid Body, 17" T. $450.00

(Left)
(D-N.Y. '76)
German Fashion Doll, Kid Body, Dome Head Under Wig, P.W. Eyes, 17" T.......$450.00

(Right)
(D-N.Y. '76)
German Doll, P.W. Eyes, Straight Wrists, Ca. 1861, 20" T.......................$700.00

(Left)
(D-N.Y. '76)
Kley & Hahn German Character Boy Doll, Toddler Body $350.00

(Right)
(D-N.Y. '76)
"Belton" German Doll, Straight Wrists, W/ Characteristic 3 Holes In Top Of Flat Head, 12" T. $350.00

(Left)
(D-N.Y. '76)
German Doll, Possibly Kestner, Straight Wrists, 22" T. $750.00

(Right)
(D-N.Y. '76)
German Shoulderhead Doll, Kid Body, Bisque Hands, 22" T. $450.00

(Left)
(D-N.Y. '76)
German Doll, Mkd. "P. Schmidt," P. W. Eyes, 16" T. $275.00

(Right)
(D-N.Y. '76)
Bergman Doll, Early 20th C., 22" T...$350.00

Evelyn Phillips

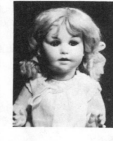

(Left)

(D-N.Y. '76)
French Depose, Unmarked, Ca. 1880, 33" T
.... $550.00

(Right)

(D-N.Y. '76)
French Depose, Molded Brow, 17" T. $300.00

(Left)

(D-N.Y. '76)
French Girl, Small, P.W. Eyes, 15" T. $700.00

(Right)

(D-N.Y. '76)
Armand Marseille Doll, Large Size, Ca. 1920, 40" T. $225.00

(Left)

(D-N.Y. '76)
French Milliner's Model, Kid Body, Papier Mache Head, 16" T. $450.00

(Right)

(D-N.Y. '76)
French Doll, Steiner, P.W. Eyes, Straight Wrists, 22" T. $650.00

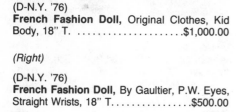

(Left)

(D-N.Y. '76)
French Fashion Doll, Original Clothes, Kid Body, 18" T. $1,000.00

(Right)

(D-N.Y. '76)
French Fashion Doll, By Gaultier, P.W. Eyes, Straight Wrists, 18" T...............$500.00

(Left)

(D-N.Y. '76)
SFBJ French Doll, P.W. Eyes, 13" T. $275.00

(Right)

(D-N.Y. '76)
French Fashion Doll, Gaultier, Bisque, Swivel Neck, Kid Body, Bisque Arms, 10" T. $1,100.00

(Left)

(D-N.Y. '76)
Belton French Doll, Straight Wrists, Usual 3 Hole Mark On Head, 16" T..........$750.00

(Right)

(D-N.Y. '76)
French Fashion Doll, Kid Body, Swivel Neck, 18" T. $900.00

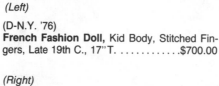
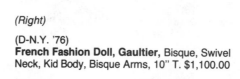

(Left)

(D-N.Y. '76)
French Fashion Doll, Cloth Body, Head Mkd. "F. G.", Glass Eyes, 18" T. $800.00

(Right)

(D-N.Y. '76)
French Fashion Doll, P.W. Eyes, Old Clothes, 12" T. $650.00

(Left)

(D-N.Y. '76)
French Fashion Doll, Kid Body, Stitched Fingers, Late 19th C., 17"T. $700.00

(Right)

(D-N.Y. '76)
Armand Marseille Character Baby, Bent Legs, Sleepy Eyes, 16" T. $225.00

(Left)

(D-N.Y. '76)
Tete Jumeau Doll, 23" T. $1,200.00

(Right)

(D-N.Y. '76)
Jumeau Doll, Unmarked, Paperweight Eyes, 26" T. $650.00

Evelyn Phillips

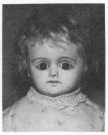

(Left)

(D-N.Y. '76)   *Evelyn Phillips*
Papier Mache Doll, Waxed, Straw Body, Orig. Clothing, 20" T. $225.00

(Right)

(D-N.Y. '76)   *Evelyn Phillips*
Papier Mache Doll, Early Clothes, Ca. 1875, 19" T. $175.00

(Left)

(D-N.Y. '76)   *Evelyn Phillips*
Wax Doll, Molded Boots W/Tassels, Orig. Clothing, Ca. 1880, 18" T. $250.00

(Right)

(D-N.Y. '76)   *Evelyn Phillips*
Wax Doll, Pupiless Glass Eyes, Orig. Clothing, Some Age Cracks, Ca. 1890, 16" T. ..$300.00

(Left)

(D-N.Y. '76)   *Evelyn Phillips*
K*R Baby Doll, Mkd., First Of Character Dolls, 14" T. $300.00

(Right)

(D-N.Y. '76)   *Evelyn Phillips*
Rag Doll, Painted Features, Hair Braided Fabric, Hand Loomed Dress, Ca. 1850 ....$75.00

(Left)

(D-N.Y. '76)   *Evelyn Phillips*
Armand Marseille Doll #323 "Googlie", Rough Body, 6½" T. $475.00

(Right)

(D-CO. '76)
Rose O'Neill Bisque Qewpie, 9½" T. $145.00

(Left)

(D-FL. '76)
Doll, "Buddy Lee", Orig. Clothing ...$100.00

(Right)

(D-N.Y. '76)   *Evelyn Phillips*
Handwerck, Sleepy Eyes, 33' T. $325.00

(Left)

(D-N.Y. '76)   *Evelyn Phillips*
Steiner Doll, Mkd. "FIRE A-4",Ca. 1890, 10" T.
.... $1,100.00

(Right)

(D-N.Y. '76)   *Evelyn Phillips*
Simon & Halbig Doll, P.W. Eyes, Orig, Clothing
.... $350.00

(Left)

(D-N.Y. '76)   *Evelyn Phillips*
Rabery & Delphieu Doll, Wind-Up Walker W/Head Made By Kestner, 18" T. $750.00

(Right)

(D-N.Y. '76)   *Evelyn Phillips*
Bru. Jne, Mkd. W/Dot & Crescent, Kid Body, Bisque Hands $3,500.00

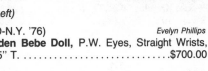

(Left)

(D-N.Y. '76)   *Evelyn Phillips*
Eden Bebe Doll, P.W. Eyes, Straight Wrists, 25" T. $700.00

(Right)

(D-N.Y. '76)   *Evelyn Phillips*
Bisque Head, Glass Eyes, Swivel Neck & Composition Body, 5" T. $110.00

(Left)

(D-N.Y. '76)   *Evelyn Phillips*
Simon & Halbig Doll, #1000 Dep., Shoulder-head Bisque, Kid Body $275.00

(Right)

(D-N.Y. '76)   *Evelyn Phillips*
Simon Halbig Doll, Negro, 15" T. $450.00

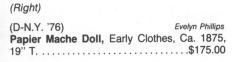

   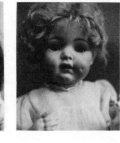  

(Left)

(D-N.Y. '76)   *Evelyn Phillips*
Kestner Boy, Comp. Body, Bisque Head, 16" T.
.... $225.00

(Right)

(D-N.Y. '76)   *Evelyn Phillips*
Jumeau Doll, Unmarked, Early 1900s, 18" T.
.... $475.00

(Left)

(D-N.Y. '76)   *Evelyn Phillips*
Gebruder Doll, Straight Wrists, P.W. Eyes,
20" T. $800.00

(Right)

(D-N.Y. '76)   *Evelyn Phillips*
K*R #121, Bent Leg Baby W/Orig. Clothes,
21" T. $350.00

(Left)

(D-N.Y. '76)   *Evelyn Phillips*
Greiner Doll, Mkd., Blonde W/Orig. Clothes,
Ca. 1872, 27" T. $400.00

(Right)

(D-N.Y. '76)   *Evelyn Phillips*
SFBJ #237, Character Boy Doll, Flocked Hair,
Glass Eyes, Comp. Body, 15" T. ...$1,100.00

(Left)

(D-N.Y. '76)   *Evelyn Phillips*
Bru. Jne #5, Kid Body, Bisque Arms, Wooden
Legs $3,800.00

(Right)

(A-MA. '76)   *Richard A. Bourne Co. Inc.*
Bisque Mechanical Doll, German, Swimming
Sailor, Bisque Head, Wooden Hands & Feet,
Sm. Chip On Back Of Hat...........$275.00

(A-MA. '76)   *Richard A. Bourne Co. Inc.*
(Left to Right)
Papier Mache Doll, Cloth Body W/Kid Arms,
Cloth Legs, Slight Crazing Of Papier Mache,
31½" T. $300.00
Wooden Boy Doll, Carved, Wood Body &
Hands, Cloth Legs & Feet, Chipped Nose & Ear,
22½" T. $180.00
Bisque Baby Girl Doll, Kid Body, Arms &
Legs, 26½" T.......................$120.00
Bisque Doll, Japanese, Morimura Bros., Com-
position Body & Limbs, 19½" T. $120.00

(Left)

(D-KS. '76)
KACHINA DOLLS, Ca. 1950
(Row I, Left to Right)
Warrior, Sgn., 12½" T...............$65.00
Butterfly, 11" T....................$65.00
Kiowa Warrior, 13" T. $50.00
(Row II, Left to Right)
Eagle, Sgn., 11¼" T. $90.00
Pueblo Kachina, 6½" T. $25.00
Raven, 10" T. $75.00

(Right)

(A-MA. '76)   *Richard A. Bourne Co. Inc.*
German Bisque Doll, Mkd. '109-15 DED'';
Blond Wig, Composition Body, Orig. Black
Socks & High Boots; Chip Over L. Eye, 28" T.
.... $125.00

(A-MA. '76)   *Richard A. Bourne Co. Inc.*
(Left to Right)
Bisque Doll, German, Marked "Darling/3",
Bisque Head, Hands & Arms, Kid Body, Cloth
Feet W/Shoes, Old Costume, 24" T. ..$100.00
Bisque Doll, German, Bisque Hands, Kid Body
& Upper Legs, Cloth Lower Legs & Feet, 25" T.
...................................$35.00
Bisque Doll, German, Kid Body, Bisque Hands,
Cloth Legs & Feet W/Leather Shoes, Missing
Forefinger Of Right Hand, Sm. Tear In Kid On
Back, 20" T. $140.00
Flora Dora Doll, German, Bisque Head &
Hands, Cloth Feet, Four Fingers On Right Hand
Broken Off, Some Retouching, 23" T. ..$85.00

(A-MA. '76)   Richard A. Bourne Co. Inc.
DOLLS
(Row I, Left to Right)
French Doll, Bisque Shoulder Plate, Swivel Neck, Kid Body, 12" T. $400.00
French Doll, Bisque Shoulder Plate, Blond Skin Wig, Kid Body, Bisque Hands, 12" T. .$400.00
French Doll, Solid Head, Blond Wig, Kid Body, Arms & Legs, 14½" T. $200.00
(Row II, Left to Right)
French Doll, Bisque Head, Swivel Neck, Blond Mohair Wig, Mkd. "WD/O", 11" T. $500.00
French Doll, No Wig, Bisque Head, Hands & Arms To Above Elbows, 9½" T. $90.00
French Doll, Made Into Doorstop W/Part Of Torso Only, No Lower Limbs, Blond Wig, Sleeping Brown Eyes, Bisque Arms, 11" T. . .$50.00

(A-MA. '76)   Richard A. Bourne Co. Inc.
(Left to Right)
Wax Over Composition Doll, Brown Human Hair Wig W/Braid In Back, Blue Eyes, Cloth Body, Comp. Arms & Legs, Left Hand In Poor Cond., Both Feet Broken & Poorly Repaired, Surface Checks Back Of Neck, 29" T. $100.00
Wax Over Composition Doll, Brown Human Hair Wig, Black Eyes, Cloth Body, Wood Hands & Arms, Comp. Feet & Legs, Painted On Shoes & Socks, Cloth Body Patched In Several Places. Toes Cracked & Chipped, Mar On Left Hand, 25" T. $60.00
Wax Over Composition Doll, Molded Wax Ears, Pierced Ears W/1 Earring, Brown Wig W/High Hair-Do, Braided On Back Of Neck, Blue Eyes, Cloth Body, Comp. Arms & Legs, Boots Painted On, Voice Box Does Not Work, 25½" T. $170.00

(A-MA. '76)   Richard A. Bourne Co. Inc.
(Row I, Left to Right)
French Child Doll, Bisque Shoulder Plate, Swivel Neck & Head Mkd. "F.I.G.", Blond Wig W/Braids & Curls, Lge. Blue Stationary Eyes, Pierced Ears & Earrings, Kid Body & Feet, Composition Hands, No Dress, Apron Only, Knees Covered W/Brown Kid, Possibly Due To Breaks In Orig. Kid, Flaking On Hands, 16" T.$1150.00
French Doll,Mkd. "C/E/" On Back Of Neck, Probably Jumeau, Bisque Shoulder Plate, Swivel Neck, Blond Wig, Gray-Blue Stationary Eyes, Pierced Ears, Cloth Body, Kid Arms, Cloth Legs & Feet, Kid On Right Hand Needs Re-Sewing, 20" T. $1250.00
French Doll, Mkd. "1010" On Back Of Head, Bisque Shoulder Plate, Swivel Neck, Blond Wig, Gray Stationary Eyes, Pierced Ears, Kid Body, Bisque Hands, Cracks Behind Both Ears, 21" T. $500.00
(Row II, Left to Right)
French Doll, Head Mkd. "R/S.F.B.J./301/ Paris/8", Blond Curly Wig, Brown Sleep Eyes, Pierced Ears, Composition Body, Arms & Lower Legs, Upper Legs Of Wood, Wears Petticoat Only, 20" T. $300.00
French Doll, Mkd. On Shoulder Plate "639-9", Blond Wig, Blue Stationary Eyes, Closed Mouth, Dimple On Chin, Cloth Body, Kid Arms, 22" T. $450.00

(A-MA. '76)   Richard A. Bourne Co. Inc.
DOLLS
(Left to Right)
Composition Head Doll, Mkd. "Greiner's/ Patent Doll Heads, No. 5/, Pat. 158, Ext. 72", 21" T. $175.00
Composition Head Doll, Mkd. "M & S/Superior /201", Cond. Fair, 10" T. $60.00
Composition Head Doll, Mkd. Greiner, Clothing Orig., Kid Hands & Arms Not Orig., Cond. Fair, 21" T. $70.00

(A-MA. '76)   *(Left to Right)*
Jumeau Doll, Signed "Depose E 7 J", Body Signed "Jumeau Madeille d'or Paris", Brown Wig, Brown Eyes, Closed Mouth, Pierced Ears, Comp. Body, Arms & Legs, Clothing Could Be Orig., Fingers Worn On Both Hands, Upper Legs Not Alike, 16" T. $650.00
Jumeau Doll, Marked "Depose/Tete/Jumeau/ 7", W/Label "France" & "Bebe Jumeau", Blond Wig, Brown Eyes, Pierced Ears W/Earrings, Closed Mouth, Comp. Body, Arms & Legs, Clothing Not Orig., Socks & Shoes One Of Which Is Marked "Paris/Depose", Legs Not Orig., & In Poor Condition, 17½" T. $650.00
Jumeau Doll, Marked "Depose/Tete Jumeau/ Bte SGDG/8", Body Marked "Bebe Jumeau Diplome d'Honneur" On Label On Back Of Body, Blond Wig, Blue Eyes, Pierced Ears W/Earrings, Comp. Body, Arms & Legs, Only One Shoe Which Is Signed "E. J. Depose", Head Cracked Across Forehead & Reglued, 13" T. . .$450.00
Jumeau Doll, Marked "Depose E 3 J", Signed On Body "Jumeau/Medaille d'or/Paris", Blond Wig, Blue Eyes, Pierced Ears, Comp. Body, Arms & Legs, 2 Breaks In Head, 11" T. $350.00

(A-MA. '76)   Richard A. Bourne Co. Inc.
French Bisque Doll By Bru, Mkd., Swivel Head, Blond Skin Wig, Pierced Ears, Brown Stationary Eyes, Bisque Arms; Wears Pants & Chemise, Possibly Orig., Orig. Socks & Shoes, 30" T. $4,300.00

(A-MA. '76)   *(Left to Right)*
Composition Head Doll, Blond Wig, Dressed As Boy, Hands Do Not Match, 14" T. . .$70.00
Composition Head Doll, Wooden Arms & Legs, Plaid Hand-Loomed Dress, Ca. 1857
. . . .$80.00

(A-MA. '76)   *Richard A. Bourne Co. Inc.*
(Row I, Left to Right)
Milliner Model Doll, Ca. 1850's, Wooden Arms
& Legs, Kid Body, Painted-On Orange Shoes,
Slight Crack In Left Shoulder, 14" T. . . .$90.00
Schoenhut Boy Doll, Stamped On Back Of
Body, "Schoenhut Doll/Pat. Jan. 17, '11 USA/
Foreign Countries", No Wig, Brown Painted
Eyes, Paint Worn On Chin & Nose, 16" T. . . . .
. . . .$210.00
Schoenhut Girl Doll, Orig. Mark On Back Of
Head & On Back, Blond Wig, Blue Painted Eyes,
Jointed Wood Body & Head, Right Leg Cracked
& Taped, 13¾" T. $150.00
(Row II, Left to Right)
Celluloid Head Doll, Mkd. "J.D.K./201/1", Kid
Body, Celluloid Hands & Feet, Blue Sleep Eyes,
Leg & One Hand Damaged, 14" T. $50.00
Lenci Boy Doll, Ca. 1915, Orig. Label & Tag,
Made Of Felt W/Brown Hair, Painted Brown
Eyes, Dressed In Felt Suit, 14¼" T. . .$150.00
Lenci Girl Doll, Ca. 1915, Matches Doll On
Left, Brown Hair, Brown Painted Eyes, Orig.
Clothes &Shoes, 14" T. $175.00

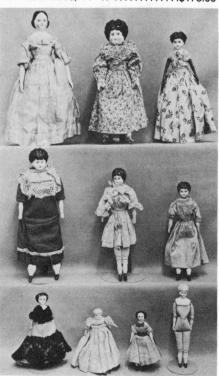

(A-MA. '76)   *Richard A. Bourne Co. Inc.*
(Row I, Left to Right)
Black-Haired China Doll, China Arms & Legs,
Cloth Body, Jenny Lind Type, Ex. Cond., 23" T.
. . . .$375.00
Black-Haired China Doll, Cloth Body, Kid
Arms, 25" T. $85.00
Black-Haired China Doll, Cloth Body, Kid
Arms, 23" T. $70.00
(Row II, Left to Right)
Black-Haired China Doll, Cloth Body, Kid
Arms, Blemish On Front Of Neck & Pitting On
Cheek, 14" T. $50.00
Blond China Doll, Cloth Body, China Hands &
Feet, Forehead Pitted, 15" T. $60.00
Black-Haired China Doll, Cloth Body, China
Arms, One Foot Missing, Minor Pitting On
Cheek, 15½" T. $35.00
Blond China Doll, Cloth Body, Bisque Hands,
Crack In One Finger, Shoulder Plate Repaired,
20" T. $60.00

← (A-MA. '76)   *Richard A. Bourne Co. Inc.*
(Row I, Left to Right)
Black-Haired China Doll, Ca. 1850, Cloth Body,
China Arms & Legs, Blue Eyes, 13" T. $175.00
Black-Haired China Doll, Cloth Body, China
Hands & Feet, Blue Eyes, #3 On Shoulder, Chip
On 2 Fingers Of Left Hand, Pitted On Leg, 13" T.
. . . .$40.00
Black-Haired China Doll, Cloth Body, Kid
Hands & Feet, Blue Eyes, 12" T. $25.00
(Row II, Left to Right)
Black-Haired China Doll, Cloth Body, China
Arms & Legs, Blue Eyes, Costume In Poor Cond.
13" T. $20.00
Black-Haired China Doll, Cloth Body, Bisque
Arms & Legs, Blue Eyes, #4 On Shoulder Plate,
Slight Crack In Left Leg, 11" T. $20.00
Black-Haired China Doll, Cloth Body, Bisque
Arms & Legs, Blue Eyes, PItting On Left Cheek,
Each Leg Cracked, 10" T. $20.00
(Row III, Left to Right)
Black-Haired China Doll, Cloth Body, Bisque
Arms & Legs, Blue Eyes, Good Cond. But
China Of Poor Quality, 7" T. $20.00
Blond China Doll, Cloth Body, Bisque Arms &
Legs, Black Eyes, 6" T. $25.00
Black-Haired China Doll, Cloth Body, China
Arms & Legs, Blue Eyes, Right Arm Repaired,
5" T. $30.00
Blond China Doll, Cloth Body, Bisque Arms &
Legs, Blue Eyes, 7½" T. $25.00

(A-MA. '76)   *Richard A. Bourne Co. Inc.*
(Row I, Left to Right)
Bisque Doll, Brown Wig, Painted Blue Station-
ary Eyes, Pierced Ears, Unjointed Kid Body,
Not Orig. To Head, Dress Soiled, 17" T. $175.00
German Bisque Doll, Mkd. "C.M. Bergman/
Waltershausen/Germany/1916/3", Blond Wig,
Blue Stationary Eyes, Composition Body & Legs,
Arms Of Wood, Shoes & Socks, 18½" T. . . . . .
. . . .$130.00
German Bisque Doll, Mkd. "Germany/Heinrich
Handwerck/Simon & Halbig/2", Brown Wig,
Brown Sleep Eyes W/Lashes, Pierced Ears
W/Earrings, Composition Body, Lower Arms &
Legs, Wood Upper Arms & Legs, 18" T. $100.00
(Row II, Left to Right)
German Bisque Doll, Mkd. "MOA (In Star)/
150/Welsch/Made In Germany/3/0", Brown Wig,
Blue Sleep Eyes, Composition Body, Arms &
Legs, 15" T. $100.00
German Bisque Doll, Mkd. "119/10X/Hand-
werck/Germany", Blond Wig, Gray-Blue Sleep-
ing Eyes, Pierced Ears, Open Mouth, Composi-
tion Body, Arms & Legs, Wears One Undergar-
ment Only, Replaced Hands, 17" T. . . .$95.00
German Bisque Doll, Mkd. "1894/AM 2 DEP",
Brown Wig, Bright Blue Sleeping Eyes, Open
Mouth W/Teeth, Kid Body, Bisque Hands, Cloth
Lower Legs, Wears Dress & Chemise, Repairs
To Kid At Hip Joints, 17" T. $90.00

(A-MA. '76)
Richard A. Bourne Co. Inc.

(Left to Right)
Composition Head Doll, Brown Wig, Cloth
Body & Legs, Leather Hands, Some Touch-Up
To Face, 10" T. $50.00
Composition Head Doll, Superior Doll, Label
Missing, Kid Body, Comp. Legs W/Painted
Boots, Comp. Hands & Arms, Some Repair,
16" T. $60.00

(A-MA. '76)   Richard A. Bourne Co. Inc.
DOLLS
(Left to Right)

German Bisque Doll, Mkd. "Made In Germany/ 370 A.M.-9-DEP/Armand Marseille", Blond Wig, Braided Around Head, Blue Sleeping Eyes, Bisque Hands & Arms To Elbows, Jointed Kid Body Stamped "Germany", Cloth Lower Legs, Dress Not Orig., Hairline Crack Left Shoulder, 27½" T. $110.00

German Bisque Doll, Mkd. "Germany/Queen Louise/10". Lt. Brown Wig, Blue Sleeping Eyes, Composition Body, Upper Arms, Hands & Legs; Wood Lower Arms, Clothes Not Orig., Fingers Repaired On Right Hand, Needs Restringing, 26" T. $120.00

German Bisque Doll, Mkd. "1078/Germany/ Simon & Halbig/S&H/11½", Blond Wig, Flirty Sleeping Eyes W/Lashes, Pierced Ears, Composition Body, Crack In Back Of Neck, 24" T. $100.00

(A-MA. '76)   Richard A. Bourne Co. Inc.
DOLLS
(Row I, Left to Right)

German Bisque Boy Doll, Mkd. "Simon & Halbig/K*R/46", Blond Wig, Brown Sleep Eyes, Pierced Ears, Comp. Body, Arms & Legs, Suit Not Orig., 1 Finger Broken On Left Hand, 18" T. $220.00

German Bisque Doll, Only Mark Is "13" On Head, Bisque Shoulder Plate, Swivel Neck, Kid Body, Cloth Lower Legs, Bisque Hands, Clothes Not Orig., Sewed On Bootees, 1 Leg Patched, Fingers Chipped, 22" T. $160.00

German Bisque Doll, Mkd. "Revalo/7/Germany", Blond Wig, Comp. Body, Legs & Hands, Wooden Arms, Repair To Back Of Neck, 20" T. $80.00

(Row II, Left to Right)

German Bisque Doll, Unmarked, Blond Wig, Kid Body & Arms, Cloth From Knees Down, Bisque Hands, Clothes Not Orig., Thumb Missing on Right Hand, 21" T. $90.00

German Bisque Doll, Mkd. "2015/3" Between Which Is Another Mark Superimposed With "W", Possibly By Wessel, Poppelsdorf, Bonn, Germany, Kid Body, Cloth From Knees Down, Bisque Hands, Clothes Not Orig., Chip On Fingers On Right Hand, 20" T. $100.00

(A-MA. '76)   Richard A. Bourne Co. Inc.
DOLLS
(Row I, Left to Right)

German Bisque Doll, Mkd. "1894 AM DEP/ Made In Germany/4", Black Human Hair Wig, Drk. Brown Sleep Eyes, Comp. Body, Arms & Legs, Orig. Clothes, Lace Socks, Silk Shoes, 17½" T. $125.00

German Bisque Doll, Mkd. "Made In/G. Germany/11", Brown Wig, Brown Sleeping Eyes, Closed Mouth, Dimple In Chin, Comp. Body, Arms & Legs, Surface Cracks Over Head, 19" T. $80.00

Bisque Doll, Mkd. "MS (In Square) / Fulper/ Made In U.S.A./12", Henna Wig, Comp. Body, Wooden Arms & Upper Legs, Upper Left Leg Replaced, Thumb On Right Hand Gone, 19½" T. $150.00

(Row II, Left to Right)

German Bisque Doll, Unmarked, Brown Wig, Brown Stationary Eyes, Pierced Ears & Earrings, Kid Body, Bisque Hands, 4 Fingers Broken On Left Hand, Dress In Poor Cond., Head In Ex. Condition, 18" T. $80.00

German Bisque Doll, Mkd. "1039 X DEP/7", Brown Wig, Blue Stationary Eyes, Pierced Ears, Comp. Body, Arms & Hands, Wooden Upper Legs, Repair Over Right Eye, 18" T. $55.00

German Bisque Doll, Mkd. "109-7½/Germany/Handwerck", Brown Wig, Brown Sleep Eyes, Pierced Ears W/1 Earring, Open Mouth W/2 Teeth, Comp. Body, Legs & Hands, Wooden Arms, Needs Restringing, 17" T. . .$120.00

(A-MA. '76)   Richard A. Bourne Co. Inc.
(Left to Right)

German Bisque Doll, "80-10" Only Mark On Head, Orig. Label In Oval On Body, "Real Kid/ I.S. Co. Germany", Blond Wig, Blue Sleep Eyes, Pierced Ears, Jointed Kid Body, Cloth From Knees Down, Comp. Lower Arms & Hands, Clothes Possibly Orig., 23" T. $65.00

German Bisque Doll, Mkd. "Made in Germany/ Armand Marseille/390-N./ASM", Brown Wig, Blue Sleep Eyes, Open Mouth, Comp. Body, Lower Arms & Legs, Wooden Upper Arms & Legs, No Shoes, Legs Repaired, 21" T. . . . . . .
. . . .$75.00

German Bisque Doll, Mkd. "Germany/Heinrich /Handwerck/Halbig/2½", Blond Braided Wig, Gray Stationary Eyes, Pierced Ears, Open Mouth, Clothes Not Orig., Leg Cracked, 21½" T.
. . . .$100.00

← (A-MA. '76)   Richard A. Bourne Co. Inc.
(Left to Right)

German Bisque Doll, Mkd. "5500/S-PB (In Star)-H/DEP/10", Brown Wig, Brown Sleep Eyes, Clothes Not Orig., Hands Do Not Match, 23" T. $125.00

German Bisque Doll, Mkd. "S & H 1079-10/ DEP/Germany", Brown Wig, Brown Stationary Eyes, Pierced Ears, Comp. Body, Arms & Legs, Clothes Not Orig., Red Shoes, One Sock, Upper Right Leg Repaired, 24" T. $120.00

German Bisque Doll, Mkd. "11 DEP.154", Brown Wig, Blue Sleep Eyes, Kid Body, Lower Legs Of Cloth, Bisque Hands, Clothes Not Orig., Kid Repaired In Several Places, Chips On Finger/, One Thumb Missing, 23" T. $80.00

(A-PA. '75)   *Pennypacker Auction Centre*
Lift Lid Salt Box, Walnut $52.50

(Left)
(D-PA. '76)
Hanging Match Box, Hand Carved, 5" H. Pa.
Dutch $45.00

(Right)
(D-N.H. '76)
Knife Scouring Box, Pine, 16½" L. . . .$85.00

(A-PA. '75)   *Pennypacker Auction Centre*
Deed Box, Wooden W/Red, Yellow & Green
Decor., Hinged Lid $225.00

(Left)
(A-PA. '75)   *Pennypacker Auction Centre*
Conestoga Wagon Box Hardware, Wrought
Iron $375.00

(Right)
(D-N.Y. '76)
Pipe Box, Pine, Dovetailed Drawer, 21" H. . . .
. . . .$265.00

(Left)
(D-WI. '76)
Hanging Salt Box, Maple & Cherry, 9" H. . . . .
. . . . $65.00

(Right)
(D-MA. '76)
Hanging Box, Orig. Red Painted Finish, Leather
Hinges Held in Place W/Pegs, 13" W.,15¼" H.
. . . .$375.00

(Left)
(D-CT. '76)
Hanging Oak Candle Box W/Hand-Gouged
Carvings, Ca. 1670, Connecticut Valley, 11¾"
W., 6½" D., 15¼" H. $1200.00

(Right)
(D-KY.)
Candle Box, Pine, Dovetailed W/Sliding Top,
7" H., 7¼" W., 8" L. $85.00

(D-KS. '76)
Pine Sewing Box, Dovetailed Drawer W/Hand
Carved Date of 1887, 5½" D., Top 8½ x 10"
. . . . $75.00

(A-PA. '75)   *Pennypacker Auction Centre*
Dome Lid Box, Decor. W/Red, Blue, Green &
White On Blue-Green Background $250.00

(Left)
(D-OH. '76)
Pipe Box, Pine, Dovetailed Drawer $55.00

(Right)
(D-MA. '76)
Hanging Wall Box, Pine, Dovetailed . .$45.00

(A-MA. '75)   *Richard A. Bourne Co. Inc.*
Oak Bible Box, American, 17th C., Orig. Hinges
Replaced W/Early Strap Hinges, Top Has Age
Split; Bottom Edge Worn & Chipped Partly
Away, 24" L., 17¼" W., 8" H. $250.00

(Left)
(A-PA. '75)   *Pennypacker Auction Centre*
Wooden Hinged Box, Lancaster Co., Sm. . . .
. . . . $170.00
(Right)
Sewing Box, Webber Style Decor., Sm. $85.00

(A-PA. '75)   *Pennypacker Auction Centre*
Wooden Bride's Box, 18" L. $360.00
Quilting Sewing Bird, Wrought Iron . . .$67.50

(A-PA. '75)   *Pennypacker Auction Centre*
Round Top Hinged Bonnet Box, Orig., 15" W.,
9½" D., 11" H. $3200.00

(D-AR. '76)
Belter-Type Chairs, New Uphol. $1200.00

(D-KY. '76)
Victorian Gothic Pulpit Chair, Ca. 1865 $85.00

(A-PA. '76)   *Pennypacker Auction Centre*
Chippendale Chairs, Set of 8, 6 Side & 2 Arm, Centennial (2 Illus.) $1,600.00

(A-MA. '76)   *Richard A. Bourne Co. Inc.*
Victorian Arm Chair, Laminated Rosewood, Carved Grape & Floral Design, Attrib. To John Henry Belter, New York City, 1804-1863, Needs Minor Regluing of Joints $1300.00
Victorian Side Chairs, Pr., Rosewood, Unrestored, Match to Arm Chair $1400.00

(A-MA. '76)   *Richard A. Bourne Co. Inc.*
(Left to Right)
Country Chippendale Side Chair, Amer., 18th C., Sq. Legs W/Molded Frontal Strip, Rush Seat, Sm. Split In Center of Crest $200.00
Queen Anne Side Chair, New England, 18th C., Walnut, Modified Balloon Seat, Seat Reupholstered, Orig. Blocking Replaced, Refinished $700.00
Country Chippendale Side Chair, Amer., 18th C., Maple, Rush Seat, Stained Mahogany, Back Broken Where It Joins Seat W/Primitive Repair, Needs Restoration $60.00

(A-OH. '76)   *Richard A. Bourne Co. Inc.*
Queen Anne Side Chair, Walnut, Balloon Seat, Curly Walnut In Splat & Shell Carving, Rhode Island $3750.00

(A-PA. '75)   *Pennypacker Auction Centre*
Couch, Turnings By Wallace Nutting .$600.00

(A-PA. '76)   *Pennypacker Auction Centre*
Victorian Chairs, Hand Carved $400.00

(A-PA. '76)   (A-MA. '76)
Pennypacker Auction Centre   *Richard A. Bourne Co. Inc.*
(Left)
Chippendale Potty Arm Chair, Mahogany $225.00
(Right)
Chippendale Side Chair, Walnut W/Upholstered Slip Seat, Amer., Ca. 1780 . . . .$300.00

(A-PA. '76)   *Pennypacker Auction Centre*
Couch, Cane Seat, Solid Splat $725.00

(D-PA. '76)
Slat-Back Armchair W/Rush Bottom, Cabriole Legs, Ca. 1730 . . . .$1200.00

(A-PA. '75)   *Pennypacker Auction Centre*
Balloon Back Chairs, Brown, All Orig., Set of 6 . . . .$720.00

(A-PA. '76)   *Pennypacker Auction Centre*
Queen Anne Side Chairs, Pr., Pierced Splats, Shells On Knees, Some Restorations .$800.00

(A-VA. '76) *Laws*
English Chippendale Rush Seat Chairs,
Set Of 8, Cyma-Scrolled Crest Rail Terminating
In Rolled Ears Over Vasi-Form Splat, Medial
Stretcher Base, 18" D., 18" W., 38" H.$850.00

(A-VA. '76) *Laws*
Honduras Mahogany Queen Anne Chair, Set
Of 6, Spoon Backs, Carved Center Splat, Slip
Seats, Cabriole Knees, Queen Anne Padded
Feet, Turned Stretchers W/Central Medial
Stretchers, Ca. 1800 ....$1,000.00

(A-VA. '76) *Laws*
Queen Anne Fiddle Back Chairs, (Set Of 6 - 2
Arm & 4 Side), Burled Walnut, Scrolled Shell &
Leaf Carved Crest, Shaped Center Splat,
Curved Formed Seat, Sculptured Skirt, Cabriole
Carved Legs W/Knees Of Shell, Leaf & Bell
Flower W/Hairy Hoof Feet, 16" D., 22" W.,
39" H., English $2,000.00

(A-VA. '76) *Laws*
Hitchcock Chairs, (Set Of 6), Orig. Hand
Grained Finish & Stenciling, Ca. 1840, 15" D.,
17" W., 34" H. $450.00

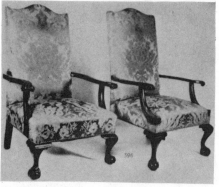

(A-VA. '76) *Laws*
Pair Of Chippendale Arm Chairs W/Cupid's
Bow Shaped Crests; Cabriole Legs W/Ball &
Claw Feet, 44" H., English $600.00

(A-VA. '76) *Laws*
Walnut Frame Armchair, 19th C., Carved
Pierced Top Crest, Needlepoint Back & Seat,
Acanthus & Floral Carved Arms, Carved &
Pierced Center Stretcher Legs, English, Ca.
1850, 22' D., 25" W., 53" H. $250.00

(A-VA. '76) *Laws*
Queen Anne Mahogany Corner Chair, 18th C.,
Mass. Origin, Pierced Back Splat Over Uphol-
stered Slip Seat, Cabriole Knee Following Into
Padded Feet, Turned Button Feet At Rear,
Ca. 1740 ....$1,500.00

(A-VA. '76) *Laws*
Queen Anne Upholstered Arm Chair, English,
24" D., 28" W., 44" H. $450.00

(D-KS. '76) *Laws*
Carpet Rocker, Orig. Covering, Fringe New,
Refinished $95.00

(A-VA. '76) *Laws*
French Walnut Side Chairs, Pr., Cathedral
Shaped Backs, Scrolled Aprons, Turned French
Feet, Separate Cushions, Replaced Corner
Blocks, Ca. 1780-1800, 22" D., 18" W., 36" H.
..................................$600.00

(A-VA. '76) *Laws*
Chippendale Sofa, Mahogany, 18th C., Camel
Back W/Semi-Rolled Arms, Box Stretcher
Base Connecting 6 Straight Legs, Recently
Upholstered, Ca. 1780, 28" D., 52" L., 44" H.
..................................$1,000.00

(A-VA. '76) *Laws*
Empire Sofa, Duncan Phyfe Style, Single Board
Carved Crest; Cornucopia Legs Terminate In
Brass Claws & Rest On Brass Casters, 97" L.,
Ca. 1800-20 ....$650.00

(A-MA. '75)   *Richard A. Bourne Co. Inc.*
Chippendale Sofa, English 18th C., Oversized, Old Sculptured Upholstery Badly Worn, Frame Intact, Approx. 8' L. $2200.00

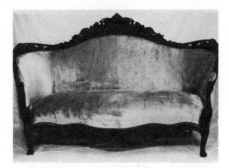

(A-PA. '76)   *Pennypacker Auction Centre*
Victorian Sofa, Hand Carved $9000.00

(A-PA. '76)   *Pennypacker Auction Centre*
Victorian Sofa, Hand Carved Back . . .$425.00

(A-OH. '76)   *Garth's Auctions, Inc.*
Federal Sofa, Mahogany, Grape Vine Carving, Upholstered in Yellow Floral Brocade, by Samuel McIntire, Salem, 82" L. $2100.00

(A-MA. '76)   *Richard A. Bourne Co. Inc.*
Empire Chaise Lounge, Mahogany, Carved Swans' Heads, Old Upholstery Worn Out, Approx. 6' Overall, ...$350.00

(A-VA. '76)   *Laws*
Chippendale Sofa, Camel Back, Fruit & Flower Scrolled Arms, Gradooned Skirt Rests On Ball & Claw Feet W/Acanthus Leaf Carved Knees 86" L., 36" D., 35" H. $350.00

(A-VA. '76)   *Laws*
Federal Sofa, Ca. 1810-20, Baltimore Origin, Legs Terminate In Heavy Brass Ball & Claw Feet W/Casters, 90" L., 34" H., 23" D.$475.00

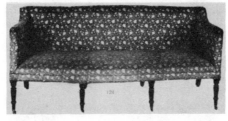

(A-VA. '76)   *Laws*
Sheraton Sofa W/Reeded Legs Retaining Orig. Brass Tips & Casters, Ca. 1800, 29" D., 75" L., 34" H. $750.00

(A-VA. '76)   *Laws*
Transitional Settee W/Chippendale Three Carved Crest Over Ribbon Backs, Scrolled Arms Rest On Cabriole Legs Ending In Padded Feet, 56" L., 40" H., 24" D. $500.00

(A-MA. '76)   *Richard A. Bourne Co. Inc.*
Victorian Lady's Chair, Finger Carved Rosewood Frame, Gold Upholstery $100.00
Victorian Sofa, Finger Carved Walnut Frame, Blue Velvet Upholstery, 69½" L. $300.00
Victorian Gentleman's Armchair, Finger Carving & Stylized Crest In Back, Walnut Frame, Minor Mars & Scratches To Finish, Upholstery Faded, Needs Replacing $135.00

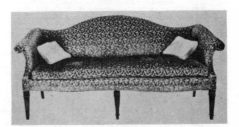

(A-VA. '76)   *Laws*
Transitional Sofa, Camel Back, Serpentine Front Rolled Arms, Blocked Legs, Down Filled Cushions, 90" L., 34" H., 23" D. $475.00

(A-PA. '75)   *Pennypacker Auction Centre*
Windsor Arm Chair, Tall $1600.00

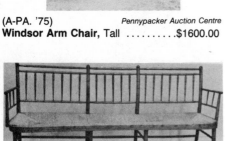

(A-OH. '77)   *Garth's Auctions, Inc.*
Sheraton Settee, Ring Turned Legs, Orig. Drk. Graining Over Red Ground, Gold Striping & Floral Stenciling, Cane Seat, 74" L. .$675.00

(A-VA. '76)   *Laws*
Maple Comb-Back Windsor Settee, Sgn. "Wallace Nutting." 18" D., 42" H., 84" L. $2,000.00

(A-MA. '77)   *Richard A. Bourne Co., Inc.*
(Left to Right)
Windsor Armchair, Early 19th C., Arrowback, Bamboo Turnings, Retains Most Orig. Paint $90.00
Windsor Side Chair, Early 19th C., Step-Down Style Back, In-The-Rough, Good Structural Cond., Old Black Paint Flaking $90.00
Windsor Youth Chair, Early 19th C., Arrowback Style, Wide Splayed Legs, Bamboo Turnings, Front Stretcher Missing, Seat Spliced W/2 Old Butterfly Insets, Retains Orig. Paint $90.00

(A-VA. '76)   *Laws*
Windsor Armchair, Butterfly, Birdcage, Maple & Hickory, 7-Spindle Back, Shaped Seat, Bamboo Turned Legs, Ca. 1800-20, 21" D., 20" W., 32" H. $375.00

(A-VA. '76)   *Laws*
Stepdown Windsor Side Chairs, Set of 6 W/Shaped Top Crests, Scooped Single Board Seats, Bamboo Turned Legs, Ca. 1800, 40" H. $375.00

(A-VA. '76)   *Laws*
Four Matching Windsor Brace-Back Side Chairs, Shaped Saddle Seats Sgn. "Wallace Nutting" $1,000.00

(A-VA. '76)   *Laws*
Birdcage Windsor Side Chairs, (Set Of 4), Maple & Pine, Shaped Seats, Bamboo Turned Legs, Ca. 1800 ....$675.00

(A-VA. '76)   *Laws*
Combed Fan-Back Windsor Chairs, Sgn. "Wallace Nutting", 46" H., Pair $800.00

(A-VA. '76)   *Laws*
Windsor Armchair, Maple & Ash, Saddle Shaped Seat, Bamboo Turned Legs & Stretchers, Signed On Bottom, "W. D. Allen", Ca. 1800, 22" D., 22" W., 36" H. $600.00

(A-VA. '77)   *Laws*
Connecticut Bannister Back Side Chair, 18th C., Scalloped & Arched Crest, 4 Reverse Turned Bannisters & Supported By Twin Acorn Finial Top Bannistered Side Supports, Reeded Seat, Bulbous Front Stretcher, Orig. Cond., Ca. 1720-40, 13" D., 20" W., 46" H. $550.00

(D-IL. '76)
Late Victorian Side Chair, (One Of 6), Refinished, Set $200.00

(A-PA. '76) *Pennypacker Auction Centre*
Half Spindle Side Chairs, Set of 6, Redecor. In Brown W/Fruit Stenciling $240.00

(A-PA. '75)
Pennypacker Auction Centre
(Left)
Arrow Back Side Chair, Cornucopia Decor., Yellow Background $350.00
(Right)
Arrow Back High Chair, Reddish Graining W/Green, Yellow, White & Red Paint, Decor. Is Late $300.00

(A-OH. '75)
Garth's Auctions, Inc.

(A-PA. '76) *Pennypacker Auction Centre*
Bent Arrow Back Chairs, Set of 6, Painted Graining Decor., Top Rail W/6½" Ovals Painted W/Early Buildings $1980.00

(A-PA. '75) *Pennypacker Auction Centre*
Settee, Decor. W/Cream Yellow Background $625.00

(A-PA. '75) *Pennypacker Auction Centre*
Mammy's Bench $275.00

(A-OH. '76) *Garth's Auctions, Inc.*
Painted Settee, Shaped Crest, Old Repaint Is Green W/Stenciled & Free Hand Fruit & Foliage, Some Repair & 2 Spindles Replaced, 71" L. $375.00

(D-NE. '76)
Hitchcock-Type Chair, One of 4 Matching, Orig. Black Finish W/Gold Stencil Decor. $300.00

(A-PA. '76) *Pennypacker Auction Centre*
Wagon Seat, Early Paint, Orig. Splat Seat, Pa., 18th C. $525.00

(A-MA. '76) *Richard A. Bourne Co. Inc.*
(Left to Right)
Windsor Bow Back Arm Chair, 18th C., Arms Terminate in Form of Human Hands, Sm. Break Extreme Left of Bow Back Repaired .. $700.00

Windsor Comb Back Arm Chair, Early 19th C., Scrolled Chestnut Arms, Refinished ...$350.00
Ladder Back Arm Chair, Fruit & Other Woods, Arms In Form Of Captain's Chair Set Between Lower Two Slats, Splint Seat, Finish Worn Around Legs & Rungs $100.00

(A-MA. '76) *Richard A. Bourne Co. Inc.*
(Left to Right)
Salem Rocker, Amer., 19th C., Restored & Redecorated $135.00
Victorian Lincoln Rocker, Cane Seat & Back. $145.00
Windsor Arrow Back Rocker, Midwestern, Early 19th C., Arms Made of Variety of Hardwoods, Refinished & Restored $200.00

(A-PA. '76) (A-PA. '75)
(Left) *Pennypacker Auction Centre*
Windsor Bow Back Chair, Saddle Seat $130.00
(Right)
Bow Back Windsor Chair, Orig. Black Paint $150.00

(A-PA. '76) (D-CT. '76)
Pennypacker Auction Centre
(Left)
Windsor Semi Comb Back Rocker, Refinished $100.00
(Right)
Hoop-Back Windsor Chair, Hickory, Pine & Maple, Ca. 1780 .... $750.00

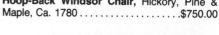

(A-OH. '76) *Garth's Auctions, Inc.*
Windsor Writing Arm Chair, Refinished W/Traces of Old Red, Replaced Drawer Under Writing Arm $2000.00

(A-PA. '75)   *Pennypacker Auction Centre*

(Left)
Moravian Plank (Peasant) Chair, Walnut, Ca. 1750-1760 ....$450.00

(Right)
Moravian Plank (Peasant) Chair, Cherry, Ca. 1750-1760, All Orig. $325.00

(A-PA. '76)   *Pennypacker Auction Centre*

(Left)
Foot Stool, Scalloped Base $37.50
Slat-Back Arm Chair, Repaired Feet .$250.00
.....................................$250.00

(Right)
Slat-Back Arm Chair $1500.00

(D-N.Y. '76)
Slat-Back Chair, Maple, Pa. Ca. 1790, Orig. Rush Seat, Refinished $225.00

(D-PA. '76)
Child's Chair, Pa. Dutch, Decorated, 18½" H., Dated 1899 .... $165.00

(A-VA. '76)   *Laws*
Wallace Nutting Pilgrim Style Armchair, Pine, Wing Back, Lift Seat, Signed & Labeled, 19" D., 24" W., 47" H. $300.00

(Right)
(A-PA. '75)   *Pennypacker Auction Centre*
Child's Potty Rocker Wing Chair, 18th C., Mahogany $325.00

(D-OH. '76)
Child's Carriage Chair, Converts to High Chair, Oak W/Carved Back, Metal Rollers ...$190.00

(D-CA. '76)
Organ Stool, Oak, Swivel Top $175.00

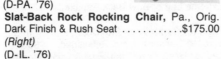

(Left)
(D-PA. '76)
Slat-Back Rock Rocking Chair, Pa., Orig. Dark Finish & Rush Seat $175.00
(Right)
(D-IL. '76)
Slat-Back Side Chair, Pa. Origin, W/Turned Finials, Bold Bulbous Front Stretcher; Orig. Untouched Condition $450.00

(D-MO. '76)   (D-OH. '76)

(Left)
Cherry Rocker, Refinished, Ca. 1897 $125.00

(Right)
Platform Rocker, Refinished $175.00

(D-KS. '76)
Oak Rocker, Pressed Back, Ca. 1900 $150.00

(A-PA. '75)   *Pennypacker Auction Centre*
Child's "Rustic" Rocking Chair, 16" W., 25" D., 25½" H. $40.00

(A-PA. '76)   *Pennypacker Auction Centre*
Hitchcock Type Chairs, Set of 6, Rush Seats, Pin Striping, Flower Decor., Ca. 1850 (2 Pictured) $720.00

(Left to Right)
Custom Georgian-Style Mahogany Dining Room Chairs, (2 Of 6), 2 Arm & 4 Side Chairs, Seats Upholstered In Red Leather, Seats Show Some Slight Wear \$650.00
Sheraton Mahogany Waiter On Stand, English, Ca. 1800, Oblong Tray W/Semi-circular Front Section, Fitted W/Brass Gallery, Turned Splayed Legs, Original, Unrestored, Cigarette Burns On Finish In Curved End .....
..................................\$400.00

Celestial & Terrestial Globes, Pr., Franklin Globe Co., Troy, N.Y., 19th C., Fitted To Cast Metal Bases, Diam. Of Globes 12", Overall Ht. 18" \$450.00
Queen Anne Walnut Tea Table, Amer., Ca. 1740-1760, Recent Blocking Between Top & Skirt, Retains Most Of Orig. Corner Blocks Behind Legs, 25" L., 15½" W., 25" H. \$2,100.00
Fan Back Windsor Side Chair, New England, 18th C., Orig. Black Painted Finish W/Gilt Highlighting & Date 1798 On Yoke \$475.00

(Left to Right)
Custom Louis XVI Style Armchairs, Pr., French, Late 19th Or Early 20th C., Upholstered In Floral Damask W/Painted Frames, Upholstery Like New, Painted Frames Flaking Considerably, 32" Overall Width, Inside Seat Width 25" \$800.00
French Directoire Tilt-Top Candlestand, 19th C., Flat Tripod Base, Fluted Stem, Marble Top W/Brass Gallery, 2 Minor Dents In Brass Gallery, Diam. Of Top: 20", Overall Height 27" \$125.00

(Left to Right)
Victorian Captian Style Arm Chairs, Set Of Four, Amer., 19th C., Oak, 1 Chair W/Handhold In Crest, Other 3 W/Solid Curved Backs, Leg Of 1 Chair Is Split (1 Illus.) \$100.00
Victorian Windsor Style Bow-Back Arm Chair, Amer., 19th C., Hardwoods, Needlework Cushion
....\$60.00
Victorian Windsor Style Bow-Back Arm Chair, Amer., 19th C., Maple & Hardwoods, Bentwood Arms & Back, Needlework Cushion \$60.00

(Left to Right)
Late Victorian Savonarola Style Armchair, W/Carved Gryphons In Back Splat & Demons' Heads Carved On Arms & Back Posts, Feet Carved In Shape Of Paws, Old Velvet Upholstered Seat, Orig. Finish Crazed & Worn .....
....\$100.00
Oak Secretary Bookcase, Late 19th C., Left Side Has Bowed Glass Door, Beveled Glass Mirror W/Shelf Above, Retains Orig. Finish, 38" W., 13" D., 68" H. \$140.00
Victorian Lady's Chair, Mid 19th C., Finger Carvings W/Rosetted Knees, Scrolled Skirt & Rococo Scrolled Crest, Unrestored, Frame Has 2 Breaks Which Are Clean & Repairable .....
....\$120.00

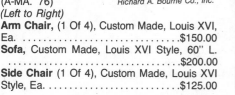

(Left to Right)
Arm Chair, (1 Of 4), Custom Made, Louis XVI, Ea. \$150.00
Sofa, Custom Made, Louis XVI Style, 60" L.
.................................\$200.00
Side Chair (1 Of 4), Custom Made, Louis XVI Style, Ea. \$125.00

(A-MA. '76)   *Richard A. Bourne Co. Inc.*
(Left to Right)
Windsor Cage-Back Side Chairs, Pr., Amer., Early 19th C., In-The-Rough, Needs Restoration (One Illus.) $200.00
Bannister Back Arm Chair, Amer., Early 18th C., Refinished in Natural Wood, Replaced Rush Seat $600.00
Fruitwood Side Chairs, Set of 6, Amer., 19th C., Signed "Made by Philip Drum in Bethel, O" (Ohio), Dated 1847, Refinished, (One Illus.) $400.00

(D-KS. '76)
Oak Office Chair, Saddle Seat $65.00

(D-KS. '76)
Pattern Back Chair, Oak, (1 of 6), Refinished, Set $350.00

(D-OH. '76)
Oak Chair (1 of 6), Orig. Finish Good, Set $120.00

(D-MO. '76)
Pattern Back Rocker, Oak, Orig. Finish $65.00

(D-KS. '76)
Pattern Back Rocker, Oak, New Seat, Refinished $90.00

(D-MO. '76)
Wicker Rocker, Orig. Shellac Finish . . .$35.00

(D-CA. '76)
Wicker Rocker, Shellac Finish Quite Worn $125.00

(D-KY. '76)
Wicker Rocker, Painted White $165.00

(D-CO. '76)
Oak High Chair, Press Back, Cane Seat $90.00

(D-MO. '76)
Oak Carriage Chair W/Press Back, Metal Wheels, Converts To Stroller, Refinished $165.00

(D-N.Y. '76)
Wicker High Chair, Orig. Shellac Finish $175.00

(A-MA. '76)　　　　　Richard A. Bourne Co. Inc.

Sheraton Mahogany Swell-Front Chest Of Drawers, Attrib. To McIntires Of Salem, Mass., Ovolu Top, McIntire Cornucopia Carvings, Top Has Lge. Split, Left Rear Foot Has Chip On Inner Part Of Turning, Left Front Leg Repaired, 44" L., 22½" W., 39" H. $450.00

(A-MA. '76)　　　　　Richard A. Bourne Co. Inc.

Hepplewhite Chest Of Drawers, Amer., 18th C., Birch, Inlaid Escutcheons, Replaced Hdwe., Refinished, 40¾" At Waist $375.00

(A-MA. '76)　　　　　Richard A. Bourne Co. Inc.

Hepplewhite Swell-Front Chest Of Drawers, Mahogany, Amer., Late 18th C., Hdwe. Probably Period Replacement Of Orig., 41" L., 23" D., 37" H. $700.00

(A-VA. '76)　　　　　Laws

Chippendale Ox-Bow Chest Of Drawers, 18th C., (Probably Charlestown, Mass.), Blocked Ends, Molded Top W/Generous Overhang, Orig. Bold Brass Pulls, Carved Ball & Claw Feet, Ca. 1770, 33" H., Case - 36½" W., 22" D. .....
.................................$6,000.00

(A-VA. '76)　　　　　Laws

Sheraton Bow Front Chest of Drawers, American, Mahogany, 4 Drawers W/Figured Veneer Facings, Cock-Beaded Moldings, Brass Bail Pulls, Swell-Top Offset W/Porringer Corners Beneath Which Are Three-Quarter Round Rope Twist Pilasters, Turned Legs W/Scrolled Skirts Between, Ca. 1800-20, 18" D., 38" W., 38" H.
.................................$625.00

(A-PA. '76)　　　　　Frank Roan III

Victorian East Lake Chest Of Drawers, Veneered, Brass Hdwe. $175.00

(A-MA. '77)　　　　　Richard A. Bourne Co., Inc.

Chippendale Maple Chest Of Drawers, 18th C., Select Tiger-Striped Maple Drawer Fronts & Sides, Flat Brcket Base, Molded Top, Old Refinishing In Natural Wood, Retains Orig. Bail Brasses, Length At Waist, 36¼", 17¾" D., 56¾" H. $2,900.00

(A-VA. '77)　　　　　Laws

Striped Tiger Maple Chest Of Drawers, 18th C., 4 Graduated Thumbnail Molded Drawers, Chippendale Cutout Bracket Feet, Ca. 1760-80, 19" D., 38" W., 41" H. $650.00

(A - MA. '76)　　　　　Richard A. Bourne Co., Inc.

Empire Gentleman's Chest Of Drawers, Amer. 19th C., Paneled Cherry Sides & Tiger Maple Facing, Maple Top, Top Drawer Ogee Molded, Legs W/Sleigh Scrolls, 41⅜" L. $400.00

(A-OH. '76)   *Garth's Auctions, Inc.*
Chippendale Chest of Drawers, Philadelphia
Walnut, Some Restoration Incl. Brasses, Tall
. . . .$825.00

(A-OH. '76)   *Garth's Auctions, Inc.*
Chippendale Block Front, Mahogany, Re-
placed Brasses, 35¼" W., 20½" D., 31" H.
. . . .$24,500.00
Brass Q. A. Candlesticks, Pr., 7¼" H.$475.00
Brass Taper Jack, Cast & Engraved Detail, 18th
C., 6¼" H. $525.00

(A-PA. '75)   *Pennypacker Auction Centre*
Chippendale Chest Of Drawers, Red Walnut,
Chester County, Restored Feet;1770 $1450.00

(A-MA. '75)   *Richard A. Bourne Co. Inc.*
Chippendale Oxbow Chest Of Drawers, Mahogany, Amer. 19th C., Replaced Right Front &
Right Rear Legs, 39" Length At Waist, 21" D.,
31" H. $2100.00

(A-PA. '76)   *Pennypacker Auction Centre*
Chippendale High Chest of Drawers, Walnut,
York County, Quarter Fluted Corners, New Wil-
low Brasses, Some Restoration, 8½" H. . . . . . .
. . . . $1350.00

(A-PA. '76)   *Pennypacker Auction Centre*
Chippendale Chest Of Drawers, Walnut, Willow Brasses, 65" H., 41" W., 22" D. $2500.00

(A-OH. '76)   *Garth's Auctions, Inc.*
Queen Anne Highboy, Walnut, Massachusetts,
Dovetailed Overlapping Drawers, Good Patina,
37½" W., 21½" D., 71" H. $12250.00

(A-MA. '76)   *Richard A. Bourne Co. Inc.*
Queen Anne Highboy, New England, 18th C.,
Cherry, Minor Restoration to Sub-Parts of Draw-
ers, 34" W., 19" D., 70" H. $1400.00

(A-OH. '76)   Garth's Auctions, Inc.

Queen Anne Highboy, Butternut W/Alligatored Varnish, Overlapping Dovetailed Drawers, Queen Anne Brasses, Minor Repair To Drawer Overlap, 37¾'' W. (At Cornice), 18¾'' D., 68¾'' H. $4400.00

(A-MA. '76)   Richard A. Bourne Co Inc.

Queen Anne Chest On Frame, Walnut, Pa., 18th C., 4 Full Width Graduated Drawers, 2 Half Width Drawers, 3 Third Width Drawers; Sm. Area Wood Deterioration On Lower Left Corner Of Bottom Drawer, Minor Restoration Necessary 37¾'' W., 21½'' D., 71¾'' H. $4200.00

(A-PA. '75)   Pennypacker Auction Centre

High Chest Of Drawers, Cherry, Broken Arch Top, 6'3'' H., 40'' W., 21'' D. $1,600.00

(A-PA. '75)   Pennypacker Auction Centre

Queen Anne Lowboy, Cherry, New Brasses
. . . . $3100.00

← (A-VA. '76)   Laws

Queen Anne Lowboy, New England Origin, Period Brasses, 18th C., 19'' D., 30'' H., 30'' W.
. . . . $3,750.00

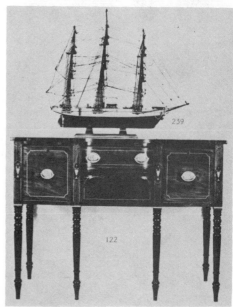

(A-VA. '76)   Laws

Three Masted Sailing Ship Model, Full Scale, Handcrafted, 36'' L., 30'' H. $170.00

Sheraton Sideboard W/Bowed Center Drawer Flanked By Two Large Drawers W/Cockbeading, Oval Brasses, Fine Light Line Inlay, Orig. Finish, Ca. 1800, 36'' H., 49'' W. $1,450.00

(A-PA. '75)   Pennypacker Auction Centre

Sheraton Sideboard, English, Late 18th C., Mahogany, Full-Depth Drawer Either End & 2 Half-Width Drawers In Center, Curly Satinwood Inlays, 52¼'' W., 23'' D., 35½'' H. . . . . . .
. . . . $950.00

(A-MA. '76)   Richard A. Bourne Co. Inc.

Victorian Walnut Bureau, Amer., 19th C., Burled Grain Walnut, 2 Sm. Box Drawers Above, Sm. Inset White Vermont Marble Top, 40'' L., 77'' H. Incl. Mirror $275.00

Victorian Walnut Commode, Amer., 19th C., 2 Paneled Doors Below W/Single Shelf Inside; Drawer W/Carved Fruit Handles, Pull-Out Towel Rod On Right Side; White Vermont Marble Top W/Backsplash & 2 Sm. Attached Marble Shelves Marble Has Slight Discoloration, 29'' L. $275.00

(D-KA. '76)
Mennonite Wardrobe, Pine W/Grained Finish In Imitation Of Oak, Cherry Trim, Breaks Down Into 15 Parts, 18" D., 47½" W., 77½" H.$650.00

(A-OH. '76)   *Garth's Auctions, Inc.*
Decorated Kas, Poplar Wood, Red Hearts & Flowers On Door Panels & "Elizabeth Hossteter 1846" Over The Doors. All Orig. W/Keys, 73" W., 20" D., 79" H. $4500.00

(A-PA. '75)   *Pennypacker Auction Centre*
Mahogany Chest Of Drawers, 37½" W., 36½" H., 19½" D. . . . .

(A- MA. '76)   *Richard A. Bourne Co., Inc.*
Louis XV Armoire, Walnut W/Two Carved Paneled Doors, Floral Carving Above Arch. Adjustable Shelves, 19th C.; 41½" W., 18" D., 7' H. $400.00

(A-VA. '77)   *Laws*
Pennsylvania Dutch Wardrobe, Overall Framed Floral Motif In The Orig. Paint, Marked M.L., 1846, Interior Has 5 Storage Comp. & 3 Drawers, 19" D., 46" W., 70" H. . .$1,000.00

(A-MA. '76)   *Richard A. Bourne Co. Inc.*
Sheraton Chest Of Drawers, Amer., Early 19th C., Birdseye Maple Drawers W/Pine Sides & Top, Spool Front Posts, Hdwe. Old But Not Orig., Refinished, 1 Escutcheon Missing, Slight Marring On Front Top Edge, 36" W. At Waist. $200.00

(A-VA. 77)   *Laws*
Chippendale Spice Chest, 18th C., Walnut, Dovetailed, Top W/Single Tombstone Carved Shaped Paneled Door, Interior W/11 Drawers, Top Interior Drawer Pulls Out From Rear For Secret Compartment Release, Chippendale Bracket Feet, 12" D., 19" W., 23" H. $1,900.00

(A-PA. '76)   *Pennypacker Auction Centre*
Chest of Drawers, Softwood, Orig. Decor., Early Berks Co., Ca. 1810 . . . . $1300.00

(A-PA. '76)   *Pennypacker Auction Centre*
Blanket Chest, Soft Wood, Green & Red Decor.,
Willow Brasses, Dated 1796 & Name $700.00

(A-PA. '76)   *Pennypacker Auction Centre*
Chest of Drawers, Hand Planed & Dovetailed
Const., Painted To Simulate Graining, Berks
Co., Ca. 1850 .... $250.00

Pennypacker Auction Centre
Chippendale Chest of Drawers, Pa., Cherry,
Fluted Quarter Columns, Ogee Feet W/Some
Restoration ....(A-PA. '76) $1700.00

(A-PA. '75)   *Pennypacker Auction Centre*
Dower Chest, Walnut, Sulphur Inlay W/Initials,
"M.K. 1765", Orig. Hdwe., Dovetailed $1500.00

(A-OH. '76)   *Garth's Auctions, Inc.*
Pennsylvania High Chest of Drawers, Walnut,
Dovetailed Cockbeaded Drawers, Fluted Quarter Columns, All Orig. Incl. Oval Acorn Brasses,
42" W., 20½" D., 63" H. $3100.00

Richard A. Bourne Co. Inc.
Chippendale Chest of Drawers, Curly Maple &
Maple, Amer., 18th C., Refinished, Hdwe. Is
Replacement, 35" W., 17¾" D., 59¾" H. ......
                              (A-MA. '76) $1500.00

(A-PA. '75)   *Pennypacker Auction Centre*
Pine Blanket Chest, Smoke Grained, 3' L. ...
.... $190.00
Stoneware Crock, Blue Decor., #3 Size .....
.... $35.00

(A-PA. '75)   *Pennypacker Auction Centre*
Blanket Chest, Orange, Yellow, Brown & Black
Decor., 26" H., 23" D., 49" W.......... $300.00
Applebutter Crock, Blue Decor., Lid Has Crack,
11" $45.00

(A-MA. '76)   *Richard A. Bourne Co., Inc.*
Pine Sea Chest, Amer., 19th C., Dovetailed,
W/Till Box Inside & Iron Bail Handles At Sides,
36¼" L. $100.00
Pine Blanket Chest, 18th C., W/Till, Flat
Bracket Base, 43½" L. $200.00

Pennypacker Auction Centre
Chippendale Highboy, 2-Pc., Curly Walnut,
Willow Brasses ....(A-PA. '76) $3,500.00

(A-PA. '75)   *Pennypacker Auction Centre*
Blanket Chest, Dated 1822 .... $325.00

(A-VA. '76)   *Laws*
Brass Rocking Cradle, Numerous Turned
Posts & Adjustable Canopy Hook, 22" W., 48" L.,
82" H. $450.00

(A-PA. '76)   *Frank Roan III*
Victorian Walnut Bed $125.00

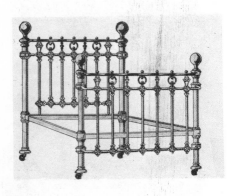

(D-CO. '76)
Brass Bed $550.00

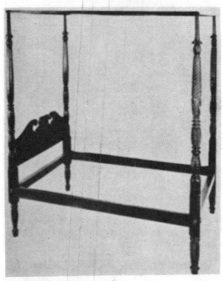

(A-VA. '76)   *Laws*
Mahogany Tester Bed W/Canopy Frame.
Posts Have Boldly Carved Acanthus Leaf,
Pineapple & Rope Twist Turnings; Matching
Foot Posts, Scrolled Headboard, Full Size,
Ca. 1800, 80" H. $300.00

(A-VA. '76)   *Laws*
Southern Cellarette, Walnut, Lift Top On Short
Tapering Legs, Single Drawer WBail Handle, Ca.
1800, 16" D., 21" W., 25½" H. $400.00

(A-VA. '76)   *Laws*
Mahogany Cellerette, 18th C. W/Molded
Bracket Base; Retains Partial Lead Liner, Ca.
1790; 17" D., 20" H., 27" W. $525.00

(D-CO. '76)
Pine Blanket Chest, Oak Grained, Hand
Wrought Hdwe., 15½" H., 18" D., 23½" L. . . . .
. . . .$150.00

(A-VA. '76)   *Laws*
Dower Chest, 18th C., Decorated, Red Paint,
3 Tulip-And-Heart Panels On Top, Again On
Front & In Oval Floral Panels On Sides; Red,
Sepia & Yellow Against Drk. Green Ground
Enhanced W/Yellow Lines, Orig. Heart-Shaped
Strap Hinges & Grab Lock, 24" D., 50" L., 20" H.
. . . .$700.00

(D-PA. '76)
Dower Chest, Dovetailed Case, Oak Grained
Finish Ex., Drawer Fronts Of Cherry, Lift-Top
Till, Sgn. In Pencil On Underside Of Chest Board
"Wm. H. Noles, Lebanon Co. Penn., 1828" . . .
. . . .$650.00

(A-VA. '76)   *Laws*
Dower Chest, Dovetailed Case, Orig. Brasses,
Bracket Feet, Lift-Top Till, Hudson River Valley
Origin, 45" W. $800.00

(A-PA. '76)   *Pennypacker Auction Centre*
Lift Top Chest, New England, Decor. In Colors;
Sheaf Of Wheat & 2 Corn Stalks, Scalloped
Apron & Brass Knobs $1900.00

(D-MA. '76)
Sea Captain's Chest, 2 pc., Pine, Dovetailed
Frame & Drawers, Secret Compartment, 35" H.,
Base 17½" D., 38" L. $1500.00

(A-PA. '75)   *Pennypacker Auction Centre*
Empire Chest of Drawers, ... $180.00

(A-PA. '76)   *Pennypacker Auction Centre*
Wood Chest, Pine, Double Lid $130.00

(A-OH. '76)   *Garth's Auctions, Inc.*
Blanket Chest on Chest, Pine, Dovetailed Con-
struction, Beaded Drawers, Till & Iron Strap
Hinges, Inside Lined W/Newspaper Pages "The
Durham Chronicle, Friday, October 11, 1850",
Grained W/Red Over Yellow Ground, 41" W.,
22" D., 46" H. $325.00

(A-PA. '76)   *Pennypacker Auction Centre*
Dower Chest, Arch Panels W/Pots Of Tulips &
Leaf Decor., Decor. Tulip Drawers, Strap Hinges,
Jaw Lock, Repaired Drawers $1100.00

(A-PA. '76)   *Pennypacker Auction Centre*
Blanket Chest, Salmon Background W/Brown
Decor. Bedminster, Bucks Co., 19th C. $250.00

(A-PA. '76)   *Pennypacker Auction Centre*
Blanket Chest, Salmon W/Black Simulated
Graining & Lge. Black Four-Pointed Stars, Berks
County $525.00

(A-PA. '76)   *Pennypacker Auction Centre*
Blanket Chest, Pa., Strap Hinges, Iron Clasp,
Stylized Graining Incl. Date "1816" . . $800.00

(A-PA. '76)   *Pennypacker Auction Centre*
Blanket Chest, Square Sunken Panels Decor.
W/Pot Of Flowers, Initialed & Dated, "G.J.B.
1835" $3100.00

(A-PA. '75)   *Pennypacker Auction Centre*
Blanket Chest, 17½" D., 21" H., 37" L. $100.00
Red Pottery Flower Pot, 6¼" $50.00

(A-PA. '76)   *Pennypacker Auction Centre*
Blanket Chest, Pa. Dutch, Painted Graining of
Orange & Black, Till & Drawer, Strap Hinges,
Engraved Lock $850.00

(A-PA. '75)   *Pennypacker Auction Centre*
Blanket Chest $480.00

(A-MA. '76)   *Richard A. Bourne Co. Inc.*

Hutch Cupboard, Pine, New Doors & Drawers, Old Finish Stained & Worn, 48½" L., 17½" D., 72" H. $225.00

(A-PA. '76)   *Pennypacker Auction Centre*

Queen Anne Corner Cupboard, American Walnut, 2-Pc., H Hinges, Scalloped Shelves, Molded Broken Arch Top $2700.00

(A-PA. '75)   *Pennypacker Auction Centre*

Wall Cupboard, Pine, Panels & Sides Decor. W/Fern Like Motif, 4" W., 6½' H. $330.00

(A-VA. '76)   *Laws*

Chippendale Glass-Faced Corner Cupboard, Cherry, 18th C., Ca. 1780-1800, 90" H. $1,900.00

(A-PA. '76)   *Pennypacker Auction Centre*

Walnut Cupboard, 2-Pc., Spoon & Plate Rack & Candle Drawers, Rattail Hinges, Lancaster Co., Ca. 1800 . . . . $2600.00

(A-PA. '76)   *Pennypacker Auction Centre*

Welsh Cupboard, Pine, 1-Pc., Red Paint, H Hinges, 26" W., 22" D., 5'8" H. $160.00

(A-OH. '76)   Garth's Auctions, Inc.

Wall Cupboard, Poplar, 2-Pc., Dovetailed Constr., Brown Graining, Orig. Hdwe. On Top Doors, Rest Has Been Replaced, 48" W., 18½" D., 81" H. $435.00

(D-MO. '76)
Oak Cabinet, Kitchen, Frosted Glass In Doors, Refinished $550.00

(A-VA. '77)   Laws
Pine Step-Back Cupboard, Ca. 1840, 19" D., 40" W., 72" H. $275.00

(D-KS. '76)
Hanging Oak Water Fountain, Metal Liner in Top, Brass Spigot, 28" H., 12" W. $125.00

(A-PA. '75)   Pennypacker Auction Centre

Corner Cupboard, Polychrome Paint In Yellow, Orange & Green, 7'1" H. $575.00

(A-OH. '76)   Garth's Auctions, Inc.
Architectural Corner Cupboard, 1-Pc., Dovetailed Drawer, Old Glass, Orig. Red & Yellow Paint, Feet Restored, 53½" W., 24½" D., 7' H. $2100.00

(A-PA. '75)   Pennypacker Auction Centre
Corner Cupboard, Lancaster Co. Pa. $1250.00
Bowl, Wooden, Orig. Red Paint, 23" D. $115.00

(A-VA. '77)   *Laws*
Step-Back Cupboard, Walnut, 2-Pc., Molded
Crown Above 2 Double Paneled Doors, Bottom
Case W/Molded Single Board Top, 2 Drawers
& Cabinet Doors, Ca. 1820, 19" D., 52" W.,
92" H. $400.00

(A-OH. '76)   *Garth's Auctions, Inc.*
Corner Cupboard,2-Pc., Turned Feet, 2 Pan-
eled Doors & 3 Dovetailed Drawers, Top W/Sin-
gle Door W/9 Panes & 2 Scalloped Shelves,
Poplar W/Reddish Brown Flame Graining &
Orig. Porcelain Knobs, Attrib. To Rupp, York,
Pa., 47" W., 24" D., 86" H. $1,300.00

(A-MA. '76)   *Richard A. Bourne Co. Inc.*
Corner Cupboard, Pine, Amer., 19th C., 2 Parts,
Lower Part W/2 Paneled Doors & 2 Shelves,
Upper Part W/2 Glazed Doors & 2 Shelves,
48½" W., 25½" D., 75½" H. $225.00

(A-VA. '76)   *Laws* ➡
Dough Trough, Pine, Dovetailed, 17" D.,
37" W., 30" H. $250.00

(A-MA. '76)   *Richard A. Bourne Co. Inc.*
Pie Safe, Maple, Amer. 19th c., Pierced Tin
Paneling, 3 Pine Shelves, Refinished 40¼" W.,
16" D., 57⅝" H. $275.00

(D-N.Y. '76)
Pine Dry Sink W/Copper Liner; Hdwe. Not
The Orig.; 5½' L., 48" H. $600.00

(A-MA. '76)   *Richard A. Bourne Co. Inc.*
Fruitwood Kitchen Cupboard, Amer., 19th
C., 1-Pc. Const., Upper Sect. W/2 Shelves, 2
Doors W/Pierced Tin Panels, Matching Panels
Each Side, 37" L., 60½" D., 68" H. . . .$250.00

(A-MA. '76)   *Richard A. Bourne Co. Inc.*
Open Faced Cupboard, Amer. 19th C., Pine, Folk Art Decor. W/Carved Eagles In Ea. Door Panel, Across Drawers & Forming Crest Across Top, Joined Disc Molding At Sides, 36½" W., 17" D., 71" H. $150.00

(A-PA. '76)   *Pennypacker Auction Centre*
Open Welsh Cupboard, New England, Pine, 3-Board, Graduated Shelves On Top, Ca. 1760, Refinished $750.00

(A-OH. '76)   *Garth's Auctions, Inc.*
Wall Cupboard, Pa., 2-Pc., Dovetailed Overlapping Drawers, Chamfered Lamb's Tongue Corners W/Reeded & Crown Molded Cornice, Reddish Brown Graining W/Beading Picked Out In Drk. Green, Replaced Door Latches, Outer Bracket Of Back Feet Restored, 50" W., 19" D., 86½" H. $7700.00

(D-PA. '76)
Step-Back Wall Cupboard, Pine, 73" H., 47" W., 20" D. $650.00

(A-MA. '76)   *Richard A. Bourne Co. Inc.*
Closed-Face Cupboard, Cherry, Midwestern, Early 19th C., Lower Section W/Paneled Doors Enclosing Lg. Cupboard W/Mid-Shelf, Above Which Is Slide-Out Shelf & 3 Sm. Drawers; Upper Cupboard W/Paneled Doors Enclosing 3 Shelves W/Plate Rails, Refinished, 41" L., 19" D., 82" H. $950.00

(D-PA. '76)
Pennsylvania Dutch Pine Cupboard, 2-Part, Original Glass Panes, 46" W., 7½ Ft. H. . . . . .
. . . .$1,200.00

(A-PA. '76)   *Pennypacker Auction Centre*
Wall Cupboard $140.00

(A-MA. '76)   *Richard A. Bourne Co. Inc.*
Open Faced Cupboard, Amer. Late 18th C.,
Pine, Normal Signs of Wear $550.00

(A-PA. '75)   *Pennypacker Auction Centre*
Chippendale Style Dutch Cupboard, Walnut,
Lge. $475.00

(D-CT. '76)
Dry Sink, Cherry, Dovetailed Drawers, 38"W..
20" D., 44" H. $850.00

(A-VA. '77)   *Laws*
Curve Back Settle, Mid 18th C., Scrolled Board
Ends, Additional Scrolling To Bottom Half Showing Away From Wall, New England Orign, 74" L.,
15" W., 60" H. $800.00

(D-OK. '76)

Amish Water Bench, Pine, 55" H., 38" W. . . . .
. . . .$650.00

(A-MA. '76)   *Richard A. Bourne Co. Inc.*
(Left to Right)
Dry Sink, Cherry, Pa., 19th C., Lower Section
W/Inner Cupboard W/Single Shelf Behind
Doors, Enclosed Recessed Top; Upper Section
W/Mid-Height Shelf & 3 Third-Width Drawers,
Refinished, 40½" W., 16" D., 56" H. . .$700.00
Sugar Chest, Cherry, Kentucky or Tennessee
Early 19th C., Top Hinged in Lge. Cupboard to
Fold Back In Half, Refinished, 30" W., 18½" D.,
35½" H. $450.00

(A-PA. '76)   *Pennypacker Auction Centre*
Pie Safe, Soft Wood, Painted Red, Tin Perforated Sides, 38" W., 48" H. $290.00

(A-PA. '76)   *Pennypacker Auction Centre*
Hanging Pie Safe, Punched Tin Decor. In Form
Of Laughing Man, Sides W/Similar Men - One
Laughing & One Frowning, Berks County . . . . .
. . . .$350.00

(D-KS.)
Pie Safe W/Pierced Tin Doors, Ca. 1850. Refinished, Poplar $195.00

(D-N.H. '76)
Hanging Wall Cupboard, Pine, New England, 4½" D., 14" W., 20" H. $290.00

(A-MA. '76)   *Richard A. Bourne Co., Inc.*
Fine Linen Press, Continental, Ca. 1800, Burled Walnut & Secondary Woods Over Oak; Two Sections, Few Minor Restorations To Veneer & Wood Necessary, 38" W., 20" D., 84" H. . . . . .
. . . .$900.00

(D-WA. '76)
Oak Spool Cabinet "Corticelli Spool Silk", 18" D., 24" H., 26" W. $300.00

(D-KS. '76)
Pine Dry Sink, 45 x 48" $450.00

(D-WI. '76)
Oak Refrigerator, Brass Hinges, Made by Challenge-Iceburg-Challenge Corn Planter Co., Grand Haven, Mich. $250.00

(D-MO. '76)
18th Century Spoon Rack, W/Candle Box & Drawer, Oak, Wax Inlay On Front, 13½" W., 28½" H. $1275.00

(D-CT. '76)
Cupboard, Pine, 3 Dovetailed Drawers, Rail Feet, 18" D., 48" L., 52" H. $550.00

(D-KS. '76)
Water Bench, Pine, Dovetailed Frame, 22" H., 28" L., 12" D. $90.00

(A-VA. '76)   *Laws*
Step-Back Cupboard, Pine & Poplar, 2-Pc., Top Case W/2 Eight Paned Doors, Bottom Case W/2 Drawers Over 2 Double Paneled Cabinet Doors, Cannonball Feet, 20" D., 53" W., 95" H. $1,000.00

(A-VA. '76) *Laws*

Chippendale Mahogany Knee-Hole Desk, 18th C., Crossband & Light Line Inlaid Molded Top, Single Top Drawer W/Central Document Drawer, Flanked By 3 Graduated Drawers, All Banded W/Line Inlay, Solid Ends & Chippendale Bracket Feet, 18" D., 34" W., 32" H. ....
...................................$1,750.00

(A-MA. '77) *Richard A. Bourne Co., Inc.*

Oak China Cabinet, Ca. 1900, Bowed Front, 3 Oak Shelves, 3-Paneled Upper Sect. W/ Beveled Leaded Clear Glass Windows In Art Nouveau Style, 20" D., 44" W., 73" H. $675.00

(A-MA. '76) *Richard A. Bourne Co. Inc.*

Victorian Walnut Dresser, Pinkish-Brown Marble Top, Burled Walnut Drawer Facing, 51¾" W., 91" H. $300.00

(A-MA. '76) *Richard A. Bourne Co., Inc.*
(Left)

Chippendale Curly Maple Chest-On-Chest, 2 Parts, Base Section W/4 Graduated Drawers & Flat Molded Top; Signed In Left Inside Of Top Drawer W/Branded Wallace Nutting Signature, Orig. & Unrestored, Width At Waist 36", 18" D., Overall, 63½" H. $1,250.00
(Right)

Chippendale-Style Curly Maple Bureau, Match To Piece On Left, Signed Inside Left Of Top Drawer W/Wallace Nutting Branded Signature, Orig. Finished Cond., 36" W., 17¾" D., 36¾" H. $700.00

Chippendale-Style Curly Maple Mirror, Fancy Carved & Gilded Tiger Maple Frame, Beveled Plate Glass Mirror, Wallace Nutting Brand Signature On Reverse Side, Orig. Cond., 42" H. ....
...................................$400.00

(A-VA. '76) *Laws*

Ornate Two-Piece China Cabinet, Mahogany, Serpentine Front, 8 Vertical Panes Of Glass Draped W/Sculpted Carving, 2 Mirror-Backed Adjustable Glass Shelves, Base W/Single Cabinet Door, 18" D., 48" W., 86" H. .$800.00

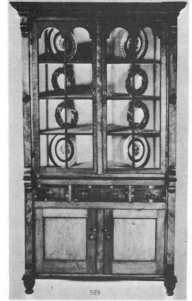

(A-VA. '77) *Laws*

Two-Piece Corner Cupboard, Cherry, Ogee Molded Top, 2 Eight-Paneled Double Doors, 1 Larger Drawer Flanked By 2 Simulated Over 2 Cabinet Doors, All W/Beaded Banding, Turned Feet, Ca. 1830, 86" H. $1,050.00

(D-MO. '76)
Corner Cupboard, Maple, Pa. Dutch, 7' H., 46" W. $2,100.00

(A-PA. '76) *Pennypacker Auction Centre*
Sleigh Seat, Softwood, Shoe Feet, Orig. Paint, ...$130.00

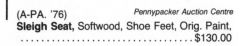

(A-OH. '76)   Garth's Auctions, Inc.
Queen Anne Desk On Frame, Cherry, Carved Flower In Drop, Dovetailed Const., Old Finish, Minor Repair, 36" W., 17" D., 42" H.; 30¼" Writing Ht., ... $5850.00

(A-MA. '76)   Richard A. Bourne Co. Inc.
Chippendale Slant-Lid Desk, Curly Maple, Amer., 18th C., Interior W/8 Drawers & 9 Pigeonholes, Refinished, Hdwe. Is Replacement, 39" L. $2200.00

(A-MA. '75)   Richard A. Bourne Co. Inc.
Chippendale Slant-Lid Desk, Attrib. to Abner Toppan, Newburyport, Mass., Last Quarter 18th C., San Domingo Mahogany W/Pine, Poplar & Cherry Secondary Woods, Interior W/6 Exposed Drawers & 3 Additional Drawers Behind A Center Ebony & Satinwood Inlaid Door, Replacement Hardware, 41½" L. $3000.00

(A-MA. '76)   Richard A. Bourne Co. Inc.
Chippendale Slant Lid Desk, Amer., Late 18th C., Cherry, Replaced Feet & Hdwe., 40½" L. . $800.00

(A-OH. '76)   Garth's Auctions, Inc.
Chippendale Desk, Curly Maple, Dovetailed Overlapping Drawers W/Orig. Brasses, Pine Interior W/Dovetailed Drawers & Pigeon Holes, Several Bails Missing, 34" W., 17" D., 29" Writing Ht. $4500.00

Laws
Queen Anne Desk, Slant-Front, Curly Maple, Writing Height 32"; 37" W., Ca. 1750-60 .... (A-VA. '76).$2,000.00

(A-PA. '76)   Pennypacker Auction Centre
Hepplewhite Slant Top Writing Desk, Mahogany, Graded Drawers, Oval Brasses, Inlaid Ivory Escutcheons, Block Chain Inlay, Interior W/Block Chain & Line Inlay, 18½" D., 37" W., 42" Overall Ht. $650.00

(A-PA. '75)   Pennypacker Auction Centre
Mahogany 3-Drawer Chest, Willow Brasses, 34½" H., 23¾" W., 17" D. $240.00

(A-MA. '76)   Richard A. Bourne Co. Inc.
Block-Front Slant-Lid Desk, Mahogany, Amer. 18th C., Flat Bracket Style Back Feet, Block & Fan Carved Lid, Interior W/8 Pigeonholes, 6 Drawers, 2 Document Drawers & Sm. Cupboard W/Fold Down Fan Carved Door, Needs Restoration, Front Legs Replacements, Block Effect Created by Applying Carved Blocks of Wood, Hdwe. Not of Period, 38" W., 19" D., 56" H. $2100.00

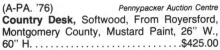

(A-PA. '76)   Pennypacker Auction Centre
Schoolmaster Desk, Pine, Early Graining, Back of Desk W/Grained American Spread Eagle $450.00

(Left)
(A-PA. '75)   Pennypacker Auction Centre
Schoolmaster's Desk, Soft Wood, 35½" H., 22" D., 24½" W. $195.00
(Right)
(A-PA. '76)   Pennypacker Auction Centre
Country Desk, Softwood, From Royersford, Montgomery County, Mustard Paint, 26" W., 60" H. $425.00

(A-PA. '76)   Pennypacker Auction Centre
Mill Desk, Decor. W/Mustard & Red Paint, ... $500.00

(A-VA. '77)   *Laws*
Mahogany Drop Panel Secretary, Interior W/
16 Molded & Sculptured Compartments; Lower
Case W/Narrow Sloped Top Framed In Satin &
Boxwood Inlay, Salem, Mass. Or Portsmouth,
New Hampshire Origin, 20" D., 41" W., 75" H.
.................................$1,900.00

(A-MA. '77)   *Richard A. Bourne Co., Inc.*
Empire Secretary, American Ca. 1820-30,
Mahogany W/Spiral-Carved Acanthus Frontal
Columns, Separate Top W/Glazed Doors In
Gothic Style, Unrestored, Retains Orig. Brass
Drawer Pulls & Hdwe., 20" D., 41½" L., 67" H.
.................................$400.00

(A-VA. '76)   *Laws*
**Chippendale Curly Maple Bonnet Top Secre-
tary Desk,** 18th C., Scrolled Bonnet Centering
A Bold Brass Finial Over Glassed Doors Reveal-
ing Several Shelves, Bottom Section W/9
Arcaded Pigeon Holes W/5 Drawers, Bold
Graining, Ca. 1780, 20" D., 36" W., 78" H. ...
.................................$3,500.00

(A-VA. '77)   *Laws*
Chippendale Knee Hole Desk, Walnut, Block
Front, Single Molded Block Board Top Over
Lge. Blocked Drawer; Central Drawer Below &
Recessed Tombstone Shaped & Shell Carved
Block Cabinet Door, Molded Cabriole Legs,
Claw & Ball Feet, 21" D., 34" W., 32½" H. ...
.................................$3,000.00
Rhode Island Block Front Bureau Mirror, Oval
Beveled Glass Mirror Framed By Mahogany
Veneer, Supported By Twin Curved Scrolled
Brackets, Drawers Supported By Ogee Bracket
Feet, Ca. 1780, 8" D., 19" L., 29" H. .$475.00

(A-VA. '77)   *Laws*
Chippendale Secretary Desk, Walnut, 18th C.,
Brass Pulls & Escutcheons, Ogee Bracket Feet,
Secret Storage Comp., Ca. 1780, 20" D., 36" W.,
76" H. $2,250.00

(A-VA. '76)   *Laws*
Walnut Ox-Bow Drop Front Desk, 18th C.,
Dovetailed Top Case, Thumbnail Molded Drop
& 4 Graduated Ox-Bow Drawers W/Applied
Cock-Beading & Appropriate Chippendale
Plates, Bails & Escutcheons, Ball & Claw Feet,
Ca. 1770, 20" D., 36" W., 41" H. ...$4,600.00

(D-CT. '76)
New England Pine Secretary, 2 Pc., Slant Writing Lid, Interior W/Single Drawer & 12 Pigeonhones W/Interesting Carved Fronts, Cherrywood Pulls On Drawer Fronts, 77" H., Base 36" W. $1,450.00

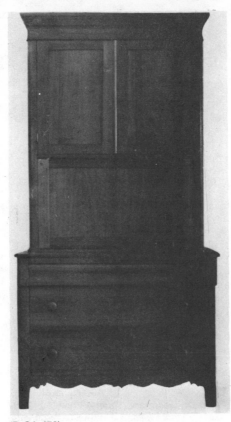

(D-CA. '76)
Pine Secretary, 72" H., 38" W. Refinished $950.00

(D-KS. '76)
Pine Secretary, Refinished, 42" W., 7' H. $650.00

(A-PA. '76)   *Frank Roan III*
Oak Secretary, 7'2" H. $425.00

(A-OH. '76)   *Garth's Auctions, Inc.*
Secretary, Two-Piece, Poplar, Dovetailed Drawers, 2 Paneled Doors, Fold Down Writing Shelf W/Fitted Interior, Upper 6 Glass Doors Are Replacements, 46" W., 22" D., 89" H. $495.00

(A-VA. '76)   *Laws*
Chippendale Secretary Desk, Cherrywood, Bonnet Top, Case W/4 Grad. Drawers, Period Brass Pulls, Ball & Claw Feet, Ca. 1770-80 Ct.; 7' H., 36" W., 20" D. $10,250.00

(D-KS. '76)

Filing Cabinet, Walnut, Roll-back Fronts on Compartments, Pat. Date May 27, '84; 76" H., 38" W. $700.00

(A-MA. '76)   *Richard A. Bourne Co. Inc.*

Slant-Lid Secretary, Cherry, Kentucky, Early 19th C., Slant Writing Lid W/Pull-Out Supports, Interior W/Single Drawer & 10 Pigeonholes; Upper Section W/2 Sm. Half-Width Drawers, Paneled Doors Enclose 3 Bookshelves, Refinished, 40" W., 24" D., 78" H. $1200.00

(A-MA. '76)   *Robert C. Eldred Co., Inc.*

Wooton Desk, Amer., 19th C., Walnut, Orig. Label On Mail Drop, 41" W., 28" D., 72" H., ...$3,000.00

(A-VA. '77)   *Laws*

Burled Walnut Davenport Desk, Top Has Lift Top Box W/Five Storage Compartments; Ca. 1830; 38" H., 44" W., 22" D.........$500.00

(A-MA. '76)   *Richard A. Bourne Co. Inc.*

Empire Sleigh Front Secretary, Mahogany, Paneled Doors & Fold Out Lid, 43" L., 22½" D., 82¾" H. $235.00

(A-VA. '76)   *Laws*

Secretary Desk, Birch, Bottom Case W/Fold Down Writing Surface, Ma. Origin Ca. 1810, 18" D., 38" W., 56" H. $700.00

(D-N.Y. '76)
Candle Screen, French, Colorful Beadwork On Needlepoint, Marble Base, 22" H. . . . $250.00

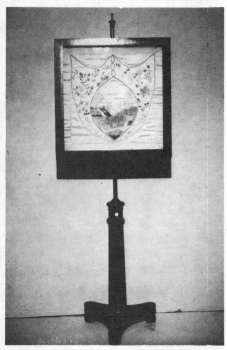

(A-PA. '75)   *Pennypacker Auction Centre*
Embroidery Work, Sq. Frame, Fire Screen, Mahogany Empire Stand Base $180.00

(A-PA. '75)   *Pennypacker Auction Centre*
(Left)
Hepplewhite Fire Screen, Inlaid Frame . . . . . .
. . . . $150.00
(Right)
Mahogany Carved Fire Screen, Painting On Velvet Of Flowers, All Orig. $77.50

(D-MA. '76)
"Gout" Stool, Pine, Cleated Top, Splayed Legs, Top 24" L., 12" W., 16¾" H. $90.00

(A-VA. '76)   *Laws*
Mahogany Tilt Top Needlepoint Fireplace Reflector, Panel W/Elaborate Fruit Bearing Tree W/Birds, Animals & Insects In Earth-Tone Colors, Supported By Turned Pedestal, Arched Padded Snake Feet, 26" W., 46" H. . .$200.00

(A-OH. '75)   *Garth's Auctions, Inc.*
Mahogany Fire Screen, Newport R.I., 56½" H. $800.00

(D-TX. '76)
Victorian Footstool, Needlework Top, 18" L. $95.00

(Left)

(A-PA. '75)   *Pennypacker Auction Centre*

Sheraton Mirror, Mahogany, W/Reversed Glass Painting $210.00

(Right)

(A-MA. '76)   *Richard A. Bourne Co. Inc.*

Sheraton Gilt Mirror, Amer. 2-Part, Reverse Upper Panel Depicts Boats In Harbor, 60" x 36" $225.00

(Left)

(A-MA. '76)   *Richard A. Bourne Co. Inc.*

Chippendale Mirror, Mahogany, Gilt Eagle Carved Pediment, Gilt Inner Border, 33" x 17" $300.00

(Right)

(A-MA. '76)   *Richard A. Bourne Co. Inc.*

Chippendale Mirror, Mahogany Gilt Circular Carving W/Gilt Inner Border, Beveled Glass, 37" x 19½" $375.00

(Left)

(A-OH. '76)   *Garth's Auctions, Inc.*

Chippendale Betrothal Mirror, Mahogany, Line Inlay Around Frame & Carved & Gilded Decor., 23" H. $1600.00

(Right)

(A-VA. '76)   *Laws*

Chippendale Mirror W/Massive Scrolled Crest & Skirt, Orig. Mercury Glass, Ca. 1780; 28" W., 54" H. $600.00

(Left)

(D-KS. '76)

Curly Maple Frame, Pegged Const., 13¼" x 15" $50.00

(Right)

(A-VA. '76)   *Laws*

Chippendale Mirror, Walnut W/Pierced Gilt Phoenix Inset; Mirror Is Parcel Gilt Lined, Ca. 1770; 18" W., 30" H. $575.00

(A-VA. '76)   *Laws*

Chippendale Three-Part Over Mirror, Mahogany, Parcel Gilt Liner, Retains Orig. Glass, Replaced Back Board, 18th C., 29" H., 50" L. $200.00

(Left)

(A-VA. '76)   *Laws*

Chevelle Mirror W/Adjustable Frame, Inlaid Shell On Cross Stretcher, Ca. 1830-40; 30" W., 68" H. $275.00

(Right)

(A-OH. '76)   *Garth's Auctions, Inc.*

Federal Architectural Mirror, Mahogany W/Curly Maple & Cherry, Corner Blocks W/Brass Medallions, Reverse Painting, 30" W., 53½" H. $230.00

(Left)

(A-VA. '76)   *Laws*

Queen Anne Mirror W/Pierced Gilt Shell Inset, Beveled Glass W/Parcel-Gilt Liner, Well Scrolled Crest & Skirt, Ca. 1760; 18" W., 34" H. $520.00

(Right)

(A-VA. '76)   *Laws*

English Mahogany Queen Anne Mirror, 18th C., Carved & Gilt Pierced Shell Insert In Scrolled Crest & Carved Gilded Shell In Shirt, Parcel-Gilt Liner Surrounds Beveled Glass, Ca. 1760, 22" W., 40" H. $650.00

(A-VA. '76)   *Laws*
(Left to Right)

English Chippendale Torchiere, Mahogany W/Rope-Twisted & Carved Pedestal; Ball & Claw Feet, Ca. 1800, 46" H. $210.00

English Regency Pedestaled Shaving Stand, Mahogany, Adjustable Mirror, Ca. 1830, 58" H. $250.00

English Torchiere, Mahogany, Turned Pedestal W/Acanthus Leaf Carving In Center; Snake-Pad Feet, Ca. 1825, 60" H. $150.00

(A-MA. '76)   *Richard A. Bourne Co., Inc.*
(Left to Right)

Georgian Mahogany Fire Screen, English, 18th C., Tripod Base W/Excellent Feet, Screen Fitted W/Pettipoint Panel Of Blue Vase Of Flowers, One Repair For Clean Break In Base, Colors In Panel Remain Quite Bold, 58½" H., Panel Size: 24" x 18" $300.00

Regency Two-Tiered Mahogany Stand (Or Dumbwaiter), English, Early 19th C., Poor Finish, Stained Top, Needs Refinishing, 36" H. $200.00

Regency Fire Screen, English, Early 19th C., Tripod Base W/Scrolled Feet & Oval Needle-Point & Pettipoint Panel Depicting Lady Reclining On Chaise Within Border Of Roses, Backboard Behind Panel New Piece Of Wood, Molding Around Panel Repaired, 43" H. Overall, Panel Size: 17½" x 21½" $200.00

(A-VA. '76) *Laws*
Dining Table W/6-16" Leaves, Ornately Carved Shell & Claw Feet, Ca. 1860, Diam. 54", 30" H., Opens to 12' L. $575.00

(A-VA. '76) *Laws*
Butterfly Table, Pegged Const., New England Origin, Ca. 1750, 25" H., 24" W., 12" L. (Closed) 34" (Open) $700.00

(A-VA. '76) *Laws*
Salem Prototype Nightstand, Mahogany, 1-Drawer W/Serpentine Shaped Top & Ormolu Corners, Serpentine Sides W/Line Inlay, Reeded Legs, 16" D., 16" W., 29" H. $275.00

Garth's Auctions, Inc.

(A-OH. '76)
Curly Maple Slat Back Chairs, Set Of 6, 4 Shaped Slats, Turned Finials & Ball Feet, New Rush Seats $2,160.00
Trestle Table, Shoe Feet, Base W/Old White Paint, Oiled Top, Top Made Removable By Addition Of 2 Supports To Underside, 43" x 96" x 29" H. $700.00

(A-VA. '76) *Laws*
Work Table, Mahogany, Massachusetts, Serpentine Top, 1-Drawer, Matched Satin Wood Panels Inlaid On All 4 Sides As Well As Ormolu Corners, Ca. 1800, 14" D., 18" W., 27½" H. $1,900.00
Queen Anne Duck Foot Corner Chair, New England Mahogany, 18th C., Turned & Blocked Cross Stretcher, Ca. 1740, 28" D., 28" W., 30" H. $1,100.00

(A-MA. '76) *Richard A. Bourne Co., Inc.*
(Left)
Cherry Rope-Leg Circular Drop Leaf Table, Early 19th C., Refinished, 34¼" L., 17¼" W. (Closed), 34¼" Diam. (Open), 28" H. .$200.00
(Right)
Cherry Commode, American, Early 19th C., Rope-Front Posts Enclosing Pair Of Paneled Doors W/Single Full-Width Drawer Above, Refinished, 29¼" L., 18' D., 32½" H. .$225.00

(D-PA. '76)
Candlestand, New England Origin, Cherry Base W/Bird's-Eye Maple Top Having Cherry Trim, Top 13½" x 21", 27½" H. $350.00

(A-VA. '76) *Laws*
Queen Anne Tavern Table, Tiger Maple, Breadboard Top & Single Contoured Drawer, New England Origin, Ca. 1740, 24" D., 31" W., 25" H. $425.00

(A-VA. '76) *Laws*
Wallace Nutting Maple Tavern Table, Bulbous Vase Turned Trestle Base, Arched Legs, 2 Turned Stretchers, Signed, 49" L., 30" W., 30" H. $425.00

(A-MA. '77) *Richard A. Bourne Co., Inc.*
Queen Anne Tavern Table, American, Early 18th C., Orig. Condition, Age Split In Top, Traces Orig. Red Paint Remain, 31¾" L., 19½" W., 26" H. $700.00

(A-VA. '76) *Laws*
Hepplewhite Pembroke Table, 18th C., Single Board Top & Sides Inlaid Top W/Double Butterfly Swings, 1-Drawer-Box, Geometric Pattern Inlay & Tapered Splayed Inlaid Legs W/Brass Fittings & Casters, Ca. 1780, 31" W., 21" H., 21" L. (Closed), 40" (Open) $600.00

(A-VA. '77) *Laws*
Six Leg Drop Leaf Table, Cherry, 19th C., Deep Drop Leaves, Tapered Bulbous Legs, Southern Origin, Ca. 1800-20, 28½" H., 47" W., 21" L. (Closed) $475.00

(A-VA. '76) *Laws*
Wake Table, Fruitwood, Oval Drops, Molded Edge, Mortise, Tenon & Pinned Const., Single Drawer, 8 Blocked & Turned Legs W/Ball Feet, Single Board Stretchers & Double Swing Gatelegs, 18" L. (Closed), 58" (Open), 78" W., 29" H.
...................................$900.00

(A-VA. '77) *Laws*
New England Queen Anne Drop-Leaf Table W/Molded Sides, Finely Scalloped Skirt; Cabriole Legs, Padded Q. A. Feet, Ca. 1750; 18½" D., 28" H., 53" W. (Closed) $1,000.00

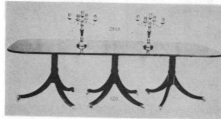

(A-VA. '76) *Laws*
Silverplate Candelabra, Pr., W/Conversion From Single To Five Holders, Elaborate Banding $175.00
Triple Pedestal Banquet Table, Mahogany, 3-Sect., Molded Top, 3 Central Pedestals, Duncan Phyfe Style Legs, Brass Claw Feet Tipped Ends & Brass Casters, 48" W., 30" H., L:W/2 Sect. 72"; W/3 Sect., 112", Has 2 Leaves, Ea. 18" $1,900.00

(A-VA. '76) *Laws*
Queen Anne Drop-Leaf Table, Small Size, Mahogany, Ca. 1840, Open 36" W., 42" L.
.................................$625.00

(A-VA. '77) *Laws*
Walnut Drop-Leaf Table, W/Single Board Top & Side Drops, Ca. 1790-1800; 19" L., 29" H., 45" W. (Closed) $350.00

(A-VA. '76) *Laws*
Queen Anne Mahogany Drop Leaf Table, Finely Scrolled Skirt, Ca. 1740, 29" H., 48" L., 16" W............................$1,400.00

(A-VA. '76) *Laws*
Sheraton Mahogany Drop Leaf Table, 6-Leg, Single Board Top & Sides, Double Swing Gate-Leg & Band Inlay On Apron, Ca. 1810, 50" W., 29" H., 24" L. (Closed), 66" (Open) ...$400.00

(A-MA. '76) *Richard A. Bourne Co. Inc.*
Victorian Music Cabinet, Cherry, Mirrored Back, Raised Trophies Of Musical Instruments On 2 Front Panels, 1 Broken Piece On Lower Door, 17⅝" W., 13½" D., 59" H. $100.00
Sheraton Drop-Leaf Table, Amer., 19th C., Fruitwood, 2 Swing Out Legs, 48" L., 24½" W., Opens To 71", 29" H. $250.00

(A-OH. '76)
Garth's Auctions, Inc.

(A-PA. '76)
Pennypacker Auction Centre

(Left)
Hepplewhite Candlestand, Cherry, Connecticut, Sq. Top W/Dovetailed Drawer & Edge Molding, Inlaid Top W/Fan Corners & Sunburst Design In Center, Drawer W/Line Inlay Front & Back, 16½" Sq., 27" H. $3500.00

(Right)
Tilt Top Table, Mahogany, Ball & Claw Feet, Carved Cabriole Legs $325.00

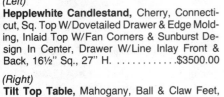

(D-CO. '76)
Small Oak Drop-Leaf Table, Ca. 1900, 28" H.
. . . . $135.00

(D-PA. '76)
Tea Table, Pa. Dutch, Pine Dovetailed Cleated Top 28" Diam., Birch Pedestal, 28" H. $650.00

(D-N.D. '76)
Victorian Table W/Marble Top, Drawer & Casters $225.00

(D-OK. '76)
Table, Drop-Leaf, Sheraton Style, Maple, Ca. 1820, 27" H. $290.00

(A-PA. '76)   *Pennypacker Auction Centre*
Drop Leaf Pembroke Table, Hepplewhite Style, Mahogany $320.00

(A-PA. '76)   *Pennypacker Auction Centre*
Drop Leaf Table, Soft Wood, In-The-Rough
. . . .$70.00

(D-N.C. '76)
Wash Stand, Maple, 15½" x 23" Top, 28" H.
. . . . $90.00

(D-N.Y. '76)
Table, Pine, Scrubbed Cleated Top, Dovetailed Drawer, Orig. Red Paint, Top 26½" x 35½", 28" H., Ca. 1820 New England $650.00

(D-PA. '76)
Hutch Table, Pine, Cleated Top, Dovetailed Drawer In Base, Top 5' x 34½", 29" H. $1950.00

(A-PA. '76)   *Pennypacker Auction Centre*
Table, Walnut, Bucks County, 2 Uneven Drawers, Restored $425.00

(D-CT. '76)
Windsor Candlestand, Swivel Top, Orig. Finish, 22" H., Raises to 28" $450.00

(D-PA. '76)
Table, Pine W/Orig. Red Paint, Scrubbed Top Cleated, Dovetailed Drawer, Legs Pegged . . . .
. . . .$650.00

(A-PA. '75)   *Pennypacker Auction Centre*

Chippendale Side Wall Table, Delaware Valley Walnut, Ca. 1780, Secondary Wood, Pine, All Orig. $450.00

(A-PA. '75)   (A-PA. '76)
Pennypacker Auction Centre

(A-MA. '75)   *Richard A. Bourne Co. Inc.*

Carved Eagles, Pr., Horace Winter, Solid Black Walnut W/Inlaid Wooden Eyes, One W/Wings Spread, 14" H. $500.00

Oval Gate-Leg Table, Cherry, Amer., Early 18th C., One Drawer At One End, Old Natural Finish W/Good Patina, All Feet Built Up 2½", Drawer Has New Facing, 42½" L., 19¼" W. (Closed), 50½" (Open), 28¼" H. $700.00

(Left)

Piecrust Tilt Top Candlestand, Philadelphia Mahogany, Orig. Iron Braces on Base $3400.00

(Right)

Candlestand, Walnut, Dish Top W/Original Iron Plate on Base, Diam. 15", 18th C.$825.00

(A-PA. '75)   *Pennypacker Auction Centre*

(Left)

Push Up Candlestick, Brass, 18th C. .$95.00

Dish Rim Candlestand, Pa. Walnut, Top 15½" D. $310.00

(Right)

Tilt Top Stand, Mahogany, All Orig., Ca. 1825 .... $220.00

(A-OH. '76)   *Garth's Auctions, Inc.*

Tilt Top Tea Table, Mahogany, Molded Claw & Ball Feet, 1-Board Dish Top, 26" D., 28½" H. $7650.00

(A-PA. '76)   *Pennypacker Auction Centre*

Tilt-Top Tea Table, Amer., 18th C., Mahogany, W/Birdcage, Finish Worn On Top Of Feet $325.00

(D-MA. '75)

New England Candlestand, Cherry, 27" H., Top 17" x 24" $285.00

(A-PA. '75)   *Pennypacker Auction Centre*

Betty Lamp, Brass, Peter Derr, Unsigned $290.00

Betty Lamp Stand, Walnut, Dish Rim $200.00

Drop Leaf Table, Pa. Walnut, Replaced Top, Wrought Iron Butterfly Hinges $600.00

(D-WY. '76)

End Table, Maple, Dovetailed Drawer, 27½" H., Top 18½" Sq., 19th C. $95.00

(A-PA. '76)   *Pennypacker Auction Centre*

Tilt-Top Queen Anne Style Table, Dish Top, Walnut, Crows Nest, 32" Top D. $500.00

(A-MA. '75)   *Richard A. Bourne Co. Inc.*

Hepplewhite Banquet Table, Amer., Late 18th C., Mahogany W/String Inlay, Center Drop-Leaf Section W/2 Separate D-Shaped Console Ends, Few Minor Restorations Necessary, Maximum Length 111", 54" W., 29" H. ...$1500.00

(A-PA. '75)   *Pennyoacker Auction Centre*

Windsor Candlestand, Montgomery Co., Pa., 12" x 12½" Dish Top, 26½" H., All Orig. $550.00

(A-VA. '76) *Laws*
Sheraton Nightstand, Cherry, Serpentine & Contoured Cornered Top, Single Drawer W/ Applied Cockbeaded Molding & Oval Brass Pull, Southern Origin, 28½" H. $400.00

(A-MA. '76) *Richard A. Bourne Co. Inc.*
Rope Leg Sewing Table, Amer., 19th C., Birch, Drop Leaves, Dovetailed Drawers $170.00
Country Sheraton Sewing Table, N.Y. State, Cherry W/Tiger Maple Drawer $100.00
Sheraton Sewing Table, Amer., 19th C., Fruitwood, 1 Drawer, Drop Leaves, Minor Wear On Finish $100.00
Hutch Table, 18th C., Pine, Circular Top Tilts Up To Make Chair-Like Back, Restored & Refinished, 46" Diam., 28¾" H. $475.00

(D-OH. '76)
Walnut Table W/Dovetailed Drawer, Refinished, Top 24" x 35", H. 29" ....$150.00 →

Richard A. Bourne Co. Inc.
(A-MA. '76)
Schoolmaster's Desk, Pine, Slant Lid, 6 Pigeonholes In Interior, 30" W., 26¼" D., 44¾" H.$150.00
Mammy's Bench, Restored & Refinished, 50" L. $150.00

(A-VA. '76) *Laws*
Sewing Stand, W/Drop Leaves, Mahogany, Ca. 1825, Fabric Covered Material Bin, 38" H. $325.00

(A-VA. '76)   *Laws*
Two-Tiered Dumbwaiter, Mahogany, Turned Grooved Serving Tiers, Vase & Urn Formed Turned Pedestal, Trifid Spider Legs W/Brass Fittings & Casters, Ca. 1830, 28" Diam., 38" H. $400.00

(A-VA. '77)   *Laws*
Lacquer Tilt Top Table, Top W/Hand Painted Center MedallionW/2 Dogs Framed By Gilded Hand Applied Flower Decor., Ebonized Pedestal & Molded Base Resting On Metal Trifid Web Feet, Ca. 1820 ....$575.00

(A-VA. '77)   *Laws*
Kutani Punch Bowl, Late 18th-Early 19th C., Exceptional Decor., 13" Diam., 6¼" H. ....
....................................$350.00
Mahogany Double-Width Washstand, Unusually High Scrolled Sides & Splash Back Finely Dovetailed, Single Board Top W/Thumbnail Molding, Sheraton Legs, Boston Origin, Ca. 1790-1800, 17" D., 26" W., 43" H.$275.00

(A-VA. '76)   *Laws*
Sheraton Mahogany Canterbury, Latticed Magazine Sections & Turned Stiles & Legs Ending In Brass Castered Feet, Single Drawer At Bottom W/Cock-Beaded Molding, Orig. Wood Pulls, 14" D., 20" L., 21" H. $450.00

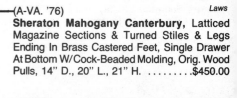

(A-VA. '76)   *Laws*
Hepplewhite Mahogany Corner Washstand, Dovetailed Back, 3 Round Cut-Outs, Scalloped Crest & Apron, Fine Line Satin Wood Inlay & Single Drawer, Square Flaring Legs W/Cross Stretchers, Takes 16" Corner, Ca. 1800, 40" H. $300.00

(A-VA. '76)   *Laws*
Chippendale Commode, Mahogany, Pierced Galleried Top W/Banded Line Inlay, 2 Cabinet Doors Over 2 Drawers & Chamfered Square Legs, Ca. 1790, 17" D., 18" W., 29" H. $500.00

(A-VA. '76)   *Laws*
Revolving Bookcase, Rosewood, Inlaid Central Medallion W/Floral And Winged Mythological Figures — Framed By 3 Fine Line Borders & Molded Top, Center Pedestal, 8 Compartments & 16 Slants W/Fine Line Inlay, 19" D., 19" W., 34" H. $275.00

(A-PA. '75) *Pennypacker Auction Centre*
Baby Coach, Wooden, All Orig. $220.00

(D-W.VA. '76)
Baby Bed, Combination Cradle & Bed, Maple, 36" L., Orig. Finish $125.00

(A-OH. '76) *Garth's Auctions, Inc.*
Child Size Buggy, Black W/Gilt Decor., 40" H. $155.00

(A-PA. '75) *Pennypacker Auction Centre*
Cradle, Walnut, Refinished $140.00

(A-PA. '75) *Pennypacker Auction Centre*
Victorian Cradle, Walnut, By Knipp of Baltimore, Md. $190.00

(A-OH. '76) *Garth's Auctions, Inc.*
Country Pine Hooded Cradle, Dovetailed, Shaped Runners, Old Drk. Alligatored Paint, 41" L. $125.00

(D-CT. '76)
Tackroom Stand, Mahogany, 36" W., 42" H., English, Ca. 1830, Used For Boots & Crops . .
. . . .$450.00

(D-CO. '76)
Spool Towel Rack, Maple $49.00

(D-N.D. '76)
Towel Rack, Maple, 36" H. $75.00

(D-OH. '76)
Bench Bed, Pine 22" D., 32" H., 73" L., Refinished $650.00

(D-PA. '76)
Bench Bed, 2 Pc., Pine W/Traces of Orig. Red Paint $600.00

(D-OH. '76)
Youth Bed, Front Extends Outward, Red & Black Sponge Decoration $300.00

(D-MO. '76)
Couch, Oak Trim Refinished, New Vinyl Cover, 28" W., 76" L. $325.00

(Left)
(D-KS. '76)
Oak Cupboard, Refinished, Orig. Glass Panes, Press Design On Top & Door Fronts, 39" W., 7' 4" H. $500.00

(Right)
(D-IL. '76)
Oak Cupboard, Refinished, 32" W., 6' 10" H. $200.00

(D-MO. '76)
Oak Roll Top Desk, Orig. Finish Good, 51" H., 33" D., 60" L. $650.00

(Left)
(D-IA. '76)
Oak Pie Safe, Refinished, Glass Doors, 32" W., 60" H. $90.00

(Right)
(D-CO. '76)
Refrigerator, Oak, Zinc Lined, Refinished, Brass Hdw., 58" H. $300.00

(D-CA. '76)
Oak Roll Top Desk, Orig. Finish, 33" D., 4' 6" W. 51½" H. $800.00

(D-IA. '76)
Oak Drop Leaf Table, Refinished, Top 42" x 54" $65.00

(Left)
(D-KS. '76)
Oak Parlor Table, Refinished, Top 16" Sq., 26" H. $35.00

(Right)
(D-OH. '76)
Oak Parlor Table, Top 16" x 16", 28" H., Orig. Finish $12.00

(D-CO. '76)
Oak Library Table, Top 30" x 48", 28" H., Refinished $45.00

(Left)
(D-MI. '76)
Oak Hall Tree, Refinished, 42" W., 86" H., Box Seat, Bevel Mirror $400.00

(Right)
(D-CO. '76)
Oak Hall Tree, Brass Hangers, Bevel Mirror, Refinished $375.00

(Left)
(D-OK. '76)
Oak Combination Desk & Bookcase, Refinished, Bent Glass In Door, Bevel Mirror & Leaded Glass In Cabinet Door, 45" W., 78" H. $475.00

(Right)
(D-CO. '76)
Combination Desk & Bookcase, Oak, 3 Bevel Mirrors, Swelled Top Drawer & Bent Glass In Door, 44" W., 79" H., Orig. Finish $650.00

(Left)
(D-NE. '76)
Refrigerator, Oak, Zinc Lined, Refinished. Brass Hdwe., 48" H. $150.00

(Right)
(D-S.D. '76)
Oak Hall Tree, Brass Hangers, Bevel Mirror, 41" W., 85" H. $350.00

AMBER GLASS is the name of any glassware having a yellowish-brown color. It became popular during the last quarter of the nineteenth century.

AMBERINA, PLATED - Considered to be the "Queen" of the Amberina family, this ware was produced by Joseph Locke in 1886. It was made for only a short time by The New England Glass Company. Plated Amberina objects shade from a soft yellowish-gold at the base to a deep fushia-red at the top, and have a creamy opal lining which almost always has a bluish cast. Another characteristic which identifies this ware is the vertical molded ribs which protrude on the outer surface of glass.

AMETHYST GLASS - The term identifies any glassware made in the proper dark purple shade. It became popular after the Civil War.

ART GLASS is a general term given to various types of ornamental glass made to be decorative rather than functional. It dates primarily from the late Victorian period to the present day and, during the span of time glassmakers have achieved fantastic effects of shape, color, pattern, texture and decoration.

BACCARAT GLASS was first made in France from 1765 by La Compagnie des Cristalleries de Baccarat — until the firm went bankrupt. Production began for the second time during the 1820s and the firm is still in operation, producing fine glasswares and paperweights. Baccarat is famous for its earlier paperweights made during the last half of the 19th century.

BOHEMIAN GLASS is named for its country of origin. It is an ornate, overlay, or flashed glassware, popular during the Victorian era.

BRISTOL GLASS is a lightweight opaque glass, oftentimes having a light bluish tint and, was oftentimes decorated with enamels. The ware is a product of Bristol, England — a glass center since the 1700s.

BURMESE - Frederick Shirley developed this shaded art glass at the now famous old Mt. Washington Glass Company in New Bedford, Massachusetts, and patented his discovery under the trade name of "Burmese" on December 15, 1885. The ware was also made in England by Thomas Webb & Sons.

Burmese is a hand-blown glass with the exception of a few pieces that were pattern molded. The latter are either ribbed, hobnail or diamond quilted in design. This ware is found in two textures or finishes: the original glazed or shiny finish, and the dull, velvety, satin finish. It is a homogeneous glass (single-layered) that was never lined, cased or plated. Although its color varies slightly, it always shades from a delicate yellow at the base to a lovely salmon-pink at the top. The blending of colors is so gradual that it is difficult to determine where one color ends and the other begins.

CAMBRIDGE GLASS - See Crown Tuscan

CAMEO ART GLASS can be defined as any glass in which the surface has been cut away to leave a design in relief. Cutting is accomplished by the use of hand cutting tools, wheel cutting and hydrofluoric acid. This ware can be clear or colored glass of a single layer, or glass with multiple layers of clear or colored glass.

Although Cameo glass has been produced for centuries, the majority available today dates from the late 1800s. It has been produced in England, France and other parts of Europe, as well as the United States. The most famous of the French masters of Cameo wares was Emile Galle'.

CANDY CONTAINERS were used for holding tiny candy pellets. These were produced in a variety of shapes — locomotives, cars, boats, guns, etc. for children.

CARNIVAL GLASS was an inexpensive, pressed, iridescent glassware made from about 1900 through the 1920s. It was made in quantities by Northwood Glass Company; Fenton Art Glass Company and others, to compete with the expensive art glass of the period. Originally called "Taffeta" glass, the ware became known as "Carnival" glass during the 1920s when carnivals gave examples as premiums or prizes.

CORALENE - The term Coralene denotes a type of decoration rather than a kind of glass — consisting of many tiny beads, either of colored or transparent glass — decorating the surface. The most popular design used resembled coral or seaweed — hence the name.

CRACKLE GLASSWARE - This type of art glass was an invention of the Venetians that spread rapidly to other countries. It is made by plunging red-hot glass into cold water, then reheating and reblowing it, thus producing an unusual outer surface which appears to be covered with a multitude of tiny fractures, but is perfectly smooth to the touch.

CRANBERRY GLASS — The term "Cranberry Glass" refers to color only, not to a particular type of glass. It is undoubtedly the most familiar colored glass known to collectors. This ware was blown or molded, and oftentimes decorated with enamels.

CROWN TUSCAN glass has a pink-opaque body. It was originally produced in 1936 by A. J. Bennett, President of the Cambridge Glass Company of Cambridge, Ohio. The line was discontinued in 1954. Occasionally referred to as Royal Crown Tuscan, this ware was named for a scenic area in Italy, and it has been said that its color was taken from the flesh-colored sky at sunrise. When trans-illuminated, examples do have all of the blaze of a sunrise — a characteristic that is even applied to new examples of the ware reproduced by Mrs. Elizabeth Degenhart of Crystal Art Glass, and Harold D. Bennett, Guernsey Glass Company of Carbridge, Ohio.

CUSTARD GLASS was manufactured in the United States for a period of about thirty years (1885-1915). Although Harry Northwood was the first and largest manufacturer of custard glass, it was also produced by the Heisey Glass Company, Diamond Glass Company, Fenton Art Glass Company and a number of others.

The name Custard Glass is derived from its "custard yellow" color which may shade light yellow to ivory to light green glass that is opaque to opalescent. Most pieces have a fiery opalescence when held to light. Both the color and glow of this ware comes from the use of uranium salts in the glass. It is generally a heavy type pressed glass made in a variety of different patterns.

CUT GLASS with its deeply cut designs and intricate patterns has been produced for centuries. The large majority of the pieces available date from the Brilliant Period of glass design — 1880-1915.

CUT OVERLAY - The term identifies pieces of glassware usually having a milk-white exterior that has been cased with cranberry, blue or amber glass. Other type examples are deep blue, amber or cranberry on crystal glass, and the majority of pieces have been decorated with dainty flowers. Although Bohemian glass manufacturers produced some very choice pieces during the nineteenth century, fine examples were also made in America, as well as in France and England.

DURAND ART GLASS was made by Victor Durand from 1879 to 1935 at the Durand Art Glass Works in Vineland, New Jersey. The glass resembles Tiffany in quality. Drawn white feather designs and thinly drawn glass threading (quite brittle) applied around the main body of the ware, are striking examples of Durand creations on an iridescent surface.

END-OF-DAY GLASS - The term identifies glass having bits and pieces of different colored glass embedded in its surface. Traditionally, the ware was made by workmen at the end of the day from the multicolored remains of the day's glass from various pots. But, research reveals that the ware was a deliberately manufactured product popular during the late 1800s.

FLASHED WARES were popular during the late 19th century. They were made by partially coating the inner surface of an object with a thin plating of glass or another, more dominant color — usually red. These pieces can readily be identified by holding the object to the light and examining the rim, as it will show more than one layer of glass. Many pieces of "Rubina Crystal" (cranberry to clear), "Blue Amberina" (blue to amber), and "Rubina Verde" (cranberry to green), were manufactured in this way.

FLORENTINE ART CAMEO GLASS is an imitation cameo glass produced around the turn of the century by Bohemian factories. Examples have a heavy white enamel decoration on a colored or Satin Glass body. The ware is an imitation of English Cameo Glass.

FRANCISWARE is a hobnail glassware with frosted or clear glass hobs and stained amber rims and tops. It was produced during the late 1880s by Hobbs, Brockunier & Company.

HEISEY glass was made from 1896 to 1958 by A. H. Heisey & Company, Inc., Newark, Ohio. The firm produced a wide variety of glasswares. The trademark is the letter "H" within a diamond shaped mark.

HOBNAIL - The term hobnail identifies any glassware having "bumps" — flattened, rounded or pointed — over the outer surface of the glass. A variety of patterns exists. Many of the fine early examples were produced by Hobbs, Brockunier & Co., Wheeling, W.Va., and The New England Glass Company.

HOLLY AMBER, originally known as "Golden Agate", is a pressed glass pattern which features holly berries and leaves over its glossy surface. Its color shades from golden brown tones to opalescent streaks. This ware was produced by the Indiana Tumbler and Goblet Company for only six months, from January 1, to June 13, 1903. Examples are rare and expensive.

IMPERIAL GLASS - The Imperial Glass Company of Bellaire, Ohio, was organized in 1901 by a group of prominent citizens of Wheeling, West Virginia. A variety of fine art glass, in addition to Carnival glass, was produced by the firm. The two trademarks which identified the ware were issued in June, 1914. One consisted of the firm's name, "Imperial", and the other included a cross formed by double-pointed arrows. The latter trademark was changed in September of the same year from the arrow cross to what was known as a "German" cross. The overlapping "IG" cipher was adopted by Imperial in 1949, and appears on practically all of their present production — including reproduced Carnival glass.

"LACY" SANDWICH GLASS -- See Sandwich Glass

LATTICINO is the name given to articles of glass in which a network of tiny milk-white lines appear, crisscrossing between two walls of glass. It is a type of Filigree glassware developed during the 16th century by the Venetians.

LOETZ GLASS was made in Austria just before the turn of the century. As Loetz work in the Tiffany factory before returning to Austria, much of his glass is similar in appearance to Tiffany wares. Loetz glass is oftentimes marked "Loetz" or "Loetz-Austria."

LUTZ GLASS was made by Nicholas Lutz, a Frenchman, who worked at the Boston and Sandwich Glass Company from 1870 to 1888 when it closed. He also produced fine glass at the Mt. Washington Glass Company and later at the Union Glass Company. Lutz is noted for two different types of glass — striped and threaded wares. Other glass houses also produced similar glass and these wares were known as Lutz-type.

MARBLE GLASS - See Slag Glass

MERCURY GLASS is a double-walled glass that dates from the 1850s to about 1910. It was made in England as well as the United States during this period. Its interior, usually in the form of vases, is lined with flashing mercury, giving the items an allover silvery appearance. The entrance hole in the base of each piece was sealed over. Many pieces were decorated.

MILK GLASS is an opaque pressed glassware, usually of milk-white color, although green, amethyst, black, and shades of blue were made. Milk glass was produced in quantity in the United States during the 1880s, in a variety of patterns.

MILLEFIORI - This decorative glassware is considered to be a special of the Venetians. It is sometimes called "glass of a thousand flowers", and has been made for centuries. Very thin colored glass rods are arranged in bundles, then fused together with heat. When the piece of glass is sliced across, it has a design like that of many small flowers. These tiny wafer thin slices are then embedded in larger masses of glass, enlarged and shaped.

MOSER GLASS was made by Kolomon Moser at Carlsbed. The ware is considered to be another type of Art Nouveau glass as it was produced during its heyday — during the early 1900s. Principal colors included amethyst, cranberry, green and blue, with fancy enameled decoration.

MOTHER-OF-PEARL, often abbreviated in descriptions as M.O.P., is glass composed of two or more layers, with a pattern showing through to the outer surface. The pattern, caused by internal air traps,is created by expanding the inside layer of molten glass into molds with varying designs. And when another layer of glass is applied, this brings out the design. When the final layer of glass is then acid dipped, and the result is Mother of Pearl Satin Ware. Patterns are numerous. The most frequently found are the Diamond Quilted, Raindrop and Herringbone. This ware can be one solid color, a single color shading light to dary, tow colors blended or a variety of colors which includes the rainbow effect. In addition, many pieces are decorated with colorful enamels, coralene beading, and other applied glass decorations.

NAILSEA glass was first produced in England from 1788 to 1873. The characteristics that identify this ware are the "pulled" loopings and swirls of colored glass over the body of the object, combined with clear or opal glass. This technique has also been used by glassblowers in Germany, Italy, France and the United States.

NEW ENGLAND PEACHBLOW - Patented in 1886 by the New England Glass Company, New England. Peachblow is a single-layered glass shading from opaque white at the base to deep rose-red or raspberry at the top. Some pieces have a glossy surface, but most were given an acid bath to produce a soft, matte finish.

OPALESCENT GLASS — The term refers to glasswares which have a milky white effect in the glass, usually on a colored ground. There are three basic types of this ware. Presently, the most popular includes pressed glass patterns found in table settings. Here, the opalescence appears at the top rim, the base, or a combination of both. On blown or mold-blown glass, the pattern itself consists of this milky effect — such as Spanish Lace. Another example is the opalescent points on some pieces of hobnail glass. These wares are lighter weight. And the third group includes opalescent novelties, primarily of the pressed variety.

PHOENIX GLASS -- The firm was establlshed in Beaver County, Pennsylvania during the late 1800s, and produced a variety of commercial glasswares. During the 1930s the factory made a desirable sculptured gift-type glassware which has become very collectible in recent years. Vases, lamps, bowls, ginger jars, candlesticks, etc. were made until the 1950s in various colors with a satin finish.

PIGEON'S BLOOD is a bright reddish-orange glass ware dating from the early 1900s.

PRESSED GLASS was the inexpensive glassware produced in quantity to fill the increasing demand for tablewares when Americans moved away from the simple table utensils of pioneer times. During the 1820s, ingenious Yankees invented and perfected machinery for successfully pressing glass. And about 1865, manufacturers began to color their products. Literally hundreds of different patterns were produced.

ROYAL FLEMISH ART GLASS was made by the Mt. Washington Glass Works during the 1880s. It has an acid finish which may consist of one or more colors, decorated with raised gold enameled lines separating into sections. Fanciful painted enamel designs also decorate this ware. Royal Flemish glass is marked "RF," with the letter "R" reversed and backed to the letter "F", within a foursided orange-red diamond mark.

SANDWICH GLASS - One of the most interesting and enduring pages from America's past is Sandwich Glass produced by the famous Boston and Sandwich Glass Company at Sandwich, Massachusetts. The firm began operations in 1825, and the glass flourished until 1888 when the factory closed. Despite the popularity of Sandwich Glass, little is known about its founder, Deming Jarvis.

The Sandwich Glass house turned out hundreds of designs in both plain and figured patterns, in colors and cyrstal, so that no one type could be considered entirely typical — but the best known is the "lacy" glass produced here. The variety and multitude of designs and patterns produced by the company over the years is a tribute to its greatness.

SATIN GLASS - The term identifies a variety of glasswares made from 1886, which were treated with hydrofluroic acid vapor to produce a smooth satin finish. Satin glass examples can be found in a variety of colors and patterns.

SCHNEIDER ART GLASS was made from 1903 through 1930 by Charles and Ernest Schneider at Epinay-sur-Seine, France. The firm is still operating, producing clear crystal glasswares.

SLAG GLASS was originally known as "Mosaic" and "Marble Glass" because of its streaked appearance. Production in the United States began about 1880. The largest producer of this ware was Challinor, Taylor & Company. The various slag mixtures are: purple, butterscotch, blue, orange, green and chocolate. A small quantity of Pink Slag was also produced in the Inverted Fan & Feather pattern. Examples are rare and expensive.

SPANISH LACE is a Victorian glassware having a distinctive white lacy design on a clear or colored ground.

STEUBEN - The Steuben Glass Works was founded in 1904 by Frederick Carter, an Englishman, and T. G. Hawkes, Sr., at Corning, New York. In 1918, the firm was purchased by the Corning Glass Company. However, Steuben remained with the firm, designing a bounty of fine art glass of exceptional quality.

TIFFANY GLASS was made by Louis Comfort Tiffany, one of America's outstanding glass designers of the Art Nouveau period, from about 1870 to the 1930s. Tiffany's designs included a variety of lamps, bronze work, silver, pottery and stained glass windows. Practically all items made were marked "L.C. Tiffany" or "L.C.T." in addition to the word "Favrille" — the French word for color.

TORTOISE SHELL GLASS - As the name indicates, this type glassware resembles the color of tortoise shell and has deep rich brown tones combined with amber and cream-colored shades. Tortoise Shell Glass was originally produced in 1880 by Francis Pohl, a German chemist. It was also made in the United States by the Sandwich Glass Works and other glass houses during the late 1800s.

VASELINE GLASS - The term "Vaseline" refers to color only, as it resembles the greenish-yellow color typical of the oily petroleum jelly known as Vaseline. This ware has been produced in a variety of patterns both here and in Europe — from the late 1800s. It has been made in both clear and opaque yellow, Vaseline combined with clear glass, and occasionally the two colors were combined in one piece.

WAVECREST GLASS is an opaque white glassware made from the late 1890s by French factories and the Pairpoint Manufacturing Company at New Bedford, Mass. Items were decorated by the C.F. Monroe Company of Meriden, Ct., with painted pastel enamels. The name Wavecrest was used after 1898 with the initials of the Company "C.F.M. Co." Operations ceased during World War I.

WHEELING PEACHBLOW - With its simple lines and delicate shadings, Wheeling Peachblow was produced soon after 1883 by J.H. Hobbs, Brockunier & Company at Wheeling, West Virginia. It is a two-layered glass lined or cased inside with an opaque, milk-white type of plated glassware. The outer layer shades from a bright yellow at the base to a mahogany red at the top. The majority of pieces produced are in the glossy finish.

(Left)
(D-IA. '76)
Vase, Spanish Lace, Pink & White, 10½" H. .
....$150.00

(Right)
(D-N.Y. '76)
New England Peachblow Vase, 10" H. . . . . . .
....$550.00

(Left)
(A-MO. '76)   *Woody Auction Company*
Carnival Glass Vase, Corn Pattern By North-
wood, Amethyst $150.00

(Right)
(A-MO. '76)   *Woody Auction Company*
Carnival Glass Vase, "Peoples" Pattern,
Blue/Green $8,100.00

(Left)
(D-FL. '76)
Opaque Vase W/Applied Crystal Decoration,
12" H. $300.00

(Right)
(D-CO. '76)
Mary Gregory Vase, Cranberry, 6½" H. . . . . .
....$175.00

(Left)
(D-IA. '76)
Phoenix Glass Vase, 8½" H., Tan Ground
W/White Flowers $35.00

(Right)
(D-AL. '76)
Cut Glass Scent Bottles, 8" L. $150.00

(Left)
(D-N.Y. '76)
Westward Ho Compote, Covered, Low Stan-
dard, 8¾" H. $150.00

(Right)
(D-IA. '76)
Three Face Sugar, Covered $90.00

(Left)
(D-CA. '76)
Butterscotch Slag Sugar Bowl $125.00

(Right)
(A-CA. '76)
Plated Amberina Bowl $2,700.00

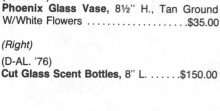

(Left)
(D-S.C. '76)
Bohemian Glass Compote, Red, Vintage
Pattern, 9" H. $200.00

(Right)
(D-LA. '76)
Tiffany Glass Sherbet, Sgn. "LCT Favrile",
5⅜" H., Gold & Opalescent, Set Of 6 (1 Illus.)
....$850.00

(D-IN. '76)
Cambridge Fruit Bowl, Crown Tuscan, Chintz
Pattern, 12" Sq. $90.00

(Left)
(D-MO. '76)
Cut Glass Toothpick Holder, Sgn. "Hawkes"
4" H. $85.00

(Right)
(D-IA. '76)
Opaque Basket W/Applied Crystal Cherries,
Amber Leaves & Handle, 6" H. $225.00

(D-N.Y. '76)
Infant Feeder, Glass $45.00

(D-FL. '76)
Blue Satin Glass Egg, Resting In Ornate Brass
Basket $450.00

(D-GA. '76)
Bride's Basket, Pink Shaded M.O.P., Silver
Basket $500.00

(D-AL. '76)
(Left to Right)
Milk Glass Atterbury Duck, Amethyst W/Glass
Eyes, 11" L. $90.00
Milk Glass Atterbury Duck, White & Amethyst
W/Glass Eyes, 11" L. $155.00

(D-IA. '76)
Burmese Lamp, Fairy, Complete W/Sgn.
Clark Base $375.00

(D-N.Y. '76)
Tiffany Plate, Gold Iridescent, Stretched Edge,
Sgn. 9½" Diam. $325.00

(D-MO. '76)
Custard Creamer & Sugar (No Cover), Intaglio
Pattern, Set $90.00

(D-MO. '76)
(Left to Right)
Milk Glass Angel Head Plate, 9" Diam.$37.50
Milk Glass Covered Compote, Chick & Eggs,
Atterbury $135.00
Milk Glass Compote W/Daisy & Button Base
. . . .$50.00

(D-FL. '76)
Milk Glass Plate W/Lattice-Edge & Trumpet
Vine Center, 10½" Diam. $55.00

(D-MO. '76)
Mother-Of-Pearl Vases, Diamond-Quilted,
Pink, 8" H. Pair $390.00
Matching Bowl, 4½" H. $175.00

(D-AL. '76)
Venetian, Latticino Glass Plate, 10" Diam.,
Pink & White $95.00

(A-OH. '76)   *Garth's Auctions, Inc.*
White Opaque Candlesticks, Pr., Crucifix,
One Has Flake On One Arm Of Cross, 11½" H.
. . . .$35.00

(A-MO. '76) *Woody Auction Company*
Carnival Glass Water Set, Lilly Of The Valley
Pattern, Amethyst $4,000.00

(D-KS. '76) *John Woody*
Carnival Glass Water Set, Purple Dandelion
....$850.00

(D-KS. '76) *John Woody*
Carnival Glass Punch Bowl (2 pcs.) & 7 Cups,
Amethyst Grape Patt. $650.00

(A-IA. '76) *Woody Auction Company*
CARNIVAL GLASS
(Row I, Left to Right)
Pitcher, Marigold, Blackberry Block Patt. .....
....$500.00
Cologne Bottles, Marigold, Northwood Grape &
Cable, Each $85.00
Pitcher, Marigold, Greek Key Patt. ...$500.00
Pitcher, Marigold, Grape Arbor Patt. ..$250.00
(Row II, Left to Right)
Sugar & Creamer, Marigold, Grape & Cable
Patt., Ea. $60.00
Tray, Marigold, Grape & Cable Patt. ..$100.00

(Left)
(D-CA. '76)
Royal Flemish Jug, Decor. W/Red, Green,
Blue, Yellow, Russet & Black W/Outline Decor.
In Gold, 8½" H. $1,450.00

(Right)
(D-WA. '76)
Amberina Pitcher, Inverted Thumbprint Pat-
tern, 7" H. $350.00

(Left)
(D-KY. '76)
Three Faces Water Pitcher, Rare ...$250.00
(Right)
(D-AL. '76)
Cut Glass Water Pitcher, Zipper Pattern .....
....$190.00

(Left)
(D-CT. '76)
Holly Amber Water Pitcher, 10" H. .$2200.00
(Right)
(A-CA. '76)
Water Pitcher, Green Cut To Clear, 12" H.,
Sterling Rim $875.00

(A-MO. '76) *Woody Auction Company*
(Left to Right)
Carnival Glass Mug, Marigold, Fisherman ...
....$125.00
Carnival Glass Mug, Amethyst, Fisherman ...
....$75.00

(Left)
(A-OH. '76) *Woody Auction Company*
Carnival Glass Mug, Green Dandelion ......
....$400.00
(Right)
(A-MO. '76)
Carnival Glass Town Pump, Purple .$425.00

(D-MA. '76)
"WESTWARD HO" PRESSED GLASS
(Left to Right)

Water Pitcher	$175.00
Covered Butter On High Standard	$135.00
Bread Tray	$90.00
Covered Sugar Bowl	$135.00
Creamer	$112.00
Spoon Holder	$85.00

(A-OH. '76)   Garth's Auctions, Inc.
(Row I, Left to Right)
Cased & Swirled Vase, Caramel Shaded Exterior W/Pale Amber Ruffled Top, White Lining, 5¾" H. $17.50
Brilliant Yellow Swirled & Ruffled Basket, Clear Applied Handle, 5¼" H. To Top Of Handle $40.00
Cased Ruffled Top Bowl, White Exterior, Dusty Rose Interior, Applied Handle Is Clear & Ribbed, 5⅜" Diam. $35.00

Cased Ribbed Vase, Brilliant Blue Exterior, White Interior, Clear Applied Feet, 6" H. $35.00
(Row II, Left to Right)
Caramel Cased Pitcher, Molded Artichoke Patt., Amber Reeded Applied Handle, White Lining, 6" H. $40.00
Ribbed & Cased Ruffled Top Vase, Yellow Swirled, Tomato Red Interior, Clear Ruffled Edge, 6⅛" H. $65.00

Ribbed Pitcher, Yellow Swirled, Interior Casing Is White W/Thin Layer Of Yellow, Then Clear Layer On Outside, Applied Clear Ribbed Handle, 7" H. $40.00

(A-PA. '75)   Pennypacker Auction Centre
(Left to Right)
Satin Glass Pattern Water Set, Blue To White Diamond Quilted Patt., 1 Tumbler Chipped $390.00
Vase, Candy Stripe White, Blue & Pink, 12" T. $190.00
Spatter Glass Water Set, Yellow, Pink & Brown, Pitcher, 3 Tumblers $75.00

(A-PA. '76)   Pennypacker Auction Centre
Blown Glass *(Left to Right)*
Vase, Pittsburgh, McKearin Pl. 22-10, Band At Top Of Geometric Devices & Swags W/Flowers and Bow Knots, Band Of Gadrooning At Base, 8½" H. $260.00
Vase, Pittsburgh, Trumpet Shape Bowl, Hollow Knob Stem, Lt. Amber, 10½" H. $150.00
Vase, Engraved, No Harm Flake On Inside Of Top Rim, 8½" H. $190.00

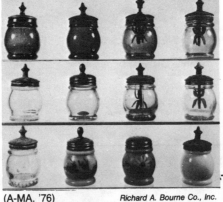

(A-MA. '76)   Richard A. Bourne Co., Inc.
CHRISTMAS SALTS
(Row I, Left to Right)
Amethyst Jar W/Orig. Plated Silver Top$70.00
Deep Sapphire Blue Jar, W/Orig. Pewter Top $70.00
Peacock Blue Jar W/Breaker & Pewter Top; Pat. Date 1877 . . . .$90.00
Pale Blue Jar W/Breaker, Orig. Pewter Top & 1877 Pat. Date $65.00
(Row II, Left to Right)
Pale Blue Salts, Pair Without Breakers, One

W/Brass Top $70.00
Amber Jar W/Orig. Pewter Top Bearing 1877 Pat. Date $70.00
Vaseline Glass Jar W/Breaker & Orig. Pewter Top & 1877 Pat. $70.00
(Row III, Left to Right)
Vaseline Jar W/Orig. Pewter Top, Never Had A Breaker, Used As Pepper Shaker $35.00
Milk Glass Decorated Salts, Pair, Neither W/Breaker, Both Have Orig. Tops $60.00
Milk Glass Salt (1 of Pr.), Both W/Orig. Pewter Tops, One W/Pat. Date 1877; One Minus Its Breaker $90.00

Rubina Verde Hobnail Water Pitcher W/
Applied Handle $300.00

(D-IA. '76)
Wheeling Peachblow Water Pitcher W/Ap-
plied Amber Handle $950.00

(A-OH. '76)　　　　　　　*Garth's Auctions, Inc.*

(Row I, Left to Right)
Barber Bottle, Cranberry W/Opalescence,
7" H. $85.00
Barber Bottle, Drk. Amethyst W/Cream Flowers,
8" H. $45.00
Barber Bottle, Opaque White W/Ceramic
Stopper W/Flakes, 9¾" H. $35.00
Barber Bottle, Blue W/Opalescent Swirls,
7" H. $65.00
Barber Bottle, Pale Yellow, Inverted Thumb-
print Patt., Neck Scratched, 7' H. $37.50
(Row II, Left to Right)
Sugar Shaker, Milk Glass, Drapery Patt., 5½" H.
. . . . $45.00
Sugar Shaker, Amethyst & White Marbelized,
5" H. $90.00
Sugar Shaker, Milk Glass, Lt. Green, Ribbed,
Brass Lid Has Split, 4½" H. $60.00
Sugar Shaker, Greentown Glass, Nile Green
Tree Of Life Patt., 3¾" H. $60.00

Sugar Shaker, Cranberry W/Opalescent Spots,
4½" H. $45.00
Sugar Shaker, White Satin Shaded To Peach
Melon Ribbed, Enameled Flowers, 4¾" H.
. . . .$55.00
Sugar Shaker, Milk Glass, Painted Green
Ground & Darker Green Enameled Moss Roses,
Pewter Lid & Threaded Ring, 5⅜" H. . .$50.00
(Row III, Left to Right)
Barber Bottle, Emerald Green W/Enameled
Flowers, 7" H. $5500
Barber Bottle, Blue Hobnail , Chipped, 7" H.
. . . . $37.50
Barber Bottle, Cobalt Blue W/Enameling &
Metal Fitting, 7¾" H. $50.00
Barber Bottle, Mary Gregory, Green W/Enamel-
ing Of Girl Picking Flowers In Her Apron, Enamel
Worn, 7¾" H. $50.00
Barber Bottle, Blue & Opalescent, 6¾" H. . . .
. . . . $45.00
Barber Bottle, Amethyst W/Enameling, 7½" H.
. . . . $35.00

(D-IA. '76)
Loetz Vase, Green Irid. W/Veined Design,
Slightly Twisted Body, 5½" H. $165.00

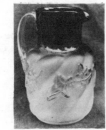

(Left)

(D-AL.)
Blue Iridescent Water Pitcher, Mkd. L. C.
Tiffany-Favrille $550.00

(Right)

(D-FL. '76)
Royal Ivy Water Pitcher by Northwood Glass
Co., Flashed Red To Clear Satin Base $125.00

(A-PA. '75)　　　　*Pennypacker Auction Centre*
(Left to Right)
MARY GREGORY GLASS
Creamer, 6", Green $105.00
Vase, 5" Green $60.00
Vase, 10", Blue $25.00
Mug, 4½", Blue $20.00

(D-AL. '76)
Imperial Glass Vase, 12" H. $250.00

(A-MA. '77)   *Richard A. Bourne Co., Inc.*
(Left to Right)
Overlay Vases, Pr., Continental 19th C., White
Overlay On Emerald Green W/Cut Design
19½" H. $525.00
Bohemian Lidded Sweetmeat Or Pokal, Ruby
FlashW/Engraving Of Deer In Landscape Sur-
rounded By Foilate Scrollwork, 18½" H. ......
.................................$500.00

(D-CO. '76)
Tiffany Bowl, 12" Diam., Purple Iridescent,
Sgn. L.C.T. $375.00

(D-N.Y. '76)
Durand Vase, Having Drawn White Feather-
Like Decor. Over Iridescent Gold-Brown Ground,
9¾" H. $750.00

(A-MA. '76)   *Richard A. Bourne Co., Inc.*
Leaded & Stained Glass Windows, (1 of Pr.),
By John LaFarge, N.A. (American 1835-1910).
Each W/Lower Section Having Amber Panes
Enclosed Within Border Of Light Green Panes;
Upper Section Is Multicolored Representing
Cranberry Colored Fruit W/Green Leaves
Surrounded By Amethyst & Blue Panes. 40¼" x
28½" $300.00

(A-MA. '75)   *Richard A. Bourne, Co., Inc.*
(Row I, Left to Right)
Satin Glass Vase, Yellow-Green W/Enamel
Decor., Ewer Form W/Frosted Applied Twist
Handle, 10" H. $80.00
Tiffany Bowl, Iridescent Gold, Panel Design,
Signed "L.C.T. Favrile", 12" Diam., 4" H. .....
.................................$325.00
Schneider Vase, Unsigned, Multi-Colored W/
Blues, Reds & Goldstone, 7" Diam., 8⅛" H. ..
.................................$70.00
(Row II, Left to Right)
Satin Glass Fluid Lamp, Gold & White Mother-
Of-Pearl In Looped Design, One Minor Check In
Outer Casing At Side, 5¼" Diam. $50.00
Tiffany Flower Holder, Signed, Iridescent
Gold $60.00
Bohemian Vase, Amber W/Scene Showing A
Stag & Doe In Forest, 6¾" H. $55.00

(A-MA. '76)   *Richard A. Bourne, Co., Inc.*
ART GLASS

(Row I, Left to Right)
Latticinio Cologne Bottle, Red & White, No
Stopper, 2 Fine-Line Cracks In Bottom .$32.00
Latticinio Tumbler, Green & White W/Gold
Spirals $30.00
Latticinio Finger Bowl, White W/Blue & Gold
Spirals, Having Foot Extension & Ruffled Edge.
.................................$70.00

(Row II, Left to Right)
Sandwich Lutz-Type Bowl, Cranberry Glass
W/Opalescent Threading In Band Around Rim,
7 Clear Applied Artwork Feet, 5½" Diam. $50.00
Sandwich Lutz-Type Creamer, Cranberry
Glass W/Opalescent Threading Around Neck,
Clear Applied Handle, 6 Clear Applied Artwork
Feet...............................$50.00

(Row III, Left to Right)
Sandwich Lutz-Type Cologne Bottles, Pr.,
Clear W/Cranberry Threaded Band Around
Lower Half, Matching Stoppers Over Clear
Glass, 1 W/Minor Damage To Cranberry
Threading $160.00
Sandwich Lutz-Type Candy Dish, Clear Glass
W/Cranberry Threading & Applied Handle, 6¾"
Diam. $75.00

(Row IV)
Sandwich Lutz-Type Beverage Set, Tankard-
Shaped Pitcher & 5 Matching Handled Lemon-
ades, Clear Glass W/Cranberry Threading
Around Lower Third, Applied Handles, Pitcher
Features Etching Of Crane Catching Fish Amidst
Flowers, Bulrushes & Pond Lilies; Lemonades
Feature Repeat Of Bulrushes & Lily Pads With-
out Crane $250.00

(A-MA. '75)　　　*Richard A. Bourne Co., Inc.*
**COLORLESS BLOWN THREE MOLD
GLASS - AMERICAN 1820-1840**
(Row I, Left to Right)
Cream Pitcher, W/Slightly Greenish Tinge,
End Of Handle Missing, 2⅞" H. $100.00
Bowl, W/Rayed Base, Rim Diam. 4⅝" . . . . . .
. . . .$160.00
Salt, W/Rayed Base, Rim Diam. 2¾" .$150.00
(Row II, Left to Right)
Tumbler Or Flip Glass, Diamond Base, 5¾" H.
. . . .$110.00
Pint Decanter, Rayed Base, Chipped Rim,
Lacks Stopper, 7" H. $35.00
Pint Decanter, Rayed Base, Pressed Sunburst
Stopper, Chip On Stopper, 8⅛" H. $60.00
(Row III, Left to Right)
Pint Barrel-Shaped Decanter, Plain Base,
Sunburst Stopper Not Orig., Some Cloudiness
In Decanter, 8⅜" H. $70.00
Quart Decanter, Plain Base, Lacks Stopper,
. . . .$40.00
Quart Decanter, Plain Base, Sunburst Stopper
Not Orig., 10⅞" H. $60.00
(Row IV, Left to Right)
Quart Decanter, Plain Base, Sunburst Stopper
Not Orig., Slight Cloudiness Near Base, Minute
Chips On Stopper, 10¼" H. $60.00
Quart Decanter, Rayed Base, 3 Applied
Double-Ring Rigaree Neck Rings, Cloudiness
Within Decanter, Crack In Body, 11" H. . . . . . .
. . . .$30.00
Quart Decanter, Diamond Pattern Within
Label Medallion, 10¾" H. $70.00

(A-OH. '76)　　　*Garth's Auctions, Inc.*
SUGAR SHAKERS
(Row I, Left to Right)
Canary Glass, Inverted Thumbprint Patt., 5¼" H.
. . . .$35.00
Pattern Glass, Clear, Top & Base Swirled,
5⅜" H. $20.00
Pattern Glass Base, Clear, Brass Top Is Head
Of Bull Dog W/Glass Eyes, 6" H. $75.00
Pattern Glass, Clear, Press Cut Zipper, Thread-
ed Top Has Chip, 5⅛" H. $15.00
Pale Yellow W/Opalescent Swirls, 4⅝"
H. $35.00
(Row II, Left to Right)
Pressed Glass, Clear, Floral, 4½" H. . .$40.00
Light Green, Coin Spot Patt., 4⅝" H. . .$50.00
Light Blue, Swirled W/Opalescent Stripes,
4¾" H. $45.00
Clear, Coin Spot Patt., Metal Lid Has Splits,
4¾" H. $20.00
Cut Glass, Diamond & Fan Patt., Chipped Base,
4½" H. $35.00

(Row III, Left to Right)
Light Blue, Spanish Lace, 4⅝" H. $52.50
Pattern Glass, Clear, Panels & Beading, 7⅞" H.
. . . .$10.00
Pattern Glass, Clear, Waffle Patt., 5" H.$12.50
Clear, W/Verticle Ribs & Opalescent Lattice,
4⅝" H. $25.00
Pattern Glass, Clear, 4¼" H. $12.50
(Row IV, Left to Right)
Hobnail Glass, Amber, 3⅞" H. $50.00
Clear, Swirled Spanish Lace, Threaded Top Is
Rough & Lid Is Poor Fit, 4⅛" H. $5.00
Hobnail Glass, Clear, Brass Top, 4¼" H. $12.50
Pattern Glass, Clear, 4¼" H. $12.50
Light Blue, Spanish Lace, 4½" H. $60.00

(D-KS. '76)
Locomotive Glass Candy Container, 6½" L.
. . . .$25.00

← (A-OH. '76)

(Row I, Left to Right)
Vases, Mary Gregory, Pr., Amber Bowls, Blue Feet, Enameled Boys, 6" H. $50.00
Ewer, Green W/Encrusted Gilt & Flowers, Clear Applied Handle, Moser Type, 7¾" H. ..$45.00
Spoon, Enamel On Silver, Russian Hallmarked "GK" For Gustaff Klingert, 5½" L. $65.00

(Row II, Left to Right)
Covered Box, Enameled, Ormolu Fittings, Ruby Glass, Base Cracked, 2⅝" H. $35.00
Miniature Box, Enameled, Blue & White On Crystal, 2½" Diam. $15.00
Tumbler, Mary Gregory, Blue, Enameled Girl, Ground Spot On Rim, 3⅝" H. $22.50
Paneled Perfume, Sapphire Blue, Frosted & Cut, Enameled Flowers, 3¾" H. $10.00
Vase, Cranberry W/Enameling, 2⅞" H. .$5.00

(Row III, Left to Right)
Cruet, Mary Gregory, Deep Cranberry W/Clear Hollow Stopper & Applied Handle, Enameled Boy, Tiny Flakes On Base Of Stopper, 6½" H.
....$55.00
Cruet, Amethyst W/Clear Stopper & Applied Handle, Enameled Flowers, Base Of Handle Ground, Stopper Chipped, 6½" H. $25.00
Cruet, Mary Gregory, Clear, Ribbed, Stopper & Applied Handle, Enameled Boy, Tear Drop Stopper, 6⅜" H. $30.00

(D-AL. '76)
Coralene Water Pitcher, Satin Glass Body Shading From Light Aqua To Deep Aqua Blue At Top, Reeded Handle $450.00

(A-OH. '76)

(Row I, Left to Right)
Opaque White Vases W/Applied Amber Crystal Decorations, Minor Roughness On Feet, Pr. $130.00
Cased Deep Pink Vases W/Enameled Decoration, 12½" H., Pr. $50.00

(Row II, Left to Right)
Cased Glass Vase, W/Pink Interior, Applied Amber Leaves, Feet & Red Cherries, 7½" H.
......................................$90.00
Cased Glass Jack-In-The-Pulpit Vase W/Deep Purple Interior, Roughness On Feet, 6½" H. $37.50
Rose Bowl, Purple To Opalescent W/Applied Crystal Decor., 4" H. $35.00
Cased Glass Vase, Rose To Yellow W/White Interior, Applied Amber Crystal Base, Green Leaves W/Fushia & Cranberry Flowers, One Petal Broken, 8¼" H. $95.00

Richard A. Bourne Co., Inc.

(A-OH. '76)   Garth's Auctions, Inc.
(Row I, Left to Right)
Cranberry Opalescent Coin Spot Pitcher,
Applied Clear Handle, 8½" H. $45.00
Hobnail Glass Pitcher, Rubina, Applied Handle,
7" H. $125.00
Brilliant Blue Pitcher, Inverted Thumbprint
Patt., Applied Reeded Handle, 8½" H. .$35.00
(Row II, Left to Right)
Cranberry Opalescent Hobnail Pitcher,
Square Mouth, Applied Clear Handle, 7½" H.
. . . .$100.00

Cased Pitcher, Shaded White To Butterscotch,
White Reeded Handle & Lining, Deep Butter-
scotch, Ruffled Mouth, 9½" H. $170.00
Cranberry Pitcher, Honeycomb Patt., Square
Mouth, Applied Clear Handle, 8½" H. .$135.00
(Row III, Left to Right)
Cased Spatter Ribbed Pitcher, Reeded Handle,
White Lining, 7½" H. $95.00
Rainbow Coin Spot Pitcher, Clear Ribbed
Applied Handle, 8½" H. $85.00
Diamond Quilted Pink Satin Glass Pitcher,
Clear Handle, Chip On Rim, 7½" H. . . .$30.00

(A-MA. '76)
COLORED COLOGNE BOTTLES
(Row I, Left to Right)
Canary Yellow, "Star & Punty" Pattern, Period
Stopper Though Not Orig., Sm. Chip On Point
Of Foot, One Point At Shoulder Chipped. . . . . .
. . . .$100.00
Canary Yellow, Orig. Stopper & 6 Cut Panels
Around Neck $60.00
Canary Yellow Hexagonal, "Loop" Pattern,
By Boston & Sandwich Glass Co., Chip Ground
On Base, Possible Ground At Top As Well, Tip
Of Stopper W/Sm. Flake Off $65.00
(Row II, Left to Right)
Canary Yellow Hexagonal, W/Ellipses, Sm.
Chips & Roughage To Several Points Of Base,
Stopper Not Orig. $60.00
Canary Yellow Globular, "Melon" Pattern,
Steeple Stopper Not Orig. $130.00
Canary Yellow, W/Steeple Stopper, Glass Is
Sick & Has Chemical Deposits In A Number Of
Areas, Stopper Not Orig. & Chipped Twice At
Top, Sm. Nick On Base $35.00
(Row III, Left to Right)
Brilliant Yellow-Green, W/Bullseye & Ellipses,
Orig. Stopper, Top Of Stopper W/Slight Rough-
age $140.00
Brilliant Medium-Green, Octagonal Shape
W/Gold Decor. On Bottle & Stopper . .$200.00
Amber, Hexagonal Shape W/Gothic Arch Pan-
els, Orig. Stopper W/Sm. Chip On Top, Traces
Of Gold Decor. $150.00
(Row IV, Left to Right)
Overlay, Clear To Pink W/Orig. Stopper W/Gold
Decor., Stopper Broken At Neck & Reglued
. . . .$75.00
Opaque Blue, Orig. Stopper W/Gold Decor.,
Gold Decor. Worn, Sm. Nick On One Point Of
Stopper $85.00
Cranberry Glass, Melon Ribbed, Stopper Does
Not Fit Though Appears To Match $70.00

(D-KA. '76)
Water Set, Pitcher W/Six Tumblers, (One Illus.)
Stars & Stripes Pattern $450.00

(A-PA. '75)   Pennypacker Auction Centre
Cheese Cover, Blown Glass, Pidgeon Blood
Red, Walnut Cutting Board Base $120.00

◄── (A-OH. '76)   *Garth's Auctions, Inc.*
(Row I, Left to Right)
Satin Glass Vase, Shaded Apricot, Diamond Quilted Mother Of Pearl, White Lining, Clear Satin Applied Feet, Minor Roughness On Feet, 4" H. $50.00
Satin Glass Tumbler, Pink, Diamond Quilted, 3¾" H. $40.00
Satin Glass Rose Bowl, Shaded Red To Pink Lining, 3⅛" H. $45.00
Mother Of Pearl Vase, Raindrop Patt., White Lining, 4" H. $55.00
(Row II, Left to Right)
Satin Glass Pitcher, Shaded White To Rose W/ Applied Frosted Reeded Handle, White Lining, 8½" H. $145.00
Satin Glass Ruffled Top Vase, White Shaded To Peach, Diamond Quilted Mother Of Pearl, White Lining, Frosted Rim, 10½" H. ..$130.00
Satin Glass Vase, Ribbed, Shaded Pink To White, Clear Frosted Ruffled Edge, 9" H. $85.00
(Row III, Left to Right)
Burmese Bowl, Applied Feet W/Strawberry On Pontil, 6¾" Diam. $95.00
Satin Glass Covered Box, White, Blue Enameled Bird, Flowers & Clear Applied Feet, 6¾" Diam. $105.00
Satin Glass Rose Bowl, White To Rose W/ Enameled Flowers, Gilt Trimmed, White Lining, 4¾" H. $70.00

(A-OH. '76)   *Garth's Auctions, Inc.*
(Row I, Left to Right)
Amberina Diamond Quilted Tumbler, 3½" H. $60.00
Cranberry Tumbler, Paneled, 3⅝" H. .$17.50
Cranberry Tumbler, Inverted Thumbprint Patt., 3½" H. $15.00
Cranberry Tumbler, Coin Spot Patt., 3¾" H. $20.00
◄──**Rubina Tumbler,** Inverted Thumbprint Patt., Flakes On Top, 3⅝" H. $15.00
(Row II, Left to Right)
Flashed Amberina Tumblers, (4), Inverted Thumbprint Patt., All W/Rim Flakes, 3¾" H. ..
....$130.00
Blue Tumblers, (2), Thumbprint Patt., One Has Flake, Other Has Minor Roughness, 4" H. $15.00
Cranberry Tumblers, (6), Coin Spot Patt., 2 Have Minor Pin Point Flakes, 3¾" H. .$105.00
Cranberry Tumbler, Diamond Quilting, Enameled Flowers, Traces Of Gilt, Minor Rim Chips, 3¾" H. $15.00
Reversed Amberina Diamond Quilted Tumbler, One Pin Point Flake On Rim, 3⅝" H.
....$20.00
(Row III, Left to Right)
Amberina Tumbler, W/Ribbing, 3¾" H. $55.00
Cranberry Tumbler, Inverted Thumbprint Patt., Minor Roughness On Top, 3¾" H. $15.00
Royal Oak Tumbler, Minor Flake On Rim, 3⅞" H. $37.50
Cranberry Tumbler, Opalescent Swirls, Minor Rim Flake, 3¾" H. $15.00
Flashed Tumblers, (5), Inverted Thumbprint Patt., 4 Have Minor Rim Flakes, 3¾" H. ....
....$100.00
(Row IV, Left to Right)
Cranberry Tumbler, Herringbone Patt., One Sm. Pin Point Flake On Rim, 3¾" H. ..$20.00
Cased Pink Satin Tumbler, Quilted Base, 3¾" H. $20.00
Satin Cranberry Tumbler, Opalescent Swirls, 3⅞" H. $22.50
Brilliant Cranberry Tumbler, Opalescent Hobs, 3¾" H. $40.00
Flashed Amberina Tumbler, Herringbone Patt., Minor Roughness On Rim, 3⅝" H. $30.00

(A-OH. '76)   *Garth's Auctions, Inc.*
(Row I, Left to Right)
Moser Glass Vases, Pr., Pale Green W/En-
crusted Gilt & Enamel Decor., Signed "Moser",
6¼" H. $130.00
Cruets, Pr., Cranberry W/Encrusted Gilt Decor.
Highlighted W/Silver, Moser Type, Sold Indi-
vidually $170.00
(Row II, Left to Right)
Moser Glass Footed Cup & Saucer, Verre de
Soie Type, Encrusted Gilt Decor. & Turquoise
Enameling, Both Signed "Moser" $110.00
Tumbler, Clear Shaded To Blue, Encrusted
Gilt Decor., Moser Type, 3⅞" H. $55.00

Moser Glass Vase, Ribbed, Pale Amber W/
Flowers & Gilt Edge, Applied Blue Feet Have
Damage, Signed "Moser", 8⅛" H. $105.00
Tumbler, Clear Shaded To Cranberry, Encrusted
Gilt Decor., Moser Type, 3⅞" H. $55.00
Cup & Saucer, Cranberry W/Encrusted Gold
Highlighted W/Silver & White Enameled Lilies
Of The Valley $90.00

(A-MA. '77)   *Richard A. Bourne Co., Inc.*
(Row I, Left to Right)
Blown Three Mold Keene Pint Bottle, Oval,
Green, 7" H. $300.00
South Jersey-Type Gemel Bottle, Sapphire
Blue W/Opaque White Spiral Striping, 7⅜" H.
...................................$125.00
Blown Decanter, Cobalt Blue W/The Word
"Hollands" Over Grape Vine Done In Gold,
Also W/The Letter "H" Etched Into Orig. Stop-
per, 9¼" H. $60.00
(Row II)
Goblets, (3), Two Ruby Flashed Wines (2 Sizes),
And One Bohemian Goblet $75.00
(Row III, Left to Right)
Ruby Flashed Glass Pint Decanter, Vintage
Pattern Etched In Band Around Center .$75.00
Ruby Flashed Glass Quart Decanter, Vintage
Pattern Etched In Band Around Center .$70.00

(A-OH. '76)   *Garth's Auctions, Inc.*
Amberina Glass
(Row I, Left to Right)
Plate, "Baccarat", Signed, 5¼" Diam. ..$17.50
Tumbler, Inverted Diamond, 3⅝" H. ...$55.00
Wine Glass, Shades To Amber, Inverted
Thumbprint, 4¾" H. $40.00
Toothpick Holder, Diamond Quilted, 2¼" H.
...................................$100.00
Sauce Dish, Daisy & Button, Minor Roughness
On Edge, 5" Sq. $50.00
(Row II, Left to Right)
Shaped Vase, Inverted Thumbprint, Flashed,
4½" H. $65.00
Vase, Swirled Rib, Flashed, Ruffled Amber Top,
9½" H. $80.00
Vase, Signed "Libbey", Ribbed, 5" H. .$325.00

(A-MA. '77)   *Richard A. Bourne Co., Inc.*

(A-OH. '76)   *Garth's Auctions, Inc.*

(Row I, Left to Right)
Mercury Glass Vases, Pr., W/Enameling, 6¾" H. $17.50
Mercury Glass Vase, White Frosted Tropical Foliage, 8¼" H. $10.00
Bristol Glass Vase, Grey-Blue W/White Enameling & Gilt, 13¼" H. $15.00
Mercury Glass Vase, W/Enameled Bouquet, 7¼" H. $12.50
(Row II, Left to Right)
Satin Glass Vases, Pr., White W/Russet Floral Sprays, Both W/Rim Flakes 10¼' H. ...$25.00

Mercury Glass Vase, 8⅞" H. $20.00
Mercury Glass Pitcher, Clear Applied Handle, Silvering Worn In Spots, 6½" H. $37.50
(Row III, Left to Right)
Bristol Glass Vases, Pr., Frosted Ground W/Enameling, 10" H. $30.00
Mercury Glass Vases, Pr., Frosted Floral Band, 6¾' H. $12.50
Mercury Glass Compote, Gold Interior, Exterior Frosted W/Gold Band In Base & Enameled Floral Band, 7⅜" Diam., 6⅜" H. $22.50

(A-MA. '76)
(Row I)
(Left & Right)
Overlay Compotes, Pr., French, 19th C., Cobalt Blue Cut To Clear, One Perfect, Other W/Slight Rim Nick, 10" Diam., 7¼" H. $250.00
(Center)
Cut Overlay Finger Bowls & Undertrays, (1 Of 12 Bowls Illus.), French, 19th C., Cobalt Blue Cut To Clear, Minor Roughage To Rims Only, 6" Diam.........................$625.00

(Row I)
Overlay Dresser Set, (3-Pc.), Pair Of Cologne Bottles & Lidded Powder Jar, White Hand Painted Overlay Medallion W/Portraits Of Ladies Of High Fashion Applied To Emerald Green W/Overall Decor. In Gold $60.00
(Row II, Left to Right)
Cut Overlay Beaker-Form Vase, Cobalt Blue Cut To Clear In Floral & Honeycomb Cut Designs, 5⅝" H. $45.00
Cut Overlay Cologne Bottle, Possibly French, 19th C., Cobalt Blue Cut To Clear, 10" H. ...$75.00
Overlay Candlestick, Signed Libby, Emerald Green Cut To Clear, 6" H. $60.00
(Row III, Left to Right)
Overlay Quart Decanders, Pair, Emerald Green Cut To Clear, Both Missing Stoppers. $70.00
Overlay Quart Decanter, Cranberry Cut To Clear W/Etched Vintage Design In Band Around Center, Stopper Not Orig..............$65.00

Richard A. Bourne, Co., Inc.

(Row II, Left to Right)
Overlay Plates, (1 Of 6 Illus.), French, 19th C., Cobalt Blue Cut To Clear, Minimal Rim Roughage, 8½" Diam. $270.00
Overlay Compote, French, 19th C., Cobalt Blue Cut To Clear In Mirror Pattern, Minimal Rim Roughage, 10" Diam., 9¾" H. ...$200.00
Cut Overlay Undertrays & Finger Bowls, (1 Of 12 Trays Illus.), French, 19th C., Cobalt Blue Cut To Clear, 8¼" Diam. $625.00

(A-MA. '75)   Richard A. Bourne Co. Inc.

NAILSEA TYPE GLASS
(Row I, Left to Right)
Footed Pitcher, 1830-1860, Freeblown, Color-less W/Greenish Tinge, Decor. W/Bands Of Opaque White Loopings, Applied Trifid Ear-Shaped Handle, 6⅝" H. $150.00
Goblet, Ca. 1830, Freeblown, Colorless W/Greenish Tinge, Cylindrical Bucket Shaped Bowl Decor. W/Opaque White Loops, Baluster Knop Stem W/Teardrop, Circular Foot, 6¼" H. . . . . .
. . . .$110.00
Covered Sugar Bowl, Ca. 1830, Decor. W/Pink & White Loopings, Footed, Button Finial, 7⅛" H. $380.00
(Row II, Left to Right)
Vase, Ca. 1840, Freeblown, Colorless, Opaque White Looped Decor., Gauffered Rim Edged W/Opaque Brownish Red, Baluster Stem, Circular Foot, 8¼" H. $175.00
Decanter, 1860-1880, Sugar Loaf Shape, Free-blown, Colorless, Decor. W/Opaque White Loopings,Teardrop Shape Stopper, Minute Chip On Stopper, 9" H. $250.00
Footed Vase, Ca. 1840. Freeblown, Colorless, Decor. W/Pale White Looped Decor., Gauffered Rim Edged W/Opaque White & Deep Pink, Waisted Cylindrical Stem, Domed Foot, 8¼" H.
. . . .$125.00
(Row III, Left to Right)
Vase, 19th C., Freeblown, Colorless, Decor. W/Opaque White Loopings, Cylindrical Stan-dard W/Medium Lge. Ribbed Melon Knop, Domed Foot, Minor Chips On Foot, 10¼" H.
. . . .$40.00
(Cont. Upper Right)

Witch Ball & Stand, 19th C., Freeblown, Color-less, Looped Decor., Ht. Of Stand - 7½", Overall, 13" H. $180.00
Bellows Bottle On Stand, 1840-1870, Free-blown, Colorless, Decor. W/Opaque White & Pink Loopings, Applied Leaf Decor., Bands Of Rigaree, Waisted Cylindrical Standard, Domed Circular Foot, Minor Crack In Stopper, Overall Ht. - 19⅜" $350.00

(A-OH. '76)   Garth's Auctions, Inc.
(Row I, Left to Right)
Clear Flint Candlesticks, Pr., Minor Rough-ness, 10" H. $100.00
Sapphire Blue Vase, Arch Bowl, Gauffered Rim, Ringed Shank & Hexagonal Cascade Base, McKearin 200-34, 11¼" H. $475.00
(Row II, Left to Right)
Clear Vases, Tulip, Pr., 8" H. $20.00
Emerald Green Vase, Tulip, McKearin 201-40, Underside Of Base Has Several Sliver Flakes, 10" H. $450.00

(A-MA. '75)   Richard A. Bourne Co. Inc.

RUBY FLASHED GLASS
(Row I, Left to Right)
Knife Rest, Bohemian, Etched Design On All Sides, Few Minute Edge Nicks $10.00
Wines, (1 Of 20), Amer., Many Nearly Matching, 3 Brownish Color, 1 W/Tortoise Shell-Like Swirl $170.00
Finger Bowls, (1 Of 16), Amer., Many Matching, All Have Etched Grape Vine Pattern . .$250.00
(Row II, Left to Right)
Goblets, (1 Of 21), Grape Vine Etching, Heights Vary Slightly, 1 W/Minute Rim Nick . . .$250.00
Goblets, (1 Of 6), Bohemian, Matched Set W/Etched Design Of Running & Standing Deer In A Forest $125.00
Goblets, (1 Of 3), Amer., Etched Grape Design, 1 W/2 Sm. Chips In Foot $15.00
(Row III, Left to Right)
Candlesticks, (1 Of 4), Matched Set, Etched Grape Vine Design On Feet & Sockets, 7¾" H.
. . . .$275.00
Carafes, (2), Amer., Both W/Similar Grape Vine Etching, 1 W/Chip On Underside Of Rim, 6½" H.
. . . .$60.00
(Row IV, Left to Right)
Covered Cheese Dish, Amer., Decorated
. . . .$100.00
Compote, Amer., Etched Panels & Cut Base, Sm. Chips In Upper Rim, 8¾" Diam., 7⅜" H.
. . . .$125.00

(A-OH. '76)

RUBINA VERDE GLASS
(Left to Right)

Pitcher, Applied Reeded Amber Handle, Shades To Olive Amber, Inverted Thumbprint, 7¾" H.
. . . .$150.00
Vase, Ribbed, Flaring Mouth, Sm. Flake On Rim, 5" Diam., 2½" H. $65.00

(A-OH. '76)   *Garth's Auctions, Inc.*
(Row I, Left to Right)
Cranberry Glass Bell, White Rim, Clear Handle,
11¾" H. $75.00
Ruby Glass Bell, Clear Handle, Slight Swirl,
13" H. $60.00
Cranberry Glass Bell, Clear Handle, Three Leaf
Clover Finial, 13½" H. $55.00
Cranberry Glass Bell, Clear Handle, Opales-
cent Swirls, 14" H. $60.00
(Row II, Left to Right)
Cranberry Glass Covered Butter, Royal Ivy,
Flake On Finial, Minor Roughness On Edges,
5½" H. $132.00
Cranberry Glass Creamer, Royal Ivy, Clear
Applied Handle, 4½" H. $115.00
Cranberry Glass Jar, Royal Ivy, 3½" H.$55.00
Cranberry Glass Covered Jar, Royal Ivy, Pin
Point Flakes On Rim, 6" H. $105.00
(Row III, Left to Right)
Opalescent Glass Celery, Blue, 5⅝" H.$25.00
Opalescent Glass Striped Powder Dish, Clear,
Ribbed Opal, 5¼" Diam. $27.50
Cranberry Overshot Pitcher, Clear Reeded
Handle, 6¾" H. $80.00
Opalescent Glass Vase, Blue Ruffled Rim,
Orchid Base W/Opalescent Swirls, 4½" H. ...
...................................$100.00

(D-MO. '76)
Glass Bell W/Clapper (Not Shown); Having a
Gold Filled Handle W/Much Gold Decoration,
8½" H. $65.00

(D-MO. '76)
Florentine Cameo Water Pitcher, Frosted
Lime W/White Enamel Decor. $125.00

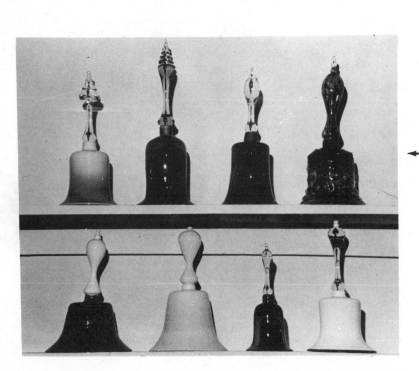

(A-OH. '76)   *Garth's Auctions, Inc.*
(Row I, Left to Right)
Burmese Glass Bell, Clear Handle W/Yellow
Tip, Yellow Rim, 12" H. $410.00
Cranberry Glass Bell, Clear Handle, 14¾" H.
...................................$55.00
Cobalt Blue Bell, Clear Handle, 12" H. $40.00
Cranberry Glass Bell, Bullseye Pattern, Hollow
End-O-Day Handle, 13¼" H. $125.00
(Row II, Left to Right)
Cranberry Glass Bell, Swirled Pattern, W/
Opaque White Handle, 10⅜" H. $60.00
Opaque White Bell, 10¼" H. $50.00
Cranberry Glass Bell, Clear Handle, 8¾" H.
...................................$35.00
Opaque White Bell, Blue Rim, Clear Handle
W/White Finial, 10¾" H. $65.00

(Row I, Left to Right)
Hobnail Glass Powder Jar, Covered, Satin Finish, Blue, Lid Has Flakes On Edge, 5⅞" H. $12.50
Hobnail Glass Open Sugar, Frosted Rubina, 4" H. $50.00
Hobnail Glass Bowl, Cranberry Opalescent, Ruffled Top, 5" Diam. $22.50
Francisware Pitcher, Amber, Applied Handle, Minor Flakes On Tips Of Hobs & Handle, 4¼" H. $15.00

(Row II, Left to Right)
Hobnail Glass Perfume, Cranberry Opalescent W/Opalescent Stopper & Hobs, Signed "Czechoslovakia", 5¾" H. $25.00

(D-N.Y. '76)
Cut Glass Water Pitcher, Intaglio Grape Pattern, Sgn. "Heisey" $275.00

Hobnail Glass Tumbler, Canary, 4" H. $20.00
Hobnail Glass Tray, Amber, 7¼" Diam. $8.00
Hobnail Glass Tumbler, Shaded Clear To Green, 4" H. $22.50
Hobnail Glass Vase, Cranberry W/Opalescent Top, 4½" H. $22.50
(Row III, Left to Right)
Hobnail Glass Compotes, Pr., 5½" Diam., 6" H. $25.00
Hobnail Tumbler, Cranberry W/Opalescent Hobs, 3¾" H. $45.00
Francisware Bowl, 9" Sq. $45.00
Hobnail Glass Tumbler, Blue Shaded To Purple, 4" H. $47.50

(Left to Right)
Burmese Glass Pitcher $60.00
Burmese Bowl & Tray, Pear Shaped W/Cover. $90.00
Burmese Glass Pitcher, 6" H., Rim Repair $35.00

(A-OH. '76)   Garth's Auctions, Inc.
Amberina Pitcher, Shades To Yellow Amber, Inverted Thumbprint, 8¼" H. $110.00

"DIAMOND THUMBPRINT" PATTERN FLINT GLASS
(Row I, Left to Right)
Wine $90.00
Champagne $130.00
Handled Whiskey, Handle Check $45.00
Sauce Dish, One Scallop Chipped $20.00
(Row II, Left to Right)
Half-Pint Decanter, (Cologne Bottle), Sm. Chip On Bottom Of Base, Stopper Not Orig. ..$50.00
Goblet $275.00
Half-Pint Bar Decanter, W/Pewter Bitters Shaker Top, 2 Small Chips & 2 Minor Bruises in Edge Of Base $90.00
(Row III, Left to Right)
Compote, 2" Crack In Bowl Where Base Joins On One Side, 7½" W., 4⅜" H. $20.00
Creamer, W/Flaring Lip, Handle Check $40.00
(Row IV, Left to Right)
Celery Vase $100.00
Quart Bar Decanter, W/Period Pewter Pouring Stopper, Shallow Chip In Center Of Bottom. $90.00

(D-IA. '76)
Wavecrest Glass Box, W/Enamel Decor., Hinged Cover, 5" H., 8" L. $450.00

(A-MA. '75)   *Richard A. Bourne, Co., Inc.*
(Row I, Left to Right)
Relish Dish, U.S. Coin Pattern, 50¢ & 25¢, 7⅜"
L. $120.00
Sauce Dish, Ring Handles, Words "For Auld
Lang Syne" Between Sprigs Of Holly & Clasped
Hands In Bottom Center $15.00
Paperweight, Sandwich Star Pattern, Cut
Knob $360.00
(Row II, Left to Right)
Flint Glass Cordial, New England Pineapple
Pattern $65.00
Flint Glass Wine, Sandwich Star Pattern .....
....$90.00
Flint Glass Mug, W/Applied Handle, Smocking
Pattern $90.00
Flint Glass Covered Sugar Bowl, Washington
Pattern, Sm. Roughage On Cover $50.00
(Row III, Left to Right)
Flint Glass Celery Vase, Ashburton Pattern,
Slightly Flaring Rim, Sm. Flake On One Scallop.
....$90.00
Flint Glass Vases, Pr., Paneled Tulip Form,
Boston & Sandwich Glass Co., 1 Has Sm. Chip
On Foot, 10" H. $70.00
(Row IV, Left to Right)
Flint Glass Covered Compote, Loop Pattern,
Sm. Mold Imperfection On One Scallop, Sm.
Flakes & Roughage On Rim Of Lid, 7" Diam.,
9" H. $70.00
Flint Glass Water Pitcher, Loop Pattern, Heavy
Applied Handle $55.00
Flint Glass Compote, Diamond Thumbprint
Pattern, 8¼" Diam., 4" H. $45.00

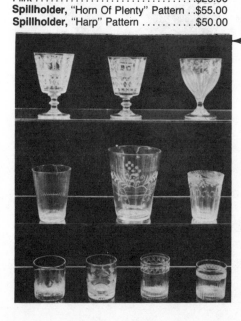

(A-MA. '76)
Richard A. Bourne Co., Inc.

PRESSED GLASS, "BUCKLE" PATTERN
Bowl, Flint, Turned-Down Rim, 9½" Diam. ...
....$100.00
Compote, Flint, Slightly Misshapen, 7" Diam.
6¼" H. $50.00

(A-MA. '76)   *Richard A. Bourne Co., Inc.*
FLINT & NON-FLINT PRESSED GLASS
(Row I, Left to Right)
Wine, "Pillar" Pattern $35.00
Wine, "Bullseye & Bar" Pattern $100.00
Wine, "Sandwich Star" Pattern $100.00
Wine, "Paneled Diamond Point" ("Hinota")
Pattern $45.00
(Row II, Left to Right)
Wine, "Ashburton" Pattern $30.00
Wine, "Ashburton" Pattern $25.00
Wine, "Prism & Crescent" Pattern $30.00
Wine, "Blackberry" Pattern, Slight Nick On
Knop $35.00
(Row III, Left to Right)
Wine, "Bigler" Pattern $30.00
Wine, "Tulip" Pattern $30.00
Champagne, "Sandwich Star" Pattern $125.00
Covered Salt, "Ribbed Ivy" Pattern, Minor
Roughage To Foot $100.00
(Row IV, Left to Right)
Covered Salt, "Sawtooth" Pattern, Non-Flint
....$35.00
Child's Mug, W/Bird & Hunting Dogs, Non-
Flint $25.00
Spillholder, "Horn Of Plenty" Pattern ..$55.00
Spillholder, "Harp" Pattern $50.00

(A-MA. '76)   *Richard A. Bourne, Co., Inc.*
MISCELLANEOUS EARLY GLASS
(Row I, Left to Right)
Egg Cup, Opaque White Or Clambroth, "Bulls-
eye & Bar" Pattern $200.00
Covered Egg Cup, Opaque White Or Clam-
broth, "Fine Rib" Pattern, Originally Sold As
Pomades, When Contents Used It Was Used
As Egg Cup $250.00
Egg Cup, Opaque White Or Clambroth, "Dia-
mond Point" Pattern $150.00
Pomade Jar, Translucent Yellow-Green,
Covered, Basketweave Design, Top Of Knob
On Cover Has Been Ground Where Finial
Apparently Was Broken Off $100.00
(Row II, Left to Right)
Cologne Bottle, Canary Yellow, "Thistle" Pat-
tern W/Thistle Stopper, Sm. Chip On Lower Part
Of Stopper Hidden By Bottle Neck $150.00
Sandwich Candleholder W/Hurricane Shade,
Opaque White Or Clambroth Base W/Applied
Handle, Brass Chimney Holder & Clear & Frost-
ed Cylindrical Chimney W/Key Pattern Around
Top, Chip In Rim Of Candle Socket, Slight Rim
Roughage $175.00
Cologne Bottle, Translucent Blue, "Basket-
weave" Pattern, Clear Stopper, Stopper Old
But Not Original $70.00

(A-MA. '75)   *Richard A. Bourne Co., Inc.*
**Colorless Flint Glass Tablewares — Late 18th
and Early 19th Century**
(Row I, Left to Right)
Rummer, Freeblown, Upper Half Of Bowl En-
graved W/Variety Of Masonic Emblems, Lower
Half W/Geometric Patt. Of Diamonds & Trifid
Motifs, 5½" H. $60.00
Rummer, Same Form As Preceding, Engraved
Motifs Vary Slightly, 5¼" H. $30.00
Rummer, Patterned In Mold, Lightly Engraved,
Initials "JMH" Within An Oval Cartouche, Sm.
Chip On Rim, 5⅛" H. $20.00
(Row II, Left to Right)
Tumbler, (Or Sm. "Flip" Glass), Cylindrical
Tapered W/Vertical Ribs, Plain Base, 4½" H. .
....$25.00
Tumbler, (Or Sm. "Flip" Glass), Freeblown,
Sketchily Engraved W/Stylized Flowers, 6" H.
....$50.00
Tumbler, Blown In A Mold & Patterned, Plain
Base, 4" H. $60.00
(Row III, Left to Right)
Tumbler, Freeblown W/Slightly Greenish Tinge,
Ground & Polished Base, Minor Chips In Rim,
3¼" H. $10.00
Tumbler, Blown In Mold To Create Rayed Base,
Finished By Blowing & Tooling, 3⅜" H. $45.00
Tumbler, Freeblown & Cut, Sm. Remains Of
Pontil Mark Evident, 3½" H. $15.00
Tumbler, Freeblown & Cut, Base Ground Flat &
Polished, 2⅞" H. $15.00

← (A-OH. '76)   *Garth's Auctions, Inc.*
(Row I, Left to Right)
Cologne Bottle, Sapphire Blue, Blown In 3-Part Mold, 5¾" H.......................$45.00
Waste Bowl, Amethyst, Bigler, Minor Roughness, 4½" Diam. $185.00
Cologne Bottle, Amethyst, Octagonal W/Panels, Ovals & Circles Blown In Tumbler Mold, Argus, 6" H. $155.00
(Row II, Left to Right)
Canary Salts, Four (2 Illus.), Cut Swags & Tassels, 2½" H. $95.00
Wine Glass, Clear Blown, Cut Panels & Wheel Engraved & Cut Decorative Bands W/Swags & Tassels, 4¾" H. $40.00
Cologne Bottle, Yellow-Green, Star & Punty, Small Bruise, 5½" H. $160.00
Wine Glass, Clear Blown, Cut Panels & Wheel Engraved & Cut Band Of Vintage, 4½" H. ....
....$40.00
(Row III, Left to Right)
Pepper Sauce Bottle, Teal Blue, 8" H. $30.00
Case Bottles, Pr., Green Blown, Wheel Engraved W/Ships & Butterflies, 5¼" H. ..$85.00
Flip, Green Blown, Wheel Engraved Ship, 6¼" H. $125.00
Decanter, Clear Blown, Wheel Engraved & Cut Design W/Swags & Tassels, 8¾" H.$55.00

(A-OH. '76)   *Garth's Auctions, Inc.*
CUT GLASS
Syrup, W/Metal Mounts, 5¼" H. $45.00
Wine Glasses, (11), Cut Stems, Signed "Hawkes", One Has ¼" Check In Rim Of Bowl, 7¼" H. $270.00

(A-OH. '76)   *Garth's Auctions, Inc.*
CUT GLASS
Bowl, Deeply Cut, Minute Pin Point Flakes, 7⅛" Diam. $35.00

(A-OH. '76)   *Garth's Auctions, Inc.*
CUT GLASS
(Row I, Left to Right)
Cruet, W/Cut Stopper, 6" H. $50.00
Cruet, W/Cut Stopper & Handle, Flattened, Globular, 7⅝" H. $40.00
Cruet, W/Cut Stopper, 7" H. $40.00
(Row II, Left to Right)
Perfume, W/Hallmarked Silver Mount, Zipper & Cane Pattern, 4¾" H. $35.00
Tall Footed Salt & Pepper Shakers, Pr., Covers For Tops Are Pressed, 5" H. ...$40.00
Syrup, W/Silver Plated Mounts, 5¼" H.$55.00
Mustard Jar, W/Cut Lid, Flange On Underside Of Lid Has Been Ground, 3¾" H......$25.00

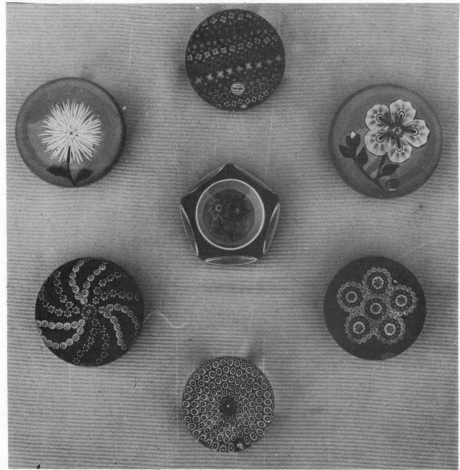

← (A-OH. '76)   *Garth's Auctions, Inc.*

Saint Louis Paperweight, White Dahlia On Mauve Ground, "S. L., 1974" $90.00

Saint Louis Paperweight, Patterned Millefiori, Purple & Green, "S. L. 1975" $80.00

Saint Louis Paperweight, White Flower On Pistachio, "S. L. 1973" $85.00

Saint Louis Paperweight, Blue Cut To White To Clear, Double Flower Center, "S. L. 1975"
.....................................$95.00

Saint Louis Paperweight, Millefiori In Flower Shape On Drk. Red Ground, "S. L. 1974" ....
.....................................$95.00

Saint Louis Paperweight, Doily & Blue Ground, "S. L. 1972" $95.00

Saint Louis Paperweight, Millefiori, "S. L. 1972 ....$85.00

(A-OH. '76)   *Garth's Auction, Inc.*

CUT GLASS

Salt & Pepper Shakers, Pr., Plated Tops, One W/Sm. Flake On Bottom $15.00

(A-MA. '75)   *Richard A. Bourne Co. Inc.*

(Row I)

Window Panes, (3 Of 16), Late 19th-Early 20th C., 3 Diff. Patterns, 2 Sizes: 4" x 5" Incl. Blue, Green & Lt. Amethyst; & 4" x 4" Incl. Amber, Lt. Green & Pale Amethyst, Slight Edge Chips ...
.....................................$130.00

(Row II, Left to Right)

Covered Dish, Atterbury Type, Contemporary, Clear Amethyst Base, Cover W/Milk Glass Head W/Teal Blue Eyes, Chip On Rim Of Base, 10¾" L. $40.00

Covered Dish, Atterbury Type, Contemporary, Milk Glass Base, Milk Glass Cover W/Amethyst Head W/Teal Blue Eyes, 10⅞" L. $30.00

(Row III, Left to Right)

Covered Dish, Amer., 19th C., Opaque Lt. Amethyst Base, Cover Same, Part Of Basket & Wings, Tail & Neck Feathers Gilded, Sm. Chip On Cover, 5½" L. $55.00

Covered Dish, Amer., 19th C., "Clam Broth" Base, Cover Same, Yellows, Browns, Reds & Orange, Sm. Chip On Base, 7" L. $55.00

Covered Dish, Amer., 19th C., Lt. Green, Part Of Basketweave & Portion Of Cover Gilded, Sm. Chip On Cover, Slight Roughage, 5½" L.
.....................................$40.00

(Row IV, Left to Right)

Covered Dish, 19th C., Custard Color, No Decor., 7½" L. $35.00

Covered Dish, Amer., 19th C., Pale Opaque Pink, Cover W/Squirrel Handle, Sm. Chip On Bowl, 5½" L. $50.00

Covered Bowl, Amer., 19th C., Pale Opaque Pink, Cover Handle In Form Of Turkey W/Tail Spread, Lg. Flake On Turkey Tail, 5½" L.
.....................................$60.00

(Row V, Left to Right)

Covered Dish, Amer., 19th C., Caramel Color, No Decor., Minor Chips, 8½" L. $55.00

Covered Dish, Amer., 19th C., Deep Amethyst W/Daisy & Button Design On Bottom, Cover W/ Reclining Cow, Minor Roughage, 6½" L.$70.00

Covered Dish, Amer., 19th C., Turkey Form, Colorless, Base W/Sq. Diamond Pattern, Cover In Form Of Head & Shoulders, Sm. Chips, Slight Roughage, 9" H. $50.00

(D-AL. '76)

Bride's Basket. In Silver Frame, Fluted Bowl Shades From Deep Cranberry On Rim to White Center W/Floral Decor.........$350.00

(D-LA. '76)

Steuben Champagne, Topaz W/ Blue Stem (1 Of 6), Set .$200.00

(A-OH. '76) Garth's Auctions, Inc.

(Row I, Left to Right)
Master Salt, Clear, 6-Panel, Tulip, Footed,
Salt, Clear, Sawtooth, Footed, Top Rim W/Minor
Chips, 3" H. $6.00
Covered Salt, Clear, Sawtooth, Footed, Sm.
Chips, 5" H. $30.00
Salt, Clear, Blown, Broken Swirl, Footed, 3" H.
................................$90.00
Salt, Clear, 6-Panel, Footed, Base W/Minor
Roughness, 3" H. $10.00

(Row II, Left to Right)
Wine Glass, Clear, Honeycomb, 4" H. .$15.00
Wine Glass, Clear, 8-Panel, 4¼" H. ...$90.00
Wine Glass, Clear, Elongated Thumbprint,
4⅜" H. $25.00
Wine Glass, Clear, Fine Rib, 4" H. $32.50
Wine Glass, Clear, Ashburton, 4½" H. .$27.50
Wine Glass, Clear, Argus, 4¼" H. $30.00

(Row III, Left to Right)
Wine Glass, Clear, 6 Panels In Base W/Diamond Point, 4½" H. $20.00
Cordial Glasses, Pr., Clear, Paneled, Sq.
Bases, 2¾' H. $4.00
Pitcher, Clear, Flint, Applied Clear Handle,
Loop Patt., 4" H. $22.50
Wine Glass, Clear, Flint, 6 Panels, 3½" H. ...
................................$27.50
Wine Glass, Clear, Flint, Horn Of Plenty, 3¾" H.
................................$27.50

(A-MA. '75) Richard A. Bourne Co. Inc.

SALT DISHES
(Row I, Left to Right)
Bird Bath, Opalescent Purple-Blue, Crack
One Side, Replaced Foot $90.00

Basket Of Flowers, Opaque Deep Purple-
Blue W/Opalescence, Chips On Four Extensions, Slight Flakes $100.00

Basket Of Flowers, Cobalt Blue W/Slight
Opalescence, 3 Scrolls Broken Off, Chips,
Some Roughage $60.00
Chariot, Silvery Opaque Blue W/Lt. Mottling,
Minor Chip $80.00
(Row II, Left to Right)
Lacy Divided, Cobalt Blue, 1 Foot Chipped Off
At Corner, Lt. Roughage.............$55.00
Gothic Arch, Med. Blue, Sm. Chips & Roughage $160.00
Light Green, Sm. Heat Check, Sm. Rim Chips
................................$70.00
Oval, Purple Blue, Slight Roughage ..$100.00

◀ (A-MA. '76)

Richard A. Bourne, Co., Inc.

BLOWN THREE-MOLD & OTHER BLOWN GLASS
(Row I, Left to Right)
Air Twist Sterm Wine, Fluted Molding Around Lower Half Of Bowl $80.00
Blown Stem Wine, W/Knop Stem $80.00
Air Twist Stem Wine, W/Flaring Rim & Wide Foot $70.00
Blown & Molded Glass Funnel, Bluish Tint & Fluted Ribbing, Rough On Sm. End $50.00
(Row II, Left to Right)
Blown Three Mold Half-Pint Decanter, Plumes Do Not Join, Stopper Of Period But Not Orig. $120.00
Clear Blown Three Mold Sandwich Half-Pint Vinegar Bottle, Period Stopper $35.00
Square Clear Blown Three Mold Pint Cologne Bottle, Plume Pattern On 2 Sides, Honeycomb Cutting Around Neck, Midwestern Style Mushroom Stopper, Slight Roughage Around Stopper, Chemical Deposit Around Lower Third Of Bottle. $50.00
Blown Three Mold Clear Hat $80.00
(Row III, Left to Right)
Clear Blown Three Mold Quart Decanter, Three-Ring Neck, Period Stopper $75.00
Clear Blown Three Mold Pint Decanter, Period Stopper But Not Orig., One-Quarter Of Stopper Bottom Chipped Away $65.00
Clear Blown Three Mold Pint Decanter, Period Stopper $200.00

(D-AL. '76)
Cut Glass Cruet, Salt, Pepper & Spooner Set, 5 Pcs. $200.00

(D-TX. '76)
CUT GLASS
(Left to Right)
Pansy Or Violet Holder, Sgn. "Libbey" $125.00
Pickle Dish, Sgn. "Libbey" $90.00
Vinegar Cruet, Sgn. "Libbey" $125.00

(D-TX. '76)
CUT GLASS
(Left to Right)
Sugar Shaker, Green Cut To Clear, Brass Lid, ... $175.00
Sugar Shaker, Intaglio Cut Flowers, Silver Lid. $95.00

(D-MO. '76)
CUT GLASS
(Left to Right)
Toothpick Holder, Sgn. "Hawks" $75.00
Barber Bottle W/Silver Top $175.00

(A-OH. '76)
CUT GLASS   *Garth's Auctions, Inc.*
Bowl, 8" Diam. $60.00

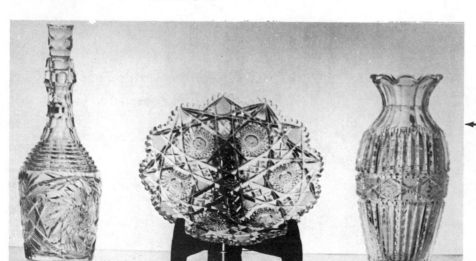

(A-OH. '76)   *Garth's Auctions, Inc.*

CUT GLASS
(Left to Right)

Decanter, W/Cut Stopper, Lge. Buzz Star, 11½" H. $140.00
Shallow Bowl, Shamrock Signature For Hawkes, Minor Rim Flakes, 10" Diam. $95.00
Vase, Notched Prism, Sm. Chip On Base, 9½" H. $50.00

Garth's Auctions, Inc.

(A-OH. '76)
SANDWICH GLASS

(Row I, Left to Right)
Toddy Plate, Lacy, Clear, Peacock Eye, Lee, Pl. 109-2, Rim Flakes, 6½" Diam. $20.00
Sauce, Lacy, Clear, Rose & Thistle, Chip On Edge, 5¼" Diam. $47.50
Dish, Lacy, Clear, Oak Leaf, Lee, Pl. 127, 5½" Diam. $20.00

(Row II, Left to Right)
Cup Plate, Lacy, Blue, 3½" Diam. $65.00
Cup Plate, Lacy, Clear, 3¾" Diam. $12.50
Cup Plate, Lacy, Opalescent, 3⅝" Diam. . . . . . .
. . . .$52.50
Cup Plate, Lacy, Clear, 3⅝" Diam. $17.50
Cup Plate, Lacy, Blue, "Henry Clay", 3⅝" Diam.
. . . .$85.00

(Row III, Left to Right)
Cup Plate, Lacy, Clear, 3¼" Diam. $17.50
Honey Dishes, Pr., Flint, Clear, Baby Thumbprint, Edges Are Rough, 4" Diam. $20.00
Honey Dish, Lacy, Clear, 4⅜" Diam. . .$14.00
Cup Plate, Lacy, Clear, 3⅜" Diam. $11.00

←(A-OH. '76)   *Garth's Auctions, Inc.*
Cut Glass Nappie, Minor Roughness, 6" Diam.
. . . .$30.00

Garth's Auctions, Inc.

(A-OH. '76)
CUT GLASS

(Left to Right)
Tumbler, Cane Patt., 3½" H. $17.50
Tumbler, Zipper & Fan Patt., 3¾" H. . .$17.50
Bowl, Brilliant & Deep Cutting, 9" Diam.$105.00

Tumbler, Buzz Star, Flake On Base, 4" H.
. . . .$15.00
Tumbler, 3¾" H. $17.50

(A-OH. '76)   *Garth's Auctions, Inc.*
CUT GLASS

Creamer & Sugar $50.00

(A-OH. '76)   *Garth's Auctions, Inc.*

SANDWICH GLASS

Bowl, Lacy, Clear Smokey, Midwestern, #442 In Corning Exhibition Of 1954, 7½" Diam. . . . .
. . . .$100.00

(A-MA. '75)   *Richard A. Bourne Co. Inc.*

LACY SANDWICH GLASS
(Row I, Left to Right)
Bowl, Ca. 1830-1840, Princess Feather Design W/Stylized Flowers In Base, Minor Damage, 6½" Diam. $60.00
Octagonal Plate, 1830-1840, Acorn & Oak Leaf Pattern, Minor Roughage & Damage, 5⅛" Across The Flats $30.00
Plate, 1830-1850, 12 Sides, Shell Pattern, Minor Damage, 6⅛" Diam. $30.00
Plate, 1825-1850, Heart & Sheaf Pattern, Minor Edge Roughage, 6¼" Diam. $40.00
(Row II, Left to Right)
Bowl, 1830-1850, Princess Feather Pattern, Minor Chips On Scallops, 8½" Diam. . .$65.00

Plates, (1 Of 11), 1830-1850, Peacock Eye & Thistle Pattern, Minor Edge Roughness, 8" Diam. $375.00
Bowl, 1830-1850, Rose & Thistle Pattern, 1 Scallop Missing, Minor Chips, 3⅛" Diam. $35.00
(Row III, Left to Right)
Bowl, 1825-1830, Heart & Lyre Pattern, Portion 1 Scallop Missing, Minor Chips, 9¼" Diam. . . .
. . . .$90.00
Octagonal Plate, 1830-1850, Beehive & Thistle Pattern, Minor Edge Roughness, 9⅛" Across The Flats $60.00

(D-CA. '76)
Cut Glass Decanter, Sgn. "Libbey" . .$225.00

(A-OH. '76)
SANDWICH GLASS

Toddy Plate, Lacy, Olive Green, Waffle & Gothic Arch, 5⅞" Diam. $125.00

Bowl, Lacy, Clear, Lee, Pl. 105, #1, Edge Chips, 6" Diam. $25.00

Garth's Auctions, Inc.

Toddy Plate, Lacy, Brilliant Blue, Unlisted Pattern, 6" Diam. $105.00

(A-OH. '76)   *Garth's Auctions, Inc.*
SANDWICH GLASS

(Row I, Left to Right)
Cup Plate, Lacy, Clear, Eagle & "1831", Rough Edge, 3½" Diam. $22.50
Cup Plate, Lacy, Clear, Eagle, 3" Diam. $15.00
Cup Plate, Lacy, Clear, Ship, 3½" Diam. $30.00
Cup Plate, Lacy, Clear, Hearts, 3" Diam. $15.00
Cup Plate, Lacy, Clear, "Henry Clay", 3⅝" Diam. $25.00

(Row II, Left to Right)
Cup Plate, Lacy, Clear, Ship, Edge Has Chips, 3-9/16" Diam. $7.00
Salt, Lacy, Clear, Basket Of Flowers & Rosettes, Chip On One Ear, 3¼" L. $55.00
Cup Plate, Lacy, Clear, 13 Hearts, 3½" Diam. $12.50
Salt, Lacy, Clear, Rosettes In Fleur-de-Lis, 3¼" L. $20.00
Cup Plate, Lacy, Clear, Ship, Uneven Edge, 3⅝" Diam. $20.00

(Row III, Left to Right)
Cup Plate, Lacy, Clear, Maid Of The Mist, 3-7/16" Diam. $20.00
Cup Plate, Lacy, Clear, Eagle & "Fort Pitt", 3-11/16" Diam. $40.00
Salt, Lacy, Fiery Opalescent, Eagles, 3⅛" L. $280.00
Cup Plate, Lacy, Clear, Eagle, 3-7/16" Diam. $30.00
Cup Plate, Lacy, Clear, 3⅝" Diam. $12.50

SALT DISHES

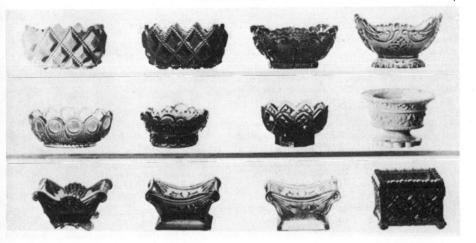

(A-MA. '75)   *Richard A. Bourne Co. Inc.*
(Row I, Left to Right)
Oval, Opaque Lt. Blue, Minor Chip ...$100.00
Oval, Deep Purple Blue, Minor Wear .$190.00
Oval, Deep Cobalt Blue $150.00
Oval Pedestal, Cobalt Blue $110.00
(Row II, Left to Right)
Peacock Eye, Oval, Peacock Blue, Sm. Chip. $200.00
Round Lacy, Drk. Green, Chips On Scallops. $45.00
Round, Deep Cobalt Blue $100.00
Round Pedestal, Silvery Opaque Violet Blue W/Mottling, Base Broken & Repaired, Crack In Rim...........................$225.00
(Row III, Left to Right)
Shell, Deep Purple Blue, Foot Chipped Off $40.00
Stag's Horn, Cobalt Blue, Minor Chip ..$70.00
Stag's Horn, Lt. Amber, Sm. Chip $200.00
Strawberry Diamond, Cobalt Blue, Chipped, Roughage $90.00

(A-OH. '76)   Garth's Auctions, Inc.

SANDWICH GLASS
(Row I, Left to Right)
Bowl, Shallow, Lacy, Clear, Heart & Lyre, Lee, Pl. 66, Chip On Edge, 9½" Diam. $70.00
Creamer, Lacy, Clear, Lee, Pl. 154, #2, Chip On Base & Top Edge Ground, 4⅜" H.....$30.00
Bowl, Shallow, Lacy, Clear, Gothic Arch, Lee, Pl. 129, 9¼" Diam. $80.00
(Row II, Left to Right)
Bowl, Lacy, Clear, Oak Leaf, Lee. Pl. 127, 7¼" Diam. $15.00
Compote, Lacy, Clear, Midwestern, 7½" Diam., 4" H. $115.00
Bowl, Lacy, Clear, Peacock Eye, Lee, Pl. 132, #1, Flake On Rim, 7½" Diam. $15.00
(Row III, Left to Right)
Covered Sugar, Lacy, Clear, Lee. Pl. 155, 6" H. $225.00
Oval Bowl, Lacy, Clear, Lee. Pl. 151, #3, Edge Chips, 10½" L. $55.00
Covered Sugar, Lacy, Clear, Gothic Arch, 3 Styles Of Arches W/Stars In Spandrels, 5¼" H. $90.00

(A-MASS. '76)   Richard A. Bourne Co. Inc.

(A-OH. '76)   Garth's Auctions, Inc.

SANDWICH GLASS
(Row I, Left to Right)
Bowl, Lacy, Clear, Amethyst Tint, Midwestern, Unlisted Patt. W/Lyres, 6½" Diam. $15.00
Octagonal Bowl, Lacy, Clear, Beehive, Lee. Pl. 136, #1, Edge Flakes, 9¾" Diam. ..$50.00
Bowl, Lacy, Clear, Princess Feather, 6⅝" Diam. $20.00
(Row II, Left to Right)
Plate, Lacy, Clear, New England, Waffle Design W/Fan Pattern, #42 In Corning Exhibition Of 1954, 9" Diam. $80.00
Candlestick, Lacy, Clear, Stepped Cascade Base, 5" H. $85.00
Bowl, Lacy, Clear, Rose & Thistle, 8" Diam. $45.00
(Row III, Left to Right)
Shallow Bowl, Lacy, Clear, Daisy, Lee. Pl. 130, 8" Diam. $80.00
Octagonal Bowl, Lacy, Clear, Rectangular W/Cut Corners, Nictarine & Star, McKearin Pl. 157, #4 Midwestern, 8" L. $75.00
Bowl, Lacy, Clear, Plume, 7½" Diam. ..$32.50

(Row I, Left to Right)
Flint Glass Egg Cups, Set Of 10, Inverted Fern Patt., 1 W/Lge. Inner Rim Chip At Top, (One Illus.) $150.00
Flint Glass Footed Salt, Inverted Fern Patt., 2 Sm. Chips On Foot $15.00
Flint Glass Sauce Dishes, Set Of 6, Inverted Fern Patt., 4" Diam.; Together W/One 3½" Sauce Or Honey Dish, (One Illus.) $40.00
Flint Glass Goblets, Set Of 6, Inverted Fern Patt., (One Illus.) $170.00
(Row II, Left to Right)
Flint Glass Covered Butter Dish, Inverted Fern Patt., 6" Diam. $50.00
Flint Glass Compote, Inverted Fern Patt., Scalloped Rim, Bruise On One Scallop, 7¼" Diam. 5" H. $40.00
Flint Glass Covered Sugar Bowl, Inverted Fern Patt. $50.00
(Row III, Left to Right)
Flint Glass Compote, Bigler Patt. Variant W/Sandwich Loop Base, 7⅜" Diam., 5½" H. $45.00
Blown Three Mold Quart Decanter, McKearin GIII-5, W/Period Blown Three Mold Stopper, One Chip In Lid At Top $65.00
Blown Three Mold Flip Glass, McKearin GII-33, Roughage On Two Points Of Pattern, 5½" H. $120.00

(A-MA. '76)   Richard A. Bourne Co., Inc.

ART GLASS TUMBLERS
(Row I, Left to Right)
Baccarat Amberina, Sgn. $40.00
Baccarat Amberina, Unsigned, Chip On Foot $40.00
Cranberry Opalescent, "Spanish Lace" Patt. $35.00
Tortoise Shell-Like Splotches $20.00
(Row II, Left to Right)
Pink Satin Glass, Diamond Quilted Patt. $50.00
Swirled Peachblow-Type Tumbler, Minute Rim Roughage $40.00
Shaded Pink W/Diamond Quilted Patt., Cased $50.00
Millefiori Patt. $30.00
(Row III, Left to Right)
Lot Of Four Assorted Tumblers Including Blue Glass Tumbler W/Enamel Decor., An Opalescent Blue Honeycomb Patt., English Purple Slag & Blue Opalescent Hobnail $15.00
(Row IV, Left to Right)
Lot Of Four Assorted Tumblers Including Blue Thumbprint W/Enamel Decor., Amber Tumbler W/Enamel Decor., & Two Amethyst Quilted $20.00

MASTER MODEL — Pattern & Other Pressed glass. Made mostly from mahogany, these wooden models serve as both a record of the original design and for producing metal molds in which the glass was pressed.

(A-MA. '75)   Richard A. Bourne Co. Inc.

WOODEN MODELS
Goblet, "Bullseye & Bar" Pattern, 8½" H. $300.00
Goblet, Unidentified Pattern, 8" H. $60.00
Goblet, Unidentified Pattern, 8⅜" H. ...$65.00
Parfait, "Flat Panel" Pattern, 7½" H. (Illus); Together W/Wine Glass W/4 Panels & Double-Knopped Sq. Stem $60.00

American kitchenwares dating from the hearth to the Victorian coal stove has become a fascinating hobby for many collectors in recent years. Items dating from the 17th and 18th centuries have become increasingly scarce and costly, but there is still available a variety of objects dating from the last century that can be purchased at reasonably moderate prices and, there is a seemingly endless number of unique gadgets made by factories during the late 1800s well into the present century, which carry price tags within the reach of almost every collector's pocketbook.

(A-OH. '76)   *Garth's Auctions, Inc.*
Marzipan Board, Mahogany, The Arms Of New York, Signed "J. Conger", Also Marked "J. Y. Watkins, N.Y.", 16" x 25" $2,600.00

(A-OH. '76)   *Garth's Auctions, Inc.*
(Row I, Left to Right)
Wooden Covered Box, Old Drk. Green Paint, 3½" D. $185.00
Wooden Bowl, Carved Signature & Date "1803, OAS", 6½" L. $145.00
Miniature Coffin Shaped Box, 4" L. ..$65.00
(Row II, Left to Right)
Miniature Wooden Footed Covered Box, Old Blk. Paint, 4" H. $75.00
Miniature Wooden Footed Salt, 20th C., Base Signed, 1¾" H $15.00
Wooden Footed Wine, 4½" H........ $45.00
Wooden Footed Salt, 3" H. $45.00
Wooden Footed Salt, 3" H. $22.50
(Row III, Left to Right)
Fish Shaped Box, Wood, Carved Detail, Sm. Piece Missing From Lid, 6¼" L. $150.00
Carved Wooden Dove, Bill Damaged .$65.00
Carved Wooden Sewing Shuttle, Shape Of Fish, Glass Eye, Brass Tack Initials "C.H.", 8¼" L. $400.00

(A-PA. '75)   *Pennypacker Auction Centre*
Butter Box, Walnut, Dovetailed, Berks Co., Signed O. Sidle, Orig. Wrought Iron Handle ...
.... $280.00

(D-KS. '75)
Cabbage Cutter, Pine, Converted to Table ...
.... $90.00

(D-MA.)
Burl Maple Bowl with insets for handles on each end. 20" L. $925.00

(D-MO.)
Chestnut Roaster, Pat. Mar. 1882 ....$45.00

(A-PA. '75)   *Pennypacker Auction Centre*
Cabbage Cutter, Curly Cherry $180.00

(D-CT. '76)
Pounce Sander, Maple, 3" H. $25.00

(D-OH. '76)
Cheese Ladder, Pine, 17" L. $55.00

(D-W. VA. '76)
GRANITEWARE
(Left to Right)
Angel Food Cake Pan, 8" Diam., Grey ......
.... $12.50
Skimmer, Brown & White $28.00

(D-CO. '76)
Coffee Mill $38.50

(D-MI. '76)
Pie Peel, Pine, 10½" W., 18" L. $95.00

Chas. Parker Co. Coffee Mill, No. 200, Pat'd. March 9, 1897, 12½" H., Orig. Paint ..$225.00

(Row I, Left to Right)
Counter-Balance Scale, Brass Pan, Buffalo Scale, Buffalo, N.Y., Pan Dented $55.00
Cast Iron Scale, Brass Pan, Howe Scale Co., Rutland, Vermont, Pat. June 18, 1887 ..$50.00
(Row II, Left to Right)
Balance Scale, Howe Scale Co. $30.00
Cast Iron Balance Scale, Victorian, 2 Brass Pans Do Not Match $50.00
(Row III, Left to Right)
Balance Scale, Ohaus, 10 lb., Counter-Weights Missing $50.00
Balance Scale, Fairbanks, 4 Oz. W/Weights $50.00
Postal Scale, Avery, Postal Rates Stamped In The Brass $50.00
(Row IV, Left to Right)
Computing Scale, Pelouze Mfg. Co., Chicago, Ill., Brass Pan, Base Slightly Rusted ...$50.00
Cast Iron Scale, 16 Oz., Brass Bank, High Scale Co., Rutland, Vermont $45.00
Hanging Scale, Brass Faced, 30 Lb., Chatillon, N.Y. $35.00
Hanging Scale, Brass Faced, 30 Lb., Salter's Number 2, Hook Missing $25.00

(Row I, Left to Right)
Brass Fireplace Trivet, Clamps, 3 Wrought Iron Legs, 12¾" L., 5" H. $60.00
Brass Fireplace Trivet, 3 Wrought Iron Legs, Pr. Of Hooks, Adjustable W/Turned Wooden Handle, 14" L., 4¼" H. $40.00
(Row II, Left to Right)
Sliding Fender Trivet, Double Hooks & Wrought Iron Frame & Reticulated Brass Trivet, 12" L. $30.00
Circular Brass Trivet, 6⅞" Diam. $10.00
Brass Hearth Trivet, 4 Brass Legs, Reticulated Top, 8⅝" L., 7" W., 6¼" H. $70.00
(Row III, Left to Right)
Steel Hearth Trivet, English, Molded Top, Minor Areas Of Rusting, 16¼" L., 15" D., 11½" H. $80.00
Brass Hearth Trivet, 3 Wrought Iron Legs, Horseshoe Shaped Stretcher, Fold-Over Hook, Turned Wooden Handle, Sm. Collar Missing From Base Of Handle, Sm. Break In Reticulated Top $55.00

(Row I, Left to Right)
Brass Coffee Mill, German, China Knob $60.00
Coffee Mill, German, Wood, Brass & Steel $45.00
Tin Coffee Mill $35.00
(Row II, Left to Right)
Brass Coffee Mill, W/Inlaid Walnut $80.00
Wood & Metal Coffee Mill, Charles Parker Co., Meriden, Conn. $45.00
Universal Coffee Mill, Metal, Orig. Label W/ Patent Date Of Feb. 14, 1905 ....$30.00
(Row III, Left to Right)
Tin Cannisters, Pr., Orig. Lettering & Decor. For Home Brand Spice, Griggs Cooper & Co., St. Paul, Minn. $100.00
(Row IV)
Tole Coffee Cannister, Diamond Brand Coffee W/Label Of Thomson & Taylor Spice Co., Chicago, Ill., Minor Dents, 19½" H., 19¼" W., 13" D. $80.00

Tin Container, Decor. W/Lid & Turned Wooden Handles, Minor Dents & Wear, 16½" H. ..$35.00
Tole Coffee Cannister, Name Of Winston Harper Fisher Co., Paint Worn, 20" H. $40.00
Tole Food Warmer Cabinet, French, Cast Iron Legs & Feet, 28" H. $100.00
Enterprise Coffee Mill, Brass Eagle Finial, 29½" H. $210.00
Tole Cannister, Partially Repainted, 17" H. $40.00
Tole Tea Cannister, Japanese Landscape Decor. W/Name "S. C. Japan", Minor Wear, 24" H. ....
.................................$170.00
Elgin National Coffee Mill, Cast Iron Base Made By Elgin National, Manufactured By Woodruff & Edwards Co., Elgin, Ill., Wooden Crank Handle Is Replacement, Lid To Brass Top Missing, 61¾" H. $190.00

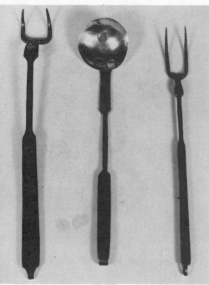

(A-PA. '75)   *Pennypacker Auction Centre*

IRON *(Left to Right)*
Butchering Fork $17.50
Ladle, Brass Bowl, Lge. Copper Rivets ....
.... $75.00
Fork, Early $80.00

A-PA. '75)   *Pennypacker Auction Centre*

Wafer Iron, Long Handle, Ca. 1835-1860 ....
.... $315.00

A-PA. '75)   *Pennypacker Auction Centre*

(Left to Right)
Hanging Spit W/Wagon Wheel Style Turner,
Brass & Wrought Iron W/Name-Nicholas Patent,
Windup Type $80.00
Trammel W/Brass & Wrought Iron Holder,
Rachet Style $27.50
Fireplace Pot Holder, Wrought Iron, Rat-tail
Handle $45.00

(A-PA. '75)   *Pennypacker Auction Centre*

Spatula, Wrought Iron W/Brass Inlay, Engraved W/Amer. Eagle W/Shield Breast &
Holding Key In His Talons $250.00

(A-PA. '75)   *Pennypacker Auction Centre*
(Left to Right)
Skimmers & Ladle, Brass & Wrought Iron ...
.... $42.50; $95.00; $40.00; $50.00

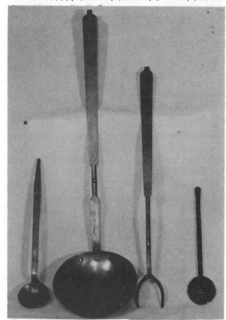

(A-PA. '76)   *Pennypacker Auction Centre*
WROUGHT IRON *(Left to Right)*
Taster Ladle, Dated 1858 .... $105.00
Fork & Ladle Set, Brass Inlay, Initials "I.H." ..
.... $180.00
Pie Crimper, Cut Design $65.00

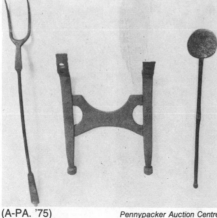

(A-PA. '75)   *Pennypacker Auction Centre*
IRON
(Left to Right)
Toasting Fork, Line Decor. $37.50
Shoe Scraper, Faceted Ball Terminals ....
.... $45.00
Salamander/Spatula, 18th C. $70.00

(A-PA. '76)   *Pennypacker Auction Centre*

Revolving Tin Spice Stand, Orig. Red Paint
W/Gold Trim $70.00

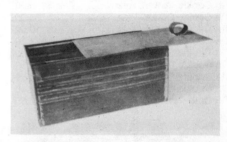

(A-PA. '76)   *Pennypacker Auction Centre*
Tin Candle Box W/Sliding Lid & Ring Handle,
10" L. $50.00

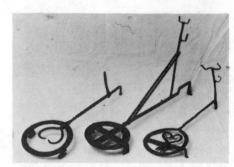

(A-PA. '75)   *Pennypacker Auction Centre*
(Left to Right)
Fireplace Pot Holders, Wrought Iron ....
.... $32.50; $40.00; $37.50

(A-OH. '76)   *Garth's Auctions, Inc.*

Wrought Iron Wafer Iron, Church Design One
Side, Pinwheel On Other, Date "1765", Initialed
"M.N.", 27" L. $390.00

(A-OH. '76)   *Garth's Auctions, Inc.*

Tin Cookie Cutter, Tulip $67.50
Tin Cookie Cutter, Large Pipe $160.00
Tin Cookie Cutter, Star $22.50
Tin Cookie Cutter, Turkey $115.00
Tin Cookie Cutter, Pipe $65.00
Tin Cookie Cutter, Tulip $110.00
Tin Cookie Cutter, Bird $27.50
Tin Cookie Cutter, Eagle $85.00
Tin Cookie Cutter, Bird $22.50
Tin Cookie Cutter, Scalloped Circle ...$22.50
Tin Cookie Cutter, Seated Animal ...$22.40
Tin Quilt Pattern, Flower Shape $100.00

(A-PA. '76)   *Pennypacker Auction Centre*

Tin Coffeepot, Punched W/Design Of An Urn W/Tulips & Daisies, Goose Necked W/High Dome & Brass Finial $2000.00

(Left)

(D-KS. '76)
Tin Coffee Grinder, Orig. Red Paint Worn, ...$32.50

(Right)

(D-N.H. '76)
Tin Churn, Wooden Handle, 14" H. ...$55.00

(A-OH. '76)   *Garth's Auctions, Inc.*

(Row I, L-R)
Copper Food Mold, Washed W/Tin, "R. Mc. V. 18" $60.00
Tin Food Mold, Lamb, "Made In Germany", 13" L. $35.00
Tin Cookie Cutter, Horse, 7¼" L. $47.50
(Row II, L-R)
Tin Food Mold, Rooster, 9¾" H. $35.00
Tin Funnel $15.00
Tin Food Mold, Fish, 9½" L. $67.50
Tin Food Mold, Lobster, 10¼" L. $55.00
(Row III, L-R)
Tin Food Mold, Chicken, "Made In Germany", 5¾" H. $30.00
Tin Food Mold, Fish, 12" L. $35.00
Tin Food Mold, Turkey, "Made In Germany", 7¾" H. $35.00

(D-MO. '76)
(Left to Right)
Chamber Pail & Pitcher (Matching Foot Tub Not Shown), Tin W/Painted Mustard Graining 3 Pc. Set $150.00

(D-CT. '76)
Hanging Egg Safe, Pine, Holds 2 Doz. Eggs . 9" W., 13½" H. $90.00

(A-OH. '76)   *Garth's Auctions, Inc.*

Tin Cookie Cutter, Heart W/Crimped Edge $24.00
Tin Food Mold, Comet $13.00
Tin Cookie Cutter, Hexagonal & Plain Circle (Not Pictured) $2.50
Tin Cookie Cutter, Star $25.00
Tin Cookie Cutter, Man $25.00
Tin Cookie Cutter, Man W/Upraised Arms, 8" H. $107.50
Tin Cookie Cutter, Crimped Oval $15.00
Copper Food Mold, Melon Ribbed $60.00
Tin Cookie Cutter, Woman $21.00

(D-N.H. '76)
Tin Bucket, 6½" H. $35.00

(D-MO. '76)
Tin Fish Mold, 10½" L. $45.00

(A-PA. '76)   *Pennypacker Auction Centre*
(Left to Right)
Tin Cake Pan $18.00
Tin Flour Dredge $36.50

(D-CO. '76)
Pie Peel, Pine, 17½" L., 11" W. $85.00

(D-CT. '76)
Breadboard, Curly Maple, 21¾" Diam. W/4"
Stub Handle $145.00

(D-NE. '76)
Breadboard, Pine, Refinished, 19½" L. $22.50

(D-PA. '76)
Breadboard, Walnut $35.00

(D-N.Y. '76)
Breadboard, Maple, 12" Diam. Type Used For
Cutting Bread At Table $75.00

(D-KS. '76)
Breadboard, Maple, 12½" Diam. Deep Carved
W/Two Kinds Of Wheat, Sunflowers, Acorns,
Oak Leaves And The Word "Bread" . .$150.00

(D-WA. '76)
Chopping Bowl, Pine, 4" D., 15" W., 26" L. . .
. . . . $125.00

(D-MO.)
Meat Board, Walnut W/3 Hand Forged Hooks,
21" L. $75.00

(D-MA. '76)
(Left to Right)
Spice Container, Maple, 4 Compartments W/
Cover $190.00
Hanging Salt Box, Pine, Dovetailed, Sgn.
"F. M. 1725" $250.00
Tankard, Pine W/Maple Cover, Ash Bands,
6¼" H. $150.00

(D-N.Y. '76)
Piggin, Staved, Oak, 15½" H. $90.00

(D-N.H. '76)
Nutmeg Grater, Maple, 4½" H. $45.00

(D-CA. '76)
Rolling Pin, Maple, 18½" L. $20.00
Rolling Pin, Curly Maple, 16¾" L. $45.00

(D-MT. '76)
Scoop, Pine, Refinished, 11" L. $45.00

Left to Right
(D-PA. '76)
Brass Ladle, Iron Handle $65.00
(D-MO. '76)
Brass Ladle, Iron Handle $75.00

(Left)
(A-PA. '76)   *Pennypacker Auction Centre*
Yarnwinder, Pa., Red & Black Decor .$150.00
(Right)
(D-OH. '76)
Washing Dolly, Pine & Oak, 32" H. ...$45.00

(Left)
(A-PA. '76)   *Pennypacker Auction Centre*
Wooden Salt Box, 6¾" H., Repaired Shrink-age Crack ....26.$90.00
(Right)
(D-N.Y. '76)
Wooden Keg, Bottom Made From One Piece Of Wood, 8" H. $150.00

(D-VT. '76)
Wash Board, Pine, 22" L. $75.00

(Left)
(D-MO. '76)
Coffeebean Roaster, 30" L., Projecting Point Was Placed On Hearth & The Cylindrical Head Was Rotated By Long Handle $85.00
(Right)
(D-MN. '76)
Cast Metal Cookie Mold, Attached Wooden Back 5½" W., 11" L. $65.00

(D-KS. '76)
(Left)
Coffee Grinder $60.00
(Right)
Coffee Grinder, French $32.00

(D-MO. '76)
Cabbage Cutter, Poplar, Heart At Neck, W/ Wooden Adjusting Screw $85.00

(A-PA. '76)   *Pennypacker Auction Centre*
Cabbage Cutter, Walnut, Montgomery County, Ca. 1880 ....$140.00
Cabbage Cutter, Pine, Confrontal Birds Form-ing Heart At Necks $100.00
Cabbage Cutter, Walnut, Quakertown, Bucks Co., Dated 1883 ....$150.00

(D-MO. '76)
Rumlet, Metal Bands, Refinished $22.50

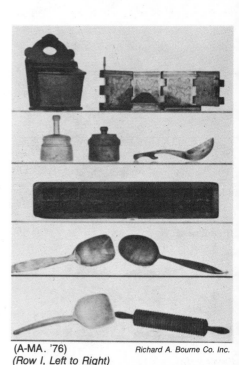

(A-MA. '76)   *Richard A. Bourne Co. Inc.*
(Row I, Left to Right)
Pine Hanging Salt Box, Hinged Lid, Script On Front Dated 1871, Orig. Red Paint, 11" H., 8" W. $110.00
Wooden Butter Mold, 3 Basic Parts, Inside W/Floral Carved Crown & Date "1881", Orig. Graining $160.00
(Row II, Left to Right)
Butter Molds, (2), One Floral Carved, One Pineapple Carved, One W/Age Split ...$40.00
(Row III)
Fruitwood Cookie Board, 18 Different Carvings Incl. Human Figures, Fowl, Fish, Animals, Wind-mill, Etc., 26¾" L. $160.00
(Row IV & V)
Woodenware, 3 Ladles W/Rolling Pin, Lge. Spoon Ladle Has Old Repair For Age Split, Sm. Chips In Rolling Pin $50.00

(A-KS. '76)
Graniteware Collander, Blue/White, 9" Diam., 4" H. $26.50
Graniteware Bun Tray, Mkd. "Graniteiron Ware, Pat. May 30, '76 & May 8, '78, Grey, 13" L. $38.50

(D-KS. '76)
"Bushel & A Peck" Basket, Raised Bottom ..
.....................................$85.00

(A-PA. '76)   *Pennypacker Auction Centre*
Rocking Butter Churn, Early Blue Paint, 18th
C. $260.00

(D-N.Y. '76)
Buttermold W/Deeply Carved Sheaf Of Wheat,
½ lb., Maple $65.00

(A-OH. '76)   *Garth's Auctions, Inc.*
(Row I, Left to Right)
Butter Print, Wooden, Deeply Cut Stylized
Flower W/Star, 4" D.................$145.00
Maple Sugar Mold, Wooden, Fish, 11" x
5" $175.00
Butter Print, Wooden, Deeply Cut Swirled Design, 4" D. $155.00
(Row II, Left to Right)
Miniature Butter Print, Star, 2⅛" D. ..$45.00
Miniature Butter Print, "T", W/Handle $165.00
Miniature Yellowware Mold, Horse ...$45.00
Candy Mold, Metal, Fish, 6½" L., 2¼" W. $45.00
Miniature Butter Print, Leaf W/Handle $115.00
Miniature Butter Print, Floral W/Handle, 2½"
D. $75.00
Miniature Butter Print, Fruit W/Handle, 2"
D. $160.00
(Row III, Left to Right)
Butter Print, Wood, Star, Handle Missing,
3⅛" D. $45.00
Butter Print, Wood, Star, 3½" D. $55.00
Cast Lead Mold, 6½" L., 3" W. $115.00
Butter Print, Wood, Handle Missing, 3¾" D. ..
.....................................$50.00
Butter Print, Wood, Flower, 3" x 4" ..$125.00

(D-MA. '76)
Apple Tray, Pine, 21" L., 15" W., 3" D. $85.00

(D-VT. '76)
Maple Sugar Molds, Carved Beavers, 3½" W.,
5¾" L. $65.00

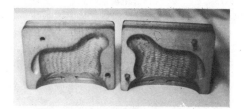

(A-PA. '75)   *Pennypacker Auction Centre*
Butter Mold, Cow Pattern, Lge. $80.00

(D-ME. '76)
Wash Board, Pine & Maple, 18" L., 12½" W.
At Bottom $65.00

(D-MI. '76)
Meat Board, Oak, 26" L. $55.00

(A-PA. '75)   *Pennypacker Auction Centre*
Scalloped Board W/Wrought Iron Cutter,
Marked H.H.S.T., 1785 ....$100.00

(D-MD. '76)
Wooden Tub, Staved Construction, 17" D. ...
9" H. $135.00

(D-PA. '76)
Meat Board, Pine W/8 Hand Wrought Iron
Hooks, 8" H., 25" L. $65.00

(D-MA. '76)
Cranberry Picker, Maple, Mkd. "F.L. Buckingham Mfg., Plymouth, Ma.", 21" H., 19½" W. ..
.....................................$150.00

(A-OH. '76)   *Garth's Auctions, Inc.*
(Row I, Left to Right)
Wooden Butter Print, Stylized Tulip, 4¼"
D. $100.00
Wooden Butter Print, W/Star On Small End &
Tulip On Lge. End, 3" x 4" D. $185.00
Wooden Butter Print, Tulip, Stars & Leaves,
Handle Missing, 4¾" D. $105.00
(Row II, Left to Right)
Wooden Maple Sugar Mold, Duck & Little
Man, 3¾" x 6¾" $85.00
Burl Sauce, 5¼" D. $150.00
(Row III, Left to Right)
Wooden Butter Print, Heart Shaped Leaf W/
Turned Handles, 4⅝" D. $125.00
Wooden Butter Print, Double W/Geometric
Design On Small End & Heart On Lge. End,
2½" x 3¼" D. $195.00
Wooden Butter Print, Song Bird, Turned
Handle, 4¼" D. $205.00

(A-PA. '76)   *Pennypacker Auction Centre*
BUTTER PRINTS *(Left to Right)*
Tulip, W/Stars & Pointed Ovals, 4¾" ..$90.00
Double Sheaf of Wheat, Notched Carving,
2¾" x 4¾" $40.00
Molds, 1 W/Pineapple & Leaves, 3"; 1 W/2
Dahlia Like Flowers, Leaves & Notched Edge,
3½" $55.00

(A-PA. '76)   *Pennypacker Auction Centre*
Eagle Butter Print, Deep Free Form, 4" D. ....
.....................................$130.00
Tulip Butter Print, Star Design, 3¾" D. ......
.....................................$105.00
Cow Butter Print, Free Form Design, 5" D. ...
.....................................$130.00
Butter Paddle & Print, Shaped From One
Piece Maple, Mold Forming End of Handle ...
.....................................$310.00
Butter Print, Design of Face Formed W/Stars
& Tulips, Lancaster Co., Oval $260.00
Elliptical Butter Print, Wheat, Fern & Flower
Design $150.00

(A-PA. '76)   *Pennypacker Auction Centre*
MINIATURE BUTTER PRINTS *(Left to Right)*
Dahlia Like Flower Over 2 Leaves & 2 Outer
Bands of Carved Notching $60.00
Rose Bud W/Leaves 2" H. $60.00
Two Molds W/Circular Device W/Rays In Cen-
ter Running Into Diamonds In Outer Half of
Circles, 3¼" Circular; 3⅛" Square $55.00

(A-PA. '76)   *Pennypacker Auction Centre*
BUTTER PRINTS *(Left to Right)*
Spray of Leaves & Flowers, Gouge Cut Bor-
der, 4" D. $85.00
Sheaf of Wheat, Carved, Primitive, 4¼" D. ...
...................................$45.00
Circular Center W/Veined Swags & Slanting
Radial Cut Band on Shoulder, 4" D. ...$65.00
Swan, 2 Concentric Circles At Edge, 3¼" D. ...
.....................................$60.00

(A-PA. '76)   *Pennypacker Auction Centre*
BUTTER PRINTS *(Left to Right)*
Sheaf of Wheat, Sprays, Half Moon Shape,
Notched Carving Around Edge $95.00
Six-Pointed Star, Carved, Notched Work &
Swags, 4¼" D. $270.00
Sheep, W/Tiny Head, Floral Sprays, Deep
Carving, 3¼" D. $290.00

(A-PA. '76)   *Pennypacker Auction Centre*
BUTTER PRINTS *(Left to Right)*
Seven-Pointed Star, Trefoils & Cut Border
Band, 4" D. $55.00
Tulip & Stars, Carved, Primitive, 1" D. 4¾"
D. $190.00
Double Print, Eagle W/Stars & Carved Acorn,
Rect., 3" x 4½" $275.00

(D-PA. '76)
Fruit Grinder, Pine & Maple W/Burl Head ....
.....................................$150.00

(A-OH. '76)   *Garth's Auctions, Inc.*
Wooden Butter Print, Round, Eagle, 4" D. ...
...................................$65.00
Ivory Pen, Carved Open Work Initials "L.A.B.",
7¾" L. $45.00
Ivory Busk, Incised Eagle, Ships & Stars,
8¼" L. $130.00
Wooden Butter Print, Round, Star, 3¾" D. ..
...................................$135.00
Carved Wooden Busk, Inlaid Star & Carved &
Punched Designs W/Date "1771", Heart Cut Out
Has Space Carved Out Behind To Accept Minia-
ture, Wood Has Split, 14" L. $185.00
Wooden Butter Print, Round, Primitive Tulip,
3¾" D. $155.00
Wooden Butter Print, Round, Star, 2½" D. ...
...................................$145.00
Silver Ladle, Turned Wooden Handle, Hall-
marks & Wedding Monogram "IWS", 15" L. ...
...................................$100.00
Wooden Butter Print, Round, Sheaf Of Wheat,
4½" D. $55.00
Wooden Traveling Mirror, Oval & Round Mir-
ror Each Bordered By Inlay, Oval Mirror
Cracked $75.00

(D-N.Y. '76)
Wooden Tea Caddy, Orig. Yellow & Red Paint,
4½" H. $125.00

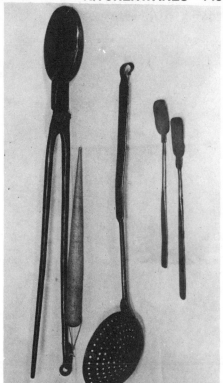

(A-PA. '76) *Pennypacker Auction Centre*

WROUGHT IRON *(Left to Right)*
Wafer Iron, W/Wooden Tool Used to Roll
Wafer from Iron $400.00
Ladle, Dated 1836 .... $100.00
Spatulas, Pr., Initialed & Decor. W/Wiggle-
Work $115.00

(A-OH. '76) *Garth's Auctions, Inc.*

Chopping Knife, Initialed "Z.P.S.", Wooden Handle $37.50
Chopping Knife, Unusual Shape Blade $27.50
Pastry Cutter, Shape Of Fish, Curly Maple Body & Whale Bone Wheel, 7" L. $575.00
Wrought Iron Spatula, 12¾" L. $30.00
Brass Pan, Wrought Iron Long Handled Holder, 13¼" L. $100.00
Hanging Spoon Rack, Lift Top Compartment, Old Green Paint, 27" L. $625.00
Pewter Spoons, (6) $75.00
Pewter Spoons, (5), Twisted Handles, Back Of Bowl Hallmarked & Initialed "N. R." $100.00

(A-PA. '76) *Pennypacker Auction Centre*

WROUGHT IRON UTENSILS *(Left to Right)*
Taster, Brass Bowl, Engraved & Dated, Initialed
B.V., 12" L.; **Matching Fork,** *(Far Right),* En-
graved W/Circles & Dated 1835, 11" L. $600.00
Fork, Engraved, 18½" L. $280.00
Taster, Brass Bowl, Inlaid Brass Rectangle On
Handle, 11" L. $330.00
Fork, Engraved Initials J.H. & Date 1828,
18" L. $200.00

(A-PA. '75) *Pennypacker Auction Centre*

Wrought Iron Trivet, Three-Penny Feet .....
.... $95.00

(D-MT. '76) (D-OH. '76)
(Left)
Trivet, Hand Wrought, Penny Feet ... $45.00
(Right)
Iron Trivet, 12¼" L. $45.00

(D-N.Y. '76)
Maple Sugar Container, Screw Top, Orig. Old Red Painted Finish, 5" H., 10" Diam. .$125.00

(D-N.Y. '76)
Sugar Bowl, Maple, 5½" H. $200.00

(D-N.H. '76)
Maple Sugar Bucket,Orig. Untouched Cond., 9½" H. $350.00

(D-N.Y. '76)
Knife Box, Cherry W/Burl Ends, Dovetailed, 6½" W. At Base, 13" L. $145.00

(D-OK. '76)
Graniteware Coffee Pot, Blue $18.00

(D-KS. '76)
Bentwood Churn, Oak, Made By M. Brown Co., Complete & Working $175.00

(A-PA. '75)   *Pennypacker Auction Centre*
(Left to Right)
Wooden Sugar Bucket $290.00
Miniature Splint Basket, Colored $45.00
Wooden Butter Paddle, Butter Mold Handle...........................$200.00

(D-N.H. '76)
Maple Sugar Molds, Pine, 3½" W., 11" L. ...
...................................$125.00

(D-TX. '76)
(Left to Right)
Mortar & Pestle, Maple, 5½" H. $35.00
Mortar & Pestle, Cherry, Salesman's Sample .
...................................$45.00

(D-MO. '76)
Graniteware Muffin Pan, Bright Blue & White W/Black Trim On Sides $28.50

(D-IL. '76)
Wooden Handle Forks, All W/Decorative Metal Inserts, Ca. 1885, Ea. $3.00

(D-KS. '76)
Lemon Squeezer, Maple W/Lignum-Vitae Heads $75.00

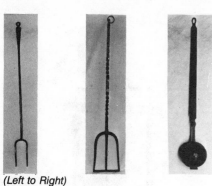

(Left to Right)
(D-PA. '76)
Iron Meat Fork, 22" L. $65.00
Iron Peel, Hand Wrought, 28" L. $100.00

(D-KS. '76)
Soap Saver, Sheet Iron W/Perforated Head,
22" L. $45.00

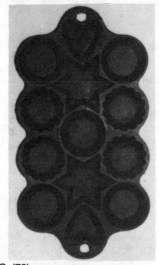

(D-MO. '76)
Iron Muffin Pan, Marked "Reids, Pat. July 18,
1871 . . . .$35.00

(A-PA. '75)   *Pennypacker Auction Centre*

Fireplace Trivets
Iron Trivet $30.00
Brass Trivet $42.50
Iron Trivet $15.00

(D-MO. '76)
Copper Apple Butter Kettle, Dovetailed, Iron
Bail, 15¼" H., 22½" Diam. Top $290.00

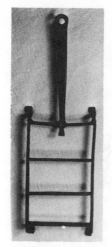

(Left to Right)

(D-KS. '76)
Iron Trivet, Wrought, Sgn. "Bergh" & Dated
1847 . . . .$75.00

(D-MO. '76)
Iron Ice Tongs, 12" L. $18.00

(D-N.M. '76)
Copper Pan, Qt. Size, Dovetailed $90.00
Copper Skillet, Iron Handle $60.00

(D-IL. '76)
Copper Teakettle, 20th C. Stripped . . .$29.00

(D-WA. '76)
Copper Measure, Tinned, 7¼" H. $38.50

(D-CT. '76)
Wrought Iron Scraper, Dough Trough, 5½" L.
. . . .$45.00

(D-CT. '76)
Iron Gooseneck Teakettle, Mkd. "3 Quart"
Impressed In Base $150.00

(D-N.H. '76)
Skillet, Copper, Tin Lined W/Iron Legs, 7" H.,
Used Over Open Fire, 18th C. $90.00

(D-MO. '76)
Copper Candy Kettle, Iron Handles, Top 18"
Diam., 14" H. $175.00

(A-MA. '76)   *Richard A. Bourne Co. Inc.*
(Left to Right)
Copper Dipper, 5¾" H., Handle - 16¾" L.
. . . .$50.00
Copper Container, Hanging Extension, Leaded
Interior, 7" Diam., 11¾" H. Incl. Extension . . . .
. . . .$65.00
Copper Sieve, Hand Punched Holes, 2 Copper
Strap Handles, 11⅞" Diam. $45.00

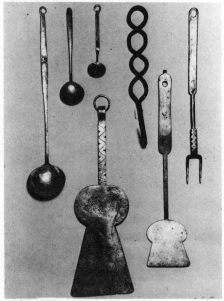

(A-OH. '76) Garth's Auctions, Inc.

Brass & Wrought Iron Taster, 11½" L. . . . . . .
. . . .$75.00

Brass & Wrought Iron Taster, 6" L. . . . . . .
. . . .$95.00

Copper & Wrought Iron Taster, 4¼" L. . . . .
. . . .$45.00

Wrought Iron Spatula, Tooled Handle, 11½"
L. $75.00

Wrought Iron Hook, For Adjustable Hanging,
8½" L. $105.00

Wrought Iron Spatula, Handle Signed "J.C.
Fox", 12" L. $55.00

Wrought Iron Fork, Tooled Work, ... $45.00

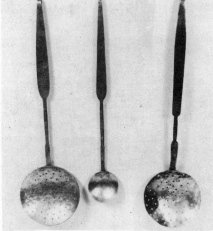

(A-OH. '76) Garth's Auctions, Inc.

Strainer & Tasting Ladle, Wrought Iron
Handles W/Punched Initials "J.W.", Brass
Bowls $180.00

Straining Ladle, Wrought Iron Handle, Copper
Bowl, Marked "S. Biehler" $80.00

(D-KS. '76)

Cheese Ladder, Pine, 26" L. $45.00

(A-OH. '76) Garth's Auctions, Inc.

(Row I, Left to Right)
Wrought Iron & Brass Taster, 11" L. $70.00
Wrought Iron & Brass Spatula, 12½" L. . . . .
. . . .$35.00
Wrought Iron & Brass Spatula, W/Matching
Fork, Stamped Ornament On Handle, 9½" L. .
. . . . $165.00
Wrought Iron Sugar Nippers $52.50
Wrought Iron Spatula, Heart Hanger, 12½"
L. $105.00

(Row II, Left to Right)
Wrought Iron & Brass Skimmer, Tooled
Handle, 16½" L. $90.00
Wrought Iron Fork, Tooled Handle, 16½" L. .
. . . . $70.00
Wrought Iron Fork, 19" L. $430.00
Wrought Iron Fork, Heart Design Hanger,
14" L. $65.00
Wrought Iron Taster, Tooled Handle . $45.00

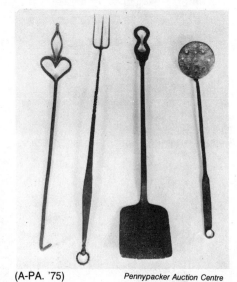

(A-PA. '75) Pennypacker Auction Centre

Fireplace Poker $36.00
Wrought Iron Toasting Fork, Marked J.R.
Lambleth $100.00
Iron Shovel, ... $70.00
Wrought Iron Spatula/Strainer $45.00

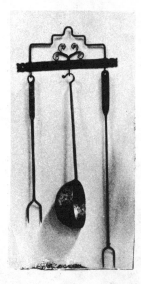

(A-OH. '77) Garth's Auctions, Inc.
WROUGHT IRON
(Left to Right)
Utensil Rack $135.00
Fork, 18¾" L. $40.00
Strainer W/Decor. On Handle $45.00
Fork W/Stamped Initials On Handle . . .$50.00

(A-PA. '76) Pennypacker Auction Centre

(Left to Right)
Iron, Trivet $60.00
Trivet $55.00
Swinging Fireplace Pine Knot Burner, 13" x
14" $300.00
Trivet $50.00
Trivet $30.00

(A-PA. '76) Pennypacker Auction Centre

Iron, Gridiron, American $85.00
Grisset, Early Pa. $100.00

For the lighting enthusiast, there exists an immense range of interesting collectibles and accessories, most of which are readily adaptable for modern decorative and functional usage. The fancy lamps of the Victorian era and the Art Nouveau period are presently enjoying the greatest popularity.

(D-MO. '76)
Tin Sconce W/Glass Covering, Pin Hinged Opening, 14" H. $95.00

(D-KS. '76)
Embossed Tin Sconce, Circus, Orig. Painted Finish, 15" H. $145.00

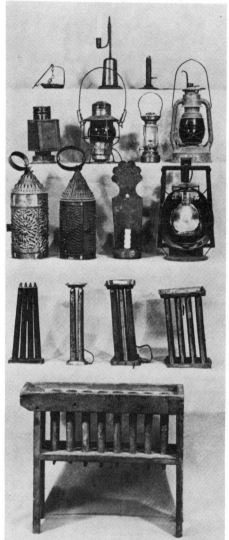

(A-MA. '76)   Richard A. Bourne Co. Inc.
(Row I, Left to Right)
Iron Betty Lamp, Amer., W/Hook & Pickwick .
. . . .$75.00
Iron Rush And Candlelight Holder, 18th C., Turned Oak Base Is Old Replacement, 12" H.
. . . .$80.00
Hog Scraper Candlestick, W/Ejector, Worn, 5¼" H. $22.00
Iron Miner's Candleholder, Hand Wrought W/Spike, Hanging Hook & Clamp-Like Holder, 11" L. $55.00
(Row II, Left to Right)
Tin Kerosene Lamp, Ruby Lamp No. 2, Shutter Over Red Glass Pane, Sm. Dent In Base, 8¾" H.
. . . .$17.00
Railroad Lantern, Blue Glass Globe W/Name Of "Adlake Kero", 9¾" H. $20.00
Kerosene Lantern, Dietz Scout, 7½" H. .$35.00
Railroad Lantern, Dietz Little Wizard, Red Globe, Some Rusting, Sm. Dents, 11¼" H. . . .
. . . .$10.00
(Row III, Left to Right)
Pierced Tin Candle Lantern, 15½" H. .$50.00
Pierced Tin Candle Lantern, Minor Rusting, 16" H. $75.00
Tin Hanging Candle Sconce, 14" H. .$140.00
Kerosene Lantern, Dietz, Cone Projector, Electrified, 14" H. $20.00
(Row IV, Left to Right)
Tin Candle Mold, 4-Section, For 10" Candles, Slightly Rusted, Handle Missing $20.00
Tin Candle Mold, 4-Section, For 10" Candles, Slightly Rusted $20.00
Tin Candle Mold, 12-Section, For 10" Candles, One Rod For Tying Candles, Applied Handle .
. . . .$40.00
Tin Candle Mold, 12-Section, For 10" Candles, Slightly Bent, Handle Missing, Slight Surface Rust $35.00
(Row V)
Candle Mold, 24-Section, Wooden Base W/24 Pewter Inserts, For 9" Candles $360.00

(A-OH. '76)   Garth's Auctions, Inc.
Candle Sconce, Punched Tin, 13½" H. . . . . . .
. . . .$325.00
Candle Sconce, Toleware, Black Ground W/ Worn Red & Yellow Decor., 7½" H. . . .$350.00

(D-S.D. '76)
(Left to Right)
Tin Candle Holder, Push-up, ...$22.50
Tin Lantern $32.50

(D-PA. '76)
Brass Miner's Lamp, 2½" H. $25.00

Garth's Auctions, Inc.

(A-OH. '76)
(Row I, Left to Right)
Candle Burning Coach Lamps, Pr., Beveled Glass, 12" H. $50.00
Tin Candle Lantern, 12¼" H. $45.00
(Row II, Left to Right)
Iron Grease Lamp, Tooled Hanger $75.00
Iron Sticking Tommy Candle Lamp $27.50
Brass Candlestick, 8⅝" H. $15.00
Iron Grease Lamp, Chicken Finial $40.00
Iron Double Crusie Lamp, Replaced Hanger $20.00
(Row III, Left to Right)
Lamp, Clear Honeycomb Font, Brass Stem, Marble Base, Not Centered On Marble Base ..$25.00
Lamp, Clear Font, Brass Stem, Marble Base $25.00
Lamp, Frosted Cut To Clear Font W/Brass Trim, Pot Metal Figural Stem, Cast Iron Base, 10" H. .
....$20.00
Lamp, Clear Font, Brass Stem, Cast Iron Base, Stem Is Repaired, 10¼" H. $7.50

Richard A. Bourne Co. Inc.

(A-MA. '75)
(Row I, Left to Right)
Whale Oil Lamp, Amer., Ca. 1835, Colorless Glass W/Pressed Quatrefoil Base W/Scroll & Shell Design, Joined To Font By Tooled Ribbed Knop, Brass Collar, 11½" H. $75.00
Fluid Burning Lamp, Amer., Ca. 1845, Colorless Glass W/Sq. Pressed Base W/Octagonal Stem Joined By Lg. Bladed Knop To Pear-Shaped Font W/Cut Panel & Punty Design, Britannia Collar, Chips On Base, Internal Crack In STem, 11¾" H. $50.00
Whale Oil Lamp, New England, Ca. 1850-1860, Pressed Greenish-Yellow Glass W/Hollow Sq. Base Joined By Knop To Font W/Ellipse & Punty Design, Double-Drop Whale Oil Burner, 10⅞" H.
....$400.00
(Row II, Left to Right)
Whale Oil Lamps, *Pr., Amer., Ca. 1830, Colorless Glass W/Sq. Foot W/Curved Chamfered Corners & Scalloped Sides Joined By Button Knop To Freeblown Pear-Shaped Font, Minor Chips, 7⅞" H.* $250.00
Fluid Burning Lamp, Amer., Ca. 1850, Hexagonal Curved Foot W/Hexagonal Stem, Cylindrical Ribbed Font, Brass Collar, Minor Chips, 10⅝" H. $100.00
Fluid Burning Lamp, Amer., Ca. 1860, Colorless Pressed Glass Font In "Bullseye & Fleur de Lis" Pattern, Stamped Brass Standard, Sq. Marble Base, Brass Stained, Minute Chips On Marble, 9⅜" H. $100.00

← **(A-MA. '75)**   Richard A. Bourne Co. Inc.

Candlesticks, Pr., Amer., 19th C., Hexagonal Bases & Standards W/Foliate Decor., Hexagonal Sockets W/Scroll Decor., Colorless, Minor Chips, 11⅛" H. $175.00
Candlestick, Caryatid, Circular Base W/Scallops & Points, Ribbed Above, Ribbed Socket W/Petal-Like Rim, Figure W/Mat Acid Finish, Colorless, Minor Chips, 12" H. $125.00
Candlesticks, Pr., Ca. 1850, Petal & Loop Design, Slight Chip On Base Of One, 6⅞" H. .
....$85.00

(D-PA. '76)
Iron Betty Lamp, Complete ....$135.00 ➡

(A-MA. '76)   *Richard A. Bourne Co. Inc.*

Willow Style Lamp, 5 Signed Quezar Art Glass Shades, Iridescent Blue Feather Design On Iridescent Ivory Ground & Iridescent Gold Interior, Metal Base W/Bronze Finish, 21" H. $525.00

Victorian Fluid Lamp, Mount Washington Type, Decor. Pink Glass Covered Font & Matching Shade W/Yellow Band, Decor. Worn, Electrified, 21" H. Inc. Chimney $140.00

(A-OH. '76)   *Garth's Auctions, Inc.*

(Row I, Left to Right)
Cast Brass Grease Lamp, Several Cast Animals W/Elephant Base, 8½" H. $30.00
Tin Candlestick Tinder Box, W/Wrought Iron Striker Marked "J.C.", 4¼" D. $135.00
Tin Betty Lamp & Stand, Lamp Has Pick & Hook, 14" H. $200.00
Tin Two Spout Grease Lamp, Saucer Base & Handle, Lid Has Cast Pewter Finial, 8¼" H $85.00

(Row II, Left to Right)
Sheet Metal Hog Scraper Candlestick, W/Pushups, 5½" H. $50.00
Wooden Lighting Device, Adjustable W/Crimped Tin Candleholder $195.00
Pewter Whale Oil Lamp, Threads Of Burner Are Stripped, 4½" H. $95.00
Sheet Metal Betty Lamp, Embossed, Twisted & Tooled Wrought Iron Hanger $50.00

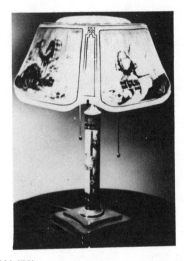

(D-N.Y. '76)
Pairpoint Table Lamp, Sgn. & Dated 1907 ...
....................................$650.00

(D-AZ. '76)
Lamp, Banquet, Cherub & Floral Decor. On White, Brass Fittings, Electrified, 30" H. ......
....................................$300.00

(A-MA. '76)   *Richard A. Bourne Co. Inc.*
(Top)
Fluid Lamp W/Pear-Shaped Font Mkd. "Patented March 4 & June 3, 1862." Opaque White W/Opaque Blue; Three Stars Within Ovals Separated By A Blue Leaf-Like Design; by J.S. Atterbury, T. B. Atterbury & James Reddick, Pittsburgh, 10½" H. $250.00

Fluid Lamp W/Swirled Lutz-Type Pear-Shaped Font; Blue & Opalescent Swirls In Clear Glass W/Large Wafer At Base Of Font (Milk Glass), 10" H. $250.00

(Left)
Sandwich Overlay Fluid Lamp W/Pear-Shaped Double Cut Overlay Font, Cranberry Cut To Clear W/Brass Fluted Stem & Typical Sandwich Double Stepped Marble Base. Cranberry Overlay Globe Possibly Original; Base 13" H., Overall 22¼" H. $375.00

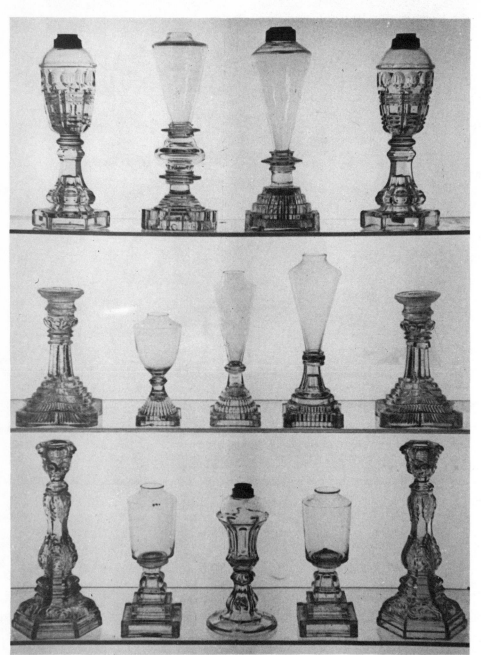

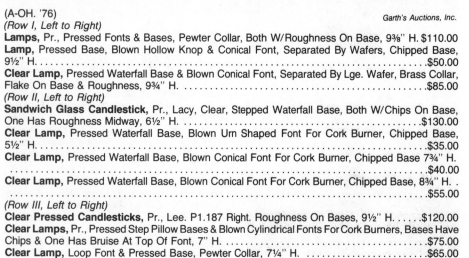

(D-CA. '76)
Table Lamp, Domed Shade W/Six Hand Painted Panels, Matching Base, Unsigned . . . .
. . . .$650.00

(D-TX. '76)
Cut Glass Table Lamp, All Orig., Unsigned
. . . .$1,800.00

Garth's Auctions, Inc.

(A-OH. '76)
(Row I, Left to Right)
Lamps, Pr., Pressed Fonts & Bases, Pewter Collar, Both W/Roughness On Base, 9⅜" H. $110.00
Lamp, Pressed Base, Blown Hollow Knop & Conical Font, Separated By Wafers, Chipped Base, 9½" H. $50.00
Clear Lamp, Pressed Waterfall Base & Blown Conical Font, Separated By Lge. Wafer, Brass Collar, Flake On Base & Roughness, 9¾" H. $85.00
(Row II, Left to Right)
Sandwich Glass Candlestick, Pr., Lacy, Clear, Stepped Waterfall Base, Both W/Chips On Base, One Has Roughness Midway, 6½" H. $130.00
Clear Lamp, Pressed Waterfall Base, Blown Urn Shaped Font For Cork Burner, Chipped Base, 5½" H. $35.00
Clear Lamp, Pressed Waterfall Base, Blown Conical Font For Cork Burner, Chipped Base 7¾" H.
. . . .$40.00
Clear Lamp, Pressed Waterfall Base, Blown Conical Font For Cork Burner, Chipped Base, 8¾" H. .
. . . .$55.00
(Row III, Left to Right)
Clear Pressed Candlesticks, Pr., Lee. P1.187 Right. Roughness On Bases, 9½" H. $120.00
Clear Lamps, Pr., Pressed Step Pillow Bases & Blown Cylindrical Fonts For Cork Burners, Bases Have Chips & One Has Bruise At Top Of Font, 7" H. $75.00
Clear Lamp, Loop Font & Pressed Base, Pewter Collar, 7¼" H. $65.00

(D-N.Y. '76)
Brass Chamber Stick W/Lever In Shaft To Push Up Candle Stump; Snuffer Attached . . . .
. . . .$125.00

Lamp, Kerosene, Brass W/Frosted Shade, Mkd. "Hinks & Sons Patent," 18" H., English $90.00

(A-MA. '76)   Richard A. Bourne Co. Inc.
(Row I)
Brass Double Student Lamp, W/Pr. Matching Green Cased Glass Shades, Shade Supports Slightly Bent, 22" H. $300.00
(Row II, Left to Right)
Astral Lamp, W/Etched Sandwich-Type Globe &Cut Crystal Prisms, Double-Stepped Marble Base, Electrified, Brass Stem & Font, 24¼" H. $250.00
Astral Lamp, W/Sandwich-Type Cut & Etched Globe, Single-Stepped Marble Base, Brass Stem & Font, Cut Crystal Prisms, Electrified, 23¾" H. $200.00

(A-OH. '75)   Garth's Auctions, Inc.

(Left to Right)
Overlay Lamp, Opaque White Cut To Rose Cranberry Font, Opaque Apple Green Stem, Brass Trim, Marble Base, 14" H. $325.00
Overlay Lamp, Opaque White Cut To Cranberry Font, Stem Is Opaque Blue Cut To Clear, Brass Trim, Marble Base, 13" H. $300.00

(D-MO. '76)
Brass Ship's Lantern, Mkd. "EG & S" 1916, 16" H. $135.00

(A-IN. '76)
Gone With The Wind Lamp, Red Satin Glass, "Washington & Lincoln" $1,700.00

(D-CO. '76)
Alladin Lamp, Model 12, Brass Fittings W/ Frosted Shade, All Orig. $165.00

(D-WY'. 76)
Gone With The Wind Lamp, Green W/White Flowers, 22" H. $225.00

(Left to Right)
French Cameo Lamp, D. Argental, Castle
Base, 24" H. $8,500.00
French Cameo Lamp, Ships, Sgn. "Daum
Nancy", 18" H. $2,500.00

French Cameo Lamp, Sgn. "Galle", Eagles . .
. . . .$6,250.00

Kerosene Lamp, Green/Blue Base W/Frosted
Shade, 12" H. $175.00

(Left to Right)
French Cameo Lamp, Sgn. "Galle", Cucoo Bird, 12" H. $2,500.00
French Cameo Lamp, Sgn. "Galle", Floral, 12½" H. $2,200.00
French Cameo Lamp, Sgn. "Galle", Jelly Fish, 10" H. $2,500.00

(Left to Right)
French Cameo Lamp, Sgn. "Muller", Mtn. Scene, 11" H. $2,500.00
French Cameo Lamp, Sgn. "Muller", Roses, 12½" H. $3,200.00
French Cameo Lamp, Sgn. "Muller", Sheep Herder, 14" H. $2,500.00

(Left to Right)
Galle Lamp, Yellow Floral, 24" H., Sgn. $2,500.00
Galle Lamp, Pink Butterfly, 26" H. $2,800.00

(D-WA. '76)
Lily Lamp, Unsigned $350.00

(D-N.Y. '76)
Metal Table Lamp W/Rainbow Glass Panels,
25" H..............................$250.00

(A-CA. '76)   *Woody Auction Company*
Tiffany "Dragonfly Lamp", Sgn. On Base,
Blue Dragonflies W/Green Eyes $7,450.00

(D-MO. '76)
Table Lamp W/Green Leaded Glass Shade
Mkd. P.L.B. & G. Co., 18" H. $350.00

(A-IN. '76)   *Woody Auction Company*
Duffner-Kimberley Wisteria Lamp, 39" H.
.................................$5,000.00

(D-N.Y. '76)
Tiffany Lamp W/Three Gold Iridescent Shades,
Bronze Base, Sgn. "Tiffany Studios, New York
319" $650.00

(D-IL. '76)
Table Lamp, Leaded Glass, Nile Scene,
Blue Green/Amber, 25" H...........$250.00

(D-CO. '76)
Table Lamp, W/Blue Slag Glass Bent Panels
Set In Metal Frame, 22" H. $300.00

(D-KS. '76)   *John Woody*
French Cameo Owl Lamp, Sgn. Daum Nancy,
32" H. $15,000.00

All types of metal objects — brass, copper, silver, pewter, Britannia, iron and tin — are in demand. And as the pendulum swings back toward a taste for country collectibles — even the old parlor stove as well as the kitchen range has suddenly become quite respectable.

Prices rise steeply for pieces of metalware that are marked and can be identified. But it is the objects of the eighteenth and early nineteenth centuries that are still the most coveted.

Richard A. Bourne Co. Inc.

(A-MA. '76)

(Row I, Left to Right)
Plated Silver Candlesticks, Pr., English, Columnar Style, 7" H. $40.00
Brass Candlesticks, Pr., English, 19th C., Octagonal Bases & Push-Ups, 7⅞" H. .$50.00

(Row II, Left to Right)
Brass Candlesticks, Pr., Sq. Bases, 1 Soldered Around Lip, Both Minus Push-Ups, 6" H.'$40.00
Brass Candlesticks, Lot Of 3, One Jack Of Diamonds Style W/Push-Up, 8" H.; One Circular Style, 6½" H.; One Low Style W/Push-Up, 5" H. $45.00

(Row III, Left to Right)
Brass Candlesticks, Pr., Queen Anne Style, Cross-Hatched Band Around Stem, 10" H. $90.00
Georgian Silver Pint Cann, Fuller White, London, 1748, Reverse C. Handle W/Foliate Scroll On Top, Weight 10 Oz. $250.00

(Row IV, Left to Right)
Brass Candlestick, Saucer-Based, Push-Up, Ejector, Snuffer Missing, 4¾" H. $45.00
Brass Candle Snuffer, Scissors Type W/ Matching Chippendale Style Tray, Minor Dents In Tray $45.00

(D-N.Y. '76)
Pewter Tablespoon (1 of 6) Unmarked, Set . .
. . . .$125.00

(A-MA. '76)   *Robert C. Eldred Co., Inc.*
COIN SILVER
(Left to Right)
Vase, By Haddock, Lincoln & Foss, Boston, 9¼" H., 5" Diam., 16 Oz., Ca. 1850 . .$110.00
Creamer, By William Thompson, New York City, 6½" H., 8 Oz., Ca. 1825 . . . .$225.00
Water Pitcher, By Wood & Hughes, New York City W/Presentation Inscription, Dated June 1860, 11½" H., 15 Oz., Ca. 1840 . . . . .$350.00
Covered Sugar Bowl, By Wood & Hughes, New York City W/Presentation Inscription, Dated 1851, 7¾" H., 14 Oz., Ca. 1840$140.00
Sugar Bowl, W/Engraved Initials, "S.V." Mkd. On Base, S & F, N.Y. W/Eagle, 17 Oz., 7½" H.
. . . .$70.00

(D-FL. '76)
Plated Silver Toothpick Holder $45.00

(D-KY. '76)
Bottle Opener, Iron, In Form Of Parrot, Orig. Paint Good $12.00

(A-VA. '76) *Laws*
Sterling Silver Coffee Service, 7 Pcs., Tray, 30" L., Pot 14" H. $750.00

(A-MA. '76) *Richard A. Bourne Co. Inc.*
SILVER
(Row I, Left to Right)
German Coffee Service, Tray, Coffeepot, Sugar & Creamer, Monogrammed & Dated 1915 . . . .$325.00
(Row II, Left to Right)
German Repousse Sterling Tea Service, Length Of Tray Incl. Handles, 30" L. .$2100.00

(D-N.Y. '76)
Silver Egg Castor, W/3 Plated Silver Egg Cups, 3 Spoons, Cut Glass Salt & Pepper . . .$225.00

(D-FL. '76)
Nut Bowl, Wm. Rogers Silver Plate . . .$75.00

(D-CA. '76)
Silver Butter Cooler, Complete, Mkd. Reed & Barton $135.00

(Left)
(D-N.Y. '76)
Coin Silver Teaspoon Mkd. "G. Baldwin" . . . .
. . . .$18.00

(Right)
(D-FL. '76)
Kate Greenaway Silver Figural Salt Shaker, 4" H., Girl W/Muff $75.00

(A-PA. '76) *Pennypacker Auction Centre*
Tin Coffee Pot, Double Conical Shape W/ Bold Ring Banding, Hinged Lid W/Brass Knob, Flaring Spout Has Dainty Heart Cutout On Top, 12" H. $105.00

(A-PA. '76) *Pennypacker Auction Centre*
Tin Water Pitcher, 8½" H. $30.00

(A-PA. '76) *Pennypacker Auction Centre*
Tin Quilt Pattern W/Fleur-De-Lis In Center & Multi. Star On Each Side, 16¾" W. $75.00

(A-MA. '76)   *Richard A. Bourne Co. Inc.*

Brass Warming Pan, Long Turned Handle & Sponge Grained Decor., Engraved Lid $170.00
Brass Folding Fire Screen, Reticulated Bottom Panels, 1 Sm. Finial Missing, Each Panel 13" W., 31" H. $70.00
Brass Lemon Top Andirons, Pr., Amer., 18th C., 1 Needs Soldering, Slightly Dented, 17½" H. $110.00
Brass Charcoal Brazier, Reticulated, Few Sm. Dents, 19" Diam., 21" H. $50.00
Brass Rail Fire Fender, 46" L. $50.00

(A-MA. '76)   *Richard A. Bourne Co. Inc.*
(Row I, Left to Right)
Copper Coffeepot, Ebonized Wooden Handle & China Finial On Hinged Lid, 10¾" W. $60.00
Copper Water Can, Tilting Handle, Hinged Lid, 11" H. $60.00
Copper Jar, Lidded, Copper Handles, Incised Date "74" One Side, Impressed Number Opposite Side, 7½" H. $50.00
Copper Boiler, Steel Bail Handles, 12" Diam., 12¼" W. $40.00
(Row II, Left to Right)
Copper Kettle, Lidded W/Copper Handles, Marked "02L" On Lid Handle, Slightly Dented, 13½" Diam., 10½" H. $50.00
Copper Boiler, Wire Handle, Wood Insulator, Minor Dents, 11½" Diam., 13¾" H. $40.00
Basin, Hand-Hammered, Steel Handles, 15¼" Diam. $50.00
(Row III, Left to Right)
Copper Kettle, Steel Bail Handle, Dovetailed Const., Sm. Hole, Minor Dents, 27" Diam., 17" H. $225.00
Copper Kettle, Riveted Const., Copper Handles, 28" Diam., 15½" H. $125.00

(Left)
(D-WA. '76)
National Cash Register, Brass, Working Cond., Ca. 1910, 10" W. $300.00

(Right)
(D-ILL.)
School Bell, Brass, Pat. 8-25-1863 . . . .$48.50

(D-IN. '76)
Iron Stove, Mkd. "Cuba Climax Stove Co., Quincy, Ill", 19½" W., 25" H., 27" L. .$175.00

(A-MA. '76)   *Richard A. Bourne Co. Inc.*
Victorian Iron Parlor Stove, Amer., 19th C., Johnson Gern Co., Troy, N.Y., Model No. 4, Minor Breaking Of Iron At Top, 2 Sm. Holes In Top Plate 34½" W., 20" D., 47" H. . . .$350.00

(A-MA. '76)   *Richard A. Bourne Co. Inc.*
Iron Stove, 19th C., Laird Norton & Co., Described As Congress Furnace, 48½" L., 15½" D., 36¾" H. $225.00

(A-OH. '76)   Garth's Auctions, Inc.
PEWTER *(Row I, Left to Right)*
Footed Bowl, Unmarked, 6" D., 4½" H. $45.00
Charger, Touch Marks & "A.B.", 16½" D. . . . .
. . . . $280.00
Hanging Salt Box, Hinge Needs Repair, 8½"
H. $195.00
(Row II, Left to Right)
Plate, Eagle In Oval Touch Marks of Thomas
Boardman, 9" D. $280.00
Teapot, "G. Richardson, Warranted", 7¾" H. .
. . . . $430.00
Basin, Marked On Wide Flange, 10" D. $155.00
(Row III, Left to Right)
Plate, Very Faint Touch, 9" D. $65.00
Vase, 10¾" H. $65.00
Soup Plate, "London" Touch Flanked by Birds
& Hallmarks Including "KW & Co.", 8½" D. . . .
. . . . $60.00

(A-OH. '76)   Garth's Auctions, Inc.
PEWTER *(Row I, Left to Right)*
Chalices, Pr., 7" H. $160.00
Flagon, Marked "Homan", 12¾" H. . . $145.00
Chalice, Faint "I.H.S." Medallion $30.00
Flagon, "Manning Bowman & Co.", 11¼" H. .
. . . . $155.00
Charger, Pitted, 16½" D. $70.00
(Row II, Left to Right)
Candlesticks, Pr., Stem Threads to Base, One
Insert Battered, 9½" H. $85.00
Plate, "Reed & Barton", 10" D. $37.50
Teapot, "Boardman & Hart", "N. York", Lid Has
Split & Battered, 8½" H. $235.00
Plate, Partial "Norwich" Touch $325.00
(Row III, Left to Right)
Plate, Thistle Touch, 9½" D. $67.50
Creamer, Handle W/Lid & Spout, Continental
Touch, Battered, 5" H. $40.00
Plate, "London" Touch, Pitted, 8¼" D. . $50.00
Creamer, Handle W/Lid & Spout, Continental
Touch, Battered, 5" H. $50.00
Plate, Knife Scratches, 9" D. 45.00

(D-PA. '76)
Pewter Coffeepot, Unsigned, 9½" H. . .$90.00

(D-PA. '76)
Pewter Teapot, Unsigned $125.00

(D-PA. '76)   (D-CT. '76)
(Left)
Pewter Coffee Pot, Unmarked, 9½" H. $85.00
(Right)
Pewter Whale Oil Lamp, Mkd. "Reed & Barton" $165.00

(A-PA. '76)   Pennypacker Auction Centre
PEWTER *(Left to Right)*
Porringer, Heart Handle, Lee or Gleason, 3¼"
D. $150.00
Porringer, 3½" D. $200.00
Plate, Joseph Danforth, Touchmarks, 18th C.,
Jacob's #95, 7¾" D. $260.00
Basin, Richard Austin, Dove & Land Touchmark, Jacob's #8, 8⅛" D. $290.00

(A-OH. '76)   Garth's Auctions, Inc.
(Row I, Left to Right)
Britannia Teapot, "Sellew & Co., Cincinnati",
Spout Repair, 9½" H. $85.00
Cast Brass Spoon Mold, W/Wooden Pliers
for Holding Hot Mold & Sample of Finished
Spoon $290.00
Britannia Teapot, "Sellew & Co., Cincinnati",
11" H. $155.00
(Row II, Left to Right)
Pewter Porringer, 2-Handled, Lid W/Cast In
Design, Finial Resoldered, 6½" D. $95.00
Pewter Vessel, Oriental, Cast Feet, 8¾" H. . .
. . . . $105.00
Pewter Porringer, 2-Handled, 6" D. . . .$70.00
(Row III, Left to Right)
Cast Brass Set of Scale Weights, Lid Has Cast
Sea Monsters & Cast Male Torso's, Exterior Of
Case Has Stamped Designs & Hallmarks, 3
Weights, Dutch, 5" D. $210.00
Pewter Hexagonal Jug, Engraved Wreath
W/"M.A." and "1804", 10½" H. $215.00
Pewter Basin, Touch Mark "Townsend & Compton", 8" D. $135.00

(A-OH. '76)   Garth's Auctions, Inc.
(Row I, Left to Right)
Pewter Candlesticks, Pr., Amer., Unmarked,
10" H. $295.00
Eagle Flag Pole Finial, Copper, Base W/
Threaded Pipe Fitting, 12½" H. $165.00
(Row II, Left to Right)
Pewter Tankard, Inside of Bottom Marked
"Compton, London", 7¾" H. $180.00
Pewter Plate, Amer., 2 Eagle Touch Marks,
"Thomas D. Boardman", Jacobs #37, 7¾"
D. $350.00
Pewter Tankard, Base Marked W/"5", A Crown
& A Lion's Head, 6½" H. $95.00
(Row III, Left to Right)
Pewter Plate, Amer., Partial Touch Mark of
"Samuel Kilborne, Baltimore", Jacobs #184,
7¾" D. $400.00
Pewter Beaker, Amer., "Boardman & Hart, N-
York", Jacobs #47, 5" H. $450.00
Pewter Plate, Amer., 2 Eagle "S.D." Touch
Marks for Samuel Danforth, Jacobs #107, 8"
D. $325.00

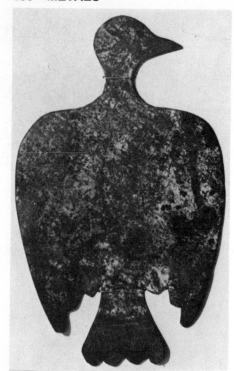

(A-PA. '76)   *Pennypacker Auction Centre*
Tin Quilt Pattern In Form Of Eagle, 6½" L. . .
. . . .$110.00

(D-OR. '76)
Lacy Iron Card Holder, 5" x 5½" $45.00

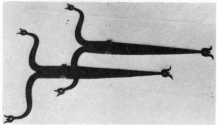

(A-PA. '76)   *Pennypacker Auction Centre*
Wrought Iron Tulip Hinges, Pr., 23" L. . . . . . .
. . . . $775.00

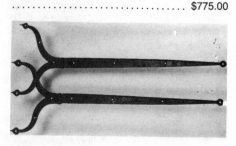

(A-PA. '76)   *Pennypacker Auction Centre*
Wrought Iron Bird Hinges, Pr., 42" L. . . . .
. . . . $110.00

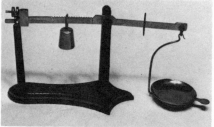

(D-N.Y.)
Fairbanks Scales Patented 1884, Brass & Iron,
. . . . $65.00

(D-KS. '76)
Iron Dead Hang, 10" L. $45.00

(A-PA. '76)   *Pennypacker Auction Centre*
Tin Cradle, 9" H., 14" L., Pa. Dutch . . .$90.00

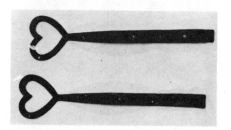

(A-PA. '76)   *Pennypacker Auction Centre*
Wrought Iron Hinges, Pr. $160.00

(A-PA. '76)   *Pennypacker Auction Centre*
Moravian Hinges, Pr., Ram's Horn, 18th C. . .
. . . . $110.00

(D-MO. '76)
Ladies' Brass Iron, French, Raised Door In
Back For Hot Coals $35.00

(D-N.Y. '76)
Iron Hitching Post, Double Horse Head . . . . .
. . . . $250.00

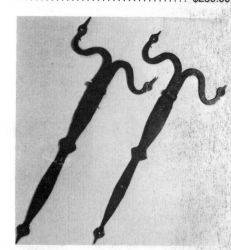

(A-PA. '76)   *Pennypacker Auction Centre*
Wrought Iron Hinges, Pr. $260.00

(A-PA. '75)   *Pennypacker Auction Centre*
Escutcheon, 18th C. $120.00

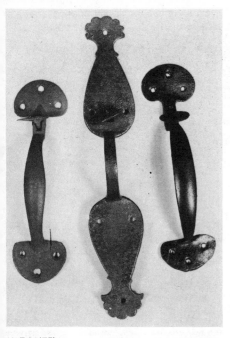

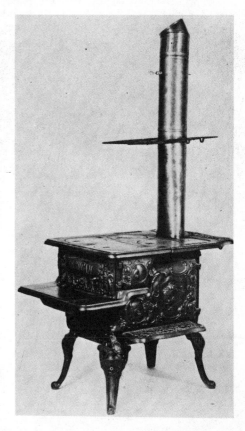

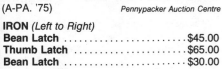

(A-PA. '75)   *Pennypacker Auction Centre*

IRON *(Left to Right)*
Bean Latch $45.00
Thumb Latch $65.00
Bean Latch $30.00

(A-PA. '76)   *Pennypacker Auction Centre*

Wrought Iron Tulip Hinges, Pr., 26" L. ......
.... $75.00

(D-MO. '76)
Copper Warming Pan, 12" Diam., Incised Bird
& Flowers On Cover, Turned Wooden Handle
Orig. $200.00

(A-MA. '76)   *Richard A. Bourne Co. Inc.*
Victorian Kitchen Range, Michigan Stove Co.,
Woodland Model No. 8-6-G, 25" W., 39" L.,
30" H. Not Incl. Pipe $225.00

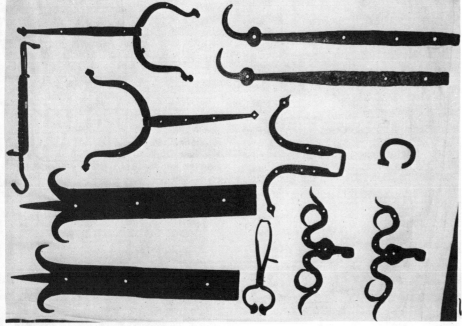

(A-OH. '76)   *Garth's Auctions, Inc.*

Wrought Iron Hinges, Rams Horn, Pr. $50.00
Wrought Iron Sugar Nippers, Pr. $55.00
Wrought Iron Hinges, Tulip Ends, May Be Reinforcing Straps Because There Is No Space For Pins,
Pr. $50.00
Wrought Iron Hinge, Single $20.00
Iron, "G" $17.50
Wrought Iron Strap Hinges, Pr. $65.00
Wrought Iron Strap Hinges, Pr. $50.00
Wrought Iron Trammel, Twisted Handle, 14" L. $95.00

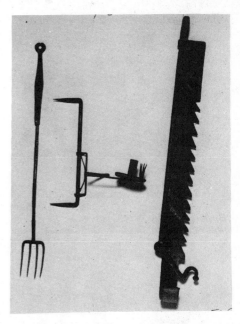

(A-OH. '76)   *Garth's Auctions, Inc.*
Wrought Iron Fork, Handle W/Tooled Design,
29" L. $30.00
Wrought Iron Lighting Device, Adjustable
Candle Arm, To Be Driven Into Wall ..$235.00
Wrought Iron Sawtooth Trammel, 34" L. ....
.... $75.00

160 MINIATURES

In every period of history, miniature objects have held a special fascination for collectors of every age group. To some, it is the nostalgic sentimental appeal related to their childhood; with others it is their attraction to small things. Today, there is a vast number of collectors of miniature objects and, the variety of examples available is almost as varied as those in almost every category of antique collecting.

(A-PA. '76)   *Pennypacker Auction Centre*

Blanket Chest, Walnut, Dovetailed W/Strap Hinges, 14½" H., 19" L., 12½" D. $210.00

(A-PA. '75)   *Pennypacker Auction Centre*
(Left to Right)
Doll Chair $27.50
Drysink, Grained, Orig. $170.00
Benches, Walnut, Pr. $25.00
Doll Chair, Orig. $27.50

(A-PA. '75)   *Pennypacker Auction Centre*
Bonnet Top Cabinet, All Orig., 16" x 23" . . . .
. . . .$100.00
Jelly Cupboard, Pine $90.00

(A-PA. '75)   *Pennypacker Auction Centre*
(Left to Right)
Welsh Cupboard, Soft Wood, Old Kitchen Paint $65.00
Bureau, Walnut $42.50
Welsh Dresser, Pine, All Orig. Red & Green Paint, 21½" H., 15½" W., 6½" D. $95.00

(A-PA. '75)   *Pennypacker Auction Centre*
Rushseat Chair $12.50
High Chair $85.00

(A-PA. '75)   *Pennypacker Auction Centre*
(Left to Right)
Doll Wardrobe $22.50
Wardrobe, Birds-Eye $37.50
Welsh Cupboard $100.00

(A-PA. '75)   *Pennypacker Auction Centre*
(Left to Right)
Empire Chest, Walnut, All Orig., 9½" W., 13" H., 8" D. $45.00
Spice Cabinet, All Orig., Brass Knobs $140.00
Chest of Drawers, Mahogany, 6" D., 11½" H., 10½" W. $80.00

(A-PA. '76)   *Pennypacker Auction Centre*
Sled, Tenon & Mortise Construction, Old Red Paint, 12" L. $75.00
Ladder Back Rocker, Splat Seat, Old Red Paint, 10" H. $100.00
Cradle, Orig. Circle Decor., Old Red Paint, 10" L. $210.00

(A-PA. '75)
(Left to Right)
Door Stop, Ohio Pottery, Brown & Yellow Lion, Lge. $60.00
Grandfather Clock, Chippendale Style Case, Hinged Top, Watch Holder Case W/Coin Silver Bulls Eye Watch, Dated 1780 . . . .$235.00
Chest of Drawers, Cherry, All Orig. . . .$55.00
Orig. $55.00
Wooden Figure $75.00
Crow On Stump, Ohio Pottery, E.J.E. .$57.50

(A-PA. '76)   *Pennypacker Auction Centre*
Cupboard, Orig. Grained Decor., 18" H. . . . . .
. . . .$100.00

REDWARE MINIATURES
(Row I, Left to Right)
Mug, Drk. Manganese Glaze, 2" H. $100.00
Bowl, Handled, 1½" H. $110.00
Egg Cup, Incised Decor., 2½" H. $180.00
Cup, 2" H. $80.00
Pitcher, 2½" H. $70.00
(Row II, Left to Right)
Pitcher, Drk. Manganese Glaze, 2¾" H.$80.00
Bowl, W/Line of Slip Decor., 1½" D. .$150.00
Bowl, Manganese Sponge Decor., 1½" D.
. . . .$230.00
Pitcher, Drk. Manganese Glaze, 2½" H. $110.00
(Row III, Left to Right)
Pitcher & Bowl Set, Rim Chip, 2½" H. $90.00
Jug, Handled, 3" H. $170.00
Bowl, Splash Manganese Decor., 1¾"$130.00

(A-PA. '76)   *Pennypacker Auction Centre*
Windsor Chair $105.00
Windsor Stool, 10" H. $110.00
Shaker Ladder Back Child's High Chair, Rush Seat $160.00

(D-KS. '75)   (A-PA. '75)
                            Pennypacker Auction Centre
(Left)
Step-back Cupboard, Walnut W/Veneered Drawer Fronts $175.00
(Right)
Dutch Cupboard, Refinished 330.00

Interest in Oriental items remains high — with a noticeable increase in prices of Chinese porcelains, Oriental prints and rugs. There is an increased demand for fine examples of Nippon and, enthusiasm for Occupied Japan items continues.

Richard A. Bourne Co. Inc.

(A-MA. '75)
(Row I, Left to Right)
Glass Snuff Bottle, Late Chinese, W/Reverse Painted Decor. Chip In Foot Ring $20.00
Glass Snuff Bottle, Late Chinese, W/Reverse Painted Decor. $30.00
Glass Snuff Bottle, Late Chinese, W/Reverse Painted Decor. $30.00
Porcelain Snuff Bottle, Chinese 19th C., Gourd Form W/Decor. In Orange-Red On White Porcelain, Top Possibly Jade, Signed $50.00
Carved Goldstone Snuff Bottle, Late Chinese, W/Jade-Colored Stopper $35.00
(Row II, Left to Right)
Carved Ivory Netsuke, Form Of Plump Man In Cloak & Peaked Hat Fan In Right Hand $25.00
Carved Ivory Figure, Possibly Japanese 19th C., Elderly Man Holding Gourd Tied To Stick Over His Head, Appears To Be Carved From Tip Of Tusk Or Tooth, 2¼" H. $50.00
Ivory Netsuke, Japanese 19th C., Figure Of Seated Man Eating & Looking Toward Sky $70.00
Soapstone Carving, Chinese 19th C., 4¾" L. $17.00
(Row III, Left to Right)
Plique A Jour Cabinet Vase, Japanese 19th C., Colorful Flowers & Green Leaves, Gilded Silver Foot Ring & Rim, 3⅝" H. $150.00
Satsuma Vase, Japanese 19th C., Decor. Of Dragon, 2 Deities & Child, Black & Aqua Signature On Bottom, 6" H. $80.00
Satsuma Vase, Japanese 19th C., 2 Lge. & 4 Sm. Scenes, Speckled Gold Ground, Each Scene Contains Deities, Samurai Warriors & Other Figures, 6" H. $75.00
(Row IV, Left & Right)
Cased Pair Chinese Trinket Boxes, Form Of Cranes, Each Bird Has Hollow Body, Mother-Of-Pearl Feathers, Ivory Legs & Feet, Head Of Ivory W/Inlaid Ebony & Mother-Of-Pearl Eyes, Shield-Shaped Lids, Both Birds Fitted In Brocade Box, Approx. 8" H. $350.00
(Center)
Chinese Export Porcelain Box, Late 19th C., Polychrome Decor. Of Figures In Landscape On Front & Back, 4¾" L. $45.00

Richard A. Bourne Co. Inc.

(A-MA. '75)
(Row I, Left to Right)
Bronze Figure, Japanese 19th C., Adult Elephant Being Attacked By 2 Tigers, On Teakwood Base, 10" H. $375.00
Oriental Brass Incense Burner, Chinese 19th C., Lge. Guardian Dog Finial, Engraved Scene Of Fishermen In One Panel & Hawthorne Blooms & Bird On Another, Teakwood Base, 11½" H. $80.00
Brass Figure Of Buddha, Japanese Late 19th C., 6" H. $60.00
(Row II, Left to Right)
Carved Teak Sculpture, Chinese Late 19th C., Laughing Buddha, 17½" H. $220.00
Carved Teak Sculpture, Chinese 19th C., Man Riding An Elephant, Both W/Glass Eyes, Elephant Real Ivory Tusks, 10½" H. . . . $60.00
Carved Teakwood Sculpture, Chinese 19th C., Old Man W/Glass Eyes, Sm. Chip In Lower Lip, 17" H. $180.00
(Row III)
Bronze Vases, Pr., Japanese 19th C., Raised Figures Of Exotic Birds On Sides, 14½" H. $175.00

(D-N.Y. '76)
Fruit Bowl, Mkd. "Nippon", 4½" W., 7¼" L. $35.00

(D-AR. '76)
Ornate Nippon Bowl, Mkd. 10" L., 5½" D. $125.00

(D-CA. '76)
Cloisonne Vases, Mkd. "Made In Japan";
Small Vase, 12" H. $65.00
Large Vase, 24" H. $375.00

(D-CA. '76)
Cinnabar Vase, 16½" H. $350.00

(D-CA. '76)
Satsuma Vase, 16" H. $375.00

(D-MO. '76)
Imari Punch Bowl, 8¾" H., 14¾" Diam. . . . . . .
. . . .$290.00

(A-MA. '75)   *Richard A. Bourne Co. Inc.*
(Left)
Silk Embroidery, Chinese, 19th C., Scene W/
Lge. Peacock Resting On Flower Branch &
Surrounded By Flowers, Smaller Birds & Butter-
flies, Signed Lower Left, 55" x 23½" . .$180.00
(Right)
Silk Embroidery, Chinese, 19th C., Oriental
Woman & Child W/Crane On Vivid Red Back-
ground, 48" x 27½" Sight $200.00

(A-MA. '76)   *Richard A. Bourne Co. Inc.*
CHINESE EXPORT PORCELAIN
(Row I, Left to Right)
Bowl, Late 18th C.; Five-Color Polychromed
Scenes, Each W/3 Figures, Vignettes & Land-
scapes Within Scrolled Floral Border; 10½"
Diam. $325.00
Bowl, Late 18th C.; Similar To Preceding Having
More Detailed Decor; 11" Diam. $350.00
(Row II, Left toRight)
Bowl, 18th C.; Two Large Panels Of Decor, Con-
taining Eight Figures Separated By Polychrome
& Gold Floral Decor, Bouquet Of Flowers In
Center; 2 Age Cracks; 10¼" Diam. . . .$175.00
Bowl, 19th C.; Unusually Heavy W/Five-Color
Polychrome Decor. Of Flowers On Interior &
Outside; 10" Diam. $300.00

(A-VA. '76)   *Laws*
Elaborately Carved Coromandal 2 Panel Screen, Pierced & Decorated W/Samuri Warriors In
Relief Of Ivory, Jade, Mother-Of-Pearl & Other Media On Blue Lacquered Ground; Reverse W/Ivory &
Jade Floral & Bird Decor. In Relief On Black Ground, Ca. 1850-75; 66" H., 36" W $1200.00
(Left)
Nest Of Four Chinese Teakwood Tables, Each W/Pierced Skirts Over Recessed Top; Round Legs
Joined By Fix Stretcher; Ca. 1860; 28" H. $550.00
(Center)
Imari Umbrella Stand, Ca. 1840; 25" H. $400.00
(Right)
Chinese Rosewood Temple Chair, Boldly Scrolled Sides W/Grey & Ivory Striated Marble Inset On
Back; Ca. 1860-80 . . . .$500.00
(Front)
Chinese Coffee Table, Intricately Carved & Pierced Skirt & Molded Top, Ca. 1880; 18" H., 16" D.,
44" L. $175.00

◄—(A-MA. '76)   *Richard A. Bourne Co. Inc.*
(Row I, Left to Right)
Chinese Export Porcelain Bowl, Late 18th C.;
Two Large Panels Of Landscapes Of Figures
Separated By Vignettes Of Flowers; 8" Diam.
. . . .$300.00
Chinese Export Porcelain Bowl, Late 18th C.;
Two-Panel Decoration Of Polychromed Figures
In Inter-Exterior Scene Separated By Vignettes
Of Flowers; 8" Diam. $250.00
**Pair Of Matched Chinese Export Porcelain
Square Bowls,** 18th C.; Orange Peel Texture,
Polychrome Floral Decor.; 9¾" Sq. .$1,100.00

(D-CA. '76)
Moriaga, Decor. On Red Ground W/Pastel Flowers, 12" H. $350.00

Richard A. Bourne Co. Inc.

(A-MA. '76)
(Row I, Left to Right)
Richard A. Bourne Co. Inc.
Porcelain Jar, Chinese Export, Polychrome Decor. Of Landscape W/2 Female Figures, Calligraphy On Back, Filled W/Dried Scented Flowers, 1 Sm. Nick On Rim, 3½" H. . .$25.00
Porcelain Plates, Set Of 3, Japanese, Polychrome Decor. Of Interior Banquet Scene W/Many Figures, Minor Nicks On Rims, 7¾" Diam. $35.00
Porcelain Dish, Chinese, 4-Section W/Lid, Multicolored, 5" Diam., 6½" H. $40.00
Cloisonne Cigarette Box, Chinese, Multicolored Butterflies $45.00
(Row II, Left to Right)
Kutani Bowl, Japanese, Late 18th Or Early 19th C., One Slight Age Crack, 13⅛" Diam. $100.00
Porcelain Bowl, Japanese, One Thousand Face Decor., 9⅞" Diam. $60.00
(Row III, Left to Right)
Lacquer Jewel Cabinet, Japanese, 19 Drawers W/Sm. Central Compartment & Lift Top, 7½" W., 15½" H. $60.00
Canton Porcelain Baluster Form Vase, Blue & White, Chinese, 19th C., 9¾" Diam., 16" H. $300.00

(D-N.Y. '76)
Korean Vase, 14" H. $65.00

CHINESE EXPORT PORCELAIN
(Row I, Left to Right)
Bowl, 18th C.; Elaborate Polychromed Decor. W/Figures Around Exterior & Inner Border Panel, Vignettes Of Birds & Flowers & Inner Medallion Of Landscape W/Figures; Two Minor Age Cracks From Top; 11¼" Diam. $550.00
One Of Six Small Dishes, Late 18thC.; 2 W/Age Cracks, 9" Diam. $200.00
One Of Nine Soup Plates, Late 18thC.; 2 W/Age Cracks & All W/Roughage In Varying Degrees; 9" Diam. $350.00
(Row II, Left to Right)
One Of Ten Plates, All W/Edge Chips; Match The Preceding $500.00
Pair Of Deep Dishes, One W/Age Crack; The Other W/Tiny Edge Nicks; 9¾" Diam. .$225.00
(Row III, Left to Right)
Platter, A Match To Preceding; 17¼" L. $400.00
Platter, A Match To Preceding; 13" L. $300.00

(D-AR. '76)
Noritake Bowl, Mkd., Handpainted $75.00

(A-PA. '76)
Pennypacker Auction Centre
Canton China Vases, 14¾" H., Pair .$220.00

(D-KS. '76)
Gay '90's
OCCUPIED JAPAN ITEMS, Marked
(Left to Right)
Figure $5.50
Cup/Saucer $8.50
Figure $6.50
Figure $12.50
Vase $5.00
Mustard Jar $8.00

(D-KS. '76)
Gay '90's
OCCUPIED JAPAN ITEMS, Marked
(Left to Right)
Figure, 4½" H. $8.50
Toothpic Holder $7.50
Figure $5.00
Clown Figure $7.50
Piano & Figure $12.50

(A-OH. '76) *Garth's Auctions, Inc.*
(Row I, Left to Right)
Canton Bowl, Blue & White, Reticulated, Oval, Lemon Peel Glaze, 11" L., 4" Diam. ..$225.00
Nanking Chocolate Pot, Blue & White, Strap Handle, Gilt Trim, Eggshell Glaze, 9¼" H. .....
....$275.00
Nanking Bowl & Tray, Blue & White, Reticulated, Lemon Peel Glaze, Tray Not Pictured, 8½" L., 3" H. $185.00
(Row II, Left to Right)
Oriental Export Porcelain Plates, (8), Blue & White, 2 Have Hairlines, (2 Pictured), 9" Diam.
....$155.00
Canton Covered Tureen, Blue & White, Animal Head Handles, Lemon Peel Glaze, 12" L. ....
....$475.00
(Row III, Left to Right)
Nanking Soup Plates, (3), Blue & White, Lemon Peel Glaze, 2 Have Hairline, 9½" Diam. .....
....$95.00
Oriental Export Crocus Pot, Blue & White, 9¼" H. $150.00
Nanking Plates, (4), Blue & White, Lemon Peel Glaze, 2 Have Minor Damage, 9" Diam. $150.00

(A-MA. '75) *Richard A. Bourne Co. Inc.*
(Row I, Left to Right)
Satsuma Covered Urn, Japanese 19th C., Deep Cobalt Blue W/2 Paneled Landscapes, Rim Chipped, 8½" H. $75.00
Cloisonne Covered Urn, Japanese Late 19th-Early 20th C., Flowering Tree W/Yellow Bird Perched, Blue Ground Filled W/Clouds, 10" H.
....$120.00
Cloisonne Vase, Japanese Late 19th-Early 20th C., Scene Of Cherry Blossoms W/Bird Against White Ground, 9" H. $130.00
(Row II, Left to Right)
Satsuma Vases, Pr., Japanese Late 19th C., Group Of Seated Or Kneeling Deities Against Gold & Black Landscape, Tiny Elephant Handles, Gold Seal Signature, 6" H. $155.00
Satsuma Vases, Pr., Japanese 19th C., Designs Of Lge. Flowers & Flying Birds Against Ivory Ground, Signed On Base, 8½" H. $225.00
(Row III, Left to Right)
Stasuma Vases, Pr., Japanese 19th C., Two-Panel Decor. Of Samurai Warriors, Signed In Red On Base, 10" H. $150.00
Wood & Lacquer Tobacco Box, Japanese 19th C., Silver Fittings Of Unknown Purity, Gold Decor., 8¼" L., 4¾" D., 5½" H. $170.00

(A-MA. '76) *Richard A. Bourne Co. Inc.*
(Row I, Left to Right)
Hanging Letter Box, 19th C., Oriental Figures Decor., Black Lacquer Ground, 2 Sm. Chips In Lacquer, 9¼" H. $40.00
Lacquer Desk Box, Japanese, Hinged Lid, Front & Lid W/Scenes Of Figures Of Firearms, Workers, Etc., 7⅞" L., 3½" D., 8" H. $50.00
Gold Lacquer Jewel Box, 2 Doors Enclosing 4 Sm. Compartments, 1 Drawer W/Lock & Key, 5⅝" W., 3¼" D., 7¾" H. $30.00
(Row II, Left to Right)
Lacquer Jewel Chest, Japanese, Floral Decor., 2 Sm. Chips On Back Edge, 2 Legs Reglued, 7" W., 3½" D., 10" H. $25.00
Lacquer Plate, Japanese, Interior Scene W/5 Figures, 9¼" Diam. $40.00
Lacquer Bowl, Japanese, Landscape Decor. In Center, 8⅞" Diam. $15.00
(Row III, Left to Right)
Lacquer Tray, Japanese, Scalloped Edge & Decor. Of Interior Scene Surrounded By Fans & Abstract Design, 13½" L. $45.00
Lacquer Tray, Japanese, Scalloped Edge, Ducks & Flowers Decor., Inner & Outer Edges Of Rim Are Worn, 15" L. $25.00
(Row IV, Left to Right)
Lacquer Box, Japanese, Hinged Lid, Decor. W/ Scenes Of Play & War W/Landscape Scene & 2 Figures On Top, 5½" Diam., 5½" H. ...$45.00
Lacquer Glove Box, Japanese, 19th C., Rust Colored Decor. On Cover W/Bird, Flower & Landscape W/Mount Fuji, 12" L. $20.00
Lacquer Muffin Dish, Gold Decor. Of Birds & Flowers & Cross Work On Black Ground, Minor Wear To Finish, 10½" L. $10.00

(A-PA. '76) *Pennypacker Auction Centre*
ROSE MEDALLION
(Left to Right)
Vase, W/Handles, 24" H............$400.00
Vase, W/Handles, Hairline, 24" H. $225.00

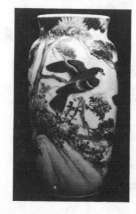

(D-FL. '76)
Oriental Vase, Japan, 16½" H. $195.00

(D-CA. '76)
Rose Medallion Punch Bowl, 16" Diam. ....
....$500.00

Fine paintings from all periods, early prints, calligraphs, silhouettes, fractures and cutouts of exceptional quality are still very much in demand. Of equal importance is the great interest today in later works of art — tinsel pictures, reverse paintings, shell work, etc. from the late Victorian years and, including fine examples of contemporary American Folk Art which oftentimes commands higher prices than comparable examples dating from the last century.

Pennypacker Auction Centre

Birth Certificate, William Schmidt, 1839, Montgomery County, Decor. W/Illus. Of Ten Commandments, Printed At 71 Race Street, Philadelphia By George B. Menz (A-PA. '76) $75.00

Pennypacker Auction Centre

Cutout, Hearts, Tulips & Birds, Orig. Frame .. ..(A-PA. '76) $170.00

Pennypacker Auction Centre

Cutout, Pa., Confrontal Birds Design Mounted Over Bright Red ....(A-PA. '76) $200.00

Pennypacker Auction Centre

Block Print, Bird & Tulip Illustration, Peter Montelius ....(A-PA. '76) $380.00

Pennypacker Auction Centre

Cutout, Tulips, Hearts & Six Pointed Stars, Mounted On Cherry Red Background, By G.W. McAllister For Emelia Flory, April 10, 1847, Bucks County ....(A-PA. '76) $275.00

Pennypacker Auction Centre

Calligraph, Red, White & Blue, American Eagle & The "Writing Hand", By Samuel Brugger ... .(A-PA. '76) $475.00

Pennypacker Auction Centre

Oil On Canvas, 10" x 14", Signed........... ....(A-PA. '75) $125.00

Pennypacker Auction Centre

Oil On Canvas, Cottage On Island W/Men On Boat Rescuing Mother & Child, 12" x 16" ....(A-PA. '75) $65.00

Pennypacker Auction Centre

Fraktur, Birth Certificate Of Mattis Meek, Lebanon County, 1829, W/Pots Of Flowers, W/ Tulip & Strawberries ......(A-PA. '76) $500.00

Pennypacker Auction Centre

Fraktur Birth Certificate, Lea Rubreckt, Feb. 20, 1819, Berks Co., By Krebs .... (A-PA. '76) $925.00

Pennypacker Auction Centre

Mennonite Fraktur, Watercolor Of Bird W/ Tulip & Other Flowers, Early Decor. Frame, Franconia, Montgomery County .... (A-PA. '76) $1100.00

Pennypacker Auction Centre

Fraktur, Inscribed "Abraham Killian, 1812, Lancaster County," 14½"x9½" (A-PA. '75) $625.00

Pennypacker Auction Centre

Fraktur, Birth Certificate Of Anna Bensinger, 1771, Orig. Decor. Frame, 18th C. (A-PA. '76) $400.00

Pennypacker Auction Centre

Bookplate, W/Face, Hearts, Distelfink & Tulip, Dated 1810 ....(A-PA. '76) $450.00

(A-PA. '76)　　*Pennypacker Auction Centre*

Fraktur, For Elizabeth Brubacher, Lancaster County; Basket Of Flowers & 4 Lge. Birds; Signed "Jacob Brubacher", Dated 1811, 7" x 12" $1600.00

Pennypacker Auction Centre

Fraktur, Statement That "John Landis Is Born, July 29, 1832", Small .....(A-PA. '76) $300.00

Pennypacker Auction Centre

Watercolor, S.S. Reurlayn Bangor, H. Jones Mate . . . .(A-PA. '75) $45.00

Pennypacker Auction Centre

Fraktur, House, Signed "Jacob Henly", 1820, ... (A-PA. '76) $1200.00

Pennypacker Auction Centre

Watercolor Portrait, Young Lady In Elaborate Dress, By Jacob Maentel, Orig. Frame, 6" x 7½" . . . .(A-PA. '76) $2100.00

Pennypacker Auction Centre

Ornamental Drawing, Watercolor, Red & Yellow Tulips, Pa., 5" x 5½"; . . . . .(A-PA. '76) $325.00

Pennypacker Auction Centre

Fraktur, Birth Certificate, Pa., Birth Of Maria Faust In 1813, Union County; Decor. W/Tulips, Birds, Hearts & Stars, By Early Centre County Artist, Full Size . . . .(A-PA. '76) $1800.00

Pennypacker Auction Centre

Watercolor, Winter Scene, By Hattie K. Brunner Dated 1968 . . . .(A-PA. '76) $1450.00

Pennypacker Auction Centre

Fraktur, Flying Angel, Benjamin Riftler, Dated 1810, Northampton County, Framed In Orig. Decor. Frame W/Finger Applied Colors Of Green, Yellow & Orange On Drk. Brown Background . . . .(A-PA. '76) $3000.00

Pennypacker Auction Centre

Fraktur, Tulip Tree W/Branches That Hold 10 Stylized Birds, Topped By Spread Eagle, Dated 1800, Attrib. To John Umble . . . .(A-PA. '76) $775.00

Pennypacker Auction Centre

Fraktur Watercolor, Distlefink Perched On Flowered Branch, Orig. Finger Daub Type Frame . . . .(A-PA. '76) $650.00

Pennypacker Auction Centre

Book Marker, Dated 1800, Pa., 3¼" x 4" . . . .(A-PA. '76) $325.00

(D-FL. '76)
Venetian Intarsia, 19th C., 8¼" x 11½" $650.00

Pennypacker Auction Centre

Portraits, Young Woman and Man, Black & White Pastel, Tinted Face Coloring, Date Around 1760, Orig. Hogarth Frames, 11" x 18" ....(A-PA. '76) $225.00

Portrait, Oil, Elaborate Frame, Ca. 1880, 34 x 40" Framed ....(D-KS. '76) $650.00

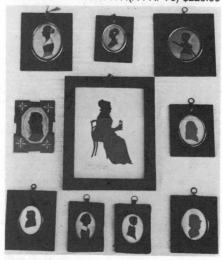

(A-OH. '76)   *Garth's Auctions, Inc.*

Reverse Painting, Italian, 18th C., 9½" x 12", Walnut Frame ....(D-KS. '76) $75.00

(A-OH. '76)   *Garth's Auctions, Inc.*

Hollow Cut Silhouette, Torso Drawn W/Pencil, "J.A. Harris LaFayette", Old Black Frame, 5" x 6¾" $85.00

Ink & Watercolor Silhouette, A Redcoat, Signed & Dated, Modern Frame 6¼" x 7½" $145.00

Hollow Cut Silhouette, Boy, Hair & Costume Drawn In, Reverse Painted Black & Gold Matt, Old Frame, 5½" x 6½" $95.00

Hollow Cut Silhouette, Boy W/Lge. Cap, Impressed "Peale", Gilt Frame, 4½" x 5½" $195.00

Hollow Cut Silhouette, Young Man, Impressed "Williams", Old Frame, 4¼" x 5¼" $190.00

Hollow Cut Silhouette, Young Man Wearing Mortar Board & Smoking, Gilt Highlights, Old Grained Frame, 5"x6" $95.00

Hollow Cut Silhouette, Major Zachary Taylor, Initialed & Dated 1832, Old Frame, 6" x 6¾" $185.00

(Row I, Left to Right)
Ink Silhouette, Young Woman Highlighted W/ Gold, Wooden Frame 5⅜"x6" $170.00
Ink Silhouette, Young Woman, Wooden Frame, 4" x 4¾" $70.00
Hollow Cut Silhouette, Child Pointing, Wooden Frame, 6¼" x 6½" $130.00
(Row II, Left to Right)
Hollow Cut Silhouette, Gentleman, Reverse Painted Glass, No Frame, 4" x 5¼" ... $95.00
Cut Silhouette, By Edouart W/Name Of Sitter & Dated 1850, Reeded Frame, 9" x 11" $350.00
Hollow Cut Silhouette, Gentleman, Cloth Background, Wooden Frame, 4¼" x 5" $45.00
(Row III, Left to Right)
Hollow Cut Silhouette, Woman W/Bonnet, Cloth Background, Wooden Frame, 4¾" x 5½" $35.00
Reverse Painted Silhouettes, Pr., Young Boy & Girl, Cardboard & Wooden Frames, 3½" x 4½" $150.00
Hollow Cut Silhouette, Woman In Fancy Hat, Cloth Background, Wooden Frame, 4½" x 5¼" $35.00

Pennypacker Auction Centre

Reverse Painting On Glass, American, Black Minstrel Presenting Calling Card "Joseph Davis" Orig. Inlaid Frame ....(A-PA. '76) $725.00

Silhouette Cut-Out, 8½ x 11" ....(D-N.H. '76) $90.00

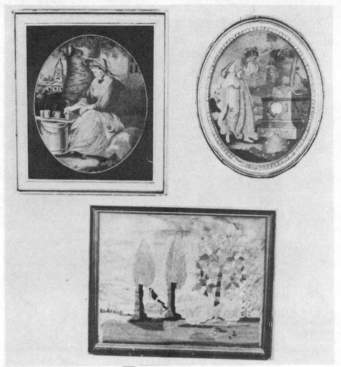

(A-PA. '76) *Pennypacker Auction Centre*
Watercolor, Boy Sitting Under Tree On Yellow Chair $800.00

(A-VA. '76) *Laws*
(Row I, Left to Right)
Embroidered Silk Scene, Young Maiden In Foreground W/Independence Hall In Distance, Orig. Oval-Shaped Mat W/Gilt Frame, Ca. 1875, Sight Size: 13" x 11" $190.00
Embroidered Silk Morning Scene, Incorporating Silver Coin W/"G.W.", (Motif Suggests The Tomb Of George Washington), Choice Example Of Lady's Work In Period Gilt Frame, Sight Size: 14" x 10"
.... $120.00
(Row II)
Lady's Stitchery Piece, On Painted Silk, Vivid Colored Bluejay Perched On Rock Amongst Several Trees W/3 Sheep In Foreground, Gilf Frame, Sight Size: 17" x 13" $65.00

(A-PA. '76) *Pennypacker Auction Centre*
Painting on Porcelain, By Ernde, Gold Leaf Frame, 5"x7½" $300.00

(A-PA. '76) *Pennypacker Auction Centre*
Watercolor, Gowan & Marx Engine Made In Phila., Pa., 1839, Green & Brown, Signed "John H. Thomas, 1848",.................. $450.00

(D-N.Y. '76)
Landscape Scenes In Oil On Satin Glass, Unsigned, Ornate Silver Frames, 8½" x 11¼", Pair $200.00

(A-PA. '76) *Pennypacker Auction Centre*
Race Horse Print, "Attla Winner Of The Derby Stakes", Dean & Co., English, Published 1842, 10" x 13½" $60.00

(D-N.H.) '76)
Tinsel Picture, Birds & Flowers On Black Ground, Orig. Gilt Frame, 12 x 15¼", Overall
.... $165.00

Pennypacker Auction Centre

Watercolor, Primitive, Orig. Decor. Softwood Frame ....(A-PA. '76) $950.00

Pennypacker Auction Centre

Watercolor, Young Girl Holding Rose, By Jacob Maentel, 8¾"x10¾" .....(A-PA. '76) $2600.00

Pennypacker Auction Centre

Watercolor Profile, Young Man Standing W/ Whip In One Hand & Hat In Other On Gaily Colored Rug, By Joseph H. Davis, New England Area, 10¾" x 8½" ......(A-PA. '76) $3200.00

(A-OH. '76)   *Garth's Auctions, Inc.*

(Row I, Left to Right)
Watercolor On Paper, Miniature, Young Woman, Brass Trimmed Wooden Frame, 4⅜" x 5½" ...
....$105.00
Double Silhouette, Man & Woman, Hollow Cut Heads & Costumes Executed In Ink, Reverse painted Black Mat W/Gilt Trim, Gilded Frame, 5¾" x 8" $115.00
Miniature On Ivory, Gentleman, Sticker On Back Identifies Likeness To "Col. Joseph Appleton Dike", Gilt Frame, 3¾" x 4¼" $135.00
(Row II, Left to Right)
Miniature On Ivory, Young Lady, Grey Background Retouched, Brass Oval Frame, 3" H. ....
....$55.00
Miniature On Ivory, Child In Red Dress, Obelisk In Background, Back Of Case Has Window W/Braided Hair, Gilt Brass & Gold Case, 3¼" H. $130.00
(Row III, Left to Right)
Pencil & Ink Drawing, Profile Of Gentleman, Reverse Painted Mat & Old Frame, Back of Frame Inscribed "Elder John Buzzer", 4½" x 5¼" $75.00
Charcoal & Pastel Drawing, Gentleman, Old Gilt Frame, 6¾" x 8" $115.00
Cut Silhouette, Young Woman, Highlighted W/Faded Gilt, "Cut W/The Mouth By Miss Honeywell", Old Gilt Frame, 5" x 6" $95.00

Pennypacker Auction Centre

Watercolor Portraits, Pa., Pair, Husband & Wife In Yellow Windsor Chairs On Colored Checkered Carpeting Beside Draped Windows W/Gaily Colored Wallpaper; His Portrait Inscribed "Abraham Baumann", Hers "Catharina Baumann", Gothic Lettering, Elaborate Scrolls, 9½" x 13½" ....
....(A-PA. '76) $4100.00

Photographic memorabilia has become one of the most popular of masculine collectibles — with prices increasing substantially with each passing year. The original common type photograph — the daguerreotype — largely gave way after the mid-1850s to the ambrotype, followed by the ferrotype or tintype — and later still a cheaper process — the paper print. With exception of the latter, all produce reverse images, causing confusion to the novice. Since the paper print and the tintype are readily identifiable, to differentiate between the daguerreotype and ambrotype, when held and moved into different positions, the daguerreotype has a brilliant silver surface and will reflect light instead of showing the image, whereas the ambrotype will look the same regardless of the position in which it is held.

The cases which held the above early photos are also popular collectibles in themselves. The most interesting are the gutta-percha cases (a pioneer plastic). Those decorated with historical scenes in relief are very much in demand.

(D-KS. '76)
The Universal Camera, B4, Rochester Optical (1886), 6½" x 8½" Plate $70.00

(D-KS. '76)
Kodak Model A, Ca. 1906, 3 B Quick Focus, 3¼" x 5½" Format $70.00

(D-KS. '76)
Premo Junior Box Camera, #3, Pat. Date 1908, 3¼" x 4¼" Film Pack $18.00

(D-N.Y. '76)
Stereoscope, French, Box Maple, 250 Cards Double Showing World War I Scenes .$325.00

(D-N.Y. '76)
Pedestal Stereoscope Viewer, Pat. Dec. 7, 1875, 30 Cards $90.00

(D-KS. '76)
(Row I, Left to Right)
Eastman Kodak, Pat. Date 1902 . . . .$25.00
Brownie Box Camera #3 . . . .$5.00
(Row II, Left to Right)
Folding Brownie, #3A, Mod. A., 1909 Pat., Ball Bearing Shutter $20.00
Kodak Premotte, B & L Rapid, Rect. Shutter, E. K. Ball Bearings, Ca. 1910 . . . .$20.00
Zeiss, #1 Konta Model, German $15.00

(D-KS. '76)
Conley Camera, 3¼" x 5½" Plate, Conley Safety Shutter, Rapid Rectilinear 3 Focus Lens, Ca. 1917 . . . .$35.00

(D-KS. '76)
Ansco #7 Model 'B'', Wollen Sak Shutter & R.R. Lens, 4" x 5" Format On Kodak 103 Or On Ensign (British) Roll Film $40.00

(D-KS. '76)
(Row I, Left to Right)
Brownie No. 2, Model A., Pat'd. 1902, Automatic Shutter, Wooden Lens Board $20.00
Conley "Kewpie" No. 3A, Sold By Sears & Roebuck $8.00
(Row II, Left to Right)
Buster Brown Box Camera, Pat'd. 1910, Made By Ansco $8.00
Argus C3, Known As "Brick" Because Of Shape $20.00
Agra Ansco, B-2 Cadet, Mkd. "Texas Centennial Celebration 1936" $12.00

(D-KS. '76)
Ziess Tessar F2.8 Super Sport Dolly, Compur Shutter (1-250), Coupled Rangefinder, Built In Exposure Meter, 12 Or 16 Exp. On 120 Film ..
....................................$50.00

(D-KS. '76)
(Left to Right)
Album, W/18 Tintypes & 9 Photos; Pat. Date May 14th, 1861, Brass Clasp, 4" x 5¾" $35.00
Album, Tooled Leather W/38 Photos & 3 Tintypes, Brass Clasp, 5¼" x 6" $45.00

(D-KS. '76)
Kodak 3A Special, Model B, Coupled Rangefinder, Optimo Shutter, Zeiss Kodak F6.3 Lens, 3¼" x 5½" Format On 122 Film $65.00

(D-KS. '76)
Ziess Super I Konta "A", Coupled Rangefinder, Compur Rapid Shutter, Ziess Tessar F3.5 Lens, 1⅝" x 2¼" Format, 16 Exp. On 120 Film $75.00

(D-KS. '76)
Kodak No. 1 Pocket, Series II, Kodak Ball Bearing Shutter, Landscape Type Lens, 2¼" x 3¼" Format On 120 Roll Film, Ca. 1922 $12.00

(D-KS. '76)
No. 1 Kodak Junior, 1914 Auto Graphic, Sliding Lock On Autographic Panel, Kodak Ballbearing Shutter, B & L R.R. Lens $12.00

(D-KS. '76)
Kodak Recomar 18 Compur Shutter, Kodak F4.5 Anstigmat Lens 2¼" x 3¼" Format, Cut Film, Film Pak Or Roll Film W/Proper Holder. Ground Glass Or Scale Focusing $45.00

(D-KS. '76)
Reflex Korelle II, Focal Plane Shutter, Shutter Speeds 2 Sec. to 500, Lens Zeiss Tessar F2.8, Focus 8 CM, Automatic Film Stop $90.00

(D-KS. '76)
Ambrotype, Leather Case $22.50

(D-KS. '76)
Ambrotype, Half Case $10.00

(D-IL. '76)
Daguerreotype, Half Case $15.00

(D-MO. '76)
Daguerreotype, Velvet Lined Leather Case $25.00

(D-KS. '76)
Cardboard Photo Of Early Country Store, 5" x 7", Ca. 1900 ....$10.00

(D-KS. '76)
Ambrotype, West Point Cadet, Hand Tinted
......................................$45.00

(D-KS. '76)
Tintype, Civil War Soldier, Gutta-Percha Case $35.00

(D-MO. '76)
Ambrotype, Soiled Leather Case $12.50

(D-KS. '76)
Daguerreotype Case, Gutta-Percha, Brown, Civil War Soldier $50.00

(D-KS. '76)
Full Plate Tintype Of House, Late 1800s,
5" x 7" $20.00

The Shaker movement in America began in 1774 when Mother Ann Lee arrived in this country from England, bringing with her a small group of ardent followers. Deliberately withdrawing from the world around them, the members of this inspired religious communal sect have given us a heritage of simplicity and beauty in their furniture, architecture and life-style.

Since the discovery of Shaker design during the late 1920s, their furniture has been a major creative force in our decorative arts heritage because it is truly the only original American style. Today, Shaker furniture and accessories are avidly sought by collectors, creating lofty auction prices when sold or found in antique shops — especially in the East.

(A-MA. '76)   *Robert W. Skinner, Inc.*
Shaker Dining Chairs, Lowback, Set Of Six $3,500.00

(A-MA. '76)   *Robert W. Skinner, Inc.*
Shaker Cupboard, Herb, Bootjack Ends, 2 Doors Above, 20 Drawers Below, Original Mustard Paint $4,250.00

(A-MA. '76)   *Robert W. Skinner, Inc.*
Shaker Trestle-Foot Dining Table, 7' L., Pine Top, Hardwood Base $5,500.00

(A-MA. '76)   *Robert W. Skinner, Inc.*
Shaker Storage Chest, 2 Parts, Original Paint $3,800.00

SHAKER BOXES *(Left Group, Top to Bottom)*
Oval, 2 Finger W/Handle, Yellow Paint $350.00
Square, Yellow Paint $80.00
Square, Yellow Paint, Dovetailed $70.00

(Center Group, Top to Bottom)
Oval, 3 Finger W/Cover, Yellow Paint $260.00
Oval, 4 Finger, Yellow Paint $360.00
Oval, 5 Finger, Natural Finish $625.00

(A-MA. '76)   *Robert W. Skinner, Inc.*
Shaker Chest, 5 Drawer, Butternut . . .$900.00

(Right Group, Top to Bottom)
Oval, 4 Finger W/Handle, Reddish Stain $260.00
Oval, 3 Finger W/Cover, Reddish Stain $320.00

(Far Right)
Oval, 2 Finger, W/Handle, Natural Wood Finish. $160.00

(D-OH. '76)
Tin Dust Pan, Large, Attributed To Shakers . .
. . . . $65.00

(D-MA. '76)
Shaker Basket, Splint, 4½" H. X.H., 6" Diam.
. . . . $80.00

(D-OH. '76)
Shaker Rocker, Maple, Refinished, Mushrooms
Missing From Arms $90.00

(D-OH. '76)
Shaker Dry Sink, Child's, Pine, 12" D., 26"
W., 31" H. $350.00

Robert W. Skinner, Inc.

(A-MA. '76)

SHAKER ITEMS
(Row I, Upper Left to Right)
Yarn Winder $110.00
Flour Sacks, From New Gloucester Mills, ...
Pr. $100.00
(Row II, Left to Right)
Oval Carrier, 2 Finger W/Handle $160.00
Oval Carrier, 3 Finger W/Handle $250.00
Oval Carrier, 3 Finger W/Handle $360.00
Bonnet $25.00
Wooden Dipper $175.00
Splint Basket W/Handle & Shaker History
Attached $130.00
Oval Box, Small, 2 Finger W/Handle .$120.00
Oval Box, Small, 2 Finger $90.00
(Row III, Left to Right)
Oval Carrier, 2 Finger W/Handle $160.00
Chest, Red Paint , Lift-Top W/Leather Handles.
. . . .$70.00
Wooden Carrier W/Handles $130.00
(Far Left)
Child's Rocker $370.00
(Center)
Chest, Pine, In Natural Wood Colors, Wooden
Handles $190.00
Boxes & Carriers *(Far Right)*
Top Carrier, Oval W/Handle $110.00
Oval Box W/Cover, 3 Finger $180.00
Oval Box, W/Cover, 3 Finger, Blue-Green . . . .
. . . .$310.00
Oval Box, W/Cover, 5 Finger, Green Paint . . .
. . . .$575.00
Oval Carrier, W/Handle, 2 Finger $110.00

Small Items Top Of Bottom Chest
(Left to Right)
Bottles, 2 W/Orig. Labels: One Witch Hazel,
One Gin $25.00
Bottles, 2 W/Orig. Labels; One "Whiskey", One
"Penny Royal Whiskey $25.00
Bottle, W/Orig. Contents & Wrapper "Wild
Cherry Pectoral Syrup $85.00
Shaker Seed Labels, 11, Lebanon, N. Y. (one
damaged) $45.00
Tin Scoop W/Wooden Handle $70.00
No. 1 Shaker Syrup Bottle $30.00

Items In Front Of Chest
(Left to Right)
Two Wooden Paddles; Together W/A
Natural Wooden Measure $30.00
Maple Sugar Molds (37 W/Oval Tin Box) . . . .
. . . .$55.00
Tin Pourer W/Spout $95.00
Oval Box, 4 Finger (Contains Above Tin Box &
Some Molds) $65.00
Dippers, Tin, Pr. $20.00
Tin Milk Can W/Cover; Together W/Scoop
(Directly Behind) $25.00
Oval Bucket, Red W/Top & Handle, Mkd.
"B. H. S." $45.00
Tin Dust Pan W/Wooden Handle $110.00
Covered Round Wooden Box $90.00

Collecting textiles is becoming more difficult with each passing day as supplies have dwindled considerably during the last few years due to the immense popularity. There is a fervent quest for fine old quilts, coverlets, rugs, tapestries, framed needlework pictures and show towels. There is even a demand for fragments of early fabric that have survived. But the qualities that make textile collecting so intriguing — beauty, skill, perception, imagination and even humor — indicate that the finest examples were very time consuming.

Pennypacker Auction Centre

Double Cloth Coverlet, Natural Cotton & Blue Wool, Stylized Flowers & Stars, Border W/ American Eagles Beneath Inscription "Liberty", Milstone, New Jersey, 1849 (A-PA. '76) $550.00

Richard A. Bourne Co. Inc.

Double Weave Coverlet, Design In Drk. Blue & Natural Color Of Medallions W/Pineapple, Leaves & Berries Alternating W/8-Pointed Stars & Border Of Birds & Weeping Willows W/ Amer. Eagle W/Wings Spread At Ea. Corner & "Delhi/1845" Beneath Eagle; Signed "Sarah Ann/Bouton", Some Browning Of Natural Color, Slight Moth Damage, Minor Damage, Seamed, 101½" L., 80" W. . . . .(A-MA. '76) $300.00

Pennypacker Auction Centre

Centennial Coverlet, Cotton & Wool, 4 Colors Depicting State Seal Of Pennsylvania On Four Corners, Also Shown Is State House In Harrisburg . . . .(A-PA. '76) $325.00

Pennypacker Auction Centre

Coverlet, Woven, Natural Cotton & Blue Wool, Attrib. To James Alexander, New York . . . .
(A-PA. '76) $1450.00

Garth's Auctions, Inc.

Jacquared Coverlet, Single Weave, 2-Piece, Red, Blue & Green, Corner Signed "Manufactured By Henry Oberly, Walmelsdorf, Penn.", Borders W/Urns Of Flowers & Birds, Corners W/Turkeys, 80" x 99" . . . .(A-OH. '76) $380.00

Pennypacker Auction Centre

Coverlet, Cotton & Wool, 3-Color W/"Christian & Heathen" Border, Woven By E. Heim, Womelsdorf, Berks County, 1839 (A-PA. '76) $425.00

Pennypacker Auction Centre

Double Cloth Coverlet, Natural Cotton & Blue Wool W/Border Of Pa. Dutch Hearts & Tulip Design, Dated 1841 . . . . . .(A-PA. '76) $475.00

Garth's Auctions, Inc.

Jacquared Coverlet, Single Weave, 1-Piece, Red, White & Blue Hunting Border W/Chicken & Squirrel, Signed & Dated, One Corner Has "This Coverlet Belongs To Me, Sary Meier, 1843", Other Corner Has Weaver Information: "S.B. Musselman, Coverlet Weaver, Milford, Bucks Co. No. 426", Some Stains At Top, 79" x 98" . . . .(A-OH. '76) $775.00

Coverlet W/Matching Sham, Red Velvet & Yellow Satin Border, Fine Stichery & Embroidery Throughout, Ca. 1880 62x62" . . . .
. . . .(D-CO. '75) $800.00

(A-PA. '75)   *Pennypacker Auction Centre*

Log Cabin Quilt, Barn Raising Pattern, Yellow, Red & Green Striped Border $325.00

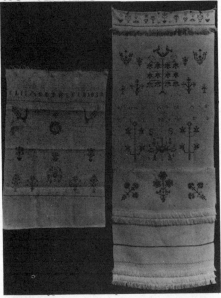

(A-PA. '76) *Pennypacker Auction Centre*

Show Towel, Pa. Dutch Embroidered Motifs Of Peacocks,Flowers, Trees, Etc. Elizabeth Lieb, 1833 .... $160.00

Linen Door Panel, Birds Perched On Trees, Flower Trees, Hearts, Etc. — Susana Steinweg, 1848, Fringed $350.00

(A-PA. '76) *Pennypacker Auction Centre*

←(A-PA. '76) *Pennypacker Auction Centre*

Hooked Rug, Pa., Free Form Design Of Two Deer In Mountain Setting $75.00

(A-PA. '76) *Pennypacker Auction Centre*

Needlework Picture, Includes Flying Birds, Buildings, Trees, Train, Boat, Stagecoach W/Horses, Men, Women & Children, & One Lone Horse Going Down The Trail; 19¼" x 14¼" Incl. Frame $475.00

(A-PA. '76) *Pennypacker Auction Centre*

Sampler, Pa., Cotton On Homespun W/Strawberries, Hearts & Tulips In Orig. Sponge Decor. Frame, By Lydia A. Kinzer, Ca. 1830 . $240.00

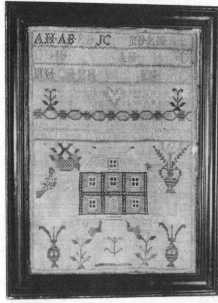

(A-PA. '76) *Pennypacker Auction Centre*

Sampler, American, House, Peacocks, Tulips, Etc. By Isabel Henderson, 1828, Dovetailed Frame $220.00

(A-PA. '76) *Pennypacker Auction Centre*

Applique Quilt, Folk Art Style W/Floral Center Surrounded By Birds, Meandering Border $245.00

(D-KS. '76)

Mennonite Quilt, 1930's, Overall Boys & Sun Bonnet Babies, 78" x 82" $125.00

(A-VA. '77)   *Laws*

Appliqued Quilt, Framed Stylized Star Motif, Rose Patterned Material On White Background, Southern Origin, Signed On Back F.L. Steel, March 28, 1878, 88" x 70" $150.00

Appliqued Quilt, Butterfly Patt. W/Diamond Shaped Border, Series Of 3 Rows Of Multi-Colored Butterflies On White Ground, 6' 6" x 7' 1" $100.00

Pieced Quilt, Stepped Star Motif, Checkered Crosswork Patt.In Drk. Blue & White, Ca. 1880, 97" x 80" $120.00

Pieced Coverlet, Carolina Basket Patt., Ea. Basket W/Reds, Blues, Yellows & Brown On White Stitched Ground, Mid-1800's, 7' x 7' 6" $150.00

Pieced Quilt, Stepped Star Motif, Each Of 36 Stars Composed Of Varying Comb. Of Blue, Red, Green, Brown, Beige, Yellow, Grey & Various Number Of Plaids, White Ground, Stitched In Various Geometric Patterns, Mid-1800's, 70" x 80" $160.00

Pieced Quilt W/Elements Of Dunkard's Path, Fool's Puzzle, Solomon's Puzzle & Wonder Of The World In Striped Red Fabric On White Ground, Ca. 1870, 74" x 84" $140.00

Patchwork Quilt, 12 Alternating Solid & Pieced Panels In Variety Of Bright Colors, 72" x 80" $40.00

(A-MA. '76)   *Richard A. Bourne Co. Inc.*

Double Weave Coverlet, Snowball Patt. W/ Pine Tree Border In Brick Red & White On Navy Blue, 89" x 78" $120.00

(A-VA. '76)   *Laws*

'Cruciform' Kazak, Scarce Green Field, 'Cruciform' Filled W/Multicolored Rosettes & Latch Hooks, 6' 2" x 9' $500.00

(A-MA. '76)   *Robert C. Eldred Co., Inc.*

Quilt, Pineapple Pattern, Blue & White, 72" x 82" $130.00

(A-VA. '77)   *Laws*

(Row I)

Persian Kurdish Tribal Rug Having Two Panels Of Opposing Diagonal Stripes In Blue, Brown, Yellow & Salmon; Ivory & Blue Floral Border; 3' 11" x 6' 7" $250.00

(Row II)

Tekke Turkoman Hatchli Prayer Rug W/ Classic Hatchli Design In Shades Of Wine Red, Blue & Ivory; 5' 1" x 3' 7" $225.00

(Row III)

Karabaugh Rug W/Powerful Design Of Three Large Star Formed Medallions In Brick REd, Yellow, Salmon On A Deep Blue Field. Geometric Borders Of Complimentary Colors Of Blue & Green; 4' 3" x 6' 8" $400.00

(A-MA. '76)   *Richard A. Bourne Co. Inc.*

Jacquard Woven Coverlet, Dusty Rose & Cream, W/Center Seam; Floral Medallions W/Rose & Geometric Border. Inscribed "Sara J. Sturdevant Of Elmira, New York." 72" x 92". $200.00

(A-MA. '76)   *Richard A. Bourne Co. Inc.*

Jacquard Woven Coverlet, Double Rose W/ Grapes & Leaves On Border; Brick Red, Navy, Blue & Forest Green On White. Sgn. By Weaver, Emanuel Ettinger - Aronsburg 1835, 96" x 78" $300.00

Pennypacker Auction Centre

Hooked Rug, Free Form Patt., Cat & 5 Hearts, Multicolored Background, 16½" x 36" .... (A-PA. '76) $220.00

Pennypacker Auction Centre

Hooked Rug, Geometric Bow Tie Pattern, Multi Colors, 27" x 57" ....(A-PA. '76) $170.00

Pennypacker Auction Centre

Hooked Rug, Profiles Of 3 Indians In Feather Head Dress, Oak Leaf & Acorn Design In Shades Of Red, Black & Brown On Neutral Background, 18" x 37" ....(A-PA. '76) $210.00

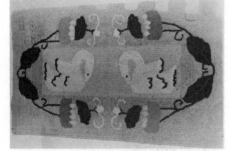

Pennypacker Auction Centre

Hooked Rug, 2 Swans & Floral Border, Pale Blue Background, 23" x 29" (A-PA. '76) $160.00

Richard A. Bourne Co. Inc.

Persian Kazvin, Blue Medallion On Red Floral Field W/Blue Borders, 4'4" x 6'6" ....(A-MA. '76) $1500.00

Garth's Auctions, Inc.

Oriental Rug, Persian, Flowering Tree & 5 Borders, Shades of Blue, Camel, Yellow & Faded Red, Some Wear, 5'6" x 8' (A-OH. '76) $175.00

Pennypacker Auction Centre

Sampler, Linen, "Eliza Lalheran", Mahogany Frame, 22"x22" ....(A-PA. '75) $170.00

Pennypacker Auction Centre

Family Register Sampler, New England, Birth Of William Bosson, Born 1766; Marriage & Death Of His 28 Year Old Wife In 1784; Remarriage To Susanna Mayo In 1784; Birth Of 14 Children & Deaths of 7; Made By Daughter, Catherine, 1807, 21" x 21½" ....(A-PA. '76) $475.00

Pennypacker Auction Centre

Sampler, New England, Ornament, Alphabets & Verses, Dated 1785, 9"x16" (A-PA. '76) $200.00

Pennypacker Auction Centre

Sampler, "Anna Kreider, 1832, Lampeter Township", 18"x18" ....(A-PA. '75) $625.00

Garth's Auctions, Inc.

Sampler, On Homespun, Vining Border W/ Adam & Eve & Serpent, Peacock, Angels, Dog, Deer, Brick House, Etc., "Ann Lee, Nov. 8th, 1796, Aged 12 Years", Modern Frame, 13¾" x 14½" ....(A-OH. '76) $560.00

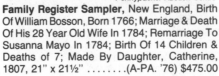

Pennypacker Auction Centre

Applique Quilt, Tulip Design In Red, Yellow & Green Calico, Natural Muslin Background . . . . (A-PA. '76) $475.00

Pennypacker Auction Centre

Applique Quilt, Pennsylvania Dutch Hearts & Tulips, Calico Materials Quilted W/Designs Of Hearts, Tulips & Butterflies (A-PA. '76) $325.00

Pennypacker Auction Centre

Pieced Quilt, 25 Stars on Drk. Green Background, Framed By Band Of Yellow Calico . . . . (A-PA. '76) $300.00

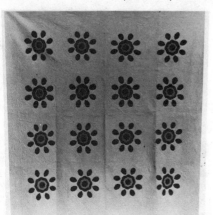

Pennypacker Auction Centre

Applique Quilt, Rose Buds On White W/Fine Quilting . . . .(A-PA. '76) $450.00

Pennypacker Auction Centre

Amish Quilt, Star Of Bethlehem Patt., Tomato Red & Shades Of Color On Brown Background, Old Amish Materials . . . . . .(A-PA. '76) $475.00

Pennypacker Auction Centre

Applique Quilt, Tulip Patt., Red, Orange & Green On White Background, Twining Border, Large . . . .(A-PA. '76) $400.00

Pennypacker Auction Centre

Pieced Quilt, Star Of Bethlehem Patt. W/8 Smaller Matching Stars . . .(A-PA. '76) $450.00

Pennypacker Auction Centre

Sampler Quilt, 49 Block, Made By Mrs. C.E. Perrine, Dutch Neck, N.J., 1875 . . . . (A-PA. '76) $475.00

Pennypacker Auction Centre

Pieced Quilt, Duck's Feet In The Mud Patt., Calico, Large . . . .(D-WI. '76) $90.00

Pennypacker Auction Centre

Hooked Rug, Free Form Patt., Roosters In Red & Grey, Black Background, 20" x 38" . . . . (A-PA. '76) $170.00

Pennypacker Auction Centre

Hooked Rug, Free Form Patt., 2 Ponies, Neutral Background, 26" x 39" (A-PA. '76) $220.00

Pennypacker Auction Centre

Hooked Rug, Free Form Patt., Lamb W/Red Ribbon, 23" x 34" . . . .(A-PA. '76) $400.00

Pieced Quilt, Log Cabin In Pink Lightning Patt. ....(D-IN. '76) $50.00

Pieced Quilt, Star Of Bethlehem, Drk. Green Background ....(D-IA. '76) $110.00

Pennypacker Auction Centre

Pieced Quilt, Star Of Bethlehem Center Surrounded W/8 Smaller Stars, Triple Border, Cotton ....(A-PA. '76) $575.00

Applique Quilt, Daisy Patt., Colors Of Red & Yellow; Pink Calico Background W/Yellow Border ....(D-MO. '76) $575.00

Pennypacker Auction Centre

Political Quilt, Constructed Around Political Bunting Used In Clay & Frelinghuysen Campaign In 1830's, Wide Border Is Early Glazed Chintz ....(A-PA. '76) $1700.00

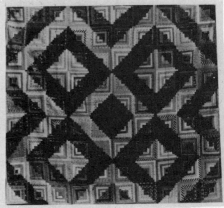

Pennypacker Auction Centre

Log Cabin Pieced Quilt, Light & Dark Pattern, Signed & Dated "1887", Miranda Worley, Cotton ....(A-PA. '76) $375.00

Pieced Quilt, Star Of Bethlehem, Tulip & Heart Design, Sawtooth Border On Drk. Green Background ....(D-IN. '76) $175.00

Pennypacker Auction Centre

Candlewick Spread, W/American Spread Eagle, Cornucopia & Pineapples Around Basket Of Fruit, Dated 1817 .....(A-PA. '76) $400.00

Pennypacker Auction Centre

Pieced Quilt, Nine-Star Variant, Green & Brown, Pumpkin Background .....(A-PA. '76) $350.00

Pennypacker Auction Centre

(A-PA. '76)
Applique Quilt, 15 White Panels Alternating W/15 Floral Panels, 70" x 84" $250.00

(A-PA. '76) *Pennypacker Auction Centre*
Applique Quilt, 12 Panels Inc. Red Circles W/Floral Green Inserts, 84" x 96" ...$240.00

Pennypacker Auction Centre

(A-PA. '76)
Applique Quilt, Pin Wheel Serrated Leaves Alternating In Red & Green W/Stars. Border Has Urns W/Red & Green Flowers, 90" x 90".
....................................$260.00

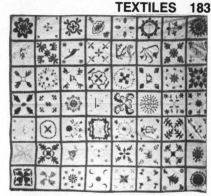

Appliqued Album Summer Spread W/49 Blocks; Includes Examples Of Trapunto; From Williamsport, Pa. Area $725.00

(A-VA. '77)   Laws
Shirvan Prayer Rug W/Central Gold Field Filled W/Botehs In Ivory, Blue, Gold, Red, Brown & Green; Border Of Stylized Trees In Blue On Brick Field. Wine Cup Border On Brown Field Flanked By Red/White Checkered Minor Borders; 6' 2" x 2' 11" $500.00

(A-VA. '76)
(Row I)   Laws
Yourouk Oriental Carpet, 4 Polar Diamond-Shaped Medallions Outlined In Ivory Enclosing Red, Ivory, & Blue Latch-Hook Devices On Soft Wine-Red Field, Retains Orig. Decor. Flat-Woven Kilim Ends, 6' 10" x 4' 4" $250.00
(Row II)
Gengi Oriental Carpet, Colorful Barber-Pole Striped Field W/Alternating Red, Blue, Green & Brown Stripes Filled W/Small Blocked Latch-Hook Devices, 7' 2" x 4' 1" $525.00

(A-PA. '76)   Pennypacker Auction Centre
Pennsylvania Cross Stitch Rug, Sgn. & Featuring Fraktur-Type Pa. Dutch Motifs Of Birds, Hearts, Tulips, Etc., 39" x 49" $1,250.00

(A-PA. '76)   Pennypacker Auction Centre
Mariner's Compass Quilt, Red & Green Calico On White Background, Seaweed Design W/ Tulips In Each Corner $475.00

(A-PA. '76)   Pennypacker Auction Centre
Pennsylvania Spread Eagle appliqued quilt with a circle of 16 tulips as a central motif $475.00

(A-MA. '76)   Robert C. Eldred Co., Inc.
Pieced Velvet Crazy Quilt, Initialed "RW", Dated 1888, Backed In Brown Flannel, 72" x 72" $90.00

(A-MA. '76)   Robert C. Eldred Co., Inc.
Appliqued & Pieced Quilt, White & Red Calico Reel Squares Alternate W/White Cotton Squares Highlighted By Feather-Wreath Quilting, Bordered W/Floral Chintz, Dated 1775, 93" x 96" $180.00

(A-PA. '76)   Pennypacker Auction Centre
Pieced Quilt, Star Of Bethlehem Patt. Surrounded by 40 Stars & Framed W/Saw Tooth Border & Wedges Of Brilliant Red $400.00

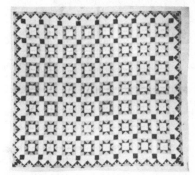

(A-MA. '76)   Richard A. Bourne Co. Inc.
Album Quilt, Lone Star Pattern W/Sawtooth Border, Red & Yellow Calico Squares, 56 Signatures, 105" x 92" $210.00

184 TOLEWARE

The term "tole" identifies the gaily decorated tinware that became popular in America during the first quarter of the last century. Decorations range from the simple to the lavish — usually decorated with colorful Pennsylvania Dutch motifs.

Collectors became interested in toleware during the thirties, and as a result, choice pieces have become scarce and expensive, especially in the east. When found through the midwest, examples can be purchased at more reasonable prices.

(A-OH. '76) *Garth's Auctions, Inc.*

Tole Teapot, Japanned Ground W/Bright Floral Design, Yellow, Green & Shades of Red, Curved Spout, 10½" H. $1600.00
Tole Teapot, Black Ground W/Tulip & Floral Decor., Red, Yellow, Black & Green, Straight Spout, 8½" H. $675.00

(A-PA. '76) *Pennypacker Auction Centre*

(Left to Right)
Child's Mug, Red W/Yellow & Black Decor., 1¾" $160.00
Mug, Red W/Dutch Tulip In Shades of Red & Leaves of Yellow & Black, 4" $500.00
Teapot, Red, Floral Decor., Both Sides $600.00
Salt Shaker, Yellow & Black Decor., 2½" $525.00
Child's Mug, Red W/Red & Yellow Decor., 1¾" $180.00

(A-OH. '76) *Garth's Auctions, Inc.*

(Row I, Left to Right)
Box, Slightly Domed Lid, Amber Colored Japan Ground W/Yellow, Green, Orange & Red Floral Decor., 6½" D., 7" H. $230.00
Document Box, Yellow Crystalized Ground W/ Band of Red, Black & White W/Red & Black Striping, 9" L., 4" D., 5½" H. $475.00
(Row II, Left to Right)
Mug, Drk. Ground Is Brown Japanning Applied To Create Striped Appearance, Red & Yellow Decor., 5¾" H. $460.00
Tray, Black Ground, Red Band & Yellow & White Decor., 12" L. $225.00
Creamer, Drk. Japan Ground W/Orange & Yellow Decor., Minor Wear, 3¾" H. .. $240.00

(A-OH. '76) *Garth's Auctions, Inc.*

(Row I, Left to Right)
Teapot, Drk. Japan Ground, Floral Design In Red, Yellow, Green & White, 8¾" H. . $800.00
Cup, Drk. Japan Ground W/Fruit & Foliage In Red, Yellow & Green, 3" H. $375.00
Teapot, Drk. Japan Ground, Floral Design In Red, Yellow, Green & White WBrush Work Detail In Black, Number 622 In Design On One Side, 8¾" H. $375.00
(Row II, Left to Right)
Deed Box, Orange-Red Ground W/Floral Brush Work Designs In Black, Yellow, Red & White, 8½" W., 4" D., 4½" H. $440.00
Tray, Drk. Japan Ground W/Floral Border W/ Red, Yellow & Green On White Ground, Black Brush Work Detail, 6" x 8¾" $350.00

(A-PA. '76) *Pennypacker Auction Centre*

(Left to Right)
Bread Tray, Red, Yellow & Green Decor., White Border $300.00
Coffeepot, Red, Yellow & Green Decor., Dome Lid, Gooseneck Spout $975.00
Bread Tray, Yellow Outlined In Red & Black, Full Size $600.00

(A-PA. '76) *Pennypacker Auction Centre*

(Row I, Left to Right)
Coffin Lid Tray, Red, Green & Yellow Decor., 12" $45.00
Coffeepot, Pa., Gooseneck, Red & Yellow Decor. $800.00
Coffin Tray, Fruit Decor., 9" $57.50
(Row II, Left to Right)
Deed Box, 6½" $50.00
Sugar, Red & Yellow Decor. $85.00
Miniature Deed Box, 4" $110.00

(A-PA. '76) *Pennypacker Auction Centre*

(Left to Right)
Deed Box, Chippendale Type Handle, Red, Yellow & Drk. Green Decor. $280.00
Fat Lamp, Early Lancaster Co., Red, Yellow & White Floral Decor. $250.00
Tea Canister, Green, Yellow & Red Decor. On White Border, 4" L. $60.00

(A-PA. '76) *Pennypacker Auction Centre*

(Left to Right)
Deed Box, Floral Decor., Red, Green & Yellow, 8" L. $300.00
Coffeepot, Goosneck Spout, Distelfink & Lge. Red Flowers, Pa. $2200.00
Deed Box, Colorful Decor., 8" L. $260.00

(A-PA. '76) *Pennypacker Auction Centre*

(Left to Right)
Deed Box, Coffin-Shape Lid, Red, White & Yellow Decor. .... $260..00
Deed Box, Border of Roses & Cherries $250.00
Coffin-Lid Bread Tray $875.00

(A-PA. '76) *Pennypacker Auction Centre*

(Left to Right)
Miniature Bun Tray, 6½" L. $250.00
Teapot, Decor. Both Sides W/Red Open Tulip $180.00
Candlestick & Snuffer, Movable Candle Raiser $525.00

(A-PA. '75) *Pennypacker Auction Centre*

Box, Orig. Decor. $85.00

All types of hand tools including cobbling, smithing, coopering and distilling, in addition to implements of the early farmstead are of great interest to the tool collector. However, the majority of tools available date from the late years of the last century and are mass-produced products.

(A-PA. '75)   *Pennypacker Auction Centre*
(Iron, L-R)
Button Hole Chisel Hammer $37.50
Two Button Hole Chisels $130.00
Larger Button Hole Chisel $75.00

(D-IN. '76)
(L-R)
Clamp, Curved $25.00
"U" Clamp, Maple $25.00

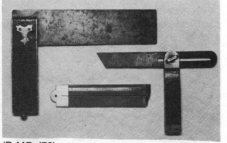

(D-MO. '76)
(L-R)
Square W/Brass Trim, Level In Handle $20.00
Ruler, Folding Type W/Brass Trim, Mkd. "Keen Kutter" $15.00
"T" Square W/Brass Trim, Mkd. "Stanley" ...
.... $15.00

(D-KY. '76)
Burl Mallet W/Oak Handle $22.50

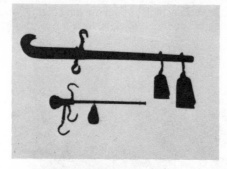

(D-MO. '76)
Iron Steelyard Scales, Top Scale $22.50
Bottom Scale $18.00

(D-MO. '76)
Draw Knife $12.00

(D-MN. '76)
Dividers, Wooden ....Ea. $25.00

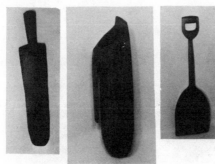

(Left to Right)
(D-PA. '76)
Flax Knife, Flax Plant Carved On Front Side, 20" L. $85.00
Whet Stone Holder, Pine W/Carving On Front, 10" L. $55.00

(D-KS. '76)
Scoop, Ash, Refinished, 37" L. $55.00

(D-NE. '76)
Monkey Wrench, 7½" L. $12.50
Vice, Small $10.00

(D-S.D. '76)
Hider's Scales, Oval Center, 3" x 3½" $55.00

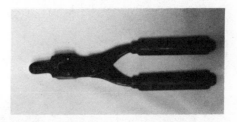

(D-CO. '76)
Bullet Mold, Mkd. Winchester, 44 Cal. .$65.00

(D-MO. '76)
Molding Plane, Pine $15.00

Anything from a pittance to a small fortune can be spent in this field of collecting nowadays. Mechanical banks and cast iron toys from the late nineteenth century have proven to be as stable as blue chip stocks. Enthusiasm for both the old and the contemporary toys — the Disney and cartoon characters for example — is especially high throughout the country. And too, because prices here are generally lower, European dealers are making sizeable purchases of American toys, limiting the supply in many areas.

(A-NE. '76)
(Row I, Left to Right)
Stake Truck-Trailer, Arcade, 11" L. $310.00
Dump Truck-Trailer, Arcade, 13" L. $290.00
(Row II, Left to Right)
Stake Truck, Arcade Model "A", 7½" L. $130.00
Dump Truck, Arcade Model "A", 7¼" L. $150.00
Wrecker, Arcade Model "A" Weaver, 8½" L. $210.00

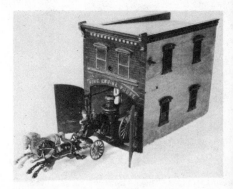

(A-PA. '76)   *Pennypacker Auction Centre*
Iron Fire Engine W/Fire House (Wood & Iron). House 15½" H., 8½" W. Separate Key Winds The Mechanism. When Lever Is Pulled, Fire Alarm Starts, Doors Open & Out Comes Horses & Fire Engine $1,300.00

(A-NE. '76)
(Row I, Left to Right)
Trencher, Kenton Buckeye, 6½" L. $290.00
Trencher, Kenton Buckeye, 8½" L. $340.00
(Row II, Left to Right)
Caterpillar, Arcade, 7¾" L. $475.00
Digger, Hubley Panama, 7" L. $420.00
Roller, Hubley Huber, 8" L. $200.00

(A-PA. '76)   *Pennypacker Auction Centre*
Cast Iron Steamer Fire Engine, 21" L. $170.00

(A-PA. '76)   *Pennypacker Auction Centre*
Cast Iron Fire Engine, "Hubley", Hook & Ladder, 32" L. $275.00

(A-NE. '76)
(Row I, Left to Right)
ALL ARCADE INTERNATIONAL TOYS
"Baby Red" Truck, 11" L. $155.00
"Baby Red" Truck, 10½" L. $180.00
(Row II)
Stake Truck, 11½" L. $110.00
Dump Truck, 11" L. $115.00
Pickup, 9½" L. $160.00

(A-PA. '76)   *Pennypacker Auction Centre*
Cast Iron Fire Engine Hose Carrier, 20½" L.
....$280.00

Rocking Hobby Horse, Wood, Stand, Smoke Grained Body & Horse Hair Tail $170.00

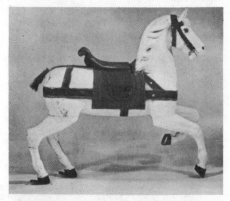

Carousel Horse, White Charger W/Carved Flying Mane & Elaborate Saddle, Orig. Horsehair Tail Mostly Disappeared, Repainted ..$600.00

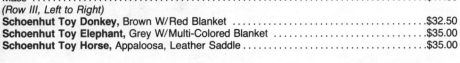

(Row I, Left to Right)
Schoenhut Jointed Wooden Clown, Composition Face, Dressed In Cloth, Six Pieces Circus Equip., Ear Missing On Clown $30.00
Schoenhut Jointed Wooden Clown, Composition Face, Dressed In Cloth, Six Pieces Circus Equip., Ear Missing On Clown $45.00
(Row II, Left to Right)
Toy Paper Soldiers, In Wooden Box, Civil War Toys Belonging To George Boswell, Worcester, Mass. $15.00
Cast Iron Clown Bank, Worn Polychrome, 6¼" H. $22.50
Toy Paper Soldiers, In Wooden Box, Civil War Toys Belonging To George Boswell, Worcester, Mass $17.50
(Row III, Left to Right)
Schoenhut Toy Donkey, Brown W/Red Blanket $32.50
Schoenhut Toy Elephant, Grey W/Multi-Colored Blanket $35.00
Schoenhut Toy Horse, Appaloosa, Leather Saddle..................................$35.00

Rocking Horse, Signed "P. Crandall", N.Y., Mid 19th C., ...$390.00

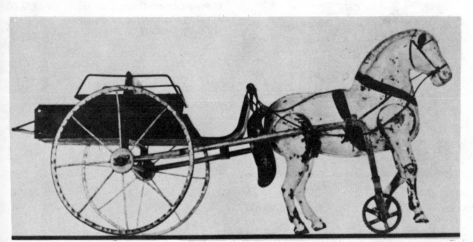

Toy Horse & Wagon, Tin $290.00

Tin Toy Wind-Up Oscillating Fan Mkd. "Made In Germany"; Orig. Paint Good & Working, 7½" W., 9" H. $90.00

(A-PA. '75)   *Pennypacker Auction Centre*
Horse & Wagon, Wooden, Orig. Decor.$55.00

(A-NE. '76)
(Row I, Left to Right)
Bell Telephone Truck, Hubley, 9½" L. $500.00
Digger, Hubley Mack Panama, 9½" L. $430.00
(Row II, Left to Right)
Digger, Hubley Mack Panama, 5" L. $205.00
Digger, Hubley Mack General, 6" L. $118.00
Digger, Hubley Mack General, 8" L. $205.00

(A-PA. '76)   *Pennypacker Auction Centre*
Cast Iron Ice Wagon, Yellow Sides, Blue Top, Red Wheels & Black Horse, 14¾" L. .$150.00

(A-NE. '76)
(Row I, Left to Right)
Gasoline Truck, Arcade Mack, 13" L. $350.00
High Lift Coal Truck, Arcade Mack, 10" L. $390.00
Dump Truck, "Hubley Mack", 11" L. $450.00
(Row II, Left to Right)
Ice Truck, Arcade Mack, 8½" L. $280.00
Ice Truck, Arcade Mack, 10½" L. $375.00
Dump Truck, Arcade Mack, 8½" L. $220.00

(D-KS. '76)
(Left to Right)
Disney Donald Duck, Rubber $32.00
Tin Dog Mkd. Occupied Japan $12.50
Wind-Up Donkey $10.00

(A-MA. '76)   *Richard A. Bourne Co. Inc.*
(Row I)
Cast Iron Toys, Lot Of Four, 2 Trucks & 2 Automobiles $100.00
(Row II, Left to Right)
Cast Iron Toy Coupe W/Spare Tire, Arcade Mfg. Co., Freeport, Ill., Black $70.00
Cast Iron Model T Sedan W/Driver, Arcade Mfg. Co., Freeport, Ill., Black, 1 Window Post Missing
. . . .$25.00
Toy Car, Rusted, Sm. Bent Areas, Steering Apparatus & Left Fender Missing $35.00

(D-KS. '76)
Windup Toy, Celluloid Dog, Tin Shoe .$35.00

Papier Mache Rabbit, 9" H., Pink Glass Eyes, ...$12.00

(D-CO. '76)
Windup Toy, Celluloid, 2 Pc. $55.00

(D-IN. '76)
Bell Pull Toy, Ca. 1880, Iron & Brass .$45.00

(A-MA. '76)   *Richard A. Bourne Co. Inc.*
(Row I, Left to Right)
Tin Wind-Up Toy, Spin-Driven, Lehmann, U.S. Patent May 12, 1903 ....$180.00
Tin Toy Train, Friction-Type, Coal Car Body Missing $20.00
(Row II)
Still Banks, Collection Of Four, 3 Buildings & 1 Safe $60.00
(Row III)
Animal Banks, Collection Of Six, 2 Lions, 1 St. Bernard Dog, 1 Horse, 1 Jackass 9 1 Pig $110.00
(Row IV)
Cast Iron Toys, 2 Steam Locomotives W/Coal Cars $50.00

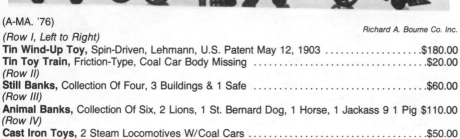

(A-MA. '76)   *Richard A. Bourne Co. Inc.*
(Row I, Left to Right)
Cast Iron Toy Fire Engine, Single Driver, 3 Horses, Paint Has Minor Wear $35.00
Cast Iron Toy Patrol Wagon, Uniformed Driver, 4 Firemen In Back, Green Wagon W/Wheels, 3 Horses $35.00
(Row II, Left to Right)
Cast Iron Steam Type Toy Fire Engine, Driver, 3 Horses $35.00
Cast Iron Toy Fire Hose Wagon, Driver & Fireman, 2 Horses $35.00
(Row III, Left to Right)
Cast Iron Toy Fire Engine, 2 Drivers, 3 Horses $40.00
Cast Iron Doctor's Surrey, 1 Driver ...$40.00

(A-MA. '76)   Richard A. Bourne Co. Inc.
(Row I, Left to Right)
Schoenhut Play Piano, Upright, Pat. Sept. 8, 1900, 6 Keys (5 Working)
7½" L. $30.00
Baby Grand Piano, Mahogany, Japanese $22.00
(Row II, Left to Right)
Schoenhut Piano, Upright, 15 Keys (13 Working), Branch Arm Candle
Holders Each Side, 16½" L. $80.00
Piano Stool, 7" Diam., 7½" H. $20.00

(A-MA. '76)   Richard A. Bourne Co. Inc.
Schoenhut Baby Grand Piano W/Stool, 22 Keys (All Working), Finish
Around Front Blistered, Hinges Missing From Front Fold-Up Flap ...
....$150.00

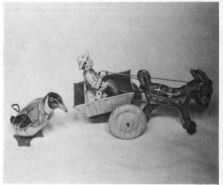

(D-CO. '76)
TIN WIND-UP TOYS
(Left to Right)
Penguin, Orig. Paint Ex., Working $28.50
Donkey W/Cart & Rider, Orig. Paint Ex.,
Working $45.00
Pecking Bird, Orig. Paint Good, Working ....
......................................$42.50

(A-OH. '76)   Garth's Auctions, Inc.
(Row I, Left to Right)
Wooden Covered Wagon Toy, Hand Made, Pulled By Pr. Of Oxen Painted Like Holsteins, Man &
Woman Passengers, Woman Has Broken Arm, 25" L. $210.00
Shoenhut Wooden Giraffe, "Knittle Collection" Sticker, 10½" H. $95.00
(Row II, Left to Right)
Shoenhut Wooden Tiger, "Knittle Collection" Sticker, 7" L. $90.00
Tin Friction Toy Fire Truck, 3 Ladders $105.00
(Row III, Left to Right)
Wood & Sheet Metal Friction Toy Locomotive, & Coal Car, Worn Red Paint, 17½" L. ...$95.00
Cast Iron "Jolly Nigger Bank", Pat. Mar. 14 '82", Base Has "Made By Shepard Hardware Co.,
Buffalo, N.Y.", 6¾" H. $135.00
Shoenhut Wooden Lamb, 7¼" L. $100.00

(D-PA. '76)
Cast Iron Toy Pump W/Attached Tank, Orig.
Paint Good, 8¼" H.; Pump Works When Primed.
......................................$65.00

(A-PA. '75)   *Pennypacker Auction Centre*
Child's Ladderback Rocker $275.00
Two China Head Dolls, Pr. $27.50

(D-KS. '76)
Captain's Chair, Child's, Oak $65.00

(A-MA. '76)   *Richard A. Bourne Co. Inc.*
TOY STOVES
(Row I, Left to Right)
Cast Iron Kitchen Range, W/Shovel, Coal Hod, Frying Pans & 1 Pot, "American" Model, 9½" L., 4½" D., 8½" H. $40.00
Cast Iron Kitchen Range, W/1 Skillet & 2 Kettles, "Prize" Marked On Oven Door, Painted W/Aluminum Paint, 2 Stove Lids Missing, 12" L., 6" D., 11½" H. $40.00
Kitchen Range, W/2 Pots & 2 Skillets, "Novelty" Model, 8¾" L., 6¼" D., 12½" H. $60.00
(Row II, Left to Right)
Kitchen Range, "Uncle Sam" Model, 1 Lid Missing & 1 Sm. Door, 20" L., 13½" D., 12¾" H. $60.00
Heating Range, Airtight Sheet Metal, 11" L., 7¾" W., 28" H. Incl. Pipe $80.00

(A-PA. '76)   *Pennypacker Auction Centre*
(Left to Right)
Doll Bed, Pa. Dutch $100.00
Wooden Soldier Holding Candle Holder In Each Hand, 11" H., Orig. Paint $60.00

(A-MA. '76)   *Richard A. Bourne Co. Inc.*
Clown Figure, Cast Iron Movable Arms & Legs, Painted Cast Iron Head, Wooden Body . . .$50.00
Stuffed Toy Pug Dog On Wheels, Victorian $25.00

(A-PA. '76)   *Pennypacker Auction Centre*
Doll Bed, Pine, In-The-Rough, 18½" L. $50.00

Richard A. Bourne Co. Inc.

(A-MA. '76)
(Row I, Left to Right)
Child's Play Bow-Front China Cabinet, Pine, 15½" W., 9¾" D., 28" H. $50.00
Closed-Faced Welch Style Cupboard, Poplar & Pine, Refinished, 19" L., 10" D., 29" H. . .$65.00
Empire Shaving Stand, Mahogany, Adj. Looking Glass, 11" H. $40.00
Sheraton-Style Bureau, Hardwood, Mortised Drawer Const., Refinished, 18" L., 9" D., 16½" H. . .
. . . .$40.00
(Row II, Left to Right)
Child's Pillow-Back Hitchcock Side Chair, Rush Seat, Stenciled Decor., 25½" H. $90.00
Drop-Leaf Dining Table, Pine, 29½" x 18½" (Leaves Closed), 35" L., (Open, 19" H.) $60.00
Child's Captain Style Arm Chair, Cane Seat & Back, Refinished, 20" H. $85.00

Richard A. Bourne Co. Inc.

(A-MA. '76)
DOLL'S TRUNKS
(Row I, Left to Right)
Metal-Bound Trunk, Contains Few Doll's Clothes, 10¼" L. $35.00
Saratoga Style Trunk, Contains Doll's Clothes & Tin Doll's Table Service, 1 Handle Broken Off,
20½" L. $30.00
Saratoga Style Trunk, Contains Material For Doll's Clothes, Name "Rosie" On One End, 12" L. . .
. . . .$70.00
(Row II, Left to Right)
Saratoga Style Trunk, Key, Contains Knitted Doll's Clothes, 16" L. $50.00
Saratoga Style Trunk, Hinge At Back Torn, 16¼" L. $30.00
Trunk, Contains Doll's Clothes, Leather Handles Missing At Both Ends, 16" L. $55.00

(D-FL. '76)
Wire Doll Carriage Ca. 1880 . . . .$95.00

(A-MA. '76)   *Richard A. Bourne Co. Inc.*
Bent Wire Ice Cream Set, 4 Pcs., Two Chairs
W/No Upholstery, Table - 17" Diam., Tallest
Chair 24¼" H. $60.00

(A-PA. '75)   *Pennypacker Auction Centre*
Windsor High Chair, Minor Repair . . $230.00

(D-PA. '76)
Doll Cradle, Pine, Orig. Decor., Pegged, Ca.
1850 . . . .$150.00

The weathervane is one of the oldest of weather instruments. The first produced here were made by amateur wood carvers and later by skilled craftsmen in wood and metal. Today, the early examples are classified as folk art of the finest sort, for both their construction and the originality of their design.

More elaborate than the vane, is the interesting whirligig with its moving parts which can be twirled or rotated. When mounted on an upright rod, these devices will rotate in the wind.

(A-PA. '76)   *Pennypacker Auction Centre*
Wooden Whirligig, Pa. Dutch, Six Amish Men Who Move When Wind Blows, Horse Also Moves,
....$1600.00

(A-PA. '76)   *Pennypacker Auction Centre*
Wooden Whirligig, Man Operating Pit Saw, Tenon & Mortise Const.,.............$260.00

(A-PA. '75)   *Pennypacker Auction Centre*
Weathervane, Sheet Iron $160.00

(A-PA. '76)   *Pennypacker Auction Centre*
Weathervane, Copper, Running Horse W/Zinc Molded Head $370.00

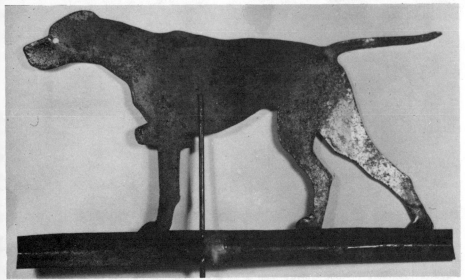

(A-PA. '75)   *Pennypacker Auction Centre*
Weathervane, Sheet Iron $180.00

(D-N.Y. '76)
Whirligig, Wooden, 15" L. Orig. Paint Good $75.00

(A-MA '76)   *Richard A. Bourne Co. Inc.*

Victorian Cow Weathervane, Tin W/Cast Iron Pointer & Glass Ball On Mount, Cow & Iron Rusted But Solid, 28¾" L. $110.00
Copper Running Horse Weathervane, Gilt Remains W/Lead & Copper Showing Through Where Flaked Off, Minor Dents, Slight Opening Of Seam, 32½" L. $175.00
Horse Weathervane, Copper & Gilded, By J. Harris & Son, Boston & N.Y., Minor Dents, 37" L. $800.00

(A-OH. '76)   *Garth's Auctions, Inc.*

Weathervane, Carved Wooden Horse & Rider, Stylized Treatment W/Minimum Of Carving, Man Wears Top Hat & Mustache, Horse Has Painted Reins, Black W/Red Harness, Man Painted Drk. Green W/Blk. & Traces Of Lt. Color On Face, Repair To Base, 19th C. American Folk Art, 58" L. $4550.00

(A-PA. '76)   *Pennypacker Auction Centre*

Wooden Whirligig, Bowlegged Man W/Name "Jim" Painted On Arm $625.00
Tin Whirligig, Two Men Chopping & Sawing Wood $230.00

(A-PA. '76)   *Pennypacker Auction Centre*

Wooden Whirligig, Man Churning Butter, Orig. Mounting Pole $210.00

(A-PA. '75)   *Pennypacker Auction Centre*

Rooster Weathervane, Tin $115.00

(A-PA. '76)   *Pennypacker Auction Centre*

Gaily Colored Weather Vane In Shape Of Steer, Sheet Metal, 28½" L. $160.00

(A-PA. '76)   *Pennypacker Auction Centre*

Tin Running Horse, Base 33½" L. $90.00

(A-PA. '76)   *Pennypacker Auction Centre*

Weather Indicator W/Hand Carved Man & Woman, Gun, Powder Horn, Hunting Bag & Carved Decor. On Roof $55.00

(A-PA. '76)   *Pennypacker Auction Centre*

Goat Weather Vane, Sheet Metal, 12½" L., Mounted On Rod W/Wood Base, Tail & Portion Of One Horn Restored $50.00

The inventive craftsmanship of the American wood carver has contributed much to our cultural history. Although most examples are quite primitive, there are those which have been intricately carved and well-executed. During recent years, interest in American Folk Art has brought about much appreciation for the fanciful objects created by these naive, non-academic artists and craftsmen.

As a result of the interest in this field today, even the contemporary objects being created have proven to be good investments with true profit potential.

(A-PA. '75)   *Pennypacker Auction Centre*
Carved Bird, Orig. Painted Decor. $80.00

(A-PA. '75)   *Pennypacker Auction Centre*
Carved Wooden Eagle, 16½" Wing Spread . .
. . . . $165.00

(D-KY. '76)
Handcarved Rooster & Barrels, Larger Used for Cigars, Small Barrel for Matches, Ca. 1900
. . . . $75.00

(A-PA. '76)   *Pennypacker Auction Centre*
Wooden Mouth Organ, Hand Carved, One Octave 6" x 5¾"; Small Whistle Included . .
. . . . $50.00

(A-PA. '76)   *Pennypacker Auction Centre*
(Left to Right)
Carved North American Quail, Mounted On A Natural Lichen, Painted $325.00
New York Bird Tree, 5 Orig. Painted Song Birds Mounted On Sassafras Branch, Ca. 1880 . . . . .
. . . . $1050.00
Carved Cock Robin Toy, Mounted & String Controlled To Lift Head & Tail, Painted . . . .
. . . . $350.00

(Left)
(A-PA. '76)
Uncle Sam Wooden Cookie Cutter, Decorated 12" H. $390.00
(Right)
(A-PA. '75)   *Pennypacker Auction Centre*
Carved Wooden Eagle, 25" Wingspread . . . . .
. . . . $425.00

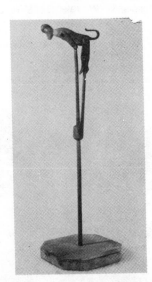

(A-PA. '76)   *Pennypacker Auction Centre*
Carved Wooden Monkey Acrobat, Mounted On Stick, When Pushed Up & Down, Monkey Performs $52.50

(A-PA. '76)   *Pennypacker Auction Centre*
Hand Carved Baseball Player Holding Bat, Attributed To Thomas V. Brooks)1828-1895), Orig. Paint, 30" H. $1,850.00

(A-MA. '76)   *Richard A. Bourne Co. Inc.*

DECORATIVE CARVINGS (Contemporary)
(Row I)
Life-Sized Black-Bellied Plover. By Lloyd Johnson. $100.00
Lesser Yellowlegs. By Delbert ("Cigar") Daisey $200.00
Life-Sized Plover. With Turned Head, By Delbert ("Cigar") Daisey, Signed $80.00
(Row II)
Life-Sized Willet. By Delbert ("Cigar") Daisey, Signed $80.00
Robin Snipe. By Delbert ("Cigar") Daisey, Signed $70.00
(Row III)
Hudsonian Curlew. By Delbert ("Cigar") Daisey, Signed $110.00
Life-Sized Curlew. By Delbert ("Cigar") Daisey, Signed $160.00
(Row IV)
Life-Sized Carving Of A Striped Bass (Rock Fish). By Gary Geberson (Port Republic, New Jersey), Excellent Detail And Even Scales Carved Into The Body Of The Fish. Overall Length 29 Inches $450.00

Garth's Auctions, Inc.

Windsor Fan Back Side Chair, Simple Crest, Old Brown Paint $450.00
Windsor Foot Stool, Old Varnish Finish, 14" L. $210.00
Copper Tea Kettle, Amer., Dovetailed Constr., Handle Stamped "I. Roberts (Israel), Phila.", Replaced Lid $185.00
Country Chinese Chippendale Card Table, Birch W/Molded Legs, Fret Work Brackets, Simple Apron, Old Worn Finish, One Bracket Old & Rest Replacements, 32" W., 13½" D., 28" H., Opens To 32" x 27" $950.00
Brass Queen Anne Candlesticks. Pr., Sm. Hole In Base Of Each, Old Repair, 9" H. ... $415.00
Historical Blue Staffordshire Platter, Reticulated Border, Impressed Ship & "A. Stevenson, Warranted Staffordshire", English Scene Of Country Estate & Haymaking, 10¼" L. $210.00
Pastel Portrait, Young Gentleman In Blue Coat, Gilt Frame, Boston, 11"x13" $200.00
Chippendale Scroll Looking Glass, W/Gilt Phoenix, One Ear Broken & Reglued W/Sm. Piece Of Veneer Missing, 29" H. $750.00

Garth's Auctions, Inc.

CURLY MAPLE
Kentucky Rifle, Curly Maple Full Stock, Percussion Lock, Barrel Marked "G.F." Engraved Brass Patch Box, Silver Inlays, 41" L. Barrel, 56" Overall. $1200.00

Oak Sewing Cabinet W/"Domestic Sewing Machine" (Working) Pat. Date May 16, 1863, Case 35" H., 20" D., 26½" W. $275.00

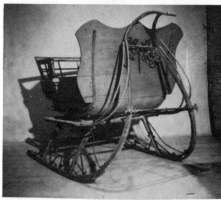

Pennypacker Auction Centre

One Horse Sleigh, Decor. W/Orig. Color Of Red & Yellow W/Drk. Tulips, Settee Type Wagon Seat, Forged Scroll Iron Around Base $525.00

Pennypacker Auction Centre

Beaded Bag, Initials & Date "MAW/1837" $35.00

(A-PA. '75) *Pennypacker Auction Centre*

Stoneware Crock, Blue Flower Decor. $45.00
Marble Top Victorian Table, Walnut, Lge.
.... $170.00

(A-OH. '76) *Garth's Auctions, Inc.*

Hepplewhite Mahogany Sideboard, Figured Wood W/Line Inlay, Rebuilt, 72" L., 21½" D., 41" H. .... $ 700.00
Girandoles, *(Left to Right),* Pr., Stepped Marble Bases & Gilt Brass Figure of Bearded Man Carrying Staff W/Cross, "Dietz Patent 1851", 16" H. $150.00
Girandole, W/5 Candle Arms, Marked W/"Dietz Patent, 19¾" H. $150.00

(A-PA. '76) *Pennypacker Auction Centre*

Queen Anne Style Cradle, Walnut, Acorn Posts & Cutout Hearts On Sides $170.00
Rhode Island Windsor Sewing Chair, Old Black Paint. $100.00

(A-OH. '75) *Garth's Auctions, Inc.*

Hepplewhite Sideboard, Mahogany, Tapering Legs W/Double Line Inlay, Figured Veneer W/Triple Line Inlay Around Drawers & Doors, Inlaid Flutes At Top Of Leg Posts, Replaced Brasses, 72" L., 29" W., 40½" H. $1750.00
Knife Boxes, Pair, Inlaid Mahogany, Bands of Inlay, Interior Has Inlaid Fan On Lid & Compartmentalized Divider Is Also Inlaid, Minor Repair, 15½" H. $750.00
Rose Medallion Platter, 16¼" L. $150.00

(A-PA. '75) *Pennypacker Auction Centre*

Coffee Mill, Wrought Iron Hdwe., Brass Pull, Wooden Pinned $85.00
Knife Box, Walnut, Dovetailed $95.00
Tavern Table, Walnut $575.00

(A-OH. '76)   Garth's Auctions, Inc.

Birdcage Windsor Side Chair, Refinished, Seat Made From 2 Pieces of Wood . . . $45.00
Hepplewhite Oval Top Tavern Table, 2-Board Top, Old Reddish Paint, 24½"x35"x28" H. $350.00
Round Woven Basket, Wooden Handle, 17½" Diam. $30.00
Wooden Chalice, 9" H. $20.00
Oval Wooden Storage Box, 11" L. . . . $85.00
Mortar & Pestle, Lignum Vitae, Mortar Is 6¾" H. $50.00
Woven Basket, 13"x11½" $40.00
Oil On Canvas, Painting Of Barnyard Scene, Pups, Kittens & Baby Chicks, "M.B. Handford 1896", 22½" x 36" $170.00

(A-OH. '76)   Garth's Auctions, Inc.

Banjo, Dated "Pat. Jan. 4, '87" . . . .
. . . . $50.00
Settle Bed, Pine, Shaped Crest & Spindles, Front Folds Down, Refinished & Some Restoration, 69" L. $175.00
Stoneware Jar, Stenciled "A.P. Donaghaugh, Parkersburg, W.Va., 2-Gal. $20.00
Child's High Chair, Primitive, Refinished, Woven Seat $55.00
Stoneware Crock, Crude Design, Br. Blue Cobalt Slip, Hairlines, 4-Gal. $55.00
Stoneware Jar, Stenciled "Henry Sentz, 185 Spring Gard...Ave. Allegheny, Pa.", 3-Gal. . . . .
. . . . $35.00
Bellows, Brass On Wood W/Embossed Design & Deer, Leather Has Deteriorated . . . .
. . . . $25.00
Iron Keys, Three $9.00

(A-OH. '76)   Garth's Auctions, Inc.

Writing Arm Chair, Writing Surface Supported By 2 Turned Posts That Are Later Additions, Refinished & Foot Rest Removed $70.00
Iron Cat Boot Scraper, Early 20th C. . . $32.50
Knife Box, Cherry, 2-Section, Dovetailed . . . . .
. . . . $40.00
Blanket Chest W/Till, Pine, Dovetailed, Worn Green Paint, 29½" W., 15½" D., 13" H. . . . . . .
. . . . $85.00
Carved Book Box, Walnut W/Birdseye Veneer Page Ends, 10¼" x 12½" $40.00
Hanging Tin Match Holder $12.00
Sheet Metal Indian, 13½" H. $25.00

(A-OH. '76)   Garth's Auctions, Inc.

Kentucky Rifle, Curly Maple, Full Stock, Percussion Lock, Barrel Marked "G.F.", Engraved Brass Patch Box, 20 Silver Inlays, 41" Barrel, 56" Overall $1200.00
Tole Flask, Worn Red Paint, 8¼" H. . . . $15.00
Iron Bound Box, Dovetailed & W/Till & Handmade Hinges, Bear Trap Lock & Straps, Painted Decor. Is Green W/Polychrome Floral Designs On Ends, Top & Front; Initials & Date, "D.L.D.H. 1843", Paint On Top Worn, 20" W., 12" D., 11" H. $180.00
Chalkware Deer, Red & Blk. Paint, 9" H. . . . . . .
. . . . $200.00
Tole Deed Box, Japanned Ground W/Floral Decor. On 4 Sides In Red, Green & Yellow, 8¾" x 5" x 5¼" $275.00
Wooden Candlestand, Threaded Post W/Adjustable Shelf & Arms W/2 Metal Candleholders, Refinished, 42" H. $925.00
American Barometer, Mahogany W/Flame Grain Veneer, Face Is Marked "Kendall Brothers N. Lebanon, N.Y.", Mercury In Orig. Reservoir, 1 Sm. Piece Of Veneer Missing From Around Glass, 35" H. $475.00
Courting Mirror, Orig. Box, Reverse Painted Glass Is Red, Green, Yellow & Blk. W/White Background, Glass Cracked But Intact, 12¼" x 17¼" $650.00
Mirrored Candle Sconce $175.00

(A-OH. '75)   Garth's Auctions, Inc

Fan Back Windsor Side Chairs, Pr., Worn Black Paint Shows Green & Red Underneath $1400.00
Candlestand, Painted, Reddish Black Graining, 18¼" x 13½" x 23¾" H. $500.00
Shaker Type Wooden Box, Top Branded "L. Mulford", 8" L. $85.00
Tin Candlestick, W/Push Up, 7½" H. . $175.00
Pin Prick Watercolor, Crucifix W/Angles & Floral Vining Border, 19" x 22½" $175.00
Bennington Name Plate Frames, Green, Blue & Brown, Flint Enamel Glaze, 4¾" x 8¾", each $250.00

(A-OH. '76)   Garth's Auctions, Inc.

Arrowback Side Chairs, Set Of 6, Orig. Pumpkin Paint W/Free Hand Decor. In Blk., Yellow & Drk. Red $900.00
Wooden Round Bucket, Old Red Paint . . . . . .
. . . . $35.00
Wooden Decoy, Red Head Drake, Worn Orig. Paint $25.00
Apothecary Drawers, Pine, Dovetailed Case & 28 Dovetailed Drawers, Worn Birdseye Graining, 5 Knobs Replaced, 30" W., 8½" D., 36" H. . . .
. . . .$625.00
Fraktur Certificate, Hand Executed W/Eagles, Tulips & Stars; Red, Blue, Yellow & Black; Never Filled In; Edges Uneven, Framed, 9½" x 14½" $475.00
Stoneware Pitcher, Salt Glaze, Lady Liberty W/Eagle & Shield In Relief On Both Sides, Handle Has Hand, 10" H. $105.00
Ironstone Platter, Sponge Decor., Blue & White, 14" L. $80.00
Stoneware Pitcher, Sponge Decor., Blue & White, Eagle & Shield In Relief On Both Sides, 8¼" H. $105.00

Hepplewhite Birch Stand, One Board Top W/Glue Blocks Reattached, 18¾" x 19" x 28½" H. $140.00

Stoneware Tureen, Farming Scenes In Applied Relief, Lid W/Embossed Leaves, Full Figure Lion Handle, Hairline In Lid, 12½" L. .. $55.00

Hitchcock Side Chair, Orig. Decor. Worn, Worn Cane Seat $85.00

Dome Top Wooden Box, Covered In Wallpaper, Hand Made Tin Hinges & Clasp, Wallpaper Faded & Worn, 11¼" W., 7¼" D., 5½" H. $17.50

Sewing Box, Mahogany On Pine, Inlaid Silver, Brass & Mother Of Pearl, Brass Ball Feet Replaced, 1 Drawer W/Ivory Knob & Pin Cushion, 12" L., 5" W., 7¼" H. $45.00

Oil On Canvas, Oval, Painting Of Young Girl, Orig. Stretcher, 12¾"x16" $160.00

Candlestand, Pine & Birch, Round Top Raises & Lowers On Threaded Post, Post Incomplete, Probably Originally Having Had Attached Candle Holder, 13½" D., 28" H. $275.00

Bow Back Windsor Arm Chair, Repair To Bows, New Drk. Paint $700.00

Red Breasted Shore Bird, 11" H. ... $100.00

Oil On Canvas Painting, "Washington, Feb. 22nd, 1732 - Dec. 27, 1799", Backed On Masonite & Some Repair, Bright Colors, Gilt Frame, 24--x30" $110.00

Picture of Washington, Background Is Hand Colored Print, Figure & Flag Are Stump Work, Signed, 12"x14½" $175.00

Candlestand, Old Blue Paint, 15½" x 5¾" x 25½" H. $900.00

Step Down Windsor Side Chair, Black W/Orig. Decor In Red & Yellow W/Vining Leaves & Flowers On Crest, Decor. Repeated On Front Of Legs & Seat $360.00

Chalk Seated Dog, Old Paint, Green, Red & Black, 6" H. $135.00

Sampler, On Homespun, Alphabets, Birds, Flowers & Brick House, "Elizabeth Wests Work, Aged 10", Some Wear, Framed, 17" x 17½" $450.00

Theorem On Velvet, Basket Of Flowers, Shades Of Blue, Rose, Yellow & Tan, Old Gilt Frame, 7½"x9¾" $160.00

Miniature Foot Stool, Legs Mortised Through Seat, Heavy Green Paint Flaked & Showing Red Underneath, 8" L. $115.00

Child's Rocker, Blue W/Red Arms, White Striping & Free Hand Floral Decor. On Crest $135.00

Candlestand, Turned Pedestal W/Iron Legs & Feet, Traces Of Old Red Paint $85.00

Toy Wooden Poodle, Jointed Legs, Orig. White Paint W/Painted Face $65.00

Tin Candle Sconce, Oval Reflector $190.00

Windsor Arm Chair, Bamboo Turnings, Drk. Green Paint $275.00

Country Hepplewhite Work Table, Pine, 2-Board Top, Base Grained In Imitation Of Curly Maple, 36"x27½"x29" H. $110.00

Wooden Sugar Bucket, Stave Const., Traces Yellow Paint, Bottom Stamped "Hirsch Bros. & Co., Louisville, Ky.", 10" H. $37.50

Sewer Tile Seated Dog, Hand Molded W/Open Feet, Tooling Around Face, Signed & Dated: "Manuel Fond ... iest, Dennison, Ohio, 1918", Repair On Base, 9¾" H. $27.50

Tramp Art Frame, Hearts & Stars W/Gold Paint, 26½"x28½" $90.00

Tramp Art Shaving Stand, Drawers, Shelves & Other Containers For Sundries, 2 Drawers Signed "Pat Rimpus Of Hamburg & Foreign Glen", 22" W., 8½" D., 27" H. $85.00

Iron Scraper, Turned Wooden Handle, 26" L. $20.00

Ladder Back Side Chair, Traces of Red Paint, Woven Split Seat, Chipped $95.00

Country Queen Anne Table, Maple Base & One Board Pine Top, Refinished, 18" x 28" x 26" H. $550.00

Woven Basket, Wooden Swing Handle, 13½" Diam. $185.00

Walnut Tray, Dovetailed, Turned Feet, 10" Sq., 5" H. $55.00

Fraktur, "Mary's Tune Tenor", Red, Yellow, Blue & Green, Paper Damaged at "M", New Frame, 8¾" x 13½" $160.00

Tin Sconces, Pr., Oval Reflectors, 9¼" H. $450.00

Hanging Salt Box, Poplar, Dovetailed, Fishtail Crest, Old Drk. Paint, Repair At Wooden Hinge, 12½" H. $200.00

(A-OH. '76)   *Garth's Auctions, Inc.*

Blanket Chest, Pine & Poplar, Dovetailed, Till & Old Reddish Stain, Hinges Replaced . $105.00
Tin Candle Mold, W/Handles, 24-Tube $120.00
Rye Straw Basket, 11¾" D $32.50
Candle Mold, Pine Stand & 18 Pewter Tubes, 1 Tube Broken $300.00
Redware Turks Head Baking Mold, Brown Speckled Glaze, 8½" D. $40.00
Redware Dish, Squiggly Green Lines, 6¼" D. $45.00
White Clay Pie Plate, Drk. Chocolate Glaze, Coggled Edge, 11" D. $30.00
Wooden Bowl, 34" L. $75.00
Bread Board, 24" L., 17" W. $32.50
Brass Bed Warmer, Turned Wooden Handle, Engraved Lid, 45" L. $210.00

(A-OH. '76)   *Garth's Auctions, Inc.*

Country Corner Chair, Old Drk. Paint, Woven Split Wood Seat Needs Repair $250.00
Butterfly Table, Oval Top W/Butterfly Hinges, Refinished W/Traces Old Red Paint, 13½" x 31" W/13" Leaves, 26" H. $3100.00
Wooden Storage Box, Round, Painted Red W/Black, Yellow & Blue Brush Work Design, 11" D. $115.00
Tole Coffeepot, Drk. Japan Ground W/Decor. In Yellow, White, Red & Green, Ground Has Some Wear, Finial Missing, 10½" H. $675.00
Wooden Horse Weathervane, Weathered Red & Black Paint W/White Underneath, 21½" L... .... $255.00
Oil On Artist Board, Painting Of Red Farm House, Attached Buildings & Barn, Gilt Frame, 18"x23"............................... $105.00

(A-OH. '76)   *Garth's Auctions, Inc.*

Wooden Goose Decoy, Black & White Paint, 25" L. $75.00
Blanket Chest, Pine, Dovetailed Drawers, Wrought Iron Strap Hinges & Till W/Missing Lid, Refinished & Replaced Brasses, 41" W., 18½" D., 44½" H. $225.00
Hand Carved Wooden Bowl, 39½" L. $65.00
Wooden Horse Weathervane, 20th C., 29" L. $85.00

(A-OH. '76)   *Garth's Auctions, Inc.*

Corner Cupboard, Poplar W/Late Red Paint, Attrib. To The Zoarites, 43¼" W., 23" D., 60" H. $525.00
(Row I) **Stoneware Crock,** Bird In Cobalt, 1½ Gal., 2 Flakes Top Edge $100.00
(Row II) **Stoneware Jar,** Bright Blue Floral Leaf Design, "Norton & Co. Bennington, Vt.", 1½ Gal., Lid Has Hairlines $165.00
(Row III, Left to Right) **Stoneware Jar,** Tulips & "Cowden & Wilcox, Harrisburg, Pa.", Minor Flakes Around Lip, Missing Lid $80.00
Stoneware Jar, ½ Gal., W/Blue Brushed Decor., Lid $55.00
(Row IV) **Stoneware Jar,** Blue Brush Work At Handles, 11½" H. $35.00

(A-OH. '76)   *Garth's Auctions, Inc.*

Wooden Hay Fork, Made From One Piece Of Wood, 60" L. $65.00
Stoneware Jar, Stenciled Label: "Donoghho, Parkersburg", 5-Gal. $25.00
Pie Safe, Poplar, Refinished Except For Tin Panels Punched W/Primitive Baskets Of Flowers, Dovetailed Drawer & Solid Ends, One End Piece Of Gallery Replaced, 40" W., 16" D., 56½" H. $175.00
Wooden Screen Topped Cover, For Drying Apples, 11½"x21" $17.50
Cabbage Cutter, Dovetailed Sliding Hopper, 33" L. $105.00
Woven Split Wood Basket, Round, Wooden Handle, 7½" D. $30.00
Woven Split Wood Basket, Round, Wooden Handle, 9" D. $22.50
Woven Split Wood Basket, Round, Wooden Handle, 12" D. $20.00

(A-OH. '76)   *Garth's Auctions, Inc.*

(Row I, Left to Right)
Copper Pitcher, 7¾" H. $27.50
Copper Food Mold, Swirled Design, Zinc Lined, 8¼" D. $40.00
Copper Pitcher, 10" H. $45.00
(Row II, Left to Right)
Copper Food Mold, 7" D. $35.00
Block Tin Colander, Ring Legs, 6" D. $35.00
Tin Food Mold, Heart Design, Plated W/Copper $57.50
(Row III, Left to Right)
Copper Pitcher, Two, 6" & 4¾" H. ... $50.00
Tin Food Mold, Hexagonal Columns & Points, 7" H. $35.00
Copper Pitchers, Two, 6" & 4¾" H. .. $40.00

(A-PA. '76) *Pennypacker Auction Centre*

Axe Holder, Wrought Iron, Fish Form W/Incised Decor. W/Traces Orig. Paint $1300.00

(A-PA. '75) *Pennypacker Auction Centre*

Tea Table, Child's, Tilt-Top, Carved Pie Crust Top $350.00
Bench, Old Red Paint, 48" L $250.00

(A-OH. '76) *Garth's Auctions, Inc.*

Blanket Chest, Poplar, Dovetailed Drawers, Till & Wrought Iron Strap Hinges, Bear Trap Lock & Ogee Feet Replaced, Refinished, 49" W., 23½" D., 19" H. $325.00
Stoneware Cooler, Wooden Spigot, Impressed "Hutchinson & Green", Brushed Floral Design, Old Flakes, 4-Gal. $55.00
Stoneware Churn, Impressed "N.A. White & Son, Utica, N.Y.", Drk. Blue Cobalt Bird, Lid Has Lge. Chips & Churn Has 2 Hairlines, 8-Gal. $235.00
Stoneware Jar, Blue Brushed Bird, 4-Gal. $85.00

(A-PA. '75) *Pennypacker Auction Centre*

Redware *(Left to Right)*
Pitcher, Manganese Glaze, 8¾" H. . . $200.00
Jug, Speckled Glaze, 8" H. $100.00
Pitcher, Blk. Manganese, Rim W/Reeded Band, 11½" H. $170.00
Jug, Ovid, Black Glaze, 7¾" $140.00
Jug, Redware, Bulbous, Pa., Ca. 1825, 10½" H. $140.00
Queen Anne Table, Walnut & Pine, 2-Board Top, 15" Overhang $325.00

(A-PA. '75) *Pennypacker Auction Centre*

Wooden Sewing Bird, Cherry, Orig. Homespun Material $32.50
Wrought Iron Sewing Bird, New Jersey Dutch, Orig. Material $40.00
Box, Walnut, Dovetailed $75.00

(A-OH. '76) *Garth's Auctions, Inc.*

Hanging Shelf, Pine, 36" W., 10½" D., 42" H. $400.00
(Row I, Left to Right)
Hanging Candle Box, Tin $310.00
Punched Panel From Pie Safe, Love Birds & "1868", Grained Frame, 13½" x 17½" $430.00
Wooden Pastry Decorating Wheel . . $55.00
Pig Mold, Tin, 10½" L. $155.00
(Row II, Left to Right)
Cookie Mold, Wood, Back Initialed "G.S.", 3¾" x 8" $65.00
Love Bird Mold, Tin, 11½" L. $85.00
Redware Cookie Mold, Several Animals, 6½" Sq. $335.00
(Row III, Left to Right)
Burl Bowl, 8½" D. $300.00
Rooster Mold, Tin, Only ½ $35.00
Lock Box, Tin, 7½" H. $40.00

(A-OH. '76) *Garth's Auctions, Inc.*

Curly Maple Bench, Single Board Top, 72" L., 17" W., 21" H. $205.00
(Row 1, Left to Right)
Stoneware Crock, Blue Feather Design, Impressed Signature "T.S. Balsle ...,Detroit, Mich.", Hairlines, 6-Gal. $70.00
Stoneware Flower Pot, Red Bodied, Salt Glaze W/Orangish-Green Color W/Splashes of Blue, Impressed "S.H. Sonner, Strasburg, Va.," Sm. Old Chips, 1-Gal. $50.00
Stoneware Jar, Open Handles & Blue Floral Design, Hairline, 19½" H. $115.00
Stoneware Jar, Polka Dot Bird In Blue Slip, Minor Flake On Rim, 8" H. $100.00
Stoneware Churn, Floral Design, 3-Gal., 15½" H. $60.00
Curly Maple Walking Stick, 35" Long. $45.00
(Row II, Left to Right)
American Spun Brass Bucket, Wire Handle, "Hayden's" Etc. Sm. Splits, 10¾" D. $45.00
Wooden Basket, Bottom W/Strips Of Wood Nailed Lattice Fashion, Metal Reinforced Wooden Handle, Old Red Paint, 17½" x 14" $65.00
Wooden Sugar Bucket, Stave Construction, 10" H. $40.00

(A-OH. '76)   *Garth's Auctions, Inc.*

William & Mary Chest on Frame, Early Heavy Dovetailing, Upper Right Drawer Front Replaced & Feet Restored, Orig. Brass Knobs, 36" W., 19¾" D., 41" H. $900.00
William & Mary Mirror, Veneered & Black Paint, 20½" x 22½" $445.00

(A-OH. '76)   *Garth's Auctions, Inc.*

Queen Anne Chest of Drawers, Pine, Dovetailed Const., Secret Drawer In Cornice, Replaced Brasses, Red Stain, 38" W. At Cornice, 19" D., 46" H. $1600.00
Candle Lantern, Wooden Frame W/Curved Punched Tin Back, Tin Top W/Ring, 13¾" H. $235.00
Burl Bowl, Amer., 13" D. $250.00
Maple Butter Scoop, Curly Maple, Hook On Handle For Edge Of Bowl $135.00

(A-OH. '76)   *Garth's Auctions, Inc.*

Windsor Step Down Side Chair, Old Black Paint W/Tulip Shape In Red On Seat .$145.00
Wooden Candlestand, Mortised Through Const., Crossed Base & Adjustable Octagonal Top W/Ratchet, Old Red Paint, 12" D., Adjusts From 25" to 31½" $1900.00
Wrought Iron Lighting Device, Crown Base, Rush Holder W/Candle Socket Counter Balance, 9" H. $155.00
Chip Carved Spoon Rack, Poplar, Bold & Deep Cutting, Back Shows Rosehead Nails, Old Blk. Paint Over Red, 9" W., 24" H. $725.00
Watercolor Drawing, Fraktur Like Decor. W/Tulips & Birds, Hand Drawn, Brown, Red, Blue & Yellow, Urn Dated "1823", Pine Frame W/Curly Maple Graining, 13½" x 15½" $335.00

(A-OH. '76)   *Garth's Auctions, Inc.*

Blanket Chest, Pine, Bracket Feet & Till, Brown Grained Decor. Over Ochre Ground, 37" W., 17" D., 37¾" H. $450.00
Queen Anne Side Chair, Spanish Feet, Black Paint W/Yellow Striping Over Other Colors (Incl. Red), Rush Seat $675.00
Footed Wooden Bowl, Smooth Interior, Exterior Shows Old Tool Marks, 19" L. $45.00
William & Mary Mirror, Inlaid W/Various Woods, Glass Is Replaced, 18" x 22½" $80.00
Running Horse Weather Vane, Copper W/ Weathered Gold Leaf, 29" L. $190.00

(A-OH. '76)   *Garth's Auctions, Inc.*

Hepplewhite Chest of Drawers, New England, Country, Pine, Wooden Pulls, Red Paint W/Black Graining, 39" W., 19" D., 38½" H. $1200.00
Pewter Charger, Hallmarks & Initials "E.K." on Front Rim, 16½" D. $170.00
Hanging Salt Box, Pine, Old Leather Hinges, Drk. Paint. $500.00
Pewter Charger, Initials & Crowns On Back, 16½" D. $200.00

(A-OH. '76)   *Garth's Auctions, Inc.*

Hooded Mahogany Cradle, Refinished, Rounded End Broken & Reglued, Dovetailed Const., 45" L. $160.00
Cannon Ball Rope Bed, Old Red Stain, Outside Measurements, 53½" x 77". $260.00

(A-OH. '76) *Garth's Auctions, Inc.*

Windsor Fan Back Side Chair, Shaped Crest On Back, Old Green Paint W/Minor Wear, Black Shows Underneath $190.00
Folk Art Wooden Head, Worn Polychrome Paint, 10" H. $40.00
Pine Settle, Paneled Base & Back, Arm Supports Mortised Through Arms, Shoe Feet, Old Red Stain, Lift Lid In Seat, 32" W., 14" D., 41" H. $1225.00
Copper Cow Weathervane, Cast Head, Green Patina W/Traces Gold Leaf, 29" L., 18" H. $500.00
Charcoal Drawing, Young Man, Framed & Matted, New Gilt Frame, 16" x 18" $105.00
Watercolor on Paper, Young Girl W/Floral Garlands, Reverse Painted Glass Frames A Diamond Shape, Old Pine Frame, 8½" x 10"................................. $65.00
Fraktur, Geburts Und Taufschein, Made for "Elizabeth", Born December 3, 1810, Nordhampton County, Pennsylvania; 3 Hearts Contain Text W/2 Birds, Flowers & Sun; Hand Drawn, Green, Blue, Tan & Faded Yellow & Red, Old Gilt Frame, 15" x 18½" $900.00

(A-OH. '76) *Garth's Auctions, Inc.*

Windsor Step Down Side Chairs, (3), Bittersweet Paint W/Black Striping & Stylized Floral Crest Painted In Green, Black & White, Underside of Seats Stenciled "A. Holmes," (Two Illus.) . $840.00
Chest, Poplar, Lift Lid, Sponge Grained, 25" W., 12" D., 24½" H. $125.00
Sewer Tile Seated Dog, Hand Molded, Impressed Signature, "W. Moore, Nebeville, Ohio," 11½" H. $45.00
Sewer Tile Lion, Hand Molded, Bottom Signed Free Hand, "Bert Heifner, New Philadelphia, Ohio, Nov. 6, 1900, McKinley Day," 10" L. $135.00
Pen & Ink Drawing, Lined Paper, Side Wheeler "Renown," Signed "J.O. Miller, Nov. 24, 1898 A.D.," Modern Frame, 10¾" x 14¾" $75.00
Oil On Canvas, Still Life Painting of Basket W/Tulips & Lilies of the Valley, Gilt Frame, 17½" x 22" $310.00
Pen & Ink Drawing, Lined Paper, Iron Clad, "Monitor Terror," Signed "J.O. Miller, Nov. 24, 1898 A.D.," Modern Frame, 10¾" x 14¾" $85.00

(A-OH. '76) *Garth's Auctions, Inc.*

Wooden Goose Decoy, Head & Neck Covered W/Tin, 26" L. $125.00
Pine Hutch Table, One Dovetailed Drawer, Worn Old Red Paint Over Darker Paint, Top Is 2 Boards & Scrubbed, 54" x 37½" x 28½" H. $1800.00
Woven Basket, Wooden Feet & Handles, Sm. Amount of Repair Necessary, 26½" L. $65.00
Sheet Metal Rooster, Old Multi-Colored Paint, 12" H. $360.00

(A-OH. '76) *Garth's Auctions, Inc.*

Hepplewhite Gate Leg Table, Mahogany, Band Of Inlay On End Aprons, Single Board In Top & On Leaves, 17¾" x 47¾" W/17" Leaves, 29" H. $250.00
Case of Drawers, Mahogany W/5 Dovetailed Drawers & Brass Bail, Base Signed W/Pencil "Josephine Noodside 1868", 16½" W., 7" D., 11" H. $85.00
Rockingham Bowl, Chips On Base, 13" D. $35.00
Oil On Canvas, Painting Of Ships In Winter Harbor, Signed "T.E. Baker", Cleaned, Gilt Frame, 25" x 36" $180.00
Queen Anne Mirror, Beveled Mirror Glass In 2 Sections, 38" x 14¾" $700.00

(A-OH. '76) *Garth's Auctions, Inc.*

Wooden Hissing Goose Decoy, Old Working Overpaint, 27" L. $130.00
Hutch Table, Pine & Birch, Compartment Under Seat, Refinished In Red Stain, Top Has Old Finish, 41" x 54" x 28¼" H. $1000.00
Wooden Barber Pole, Red & White Stripes W/White Stars On Blue Field, Acorn Finial, 49" H. $130.00
Carved Wooden Sea Gull, Primitive, Painted Gold, 25" Wing Span $130.00
Wooden Shovel, Blade Has Hand Painted Scene Of Farm House In Winter Landscape, Minor Damage To Blade, 39" L. $55.00

(A-PA. '75)   *Pennypacker Auction Centre*

(Left to Right)
Hickory Splint Basket $45.00
Rye Straw Basket, 11½' D. $25.00
Tin Collander · $55.00
Splint Basket $25.00
Bench, Orig. Red Paint $95.00

(A-OH. '76)   *Garth's Auctions, Inc.*
Ladder Back Side Chair, Old Rush Seat, Paint Removed To Show Old Red, Repaired Split In One Post & Back Legs Built Up 1" . . .$130.00
Round Top Hutch Table, Pine & Ash, Lift Up Compartment In Seat, Refinished, 19th C., 52" D., 28¾" H. $700.00
Stoneware Jar, Stenciled Label: "W.H.H. Clark, Maker, Swan, O.", 5-Gal. $70.00
Sheet Metal Fish, 23½" L. $140.00

(A-OH. '76)   *Garth's Auctions, Inc.*
Cast Iron Andirons, Pr., Comic Black Man & Woman, 16" H. $55.00
Blanket Chest, Pine, 6-Board, Staple Hinges Orig. Old Red Paint, 61" L., 19½" D., 25" H. $205.00
Shenandoah Pottery Jar, Redware W/Cream Slip & Green Dripping Glaze, Old Sm. Chips, 13½" H. $350.00
Charger, White Clay W/Red Slip & Trailed Decor. In Yellow Slip, 18th C., 16¼" D. . . .$125.00
Redware Jar, Drk. Brown Splotches, Drilled For Lamp, Minor Flakes, Several Bands Of Incised Lines, 10½" H. $185.00

(A-OH. '76)   *Garth's Auctions, Inc.*
Hutch Table, Pine & Poplar, 2-Board Top, Refinished 38" x 65½" x 29½" H. $525.00
(Top) Colored Horse Lithograph, "Dexter, Ethan Allen and Mate", "1872 Haskell and Allen", Framed, 24½" x 30½" $120.00
(Center, Left to Right)
Stoneware Pitcher, Crude Brushed Design, Interior Is Albany Slip, Sm. Old Chips, 2-Gal. $100.00
Stoneware Jug, Impressed Swan Highlighted In Blue, Wooden Stopper, 1-Gal. $40.00
Stoneware Pitcher, Impressed "6-Bullard & Scott, Cambridgeport, Mass.", Interior Is Albany Slip, Flake On Edge $45.00
(Bottom, Left to Right)
Redware Jug, Greenish Glaze, 2-Gal. . . . .
. . . . $40.00
Redware Flower Pot, Drk. Glaze, Edge Wear & Hairline, 9" D. $40.00
Stoneware Jar, Tulip Design, Interior Is Albany Slip, Sm. Old Chips, 2-Gal. $40.00

(A-OH. '76)   *Garth's Auctions, Inc.*
Cast Brass Spider, Handle Signed "Robert Street & Co.", Virginia, 7" D. $55.00
Country Windsor Bow Back Arm Chair, Worn Black Paint, Attrib. To Cincinnati Area . . . .
. . . . $170.00
Blanket Chest, Pine, Dovetailed Const., Decor. W/Black Brush Work On White Ground, Alligatored Surface, Missing Till, 40" W., 22" D., 19" H. $100.00
Brass Cannon On Wooden Cart, Wrought Iron Fittings, Barrel Is 20½" L. $150.00
Wagon Jack, Wooden Case & Wrought Iron Mechanism, Iron Is Tooled & Marked "C.B. 1829", Worn Old Orange Paint, Case 20" H. $145.00
Currier & Ives Print, "The Woods In Autumn", Gilt Frame, 17½" x 22½" $150.00
Wrought Iron Trivet $185.00
Wrought Iron Hook, Shape of Snake . . . .
. . . . $85.00

(A-OH. '76)   *Garth's Auctions, Inc.*
Wooden Strainer, Long Handle, Bowl Has Split $42.50
Wrought Iron Revolving Broiler $80.00
Blanket Chest, Pine, Iron Strap Hinges, Bear Trap Lock, Till W/2 Dovetailed Drawers Missing Lid, Turned Feet W/Blocks That Continue Up Into Chest, Worn Orig. Drk. Green Paint, Base Molding Old Replacement, 51" W., 23" D., 28" H. $150.00
Wooden Candle Mold, 24 Pewter Tubes, Tubes Signed "W. Webb", 21½" W., 6½" D., 17¾" H. $1150.00
Redware Plate, Clear Glaze W/Brown Streaks, Irregular Shape, Old Edge Chips, Glaze Worn, 12" D. $95.00
Utensil Rack, Pine, Wrought Iron Hooks, Old Drk. Color $65.00
Pewter Ladle, Turned Wooden Handle . . . .
. . . . $35.00
Pewter Ladle, Turned Wooden Handle . . . .
. . . . $30.00

(A-OH. '76)   *Garth's Auctions, Inc.*
Bannister Back Side Chair, Alligatored Old Blk. Paint, Rush Seat Painted White $290.00
Country Queen Anne Tavern Table, Oval Top, 2-Board Pine Top & Maple Base, Mortised Stretcher, Refinished W/Traces Old Red Paint, 36" x 26½" x 25" H. $1350.00
Burl Bowl, 15½" D. $600.00
Wrought Iron & Brass Skimmer, Iron Handle Signed "Silvius", 21" L. $110.00
Hanging Poplar Box, Dovetailed W/Shaped Crest & Old Red Paint, 2-Sect. Compartment W/Lift Lid & Dovetailed Drawer, 13½" W., 8" D., 11½" H. $290.00
Chalk Standing Dog, Damaged, 7" H. . . . .
. . . . $65.00
Wrought Iron & Brass Strainer, 9½" D., 18½" L. $125.00

(A-OH. '76)   *Garth's Auctions, Inc.*

Country Chippendale Side Chairs, Pr., Birch
W/Worn, Old Drk. Brown Paint, Rush Seats
Have Some Age & Painted Yellow $90.00
Blown Glass Demijohn, Green, 24" H. ......
....$100.00
Oil On Canvas, Young Lady On Garden Terrace
Black Dress & Pearls, Holds Rose, Cleaned &
Rebacked on Board, Gilt Frame, 18½" x 23" ..
.... $175.00

(A-OH. '76)   *Garth's Auctions, Inc.*

Tilt Top Mahogany Tea Table, 30" Diam.,
28½" H. $250.00
Oval Wooden Storage Box, Wallpaper Cover-
ed, Blue Paper W/Flowers & Peacocks, 17½"
L. $75.00
Mahogany Screen, 2 Sliding Panels Covered
In Faded Green, 35½" H. $45.00

(A-OH. '75)   *Garth's Auctions, Inc.*

Goose Decoy, Stripped & Refinished, Body One
Piece Of Wood, 37½" L. $45.00
Goose Decoy, Stripped & Refinished, Bottom
Initialed "JT", 23" L. $45.00
Spinning Wheel, Reddish Paint, 90" L. Over-
all $170.00
Iron Brace & Bit, Turned Wooden Handle ....
.... $5.00
Wrought Iron Chain Trammel $30.00
Iron Auger, Wooden Handle $2.00
Hand Made Wrought Iron Pipe Tongs, 2 Pr.,
One W/Tooling & Initials $10.00
Iron Broad Axe, Signed $22.50

(A-OH. '76)   *Garth's Auctions, Inc.*

Country Hepplewhite Table, Dovetailed, Swing
Leg, Bottom of Drawer Replaced, Old Brass
Pull $140.00
Wooden Decoy, "Decoy's Unlimited, Erie,
Penna.", 22" L. $17.50
Sheraton Side Chair, Grained Seat, Black
Ground W/Stenciled Decor........... $45.00
Sheet Metal Lantern, Beveled Round Glass,
Oil Burner & Reflector, 9¾" H. $25.00
Pine Box, Dovetailed, Orig. Brown Paint W/
Yellow Striping, Brass Bail Handle Replaced,
12"x6"x5½" $25.00
Sheet Metal Candle Lantern, 11" H. Exclusive
Of Handle $55.00
Watercolor, Tulip & Leaf, Green, Red & Yellow,
Framed, 9½"x11½" $65.00

(A-OH. '76)   *Garth's Auctions, Inc.*

(Row I, Left to Right)
Miniature Cast Iron Kettle & Skillet . $12.50
Miniature Cast Iron Swan Shaped Iron $5.00
Cast Iron Toy Cook Stove, Stove Plates &
Shelves $25.00
Miniature Cast Iron Tea Kettle & Pan W/
Handle $20.00
(Row II, Left to Right)
Cast Iron Mechanical Bank, Lion & Monkey,
Monkey Missing One Arm, Lion Needs One Eye,
9¼" H. $185.00
Chalk Cat Bank, 6¾" H. $22.50
Tin Building Bank, "Bank", 4½" H. .. $17.50
Cast Iron Mechanical "Uncle Sam Bank", Worn
Orig. Paint, 11" H. $60.00
(Row III, Left to Right)
Cast Iron Bank, Aunt Jemima, 5¾" H. . $7.50
Cast Iron Boots, Pr., "Sollecin Co., New York"
.... $42.50
Brush & Dust Pan, Attrib. To The Shakers ...
.... $27.50
Cast Iron Bank, Policeman, Worn Paint, 5½" H.
.... $7.50

(A-OH. '76)   *Garth's Auctions, Inc.*

Arrow Back Arm Chair Rocker, Refinished ..
.... $75.00
Sheraton Mahogany Stand, Dovetailed Draw-
er, 2 Galleryed Shelves, 15½" Sq., 32½" H. ..
.................................$240.00
Salt Glazed Teapot, Embossed, Lt. Green,
Floral, Britannia Lid, 10" H. $37.50
Salt Glaze Pitcher, Embossed, Lt. Blue, Drink-
ing Scene & Man On Horseback Being Attacked
By 2 Flying Women, Impressed Mark "Published
By W. Ridgeway & Co., Hanley, October 1,
1835", Cracked, Britannia Lid, 8¾" H. $30.00
Ironstone Pitcher, Blue Transfer, Britannia
Lid, English Registry Mark I "Furnival", 7½" H.
.................................$17.50

(A-OH. '76)   *Garth's Auctions, Inc.*

(Row I, Left to Right)
Wooden Horse Pull Toy, Primitive, Drk. Paint,
Leather Ears, 10½" L. $230.00
Cast Iron Bank, "The Home Savings Bank,
Detroit, Mich.", Old Blue & Gold Paint, Clasp On
Door Incomplete, 10½" H. $85.00
Team of Carved Wooden Oxen Pull Toy, Back
Two Wheels Unpainted, Ears Incomplete, 10¾"
L. $135.00
(Row II, Left to Right)
Wood Carving, Man Holding Building, Oak,
20th C., 10" H. $35.00
Wooden Grasshopper Pull Toy, Moving
Parts, 10" L. $65.00
Wooden Kitchen Masher, Ornamented Handle
12¼" L. $15.00
Wooden Acrobat $20.00
(Row III, Left to Right)
Carved Wooden Chain, Ea. Link W/Chip
Carving $35.00
Carved Wooden Dice, Black & Silver, 5¼" ...
.... $10.00

(A-OH. '76)   *Garth's Auctions, Inc.*

Queen Anne Side Chair, Spanish Feet, Old Drk. Graining W/Red Showing, New Rush Seat. $190.00

Wrought Iron Knife Blade Andirons, Pr., Brass Urn Finials & Penny Feet, Sm. Hole In Ea. Finial, Back Rods Extended, 23" H. $225.00

New Hampshire Chest of Drawers, Pine, Dovetailed Drawers, Beaded Frame, Replaced Brass Knobs & Refinished W/Traces Of Green, 32" W., 17" D., 36½" H. $635.00

Tole Tray, Reticulated Gallery, Black Ground W/Gold Stenciled Border & Free Hand Painting Of Fruit, Pillars, Arches & Drapes In Center, 14½" x 19¼" $130.00

Queen Anne Side Chair, Spanish Feet, Some Curl Shows Beneath Old Paint, New Rush Seat $225.00

Currier & Ives Print, "Chappaqua Farm, West Chester County, New York", Framed, 12½" x 16½" $60.00

(A-OH. '76)   *Garth's Auctions, Inc.*

Pine Hanging Shelf, Scrolled Ends, Late, 21" W., 8" D., 30" H. $70.00

(Row I, Left to Right)
Sheet Metal Candle Lantern, Worn Pale Green Paint, 11½" H. $57.50
Tin Candle Mold, 6 Tubes W/Handle, 9¾" H. $25.00
Sheet Metal Candle Lantern, Black Paint, 12" H. $20.00

(Row II, Left to Right)
Tin Candle Mold, 6 Tube, Handle & Ring Hanger, 10¾" H. $32.50
Powder Horn, Incised Compass Design & Crescent & Lizard $45.00
Tin Shadow Box Frame, Sides Have Reverse Painted Glass Panels Decor. W/Red & Green, Tin Corners Are Primitively Tooled Fans, 4½" x 6" $75.00

(A-OH. '76)
Garth's Auctions, Inc.

(A-OH. '76)   *Garth's Auctions, Inc.*

Bucket, Stave Construction, Old Yellow Paint $37.50

Shaker Arm Chair Rocker, Worn Orig. Drk. Finish, New Olive Green Tape Seat .. $250.00

Shaker Storage Box, Wooden, 15½" L. $130.00

Shaker Storage Box, Wooden, 11" D. $100.00

Demilune Table, Pine Top & Ash Legs, Attrib. To Shaker, 26" W., 15" D.. 25" H. ... $225.00

Shaker Sewing Box, Wooden, Fabric Lined Interior W/Cake Of Beeswax & Sm. Strawberry Shaped Pin Cushion Attached To Sides, 10¼" L. $265.00

Storage Box, Wooden, "E. Payson, Westbrook", 6¾" D $15.00

Shaker Thread Caddy & Pin Cushion, 5" D., 6" H. $55.00

Pencil Drawing, "Lake Windermere", Framed, 12½' x 16½" $12.50

Oil On Canvas Portrait, Woman W/Lace Collar, Orig. Gilt Frame, 16½" x 18½" $150.00

Sheraton Side Chairs, Pr., Black Paint W/Yellow Striping & Free Hand Gilt & Red Decor. Is Old But Not Orig., Old Rush Seats $100.00
Wash Stand, Pine, 1 Dovetailed Drawer, Scalloped Gallery, Orig. Yellow Paint W/Green & Black Striping & Free Hand & Stenciled Fruit & Foliage, 18" W., 16" D., 36½" H. $160.00
Chalk Dog, Red, Brown, Black & Yellow, Repair On One Front Leg, 14" H. $80.00
Currier & Ives, Lithograph, Folio, "Sunny Side," Residence of Late Washington Irving Near Tarrytown, N.Y.," Ogee Frame, 22½" x 27½" $150.00
Currier & Ives, Lithograph, Folio, "View Of Harper's Ferry Ca. (From Potomac Side)," Gilt Frame, 21" x 27¼" $260.00

(A-OH. '76)   *Garth's Auctions, Inc.*

Foot Warmer, Punched Tin Panels & Wooden Frame, Interior W/One Long Pan, 10½" x 16½" x 7" H. $165.00
Wooden Mortar & Pestle $45.00
Rye Straw Basket, 17" D. $52.50
Case of Drawers, Pine, Dovetailed Const., 4 Interior Drawers W/Leather Loop Pulls, Sm. Iron Strap Hinges, 16½" W., 14" D., 22" H. $140.00
Redware Loaf Pan, Worn Yellow Decor. Of Wavy Lines, Coggled Edge, Old Cracks, 13" L. $160.00
Writing Arm Chair, Plank Seat, Drawer Under Writing Surface, Worn Red Paint $400.00

(A-OH. '76)   *Garth's Auctions, Inc.*

Pewter Cupboard, Pine, Open, Beaded Frame, Old Red Stain, Bottom Board Is Replacement, 43¾" W., 17½" D., 86½" H. $500.00

(Row I, Left to Right)
Pewter
Salt, 2½" H. $60.00
Charger, Hallmark "B & Co.", 12¼" Diam. . . .
. . . . $95.00
Tankard, "Quart", 6¼" H. $80.00
Sauce Pitcher, 5½" H. $30.00
Bowl, 3¾" D. $10.00
Charger, 12" D. $95.00
(Row II, Left to Right)
Cups, Pr., 2¾" H. $115.00
Plate, 8¾" D. $35.00
Tankard, Marked, "W.R.", W/Crown & 3 x's; Mark On Handle Indistinct, 6½" H. $85.00
Basin, Touch Mark W/Lion, Cross & "Caz", Also "Herspe ...", 11½" D. $105.00
Tankard, Marked "V.R." W/Shield, "1 Qt. Imperial", 6¼" H. $85.00
Plate, Touch Mark "I.G.",   Knife Scratches, 8¾" D. $45.00

(Row III, Left to Right)
Plate, "London" Touch & "Samuel —" & "S. Elles", Rim Marked "D.C.", 9½" D. $65.00
Chalises, Pr., Inscribed "Associate Cong. N Edin. R 1753", 8¼" H. $370.00
Basin, 8" D. $52.50
Plate, 3 Touch Marks Incl. "Made In London" "In Cheapside London" & Third Not Clear, Pitted Surface, 9" D. $35.00

(Row IV, Left to Right)
Drinking Cup, 2-Handled, Inscribed "Inter Scholastic Games 1871, Flat Race 100 Yds. (Open) 2nd Prize, Won By ———— " Glass Bottom Cracked, 6¾" H. $40.00
Charger, Center W/Embossed Coat Of Arms, Rim Marked "JA, GL, JA, DE", Loop For Hanging, 13¾" D. $45.00
Compote, Some Repairs, 7¼" D., 7¼" H.
. . . .$20.00

(A-OH. '76)   *Garth's Auctions, Inc.*

(Row I)
Copper Pans, Set of Six, Cast Iron handles $245.00
(Row II, Left to Right)
Carved Wooden Bird, Glass Eyes, Worn Paint, Repaired Tail, 6" H. $150.00
Tin Candlestick Inserts, Pr., Leaf Design W/Worn Green Paint $85.00
Carved Wooden Rooster, Red, Yellow & Black, 7¾" H. $310.00
Carved Wooden Bird, Painted Drk. Green, Brown & Black, 6¾" H. $260.00
(Row III, Left to Right)
Pratt Pitcher, 4 Colors, One Side Shows Man Drinking, Reverse Is Male Nude, Sm. Hairline At Spout, 5½" H. $200.00
Wooden Donut Cutter, 4½" H. $30.00
Wooden Adjustable Candlestand, Base Signed In Pencil, 5¾" D. $170.00
Cast Iron Eagle Snow Birds, Three (2 Illus.) $79.50

(A-PA. '75)   *Pennypacker Auction Centre*

Bronze Figure, Marked 1759 to 1796 Burns, Signed "F.W. Pomeroy, Sculptor 1890", 16" T.
. . . . $190.00
Bronze Dog, Signed P. Lecourtier . . . $110.00

Stoneware Jug, Impressed "New York Stoneware Co., Fort Edwards, N.Y.", Floral Design In Cobalt, 2-Gal. $75.00
Birch Table, 1 Dovetailed Drawer, 1-Board Breadboard Top, Reddish Brown Paint, 24" x 18" x 27" H. $925.00
Slat Back Arm Chair Rocker, Old Worn Green Paint Over Orig. Red, Worn Split Wood Seat . .
. . . .$395.00
Sewing Box, Drum Base W/Drawer, 2 Tiers Of Whale Bone Tipped Pins For Spools Of Thread, Pin Cushion Finial; Black Ground W/Red Poinsetta Like Flowers & Green Leaves, Paint Shows Wear On Tiers, 9¼" D., 12" H. $400.00
Shaker Wooden Basket, Round W/Handle, Fabric Lined, 6¾" D. $75.00
Federal Two-Part Mirror, Reeded Pilasters, Chip Carved Corner Blocks & Molded Cornice, Reverse Painting Of Tiger & Palm Trees Is Cracked, 10" H. $275.00
Poplar Hanging Box, 2 Compartments, Old Red & Brown Paint W/Worn White Striping, 11" W., 10" H. $170.00

(A-OH. '76)   *Garth's Auctions, Inc.*

(A-OH. '76)   *Garth's Auctions, Inc.*

Hepplewhite Stand, Cherry, Unusual Inlay, Top Is Old Replacement, Refinished & Replaced Knob, 15" Sq., 28½" H. $295.00
Oval Wooden Storage Box, Drk. Green Paint, 7¾" L. $30.00
Round Wooden Storage Box, Drk. Green Paint, 6" Diam. $20.00
Salem Rocker, Modern Blk. Paint $40.00
Printed "Geburts Und Taufschein", 1850 Birth In Berks Co., Pa. Printed In Reading By "Johann Ritter", Faded Hand Coloring, Paper Wrinkled & Stained, New Painted Frame, 15¾' x 18¾" $35.00
Sewing Box, 1 Drawer & Compartment For Thread, 5⅞" H. $25.00

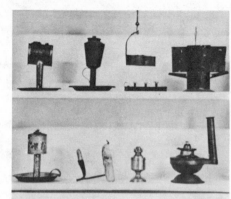

(A-OH. '76)   *Garth's Auctions, Inc.*
(Row I, Left to Right)

Tin Lamp, Saucer Base & Horizontal Font, Ring Handle, 6½" H. $50.00
Tin Lamp, Saucer Base W/Carrying Handle On Stem, Conical Base & Single Tubular Burner, 7½" H. $35.00
Betty Lamp, Sheet Iron, Wrought Iron Hanger, Wick Support Missing $27.50
Tin Lamp, Flat Rectangular Font W/3 Wicks, 5¾" x 2¼" $45.00
Tin Lamp, Wicks Held On Each Side, Drippings Caught By Trough In Base, Old Japanning, 6¼" H. $155.00
(Row II, Left to Right)
Tin Lamp, Saucer Base W/Ring Handle, Cylindrical Font & Whale Oil Burner, Traces Of Old Paint, 7"f H. $30.00
Candle Holder, Wrought Iron, To Be Pounded Into Wall, Displayed In Weathered Piece Of Wood $60.00
Miniature Brass Lamp, Acorn Kerosene Burner & Chimney, 7½" H. $22.50
Kerosene Lamp, Sheet Metal, Stamped "Tubular Lamp", Last Pat. Date "July 25, 1878", 8½" H. $25.00

(A-OH. '76)   *Garth's Auctions, Inc.*
Woven Split Wood Basket, Oval W/Wooden Handles, 18" x 23" $40.00
Curly Maple Side Board, Dovetailed Drawers, Orig. Hdwe., 62" W., 19¼" D., 61" H. To Top Of Gallery $425.00
Rye Straw Basket, Round W/Wooden Carrying Handle, 17" Diam. $55.00
Stoneware Pitcher, Salt Glaze Did Not Mature Correctly Leaving An Interesting Surface, Hairline Damage, 9" H. $25.00
Wooden Bowl, Round, Age Check, 15" Diam. $12.50

(D-PA. '76)
Early Shaving Brush, Maple Turned Onion Top; Upper Portion Of Brush Wrapped With String, 6" L. $18.00

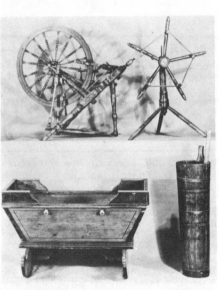

(A-MA. '76)   *Richard A. Bourne Co. Inc.*
(Row I, Left to Right)
Flax Wheel, Carved, Patented W/Words "Loso" & Painted Initials "R E D", Dated 1831, Retains Most Orig. Green Paint & Parts $125.00
Yarn Winder, Retains Most Orig. Green Paint & Parts $60.00
(Row II, Left to Right)
Pine Cradle W/2 Porcelain Knobs On Each Side, 36" L. $110.00
Wooden Butter Churn, Iron-Bound, Normal Wear & Patina, 31¼" H. $100.00

(A-OH. '76)   *Garth's Auctions, Inc.*
Iron Fork, Long Handled $17.50
Fireplace Mantle, Pine, Refinished & Top Shelf Replaced, 47¾" H., 58" W. $350.00
Cast Iron Fireplace Grate, Coal Burning $35.00
Wrought Iron Hinges (4) $15.00
Wrought Iron 4-Prong Hook $20.00
Wrought Iron Fireplace Tongs, Pr. ...$15.00
Cast Iron Tea Kettle $16.00
Tin Food Mold W/Copper Eagle At Bottom, Copper Washed W/Tin $45.00
Copper Tea Kettle, Dovetailed Bottom $205.00
Block Tin Coffee Pot, 8⅜" H. $10.00

(A-OH. '76)   *Garth's Auctions, Inc.*
Three-Legged Stool, Heavy Round Top, 24¾" H. $165.00
Bow Back Windsor Arm Chair, Worn Red & Blk. Paint $475.00
Candlestand, Pine, Late Drk. Red Paint, 22½" H. $170.00
Candle Sconces, Tin, Pr., Ea. W/Double Candelabra & Rayed Reflector $1,525.00
Hanging Open Salt Box, Old Drk. Paint $175.00

(A-OH. '76)   *Garth's Auctions, Inc.*

Cast Iron Deer, Ex Samaha Collection, 18" H.
.... $375.00
Table, Primitive, Base Has Old Red Paint, 24"
x 37½" x 27" H. $310.00
Wrought Iron Sawtooth Trammel, 49" H. ...
.... $75.00
Redware Mug, Clear Glaze W/Brown Speckles
.... $25.00
Redware Loaf Tray, "Washington & Lafayette"
In Yellow Slip, Sawtooth Edge, 14½" L. ......
.... $1500.00
Redware Mug, Clear Glaze W/Brown Speckles,
3 Tooled Rings Around Base, Old Hairline &
Chip At Handle, 4⅜" H. $30.00
Wrought Iron Trammel, Underside Of Top
Hook Marked "W", 39" L. $45.00
Tin Candle Sconce, Crimped Top & Base,
13½" H. $135.00
Chopping Knife, Wooden Handle, Blade
Signed "Wm. Greaves & Sons," $25.00
Tin Candle Sconce, Flared Back, Top & Base
Have Crimping, 12" H. $100.00

(A-OH. '76)   *Garth's Auctions, Inc.*

Pennsylvania Settle Bench, Base W/Storage
Compartment & Lift Lid, Pine & Birch W/Several
Coats Old Worn Paint, Red On Top, 57" W., 20"
D., 45" H. $550.00
Turned Wooden Bowl, Exterior Has Yellowish
Stain, 18" D. $75.00
Ovoid Stoneware Jar, Handles, Simple Flower
Design, Old Chips Around Top, No Lid, 11¼" H.
.... $65.00
Sheet Metal Stick Up Goose Decoy, Worn
Paint, 24¾" L. $100.00
Stoneware Jar, "Evan R. Jones, Pittston, Pa.",
Flower In Cobalt, Chip On Rim, 1½ Gal. ......
.....................................$80.00

(A-OH. '76)   *Garth's Auctions, Inc.*

Country Captain Chairs, Pr., Worn Drk. Paint
W/Yellow Striping $170.00
Primitive Pine Bench, Cleaned Down To Old
Red, 34" L., 11¾" W., 14½" H. $55.00
Wooden Duck Decoy, Orig. Paint, 13½" L. ..
.... $45.00
Wooden Duck Decoy, Redhead, 15" L. ......
.... $40.00
Wooden Hobby Horse, Orig. Decor. W/Red
Rockers & Black & White Body, Worn Harness,
Saddle & Ears, Rope Tail $155.00
Toy Wooden Bucket, Painted White W/Red
Horse, Stars & Flag, Also "Truth & Good Boy",
5¾" D $37.50
Sampler, On Homespun, Birds, Flowers, Ever-
greens, House, Verse & "Sophia Redrup, March
1832", Old Repairs, Brown, Green, Blue &
Yellow, Framed, 15½"x19¼".........$110.00
Wrought Iron Fork, For Dispensing Nails,
Signed "M. Moles", 17¾" L............$60.00
Spencerian Pen & Ink Certificate, "Bon Voy-
age Via New York, Philad., And Boston, 1871,
Compliments Of Thomas Shotton", 10" x 12¾"
.... $85.00
Wrought Iron Spatula, 17" L. $50.00

(A-OH. '76)   *Garth's Auctions, Inc.*

Iron Kettle Stand, Penny Feet, Traces White
Paint, 12" H........................ $35.00
Wrought Iron Stationary Broiler, Heart De-
sign $75.00
Pine Dry Sink, Low Gallery Back W/Shelf, Re-
finished, 56" L., 20" W., 45" H. $220.00
Redware Apple Butter Jar, Glazed Inside &
Out, 8½" H.......................... $30.00
Stoneware Crock, "3" & Flourish, 3-Gal. .....
.... $30.00
Stoneware Jar, W/Lid, Cream Colored Glaze,
7½" H.............................. $8.00
Tin Candle Mold, Eight Tube $20.00
Wrought Iron Toaster, 16½" L. $15.00
Tin Candle Mold, Four Tube $20.00
Stoneware Bottle, 9¼" H. $3.00

(A-OH. '76)   *Garth's Auctions, Inc.*

Tin Lighting Device, Adjustable, Wooden Base,
Space For 2 Candles W/Crimped Pans & Spring
Clamp That Holds Arm In Position, 34" H. ....
.... $425.00
Windsor Stool, Bamboo Turnings, Old Red
Paint $65.00
Pip Squeak W/Composition Rooster, Mustard
W/Black, Red & White, Bellows Need Repair,
Chicken Has Minor Repair, 8" H. $75.00
Walnut One Drawer Stand, Dovetailed Drawer
W/Opalescent Knob, One Board Top, Refinish-
ed, 17"x19¼"x29½" H. $130.00
Arrow Back Arm Chair Rocker, Refinished ..
.... $150.00
Bellows, Drk. Green W/Stenciled & Free Hand
Fruit & Foliage, Leather Is Worn, 16½" L. ....
.... $65.00
Rockingham Spittoon, Chips Around Top Edge
13¼" Diam.......................... $30.00
Cut Out W/Silhouette In Center, Border De-
sign W/Eagle, Hearts, Stars, Crescent Moons
& Vining Tulips, Old Frame, 15" Sq. ....
.....................................$400.00
Pine Hanging Box, 1 Drawer, Cut Out Work,
Old Red Paint, 19th C., 14" H. $85.00
Cut Out, Eagles Carrying Arrows In One Talon
& American Flag In The Other, Pots Of Flowers
At Bottom Edge, Old Frame, 10" x 12" ....
.... $155.00

(A-OH. '76)   *Garth's Auctions, Inc.*

Bannister Back Side Chair, Modern Blk. Paint
& Rush Seat $425.00
Woven Basket, 17" L. $55.00
Walnut Press, 26" W., 14" D., 58" H. ....
.... $500.00
Bannister Back Side Chair, Modern Blk. Paint
& Rush Seat $475.00

(A-OH. '76)
Pine Hanging Shelves, Sm. Set, 24" W., 4" D. $50.00
(Row I, Left to Right)
Duck Pip Squeak, Composition Body, 6" H. $120.00
Wind Up Rocking Horse, Wooden, 7" H. $95.00
Bird Carving, Wooden, Tin Base, Blk, Bird W/Grey Beak, 6½" H. $65.00
(Row II, Left to Right)
Miniature Wooden Decoy, 7" L. $85.00
Cat Pip Squeak, Composition Body Is Cracked, 3½" H. $45.00
Miniature Wooden Decoy, "Made By Ken Harris, Woodville, N.Y.", 7" L. $145.00
(Row III, Left to Right)
Bird Pip Squeak & Pull Toy, Wooden, Orig. Polychrome Decor., Leather Has Deteriorated, 6½" L. $215.00
Miniature Bird Carving, "Killdeer K. Kitahota", 2½" H. $40.00
Pen Work Bird, W/"Mary", Old Red Frame, 5¾" x 7" $115.00
Wooden Horse Carving, 5¼" H. $40.00

(A-OH. '76)
Watercolor, W/Poem, "The Late Visitor", 12" x 15½" $300.00
Federal Mirror, 2-Section, Reverse Painting Of House, Frame Decor. W/Red & Yellow, 13½" x 21¾" $335.00
Side Chairs, Decor. W/Putty Colored Ground W/Polychrome Floral Stenciling & Olive & Black Striping, Some Wear & Repair, Set Of 6 ......
....$750.00
Pine Stand, Brownish-Yellow Sponged Decor. W/Green & Red, Dovetailed Drawer W/Divided Interior, Orig. Brass Knob, 16" Sq., 29½" H.
....$750.00
Bowl, Luster Decor. W/Polychrome Fish & Brick Red Striping, Worn Interior, Lge. Flake On Rim, 7½" Diam. $115.00

(A-OH. '76)
Bannister Back Side Chair, Worn Modern Blk. Paint, New Rush Seat $350.00
Pine Bench, Legs Mortised Through Top, Worn Red Paint, 51" L., 17" W., 19" H. $285.00
Shaker Clothes Basket, Mt. Lebanon, 16½" x 24" $85.00
Redware Vase, 2 Ribbed Handles, Tooling At Handles And Around Top, Greenish-Brown Streaked Glaze, Some Glaze Flakes, 11½" Diam. $135.00
Redware Turks Head Mold, Exterior Has Green Glaze, Interior Has Lt. Green Splotches, 11½" Diam. $95.00
Oval Basket, 13" L. $35.00
Redware Muffin Pan, Lt. Green Splotches In Clear Glaze, 7½" x 11" $100.00
Pig Cutting Board, 16" L. $45.00
Printed Textile, "Washington - First In War, First In Peace, First In The Hearts Of His Countrymen"; Eagle & Banners W/Border Depicting Naval Battles; Green, Red, Yellow & Drk. Brown; Framed, 24½" L., 29½" W. $525.00

(A-OH. '76)
Windsor Candlestand, 12 Sided Top, Worn Red & Blue Paint, 26" H., 18" Diam. ..$850.00
Woven Basket, Wooden Handle $85.00
Fan Back Windsor Rocking Chair, Old Refinishing $550.00
Shaker Sewing Box, 2 Lift Up Compartments, Orig. Yellow Paint, Sm. Repair To One Lid Flange, 15" L. $450.00
Crewel Work Panel, Painted & Grained Frame, 10" x 12" $55.00

(A-OH. '76)
Windsor Candlestand, Orig. Drk. Grey-Blue Paint W/White Striping, Old Repair To Top, 16" Diam., 27¼" H. $2,900.00
Comb-Back Windsor Arm Chair Rocker, Orig. Worn Blk. Paint W/Green & Yellow Striping, Faded Decor. On Crest Of Comb & Bow .....
....$1,450.00
Pewter Candlestick, 7" H. $300.00
Fish Watercolor, Red, Green & Blue, Grained Frame, Paper Has Tear, 9" x 14" $475.00

(A-OH. '76)
(Row I, Left to Right)
Miniature Foot Stool, Green Paint, 5" L. ......
....$70.00
Miniature Foot Stool, Red Paint $37.50
Dovetailed Box, Poplar, Yellow Brown W/Green Edgings, Center Panels Brushed W/Drk. Red & Green, Iron & Brass Lock & Brass Bail Handle, 12¼" x 5¾" x 6½" $350.00
Miniature Foot Stool, Refinished, 4" L. $25.00
Miniature Basket, Wooden Handle, 5¾" H. ..
....$65.00
(Row II, Left to Right)
Miniature Round Basket, Wooden Handles ..
....$90.00
Box W/Sliding Lid, Divided Compartment, 6" L.
....$15.00
Miniature Dovetailed Tray, 4 Sections, 7" x 4½" $65.00
Miniature Oval Basket, Some Wear, 8" L.
....$52.50
Miniature Round Basket, 5" Diam. ...$65.00

(A-OH. '76)   *Garth's Auctions, Inc.*

Table Top Desk, Poplar, Dovetailed W/Base Molding, Slant Top Lift Lid, Old Red Stain, Interior W/1 Open Compartment, 24" W., 19" D., 16" H. $85.00

Fraktur, Birth Certificate, Printed & Hand Colored, For "Jacob Diewler", German Reads: "Born 1807, September 5 In Dauphin County, Pennsylvania", Parrots, Birds & Flowers In Yellow, Green & Red, Framed, 14¼" x 17½" $290.00

Bed Warmer, Brass Pan & Lid W/Engraved Rooster & Flowers, Turned Wooden Handle, 43" L. $150.00

Country Hepplewhite Table, Round Top, Pine, Added Braces At One End Of Top, 42" Diam., 28½" H. $285.00

Rye Straw Beehive, 15" H. $105.00

Wrought Iron Wafer Iron, Ovals W/Cast Star Swirled Design, 25½" L. $125.00

Redware Bowl, Clear Glaze W/Yellow Slip & Slip Covered By Green, Band of Sponged Brown, Some Wear, 13" D. $165.00

Tin Candle Sconces, Pr., 12½" H. .. $180.00

(A-OH. '76)   *Garth's Auctions, Inc.*

Gate Leg Table, Maple Base, Curly Maple Top W/Butterfly Hinges Is Replacement, Base Refinished & Stained, Top Is Scrubbed, 29½" x 12½" W/12" Leaves, 26½" H. $3,300.00

(Left to Right)

Brass Candlestick, Lip Of Candle Socket Incomplete, 7" H. $95.00

Friesian Carved Candle Box, Wrought Iron Strap Hinges, Minor Damage To Back Mouldings 14½" x 7" x 7" $180.00

Brass Candlestick, Sm. Solder Repair, 7¼" H. $200.00

(A-OH. '76)   *Garth's Auctions, Inc.*

Birch Open Cupboard, Board & Batten Doors, 2 Shelves, 36½" W., 17" D., 75" H. ..$350.00

(Top Of Cupboard)
Carved Wooden Decoy, Old Orig. Paint, 19¾" L. $120.00
Carved Wooden Decoy, Old Paint $30.00

(Row I, Left to Right)
Pewter Porringer, Plain Handle, 5¼" Diam. $650.00
Pewter Coffee Pot, "H.B. Ward &Co.", Handle Resoldered, 9½" H. $135.00
Pewter Porringer, Cast Handle, 3¼" Diam. $80.00

(Row II, Left to Right)
Pewter Pitcher, "Hopper", 7¾" H. ...$310.00
Pewter Teapot, "J. Danforth", Repair At Hinge, Wooden Finial Missing, Jacobs #100, 6¾" H. $300.00
Pewter Teapot, Wooden Handle & Finial, Polished, Faint Touch Mark, 7½" H. $285.00

(Row III, Left to Right)
Carved Wooden Decoys, Pr., Red Breasted Merganser, Branded "Kangas", 18" L. .$60.00
Pewter Teapot, "T.S. Derby", Jacobs #126, 8¾" H. $185.00

(Below)
Carved Wooden Decoy, Fat-Humped Back Bluebill Drake, N.Y. State, 13" L. $35.00
Carved Wooden Decoy, Pintail Drake, Houghton Lake, Mich., Orig. Paint, 19½" L. ..$45.00

(A-OH. '76)   *Garth's Auctions, Inc.*

Pine Pewter Cupboard, Doors W/Battens & "H" Hinges, 45" W., 17" D., 78½" H. $3,500.00
(Row I, Left to Right)
Pewter Sugar & Creamer $25.00
Pewter Tea Pot, "London" Mark, Handle Repairs, 5¼" H. $210.00
(Row II, Left to Center)
Pewter Bowls, Unmarked $290.00
Pewter Bowl, Footed, 5" Diam. $45.00
Pewter Bowl, Unmarked, 6¾" Diam. ..$75.00
(Row III, Left to Right)
Pewter Plates, (3), 2 Pictured, "London" Mark, One Has Split, 6" Diam. $75.00
Pewter Platter, Oval, "Made In London", Sm. Split In Edge, 13¼" L. $65.00
(Row IV, Left to Right)
Pewter Plates, (3), 2 Pictured, "London" Touch & St. George & Dragon, 7¾" Diam. $150.00
Pewter Platter, Oval, "Made In London", 16" L. $170.00

(A-PA. '76)   *Pennypacker Auction Centre*
(Left to Right)
Dresden China Figurine, 9", Dancing Girl W/Pink Lace Dress $57.50
Painting on Porcelain, By Ernde, Gold Leaf Frame, 5" x 7½" $300.00
Bronze Vase, 12" T., Egyptian Figure, Signed K. K. Kunst, Ersggressere-Wier, #1316 $60.00

(D-N.H. '76)

Wax Plaque, "A Friendly Call", 10x14", Orig. Paint Good $25.00

(D-CO. '76)

Razor, Straight Edge, German, Celluloid Handle $8.00

(D-CO. '76)

Razor, Straight Edge, German, Bone Handle $6.00

(A-PA. '76)   *Pennypacker Auction Centre*

Copy Of Martin Luther Bible, 1819, Lancaster, Pa., W/Complete List Of Subscribing Families Grouped By Counties Within Pennsylvania, Ohio, Maryland & Virginia; At The End Of Old Testament Are 2½ Pages Of The Rice Family Records $340.00

(A-PA. '76)   *Pennypacker Auction Centre*

Marriage Combs, Punched Brass Decor. Of Birds, Flowers & Heart W/Date of 1834 And Initials "D.W.", Probably Lancaster Co. $300.00

(A-OH. '76)   *Garth's Auctions, Inc.*

Walnut Dry Sink, Double Doors In Base W/ Punched Tin Panels, High Back W/2 Shelves, Refinished, Strip On Right Side Of Well Is Replaced, 52½" W., 214½" D., 58" H. $600.00

(Row I, Left to Right)
Rockingham Bowl, 10½" Diam. $35.00
Carved Printing Block, For Labeling Feed Sacks, "Jacob Farmer, 1852", & Bird, 17½" L. $260.00
Rockingham Bowl, Interior Glaze Wear, 10½" Diam. $35.00
(Row II, Left to Right)
Rockingham Plate, Embossed Border, 8" Diam. $9.00
Rockingham Bowl, Edge Wear, 10½" Diam. $35.00
Rockingham Oval Dish, 10" L. $37.50
(Row III, Left to Right)
Rockingham Bowl, Interior Glaze Wear, 13" Diam., 3¾" H. $35.00
Rockingham Tray, Embossed Figures & Border, Green In Glaze, Old Chip On Edge, 8½" x 10½" $50.00
Rockingham Bowl, Flake On Base, 12" Diam. $30.00

(A-MA. '76)   *Robert C. Eldred Co., Inc.*

Fireman's Salvage Bag, Lettered "Sam'l Harris, No. 1, 1803", Chief Engineer Of Boston Fire Dept., Linen $260.00
Fire Hat, Beaver Skin, Painted, Marked "Washington 1796", Owners Initials "R.G." & "No. 14" In Gold On White Ground...........$700.00
Leather Fire Bucket, Painted Red .. $160.00
Leather Fire Bucket, Painted Red, Dated 1804 .... $180.00

(A-MA. '76)   *Richard A. Bourne Co. Inc.*

Open Faced Hutch Cupboard, 37" L., 20½" W., 76" H. $125.00

PEWTER

(Row I, Left to Right)
Plate, Amer. Late 18th C., Trace Of Touchmark Showing Three Letters On Bottom, 8½" D. $50.00
Charger, English, Trace Of Touchmark On Back, Minor Pitting, 11" D. $55.00
Communion Plate, Leonard Reed & Barton, Straight Line W/Numeral "10", Minor Repair In Rim, 10¼" D. $50.00
(Row II, Left to Right)
Plate, Amer., Unmarked, 2 Sm. Pitted Areas In Center $35.00
Charger, 18th C., Unmarked, Smooth Brim, Pitted, 12" D. $70.00
Plate, Amer., Unmarked, Initialed "MS" In Rim, 2 Sm. Fractures In Rim Resoldered, 8½" D. $35.00
(Row III, Left to Right)
Charger, Traces Of Touchmarks Faintly Visible, Repair On Approx. 5" Of Edge, Polished, 12" D. $80.00
Charger, London Scroll Touch & Several Other Touch & Hallmarks, Hammered Booge, Polished 12¼" D. $70.00

(A-PA. '76)   *Pennypacker Auction Centre*

Yarn Winder, Hickory & Poplar, Base Shaped to Form Heart $260.00

(A-OH. '77)   Garth's Auctions, Inc.

Side Chair, Spindle Back Worn Woven Split Wood Seat $30.00
Dough Box, Attached Base, Dovetailed, Sq. Tapering Legs W/Some Splay, Old Red Paint, Scrubbed Top, 20" x 25" x 28" H. $260.00
Foot Stool, Walnut, Figured Top, 18" L. $25.00
Copper Kettle, W/Handle & Lid, Dovetailed Seam, Tinned Interior, 9¼" H. $150.00
Copper Pan, Flared Sides & Wrought Handles, 7¼" Diam. $37.50
Turtle Back Bellows, Red & Black Graining W/Floral Decor. In Red, Gold & Yellow-Green, Professionally Releathered, 18" L. $135.00
Copper Food Mold, Fish $127.50
Copper Food Mold, Man In The Moon, Mkd. "G.M.T. Bro." $295.00
Copper Food Mold, Fish $72.50
Cabbage Cutter, Back W/Worn Old Red Paint & Applied Turned & Split Molding, 19" L. $165.00

(A-OH. '77)   Garth's Auctions, Inc.

Country Hepplewhite Work Table, Old Red Base, 2-Board Pine Top W/Bread Board Ends W/Traces Of Red, 33½" x 49" $370.00
Wooden Bushel Basket, Stave Const., Worn Red & Black Paint, 22" Diam. $37.50
Irnostone Apothecary Jar, Blue & White, Paper Label "Ung. Hydrarg", 10½" H. .$55.00
Hog Scraper Candlestick, Sheet Iron, Push Up Dated "1853", 5" H. $65.00
Hog Scraper Candlestick, Sheet Iron, Push Up Signed, 7" H. $65.00
Hog Scraper Candlestick, Sheet Iron, Push Up Signed, 8" H. $65.00
Wooden Bowl, W/Handles, Exterior W/Old Red Paint, 31½" L. $55.00
Zink Pineapple Finial, Worn Red Paint, Minor Damage, 12¼" H. $32.50
Wooden Hat Rack, W/Turned Hooks, Painted Yellow W/Black Stripes, 32" L. $135.00

(A-OH. '76)   Garth's Auctions, Inc.

Hearth Brush, Decor. W/Yellow W/Black Striping & Floral Design On Handle, 26" L. $95.00
Poplar Box, Decor. W/White W/Blue-Green Edge Striping & Floral Designs On Sides, Top W/Weeping Willow & Draped Tomb, Worn Paint, 11" W., 7" D., 3¾" H. $175.00
Poplar Bin, Dovetailed, Open Interior W/One Till-Like Compartment On Side, Red Paint, 36½" W., 20" D., 32½" H. $170.00
Wrought Iron Knife Blade Andirons, Brass Urn Finials, Brass Trim On Bottom Stamped "I.C.", 24" H. $475.00
Windsor Side Chairs, Three (1 Illus.), Reddish-Brown Finish $240.00
Miniature Blanket Chest, Scalloped Bracket Feet, Compass Carving On Ends & Top, "Y.O." On Front, Worn Red Paint, Leather Hinges, 10½" W., 6" D., 5¾" H. $125.00
Dome Top Box, Pine, Hand Made Tin & Wire Hinges, Old Red Paint, 6¾" W., 3½" D., 3" H. $40.00
Pine Box, Painted Yellow W/Red Striping & Red & Green Star, Top W/Hearts, Hand Written Paper Glued To Inside Of Lid States "Daniel W. Iredell, Horsehamville, Montgomery Co., March 24th, 1860", 7" W., 5" D., 5" H. $385.00
Copper Horse Weathervane, Worn Gold Leaf, 31" L. $255.00
Block Tin Tray, Oval, Punched Star Design, 20½" L. $300.00

(A-OH. '76)   Garth's Auctions, Inc.

Sheraton Chest Of Drawers, Cherry, Turned Feet, Reeded Posts, Biscuit Corners, Banded Inlay Around Base & Top, Dovetailed Cock Beaded Drawers W/Oval Brasses & Escutcheons, 41" W., 19¾" D., 39½" H. $775.00
Brass Queen Anne Candlesticks, Pr., 8¾" H. $400.00
Pine Decorated Box, Painted Yellow W/Scene Of Bird, Flowers & Butterfly In Red, Green, Black & Yellow; Red & Black Border; Red & Black Design On Sides, 8"x10"x2½' $750.00

(A-OH. '76)   Garth's Auctions, Inc.

Wooden Butter Scoop, Butter Print Handle, Flowers & Berries, 11" L. $315.00
Decorated Box, Dovetailed Pine W/Iron Hdwe., Lightly Pigmented Varnish Ground W/Stenciled Decor. In Yellow, Green & White On 3 Sides & Top, Top Also Has Oval W/Initials In A Monogram, Interior Has Bits Of Orig. Wallpaper, 24" L., 12" W., 9½" H. $550.00
Fraktur Drawing, Black Swan W/Blue Wing & Red Legs, Vining Flowers & Letters In Red, Yellow, Blue, Green & Black, Paper Has Old Repairs, Old Painted Frame, 11¾" x 17½" $1650.00
Pine Pipe Box, Dovetailed Drawer, Base Molding, Scalloped Opening W/Shaped Crest, Alligatored Varnish Over Orig. Brown Paint, 19¼" H. $925.00

(A-OH. '75)   Garth's Auctions, Inc.

Hepplewhite Bow Front Chest of Drawers, Cherry W/Flame Veneer On Facade, Line Inlay Around Drawers & Inlaid Escutcheons, 43½" W., 21½" D., 37" H. $675.00
Tole Chestnut Urns, Pr., Black Ground W/ Skating Scene In Medallion, Lion & Ring Handles 12½" H. $375.00
Nanking Platter, Blue & White, Lemon Peel Glace, 14" L. $275.00

(A-OH. '76)   *Garth's Auctions, Inc.*

Blanket Chest, Walnut, Dovetailed Const., Overlapping Drawers W/Orig. Brass Bail Hdwe., Line Inlay On & Between Drawer Fronts & On Front & Top Of Chest, Till W/Secret Compartment & Iron Strap Hinges, Found In Hebron, Ohio, 51" W., 23" D., 26" H. $660.00
Lard Press, Primitive, Old Repair To Post Where Arm Pivots $40.00

(A-OH. '76)   *Garth's Auctions, Inc.*

Wrought Iron Hooks, Adjustable Trammel, 16" L. $135.00
Wrought Iron Trivet, Wooden Handle, 10" L. $30.00
Wrought Iron Trivet, Wooden Handle, 10" L. $32.50
Wrought Iron Peel, 39" H. $95.00
Bucket Bench, Pine, Scalloped Crest, Worn Red Paint, 30" W., 10" D., 35" H. . . . $255.00
(Row I, Left to Right)
Redware Foot Warmer, Green Glaze W/White Slip Design Of Tulips & Wavy & Straight Lines, Some Slip Highlighted W/Yellow Glaze, Old Chips, 10" L. $85.00
(Row II, Left to Right)
Stoneware Jug, Stamped "Clinton Pottery", Flower & Leaf Design In Cobalt, Hairline In Handle, 1-Gal. $45.00
Stoneware Crock, "W.A. Maco..oid & Co., Pottery Works, West 12th St. N.Y.", Running Chicken In Cobalt, Old Chip On Base, 1½ Gal. $85.00
(Row III, Left to Right)
Stoneware Jar, Handles & Top, Ovoid, 3-Gal. $37.50
Stoneware Jar, Free Hand Decor. & Stenciled Advertising Label, "George Davenport, Dealer In Dry Goods, Matamoras, Ohio", 2-Gal. $85.00

(A-OH. '76)   *Garth's Auctions, Inc.*

Child's Chair, Woven Split Seat, Worn Orig. Yellow Paint, Holes For Rod To Hold Child In Place $205.00
Stool, Old Repair To Top, Worn Drk. Paint, 10½" H. $45.00
Redware Frog, Green Glaze, Old Chips Around Base $35.00
Country Hepplewhite Table, Swing Leg Supports Drop Leaf, Pine Top W/Oval Corners, Old Refinishing, 37" W., 18½" D., 28¾" H. $650.00
Comb Back Rocking Chair, Old Alligatored Blk. Paint Shows Red Underneath, Striping & Floral Decor. On Crest $225.00
Dovetailed Box, Poplar, Blk. W/Free Hand & Stenciled Floral Decor., Mirror In Lid Held By Red Molding, 14"x11"x6" $450.00
Stoneware Butter Crock, Old Chip On Lid Knob, Blue Floral Design, 9" D. $105.00
Bellows, Yellow Smoked Ground W/Red, Green & Blk. Free Hand & Stenciled Decor. $150.00
Coffee Grinder, Turned Wooden Case, 7½" $155.00
Salt Box, Walnut & Pine, Front Has Raised Panel $245.00

(A-OH. '76)   *Garth's Auctions, Inc.*

Seed Cabinet, Pine & Poplar, Dovetailed Drawers, Old Blue Grey Paint, Some Knobs Replaced & Others Missing, Molding Around Top Missing, Attrib. To Shaker Craftsmen, 50½" W., 30" D., 51" H. $395.00
Carved Oak Grotesque Lions, Pr., 4½" x 5¾" $20.00
Brass Lamp, Elongated, 2 Burners, 15" L. $45.00
Pine Trunk, Dovetailed, Canted Sides & Dome Top, Feet Restored, Crudely Carved Initials "P.O.S." & "Titusville", 28½" L., 16" W., 16" H. $80.00

(A-OH. '76)   *Garth's Auctions, Inc.*

Gate Leg Table, Oak, Mortised Stretcher Base, Drawer Missing & Opening Plugged, One End Stretcher Has Broken Tendon, English, 55½" x 20½" x 27½" H., 19½" Leaves $400.00
Silver Candlesticks, Pair, Stop Fluted Columns W/Corinthian Capitals, Touch Marks Incl. Hibernia, Harp Crowned & Makers Initial "R.W.", Richard Williams, Dublin, 18th C., 14½" H. $360.00
Papier Mache Tray, Gilt Floral Borders W/Inlaid Mother Of Pearl & Bouquet Center W/Polychrome & Mother Of Pearl, 13¼" L. $160.00

(A-OH. '75)   *Garth's Auctions, Inc.*

Open Wall Cupboard, Pine, 2-Piece, Refinished, 67" W., 81½" H., 22" D. $400.00
(Row I, Left to Right)
Stoneware Butter Crock, Embossed Fruit & "Butter", 7" D. $27.50
Stoneware Butter Crock, Embossed Daisies, 6" D. $25.00
Stoneware Butter Crock, Embossed Cows & "Butter", Wire Handle, 7¼" D. $32.50
(Row II)
Three Stoneware Bowls, Graduated, Embossed Design, 7¼" D.; 6¼" D.; 5¼" D. $21.00
(Row III, Left to Right)
Stoneware Pitcher, Embossed Grapes, 8" H. $22.50
Stoneware Spittoon, Embossed Morning Glory 7½" D. $5.00
Stoneware Pitcher, Blue Embossed Flowers On Grey Ground, 8" H. $25.00
Stoneware Bowl, Embossed Fruit, 9½" D. $15.00
Stoneware Pitcher, Embossed Swastika, 8½" H. $20.00

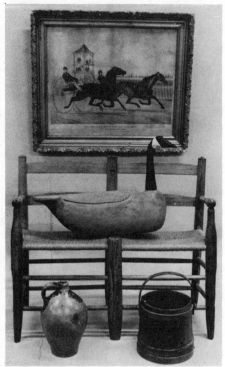

(A-OH. '76)　　　　　　　　*Garth's Auctions, Inc.*

Stoneware Jug, Ovoid, Black Glaze At Top $45.00
Wooden Sugar Bucket, Stave Const., No Lid, 9" H. $20.00
Buggy Seat, New Rush Seat, Refinished, 3½" L. $175.00
Wooden Goose Decoy, Wood & Sheet Metal Head, Grey, Black & White, 26" L. $70.00
Lithograph, Hand Colored, By "Haskell & Allen", "Fast Trotting At Mystic Park, Medford, Mass.", Gilt Frame, 28"x32" $125.00

(A-OH. '76)　　　　　　　　*Garth's Auctions, Inc.*

Country Queen Anne Side Chair, Spanish Feet, Drk. Refinishing, New Rush Seat $275.00
Wrought Iron Andirons, 8" D., 13½" H. $35.00
Cupboard, Pine & Poplar, 1-Board Door, Beaded Frame, Late Red Paint, 36" W., 19" D., 43" H. $165.00
Block Tin Coffeepot, 14" H. $60.00
Hanging Candle Box, Pine, Red & Yellow Paint, 12" W., 5½" D., 9" H. $120.00
Block Tin Coffeepot, Curved Spout, Base Flange Has Rust Damage, 10" H. $55.00
Pen & Ink Drawing, Pen Exercise In Black & Red Ink & Cut Work Featuring Birds, Feathery Foliage, Etc., 15¾" x 19½" $285.00

(A-OH. '76)　　　　　　　　*Garth's Auctions, Inc.*

Open Pine Pewter Cupboard, Scalloped Cut Out Sides, Cut Down, 49" W., 15" D., 69½" H. $550.00
Sheet Metal Boat Lantern, 3-Sided, Old Green Paint, 18" H. $135.00

(Row I, Left to Right)
Wooden Measures, Set of 4, Stave Const., 2 W/Bands, 2 W/Wires, Larger Has Metal Handles All W/Old Blue Paint, Largest Signed W/Anchor & "R.W. Richmond, Va.", 5½" H. To 10½" H. $90.00

(Row II, Left to Right)
Copper Foot Warmer, Brass Cap, Signed "B. Hawkhead, Coppersmith, Leeds", Solder Repair At Seams, 12" L. $30.00
Tin Rabbit Chocolate Mold, 12½" H. . $22.50
Copper Ale Warmer, Wooden Handle . $40.00

(Row III, Left to Right)
Wooden Maple Sugar Candy Mold, Man On Horseback, Back Of Each Half Has Carved Initials, 7" x 10¾", 2 Pcs. $105.00
Redware Mold, Shape Of Slipper, Lge. Chip, 6½" $5.00
Wrought Iron Trivet, Turned Wooden Handle $22.50
Wooden Butter Mold, Makes Cube Of Butter Decor. W/Pine Tree, Goat, Deer, Flower & Snowflake, Hinged At Top, Held By Wooden Ring $105.00

(Row IV, Left to Right)
Coffee Grinder, Oak Base W/Turned Posts & Scroll Cut Top & Bottom, Brass Hopper & Brass & Iron Handle W/Stamped Signature, 12½" H. $125.00
Redware Bowl, Base Signed "Buzz Watson", 28 Jan. 66, Camp Drum, N.Y.", Interior W/Heavy White Glaze, Chips & White Glaze Flaked, 13" Diam. $15.00
Block Tin Cash Box, Dome Lid W/Clear Glass Knob, Lift-Out Divided Tray & Secret Compartment In Lid, 9½" Sq., 11" H. $35.00

(A-OH. '76)　　　　　　　　*Garth's Auctions, Inc.*

Lantern, Paul Revere Type W/Punched Design, Ring Handle, 15" H. $75.00
Highchair, Worn Green Paint, Back Crest Split, 31½" H. $45.00
Candlestand, Maple, Dish Turned Top W/Patches Of Burl, 15" D., 25¼" H. $380.00
Tea Kettle, Copper, Dovetailed Const., Hinged Flap On End Of Spout, Handle Stamped "ABB" $95.00

(A-OH. '76)　　　　　　　　*Garth's Auctions, Inc.*

Windsor Step Down Arm Chair, Drk. Graining W/Gilt & Yellow Decor., Old But Not Original $170.00
Wire Fireplace Fender, W/Brass Rail & 3 Brass Knobs, 38½" W., 10" D., 10" H. $185.00
Table Top Desk, 3 Interior Drawers & Pigeonholes, Paneled Doors, Drk. Red W/Black Panels In Door Outlined In Yellow, Initialed "G.A.R.", Replaced Base Moldings, 35" W., 15½" D., 30½" H. $85.00
Sewer Tile Lion, Stamped "Beatrice Sewer Pipe Co.", Interior Stamped "J.M.O. Jones", Tooled Features, 11" L. $45.00
Cast Iron Mirror, Base W/Amer. Flag & Shield W/2 Ladies Supporting Oval Mirror, Old Polychrome Paint Over White Enamel, Some Flaking, 20" H. $55.00
Spencerian Penwork Lion, "Ornamental And Practical Penmanship", "Executed By Fannie Middaugh, New Parris, Ohio", Gold Frame, 25½" x 30" $220.00

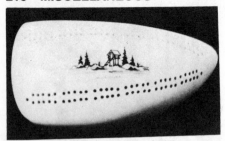

(D-CT. '76)
Scrimshaw Cribbage Board $125.00

(D-TX. '76)
Fish, Completely Made From Animal Horn, Scrimshaw-type Carving on Sides, 11" L. $65.00

(A-CA. '76)
Roger's Group "Coming To The Parson" $450.00

(A-OH. '75)   *Garth's Auctions, Inc.*
Whale's Tooth Scrimshaw, Incised Picture Of Young Woman, 5⅜" H. $175.00

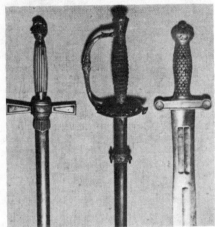

(A-OH. '76)   *Garth's Auctions, Inc.*
(Left to Right)
Sword, Brass Hilt, Ivory Grip & Ornamented By Cast Helmet & Shield, 31¼" L. $45.00
Sword, Gilt Brass Hilt, Ornamented W/Cast American Eagles & Shields, Blade Has Etched Flats & Eagles & Sheath Decor. W/Brass $105.00
Sword, Brass Hilt, Scale-Like Grip & Cast American Eagle W/Shield, 25" L. $95.00

(D-OH. '76)
Hair Wreath, Framed 12" x 16" $95.00

(D-CA. '76)
Meerschaum Pipe W/Orig. Case $65.00

(D-N.Y. '76)
Typewriter, Smith Premier No. 2 . . . . .$175.00

(A-OH. '76)   *Garth's Auctions, Inc.*
Wooden Butter Scoop, Bowl Is Burled $80.00
Cast Iron Eagle Snow Bird $17.50
Carved Wooden Toy, Dancing Man, 12" L. $85.00
Chopping Knife $12.50
Brass Pastry Cutter, Wheel On Both Ends, 7¾" L. $25.00
Chopping Knife, Wooden Handles, Blade Mkd., 10½" L. $20.00
Pastry Cutter, Turned Wooden Handle, 6¼" L. $22.50
Brass Pastry Cutter, 5½" L. $30.00

(A-MA. '76)   *Richard A. Bourne Co., Inc.*
(Left to Right)
Scrimshaw Decorated Whale's Tooth, Or Obverse, A Praying Woman, On The Reverse An Eagle Below Group Of Sm. Figures, 6" H $230.00
Scrimshaw Decorated Pan Bone, 2 Poly chromed Figures From Godey's Ladies Book 6½" W. At Base, 8½" L. $650.00
Scrimshaw Decorated Whale's Tooth, Ob verse Shows Lge. Building Below An Amer Eagle; Reverse Illustrates 3-Masted War Ship Below 2 Hearts Pierced By An Arrow Below The Bust Of Sailor, 8½" L. $550.00
Scrimshaw Decorated Whale's Tooth, Poly chrome Depiction Of Christ On The Cross 5½" L. $750.00

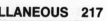

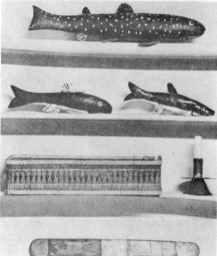

(A-OH. '76)   Garth's Auctions, Inc.
(Row I, Left to Right)

Windup Tin Toy, "Tombo, The Alabama Coon Jigger", Strauss Mfg. Co., Pat. May 24, 1910", 10½" H. $85.00

Cast Iron Toy Refrigerator, "Arcade Mfg. Co., Freeport, Ill.", Traces White Paint, 5¾" H. ....
....................................$7.50

Stuffed Toy Animal, 10" L. $7.00

Windup Tin Toy, Fireman On Ladder, "Louis Marx &Co." $70.00

(Row II, Left to Right)

Cast Iron Bulldog Bank, Old White & Brown Paint, 5¼" H. $22.50

Cast Iron Motorcycle & Rider, Worn White Paint, 6¼" L. $7.50

Cast Iron Bank, "The Wise Pit", Orig. Paint Worn, Pink Paint Around Face, 6½" H. .$35.00

Cast Iron Bank, Cat W/Ball Of Yarn, No Paint, 5½" L. $22.50

Cast Iron Mechanical Bank, "Little Joe Bank", 5½" H. $95.00

(Row III, Left to Right)

Cast Iron Bank, Seated Cat, Old Black, White & Red Paint, 4½" H. $47.50

Cast Iron Bank, Prancing Horse, Worn Gilt, 5¼" H. $22.50

Cast Iron Door Stop, Sheep, 7¾" H. ..$50.00

Cast Iron Bank, Horse, Old White & Black Paint, 4¼" H. $25.00

Cast Iron Nut Cracker, Squirrel, 4¾" H. .....
....................................$25.00

(A-OH. '76)   Garth's Auctions, Inc.

Sheraton One-Drawer Stand, Turned Legs, 1 Dovetailed Drawer, Reddish Brown Graining Over Yellow Ground, 17" x 19½' x 28½" H.
....................................$350.00

Brass Chalice, Threaded Protrusion For Mounting, Inscr. Reads "All Friends Round The Wrekin", & "Success To The Essington And Wyrley Canal", Reverse W/Snouted Animal And Latin Inscription "Ver Non Semper Viret", 12¾" H. $40.00

Cast Iron Cannon, Wood & Iron Carriage W/ Cast Iron Wheel, Barrel Is 9¼" L. $130.00

Victorian Bird Cage W/Tramp Art-Like Gingerbread, Old Yellow & Red Paint, Initialed & Dated "AB, 1896", Few Sm. Pieces Missing, Finial Is Replacement, 35" H. $140.00

Queen Anne Mirror, Mahogany On Pine, Veneer Repair, 13" x 25" $205.00

(A-OH. '76)   Garth's Auctions, Inc.
(Row I)

Fish Decoy, Wooden Body & Metal Fins, Brown, White & yellow W/Red, Signed "Miles Smith", 14" L. $25.00

(Row II)

Fish Decoy, Wooden Body & Metal Fins, Brown, White & Red, Signed "Miles Smith", 8" L. ....
....................................$20.00

Fish Decoy, Wooden Body & Metal Fins, Green, White, Yellow & Red, Signed "Miles Smith", 7¼" L. $19.00

(Row III)

Shaker Basket, Needs Minor Repair, 12¼" L.
....................................$25.00

Miniature Tin Candlestick, 3" H. $65.00

(Row IV)

Wooden Busk, Polychrome Decor. W/Gilt, 13½" L. $50.00

(A-OH. '77)   Garth's Auctions, Inc.
(Row I, Left to Right)

Wooden Storage Box, Oval, Lid Striped W/ Wide Bands Of Red, White & Blue, 7½" L. ...
....................................$15.00

Church Collection Box, Pine, Dovetailed, Old Graining, 9" x 5¼" x 4½" $22.50

Wooden Key, Worn Gold Paint, 11" L. ..$9.00

Wooden Book Box, Decor. W/Inlaid Straw, Lid W/Scene Of House & Barn, Interior W/ Mirror In Lid & 3 Compartments Covered By 2 Lids & All Decor. W/Straw, Marbleized End Paper, 6" x 4" x 2" $30.00

(Row II, Left to Right)

Poplar Box, Dovetailed, Reddish Graining Over Yellow Ground, 8" x 4" x 4½" $55.00

Bucket, Stave Const., Red W/Metal Bands Of Black W/Green, Red, Yellow & White Floral Vines, Lehn, 8½" H. $350.00

Decorated Lid, Matches Above Bucket, 8" Diam. $35.00

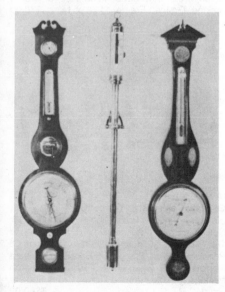

(A-VA. '76)
(Left to Right)

Banjo-Shaped Barometer, Mahogany, English, Broken Pediment Top Surmounted W/Cast Brass Finial, Beveled Glass Face Shows Dial Beneath Bearing Inscription, "T.B. Winter & Son, Newcastle-On-Tyne", Casing Has Light Wood Pencil-Line Inlay Around Perimeter, 11" W., 38" H. $250.00

Brass Gimbel Mounted Barometer, 40" H.
....................................$90.00

Banjo Barometer, Mahogany, English, Scrolled Top Over Thermometer, Bull's Eye Mirror, Several Other Meteorological Devices, Case Embellished W/Dark-Wood Inlay Around Side, Ca. 1830, 9" W., 36" H. $150.00

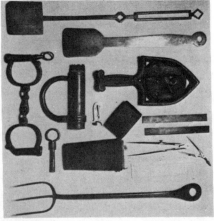

(A-OH. '76)   *Garth's Auctions, Inc.*

Iron Spatula, Cut-Out Handle, 18" L. . .$50.00
Sheet Iron Spatula, W/"M. T. Fitch" Inlaid In Brass On Handle, 13½" L. $170.00
Cast Iron George Washington Trivet, 9½" L.
. . . .$20.00
Draftsman's Tools, Cardboard Covered Wooden Case, 6 Brass &Steel Dividers &Compasses & Accessories, 1 Ivory Ruler W/Various Scales & Ebony & Brass Parallel Ruler $85.00
Brass & Steel Lancet, Signed "Philadelphia"
. . . .$50.00
Wrought Iron Fork, 17" L. $35.00
Wrought Iron Pan Lock W/Key $35.00
Wrought Iron Handcuffs W/Key $67.50

(A-OH. '76)   *Garth's Auctions, Inc.*

Powder Horn $27.50
Chopping Knife, Wooden Handle . . .$12.00
Powder Horn, Point Carved W/Face . .$22.50
Block Plane, Blade Signed & Wood W/Carved Initials, Small $13.00
Wooden Book-Shaped Box, 1 End Slides Open, 1 Pc. Wood W/Chip Carving, 6" L. . . . .
. . . .$15.00
Wooden Butter Scoop, Some Burl $80.00
Wooden Butter Print, Snow Flake Design, 4" x 5" $22.50
Folk Art Match Holder, Carving Of Man W/ Beard, Sm. Chip Off Nose $20.00
Wooden Butter Print, Round, Primitive Floral Design, 4¾" Diam. $15.00
Powder Horn, Turned Wooden End & Primitive Engraving Of Man In Top Hat & Deer . .$75.00

(D-MO. '76)
Tramp Art Hanging Comb Case, 8" W., 8½" H. . . . . .
. . . .$45.00

(A-OH. '76)   *Garth's Auctions, Inc.*

Manufacturer's Branding Iron, "I. M. Bimeler & Co.", 21" L. $87.50
Copper Hot Water Bottle $30.00
Country Curly Maple Blanket Chest, Till, 1 Drawer & Scalloped Front, Side Aprons, 27½" W., 20" D., 24½" H. $410.00
Stoneware Crock, 3-Gal., Impressed "West Troy N.Y. Pottery", Floral Design In Cobalt, Crows Foot In Base $45.00
Lighting Device, Wrought Iron, Adjustable Grease Lamp W/Penny Feet In Base, 33" H.
. . . .$145.00
Stoneware Jar, 2-Gal., Stenciled "Greensboro, Pa.", Label Blurred $35.00
Wooden Shovel, Winter Scene Painted On Scoop $75.00
Folded Cut-Out, W/Hearts, Animals & Birds, Framed, 10" x 15" $135.00
Cut-Out, On Lined Paper, Scene W/3 Cows & 2 Trees, Framed, 10" x 14" $105.00

(A-OH. '77)   *Garth's Auctions, Inc.*

Balloon Back Side Chairs, (Set Of 6), 2 Illus., Turned Legs, Plank Seat, Decor. W/Red & Black Graining W/Green & Red Striping & Free Hand Floral Decor. W/Tulips On The Crests & Splat In Green, Yellow, Blue, White & Red . . . .
. . . .$480.00
Bedside Stand, Curly Maple, Turned Legs, 2 Dovetailed Drawers & 2-Board Top, Clear Glass Pulls, 21" Sq., 27¾" H. $250.00
Terra Cotta Building Tile, Leaf Design, 7½" Sq.
. . . .$15.00
Walnut Knife Box, Scalloped Ends, Divider W/Cut Out Handle, 17½" x 9½" $80.00
Handkerchiefs, Child's, (2), "Wild Beasts" & "Birds", Framed, 1 W/Repair, 14" x 14" & 12" x 12" $100.00
Handkerchiefs, Child's, (2), "Wild Beasts" (Pictured), & "Old Mother Hubbard, Etc.", 8¾" x 10½" x 11¾" $100.00

(A-OH. '77)   *Garth's Auctions, Inc.*

Wooden Cheese Box, Round, Stave Constr., Stamped "Wm. C. Fisher", 16½" Diam. . . . . . .
. . . .$50.00
Poplar Wooden Box, Edges W/Brass Reinforcement, 25½" W., 18½" D., 31" H. . .$65.00
Tole Deed Box, Drk. Japanned Ground W/ Floral Decor. In White, Green, Orange, Red & Black, 8½" x 5¼" x 4¾" $90.00
Show Towel, Red, Yellow, Pink & Blue Embroidery On Homespun, Flowers, Birds, Hounds & Hunters Chasing Deer W/Poem "The Grass Is Green, The Rose Is Red, Here Is My Name, When Am I Dead, Elizabeth Frey, She Marked This Towel On The 4th Day Of October A.D., 1843", Applied Fringe On Bottom & Top, 16" x 62" $1,225.00
Wooden Spoon, Chip Carving Above Bowl, Initials "M.L.A.", 17" L. $20.00
Copper Food Mold, Lobster, 6½" L. . .$47.50
Watercolor, Rooster W/Colorful Plumage, From An Exercise Book, Dated "1812", Pine Frame, 9¾" x 11" $475.00
Wooden Tool, Old Red Paint, 19½" L. $45.00
Watercolor, Birds, Cut Out & Arranged Paper Background, Framed, 12" x 14" $25.00
Fraktur Certificate, Hand Done German Dedication From Sermon Book In Red & Green, Stained, Grained Frame, 11¼" x 14" . .$70.00

(A-VA. '76)   *Laws*

English Celestial & Terrestrial Globes, Pr., Signed J. Vincent, Prize Globes, London 1818; Celestial Stating Adjusted To Present Period 1800; Terrestrial Stating Accurate Positions Of Principal Known Places Of Earth To Present Period 1817, Each W/4 Turned Sheraton Mahogany Legs, Tapered Turned Cross Stretchers, 18" H. $850.00

Foot Warmer, Wooden Frame, Punched Tin Panels W/Hearts & Circles, 9¼" x 7¾" x 6"
....$40.00
Paul Revere Type Lantern, Fine Punched Decor., 15½" H. $425.00
Foot Warmer, Curly Maple W/Pan For Coals, Sliding Door Replaced $85.00
Country Queen Anne High Chest, Pine, Red Paint W/Orig. Free Hand Decor. (Wavy Lines). Some Restoration To Drawer Laps, Molding Missing Around Base, One Foot W/Minor Repair, 38" W., 18" D., 49" H. $1,000.00

Foot Warmer, Perforated Tin, Walnut Frame,
....$45.00

Wooden Cigar Store Indian Princess, Old Polychrome Paint Has Some Wear As Does Gesso On Base, "Cigars", 43" H. $1,600.00

Cast Iron Hitching Post, Black Jockey Holding Ring, Monumental Base, 35" H. $175.00
Victorian Turtle-Top Table, Mahogany Base W/Black Slate Top, 38" L., 27" W., 30½" H. ..
....$150.00
Blackamoor Figure, Kneeling Slave Supporting Giant Clam Shell, Wood Carved, Polychrome Decor., Age Splits, Needs Restoration, 36" H.
....$225.00
Victorian Dressing Table, Mahogany Frame W/ Spool Turned Legs, White Vermont Marble Top, Rosette Carved Wooden Pulls, 29" L. .$125.00

Country Jelly Cupboard, W/Board & Batten Door, Old Red Paint, 51" W., 16" D., 44" H.
....$100.00
Woven Split Wood Basket, Round Rim & Square Base, Yellow & Blue Stripes, 12" Diam.
....$10.00
Foot Stool, Pine, Mortised Constr., Refinished, 14" x 16" x 10" H. $37.50
Woven Split Wood Basket, Round Rim & Square Base, 10¾" Diam. $10.00
(Cupboard Top - Left to Right)
Pewter Teapot, Wooden Handle & Finial, Base Mkd. "Roswell Gleason", 10" H. $175.00
Miniature Blanket Chest, Pine, Dovetailed, Turned Feet & Till, Grained In Yellow & Red In Imitation Of Curly Maple, 12" x 22" x 12½" ...
....$410.00
Pewter Teapot, Wooden Handle & Finial, Handle Repaired, 10" H. $160.00
(Blanket Chest Top - Left to Right)
Pewter Cup, Unmarked, 3¼" H. $52.50
Pewter Teapot, English Touch Marks, Repairs & Tip Of Spout Battered, 5" H. $65.00
Miniature Pewter Whale Oil Lamp, Single Spout Brass Burner, 3¼" H. $130.00

(Left to Right)
Redware Herb Jar, Drk. Glaze W/Orig. Lid, 9¼" H. $150.00
Stoneware Ring Bottle, Deep Brown Glaze W/Yellowish-Orange Highlights, 10½" H. .....
....$200.00
Redware Flower Pot, Crimped Edge, Chain Coggle Around Top, "L. K. Tomlinson," 19th C.,
....$125.00
Linen Cloth, Brown & White Check, 35" x 30½",
....$65.00
Blanket Chest, Walnut, Early Pa., Orig. Hdwe.,
....$475.00

Blanket Chest, Pine, Dovetailed, Wrought Iron Hdwe., Green Ground W/4 Panels, Ea. W/ Polychrome Floral Design & Bird, Ends Have Simple Geometric Design, Top Unpainted, End Molding Of Top Incomplete, 42" L., 25" W., 22" H. $425.00
Burl Bowl, American, 21½" Diam. ...$650.00
Stoneware Jug, Ovoid, "Charlestown" Impressed W/Hearts, 16" H. $200.00

(A-MA. '75) *Richard A. Bourne Co. Inc.*

Horse Weathervane, Horse Has Six Repaired Bullet Holes W/Stand $230.00

Open Faced Cupboard, Cherry & Pine, American, 19th C., Restored & Refinished, Repainted Interior, Backboard In Upper Section A Replacement, 42½" L., 19" D., 8¾" H. . $425.00

Hitchock Side Chairs, Matched Set Of 4, Thick Plank Seats, Yellow W/Black, Green & Gold Decor., Grained Seats, Restored & Redecorated $225.00

(D-N.Y. '76)

Hand Organ, "The Improved Celestina", 13¼" x 13¾" x 15". Made By Aeolian Organ & Music Co., N.Y. $450.00

(A-PA. '76) *Pennypacker Auction Centre*

Upright Console Hurdy Gurdy, Italian, Mfg. By Luis Casali, 10 Different Musical Selections, ... $160.00

(A-PA. '76) *Pennypacker Auction Centre*

Queen Anne Tilt Top Table, Walnut, Bird Cage & 34" Dish Top $450.00
Wallpaper Hat Box, 16" H., Oval $30.00

(A-PA. '75) *Pennypacker Auction Centre*

Windsor High Chair, Minor Repair . . .$230.00
Curly Maple Nite Stand, 15½" x 19½" Top $190.00

(D-CA. '76)
"Olympia" Hand Organ W/20 Discs, Made By F. G. Otto & Son, New Jersey $750.00

(A-PA. '75) *Pennypacker Auction Centre*

Bowback Windsor Arm Chair, All Orig., Refinished $310.00
Sleeping Swans Decoy, Lge., Refinished, ...$70.00

(A-PA. '75) *Pennypacker Auction Centre*

Dish Top Candlestand, Walnut, 18th C., Orig. Iron Plate On Base, 15" Diam. $825.00
Windsor Arm Chair, Tall $1,600.00

(A-MA. '76) *Richard A. Bourne Co. Inc.*

Cased Melodeon, Walnut, By William P. Hastings, Portland, Maine $175.00

(A-OH. '77) *Garth's Auctions, Inc.*
(Left to Right)
Hanging Shelves, Miniature, Walnut, 7½" W., 7½" H. $27.50
Wooden Box, Round, Decor. W/Carved Pin Wheels & Brass Studs, Worn Orig. Brown Paint, 4¾" Diam. $230.00
Carved Wooden Rooster, 20th C. Folk Art, 8½" H. $60.00

FURNITURE CONTINUED